The Politics of the European Union

Second Edition

This introduction to the politics of the European Union uses the lens of comparative politics to explore the history, theories, institutions, key participants, policies and policy-making of the EU. The comparative approach enables students to use their knowledge of domestic politics and broader debates in political science to better understand the EU. Numerous real-world examples guide students through the material, and chapter briefings, fact files and controversy boxes highlight important information and controversial issues in EU politics to widen and deepen student understanding. The Second Edition has been updated throughout and includes the results of the 2014 European elections, and new material has been added on the Economic and Monetary Union and the Common Foreign and Security Policy. A companion website features free 'Navigating the EU' exercises to guide students in their analysis of EU policy-making.

HERMAN LELIEVELDT is Associate Professor of Political Science at Utrecht University, University College Roosevelt.

SEBASTIAAN PRINCEN is Professor of Governance and Policymaking in the European Union at Utrecht University, Utrecht School of Governance.

CAMBRIDGE TEXTBOOKS IN COMPARATIVE POLITICS

Series Editors:
Jan W. van Deth, *Universität Mannheim, Germany*
Kenneth Newton, *University of Southampton, United Kingdom*

Comparative research is central to the study of politics. This series offers accessible but sophisticated materials for students of comparative politics at the introductory level and beyond. It comprises an authoritative introductory textbook, *Foundations of Comparative Politics*, accompanied by volumes devoted to the politics of individual countries, and an introduction to methodology in comparative politics. The books share a common structure and approach, allowing teachers to choose combinations of volumes to suit their particular course. The volumes are also suitable for use independently of one other. Attractively designed and accessibly written, this series provides an up-to-date and flexible teaching resource.

Other books in this series:
KENNETH NEWTON & JAN W. VAN DETH
Foundations of Comparative Politics, 2nd edition

RICHARD GUNTHER & JOSÉ RAMÓN MONTERO
The Politics of Spain

JAMES L. NEWELL
The Politics of Italy

The Politics of the European Union

Second Edition

HERMAN LELIEVELDT
and
SEBASTIAAN PRINCEN

CAMBRIDGE
UNIVERSITY PRESS

CAMBRIDGE
UNIVERSITY PRESS

University Printing House, Cambridge CB2 8BS, United Kingdom

Cambridge University Press is part of the University of Cambridge.

It furthers the University's mission by disseminating knowledge in the pursuit of education, learning and research at the highest international levels of excellence.

www.cambridge.org
Information on this title: www.cambridge.org/9781107544901

© Herman Lelieveldt and Sebastiaan Princen 2015

First edition published 2011
Second edition 2015
Reprinted 2016

Printed in the United Kingdom by TJ International Ltd. Padstow Cornwall

A catalogue record for this publication is available from the British Library

Library of Congress Cataloguing in Publication data
Lelieveldt, Herman, 1967–
The politics of the European Union / Herman Lelieveldt and Sebastiaan Princen. – Second edition.
    pages cm. – (Cambridge textbooks in comparative politics)
Includes bibliographical references and index.
ISBN 978-1-107-11874-4 (Hardback) – ISBN 978-1-107-54490-1 (Paperback)
1. Europe–Politics and government–Textbooks.   2. European Union countries–Politics and government–Textbooks.   3. Comparative government–Textbooks.   I. Princen, Sebastiaan.   II. Title.
JN5.L45 2015
341.242'2–dc23   2015013723

ISBN 978-1-107-11874-4 Hardback
ISBN 978-1-107-54490-1 Paperback

Additional resources for this publication at www.cambridge.org/lelieveldt

Contents

PART III
EU policies: agenda-setting, decision-making and implementation

Acknowledgements

First we would like to thank our respective institutions, University College Roosevelt and the Utrecht School of Governance, both at Utrecht University, for their support and encouragement during the process of writing this book. In these research-driven times we feel blessed to have our work on a textbook to be considered by them as relevant as writing peer-reviewed articles.

We thank Jan van Deth and Kenneth Newton who as series editors entrusted us with this project. Their ideas to produce a book on the EU in a comparative politics textbook series provided a perfect match with our longstanding desire to write such a book based upon our experience teaching the EU in this fashion. John Haslam and the editorial and production teams at Cambridge smoothly managed the writing and production process. Deadlines were handled with just the appropriate amount of flexibility needed to combine our project with other commitments, while ensuring a steady progress on completing the manuscript.

In revising the text for this Second Edition, we were helped enormously by the comments and feedback we received from users over the past years. In addition, we would like to thank the lecturers who filled out the questionnaire on the first edition that was sent out by Cambridge University Press. Their observations and suggestions were invaluable for improving the text. Trineke Palm and Femke van Esch provided us with feedback on the sections on foreign policy and EMU in Chapter 8, helping us to avoid mistakes and misunderstandings in our descriptions of these complex policy fields. We also thank Ramon van der Does for his help in updating many of the book's tables and figures. Of course, any remaining errors in the text remain ours.

Middelburg/Utrecht,
January 2015

Briefings

Fact files

Controversies

Tables

Figures

Abbreviations and acronyms

AECR	Alliance of European Conservatives and Reformists
AEMN	Alliance of European National Movements
ALDE	Group of the Alliance of Liberals and Democrats for Europe
CAP	Common Agricultural Policy
CDU/CSU	Christlich Demokratische Union Deutschlands/Christlich-Soziale Union in Bayern (Germany)
CEECs	Central and Eastern European Countries
CEFIC	European Chemical Industry Council
CFSP	Common Foreign and Security Policy
CIA	Central Intelligence Agency
CJ	Court of Justice
COPS	Comité Politique et de Sécurité (Political and Security Committee)
CoR	Committee of the Regions
Coreper	Committee of Permanent Representatives
CPME	Standing Committee of European Doctors
CVCE	Virtual Resource Centre for Knowledge about Europe
DG	Directorate-General
EAF	European Alliance for Freedom
EC	European Community
ECB	European Central Bank
ECOFIN	Economic and Financial Affairs
ECPM	European Christian Political Movement
ECR	European Conservatives and Reformists Group
ECSC	European Coal and Steel Community
ED	European Democrats
EDC	European Defence Community
EDP	European Democratic Party
EEC	European Economic Community
EESC	European Economic and Social Committee
EFA	European Free Alliance
EFDD	Europe of Freedom and Direct Democracy Group
EFSA	European Food and Safety Agency
EGP	European Green Party
EL	Party of the European Left

ELDR	European Liberal Democrat and Reform Party
EMS	European Monetary System
EMU	Economic and Monetary Union
EP	European Parliament
EPC	European Political Community
EPP	Group of the European People's Party
ESM	European Stability Mechanism
ESC	Economic and Social Committee
ESDP	European Security and Defence Policy
ETUC	European Trade Union Confederation
EU	European Union
EUD	European Union Democrats
EUL/NGL	Confederal Group of the European United Left-Nordic Green Left
Euratom	European Atomic Energy Community
Europol	European Police Office
FDP	Freie Demokratische Partei (Germany)
FPÖ	Freiheitliche Partei Österreichs (Austria)
FRG	Federal Republic of Germany
GAC	General Affairs Council
GATT	General Agreement on Tariffs and Trade
GDP	Gross Domestic Product
GDR	German Democratic Republic
G-EFA	Group of the Greens/European Free Alliance
GMOs	Genetically Modified Organisms
GNI	Gross National Income
GSM	Global System for Mobile Communications
IAEA	International Atomic Energy Agency
IAR	International Authority for the Ruhr
IGC	Intergovernmental Conference
IMF	International Monetary Fund
IR	International Relations
ISS	Institute for Security Studies
JHA	Justice and Home Affairs
MELD	Movement for a Europe of Liberties and Democracy
MEP	Member of the European Parliament
MFF	Multiannual Financial Framework
MLG	Multi-level governance
NATO	North Atlantic Treaty Organization
NGO	Non-Governmental Organization
OECD	Organisation for Economic Co-operation and Development
OEEC	Organisation for European Economic Co-operation
OMC	Open Method of Coordination
Open VLD	Open Vlaamse Liberalen en Democraten (Belgium)
PES	Party of European Socialists
PP	Partido Popular (Spain)
PS	Parti Socialiste (France)

QMV	Qualified Majority Voting
S&D	Group of the Progressive Alliance of Socialists and Democrats in the European Parliament
SEA	Single European Act
SGP	Stability and Growth Pact
SPÖ	Sozialdemokratische Partei Österreichs (Austria)
TEC	Treaty establishing the European Community
TEU	Treaty on European Union
TFEU	Treaty on the Functioning of the European Union
TPD	Tobacco Products Directive
TTIP	Transatlantic Trade and Investment Partnership
UKIP	UK Independence Party
UMP	Union pour un Mouvement Populaire (France)
UMTS	Universal Mobile Telecommunications System
UN	United Nations
VAT	Value Added Tax
VLD	Vlaamse Liberalen en Democraten (Open Flemish Liberals and Democrats)
WEU	Western European Union
WHO	World Health Organization

Country abbreviations used in tables and figures

AT	Austria
BE	Belgium
BG	Bulgaria
CY	Cyprus
CZ	Czech Republic
DE	Germany
DK	Denmark
EE	Estonia
EL	Greece
ES	Spain
FI	Finland
FR	France
HR	Croatia
HU	Hungary
IE	Ireland
IT	Italy
LT	Lithuania
LU	Luxembourg
LV	Latvia
MT	Malta
NL	Netherlands
PL	Poland
PT	Portugal
RO	Romania
SE	Sweden
SI	Slovenia
SK	Slovakia
UK	United Kingdom
EU-28	All member states
EU-25	The twenty-five member states that joined up till 2007
EU-15	The fifteen – 'old' – member states
EU-12	The twelve – 'new' – member states that joined in 2004 and 2007

Preface

Why yet another textbook on EU politics? And why in a series on comparative politics? For us, the answers to these two questions are closely linked. Having taught EU politics for several years, both of us grew increasingly dissatisfied with the introductory texts on EU politics available on the market. Our dissatisfaction stemmed from two facts. First, existing textbooks on EU politics tend to be too descriptive for our liking. Vast parts of those texts are devoted to discussing the details of the EU's institutional set-up or the intricacies of EU decision-making procedures. By contrast, we are more interested in the political processes that take place within the EU. Knowledge of the EU's institutions and procedures is necessary in order to study those processes fruitfully, but our objective in teaching EU politics is to give students an understanding of how politics in the EU works, not of the EU's institutions and procedures per se. Second, most textbooks still look at the EU as a 'one-of-a-kind' system or, as it is commonly put in the EU studies literature, as an organization 'sui generis'. The focus on the EU's uniqueness makes it difficult for students to relate their understanding of EU politics to what they know about other political systems. We believe that, increasingly, the EU can best be studied from a comparative politics perspective, and that this should form the leading premise of a textbook on EU politics. In that sense, we build on the pioneering work of the one textbook on EU politics that does discuss the EU in a comparative politics framework: Simon Hix and Bjørn Høyland's *Political System of the European Union*. At the same time, Hix and Høyland's text is both too difficult as an introductory text for students who are new to the EU and looks at the EU from one specific theoretical lens – that of rational choice theory. What we were looking for was a book that we could use for undergraduate students new to the subject and that would draw upon a wider range of theoretical approaches. Hence this book.

■ Why comparative politics?

For us, the core assumption underlying a comparative politics approach to the EU is that most of the questions that can be asked of domestic political systems can also be asked of the EU – even if the answers to those questions are not always the same. The latter addition is crucial because we do not mean to imply that the EU is 'essentially' (whatever that may mean) or even just for practical purposes a 'state' or 'like a state'. What we do claim is that the kind of questions that we normally ask of domestic political systems can (and should) also be asked of the EU. These include questions such as: How are relations between the 'executive' and the 'legislative' organized? In what ways do citizen opinions play a role in political decision-making? What role do political parties play in politics? How much influence do interest groups have over policy-making? How do issues reach the political agenda? How are policies implemented once they have been adopted? It is not self-evident that these questions can be asked of any political institution. For instance, we doubt whether it would yield useful insights to ask about the role of political parties in the World Trade Organization or executive–legislative relationships in the United Nations Organization. In order for these questions to make sense, the actors that we commonly look at when studying domestic politics at least need to be present in the political system we are interested in. In the case of the EU, so we argue, this is indeed the case.

Having said that, the answers that we give to those questions will often be different in the EU than in domestic political systems. Although it makes sense to study political parties in the EU, their organization and the role they play in EU politics are quite different from the way they operate in most EU member states. Likewise, we can study executive–parliamentary relations in the EU but in doing so we will have to acknowledge that 'the executive' is much less clearly defined in the EU than in domestic politics. This, however, is exactly the point of looking at the EU from a comparative politics perspective: by asking the same questions, we can see more clearly both where EU politics is similar to domestic politics and where it is different. This is not unlike the benefit of applying a comparative politics perspective to domestic political systems – after all, no two countries are identical and in studying them comparatively we will see both commonalities and points at which specific countries are unique.

■ How this book is organized

In taking a comparative politics perspective, we have made a number of choices about the organization of the book. Since our focus is on gaining an understanding of how EU politics works, our treatment of the history, institutions and policies of the EU has been structured in such a way that it invites comparisons with other political systems and concentrates on the political dynamics of the EU.

This book consists of three parts plus a concluding chapter. The first part (Chapters 1–4) lays the foundation for studying EU politics by developing a working knowledge of the historical development of the EU (Chapter 1), theoretical approaches to studying EU politics (Chapter 2) and the institutions and procedures of the EU (Chapters 3 and 4). We do not see this knowledge as an end in itself. Although we acknowledge that an understanding of history, institutions and procedures is important for understanding political systems and political processes, we also believe that – in a political science textbook – discussions of history, institutions and procedures should be instrumental to discussions of political processes. Hence, we seek to place the EU's history, institutions and procedures within the framework of the EU's political system as a whole and we elucidate the logic behind the EU's institutional and procedural framework.

The second part (Chapters 5–7) moves on to discuss the role of three key actors in politics: citizens (Chapter 5), interest groups (Chapter 6) and political parties (Chapter 7). In these three chapters, we show what role they play in EU politics and how this compares to the roles of citizens, interest groups and political parties in domestic political systems. In this way, a better insight can be obtained of how the EU works and what it is that makes EU politics 'tick'.

The third part focuses on policies. Policies are arguably a key 'output' of any political system. It is in making policies that politics has its greatest impact on society. Therefore, much of what political actors do is linked, one way or another, to influencing policies. In discussing EU policy-making, we take a thematic approach. After an overview of policy-making and the main policy fields in Chapter 8, we take a closer look at three important aspects of policy-making processes: agenda-setting (Chapter 9), decision-making (Chapter 10) and implementation (Chapter 11). By reading these chapters, students will be equipped with the conceptual and theoretical tools that they can subsequently use to study and analyse specific policies and policy areas.

Finally, Chapter 12 brings together a number of threads woven throughout this book. It does so by reflecting on three important issues in debates on the EU. First, it takes a look into the future and shows how the insights presented in this book can help analyse developments in the EU. Second, it discusses the issue of democracy in the context of the EU. Having compared the EU with other (democratic) political systems, what can we say about the democratic credentials of the EU itself ? Finally, we come back to the comparative method itself, reflecting on the added value it has provided in this book.

■ Features to help you learn

Learning a subject is not just about substance, it is also about the appropriate ways of bringing the substance to life. Therefore, we have sought to aid students' understanding of the EU by adding a number of learning tools that link abstract concepts and theories to concrete issues and debates:

- In briefings, important issues are highlighted and background information is given without distracting from the argument in the main text.
- Fact files provide concise overviews of key facts for easy reference.
- Small boxes in the margin of the text define and explain key concepts.

- Students are engaged in debating EU politics through controversy boxes that discuss topical debates in the EU and invite students to reflect on them.
- In addition, we have developed a number of 'Navigating the EU' exercises for each chapter. In these exercises, students are encouraged to further explore EU politics by making use of the vast amounts of information now available on the Internet. Because of the changeability of Internet sources, these exercises are not included in the book itself but are available on the website www.navigatingthe.eu.

All in all, we have sought to write a book that will be attractive to students and instructors alike. It will be of interest to those studying or teaching courses in the fields of political science, government and European studies. For those, we hope to have written a book that is accessible, stimulating and clear – the kind of book we wanted to use in our own courses.

PART I

Setting the scene: origins, analytical perspectives and institutions

1 The historical development of the EU

■ Introduction

To most European citizens the Ninth of May will be a day just like any other. In Brussels, Luxembourg and Strasbourg, however, this is different. In these cities a sizeable number of people work for one of the institutions and organizations of the European Union (EU). If we follow the official historiography of the EU, their jobs found their origin in a press conference held sixty-five years ago by the French Minister of Foreign Affairs, Robert Schuman. On 9 May 1950 he proposed a plan that laid the foundation for today's European Union by proposing to set up a European Coal and Steel Community (ECSC).

In 1985 the leaders of the member states of the EU decided that it would be good to celebrate this day as Europe Day. But most citizens will not notice this. Maybe this is not surprising given the fact that the day marks a rather obscure event in history. After all, commemorating a press conference is quite different from celebrating a rebellion (like the USA's Fourth of July) or a revolution (such as France's Quatorze Juillet).

Despite its humble origins, the EU has in the meantime developed into a political system that seriously impacts the lives of these same citizens. Within a timespan of only sixty years it has established itself as a unique form of political cooperation comprising twenty-eight member states and 500 million inhabitants, with a combined income that is the world's largest. No wonder some observers have characterized the EU as a superpower, albeit a soft one: instead of conquering new territory by force as the old superpowers used to do, the EU has been able to expand because countries have been very eager to join and share in the assumed benefits of membership.

In this book we outline the current politics of the EU, but a brief overview of the way this organization has evolved is essential to better understand how it operates today. After all, many of today's political decisions will end up as historic events in tomorrow's books. A closer examination of the most significant political events that occurred in the EU's history gives us a first insight in the nature of EU politics today. We do this by examining the following questions:

- What was the historical background to several initiatives for international cooperation after the Second World War?
- What made the European Coal and Steel Community so important for European integration?
- What have been the major developments in the process of European integration when looking at the evolution of its policies, institutions and membership over the decades?
- What does the history of European integration teach us about studying EU politics today?

After reading this chapter you will have learned that the process of bringing the European countries together was a long and winding road with many fits and starts. Periods of rapid change and innovation have alternated with long stretches of gridlock and stalemate. The process was often erratic because of fundamentally different views on the nature, pace and scope of integration. While the term 'European Union' suggests that we are dealing with an organization that was swiftly put in place on the basis of a solid design, we are in fact looking at a patchwork that has been stitched together in a step-by-step fashion over the course of six decades.

■ The origins of European integration

The institutional roots of the European Union lie in the years following the Second World War. Europe was shattered, and not for the first time. European history had been marked by an almost infinite sequence of conflicts, wars and rebellions, fuelled by religious strife, imperial ambitions and nationalistic sentiments. Notable philosophers such as Jean-Jacques Rousseau, Jeremy Bentham and Immanuel Kant had already concerned themselves with this problem and come up with proposals for some type of a federation of states in order to guarantee peace and avoid war. None of these ever materialized, however.

The aftermath of the Second World War provided unusually fertile ground for new ideas for international cooperation. The war took the lives of approximately 40 million civilians and 20 million soldiers, while those that survived were faced with destruction and despair. In a speech at the University of Zürich in 1946 Winston Churchill – who had been Britain's prime minister during the war – sketched the sense of despair: 'Over wide areas a vast quivering mass of tormented, hungry, care-worn and bewildered human beings gape at the ruins of their cities and their homes and scan the dark horizons for the approach of some new peril, tyranny or terror.' Churchill's speech became historic because he proposed to 'recreate the European family in a regional structure called, it may be, the United States of Europe'. He urged France and Germany, the two arch-enemies, to take the lead in setting up such a federation.

Fears about the future were fuelled in particular by the geopolitical map of the new Europe. Following the post-war settlement, Europe was divided into two spheres of influence. An Eastern zone was dominated by the communist Soviet Union, with countries such as Poland, Hungary, Romania and Bulgaria and the eastern part of Germany. The Western part of Europe consisted of liberal democracies that were strongly supported and protected by the USA. Fears that the Soviet Union might try to expand its sphere of influence westward necessitated a swift rebuilding of Europe. Hence, the USA was supportive of many of the initiatives that were launched to foster cooperation (see Briefing 1.1). Three different types of organization emerged:

- Military cooperation found its beginnings in initiatives for a common defence such as the Western European Union (WEU) and the North Atlantic Treaty Organization (NATO).
- Political cooperation emerged via organizations such as the Council of Europe.
- Economic cooperation took root via the Organisation for European Economic Co-operation (OEEC), the Benelux and the European Coal and Steel Community (ECSC).

The legacy of the two world wars made any form of cooperation involving France and Germany extremely difficult. The most delicate and pressing issue was the German question. Germany's size and its economic potential necessitated that it recover as soon as possible. Germany's large coal resources in the Ruhr area were pivotal for Europe's recovery and for the French steel industry in particular. At the same time many feared that a resurgence of Germany could make the country belligerent again and cause new military conflict.

Fuelled by the fear of communism the USA decided that Germany needed to be integrated in the Western bloc as soon as possible. In April 1949 the western part of Germany regained its independence and was transformed into the Federal Republic of Germany (FRG). French fears were dealt with by putting Germany's coal industry under the supervision of the International Authority for the Ruhr (IAR) which would manage coal supplies from the Ruhr region. The IAR was in charge of determining the minimum amount of coal, coke and steel Germany should make available for export. Both politically and economically the IAR was not a success: the Germans still felt occupied and the method of rationing coal was not efficient. The Americans therefore urged the French to devise another scheme. It was Jean Monnet, Commissioner-General of the

Briefing 1.1

Related international organizations and their current status

The **Western European Union** (WEU) was founded through the Brussels Treaty in 1948 by the United Kingdom, Belgium, France, Luxembourg and the Netherlands. It was set up to provide for common defence in case of an attack on any of its members and prepared the ground for the foundation of NATO (see below). The activities of the WEU have now been incorporated in the EU's Common Security and Defence Policy and the Treaty was terminated in 2011.

The **North Atlantic Treaty Organization** (NATO) is a military intergovernmental alliance through which each of the members pledges support to the other members in the event they are attacked. It found its origin in a similarly named Treaty signed in 1949 by twelve Western countries including the USA, Canada, United Kingdom, France and Italy. NATO currently has twenty-eight members and is involved in several peacekeeping and reconstruction missions worldwide.

The **Council of Europe** was founded in 1949 to achieve greater unity between its members by maintaining and developing the rule of law, human rights and fundamental freedoms. It currently has forty-seven member states and is home to the European Court of Human Rights which deals with cases relating to the European Convention on Human Rights. The judgments of the Court are binding upon the member states. (Note that the Council of Europe should not be confused with the European Council, an EU institution that hosts the Heads of State and Government of the EU member states.)

The **Organisation for European Economic Co-operation** (OEEC) was set up in 1948 in order to administer the Marshall Plan, a US-funded package for economic recovery of Europe. In 1960 it was succeeded by the Organisation for Economic Co-operation and Development (OECD), which focuses on analysing and forecasting the economic policies of its thirty-four members.

The **Benelux** was founded in 1944 by the governments-in-exile of Belgium, the Netherlands and Luxembourg with the aim of forming a customs union. It was upgraded to an economic union in 1958. A new treaty expanding cooperation to sustainable development and judicial cooperation entered into force in 2010.

French National Planning Board, who came up with a plan that would pool the coal and steel production of France and Germany and create a common market.

On 9 May 1950 Monnet's scheme was presented by the French Minister of Foreign Affairs, Robert Schuman, in a declaration that is nowadays considered to be the EU's founding moment. This is how Schuman outlined this philosophy:

> Europe will not be made all at once, or according to a single plan. It will be built through concrete achievements which first create a de facto solidarity. The rassemblement of the nations of Europe requires the elimination of the age-old opposition of France and Germany. Any action taken must in the first place concern these two

countries. With this aim in view, the French Government proposes to take action immediately on one limited but decisive point. It proposes to place Franco-German production of coal and steel as a whole under a common higher authority, within the framework of an organisation open to the participation of the other countries of Europe. [...] In this way there will be realised simply and speedily that fusion of interests which is indispensable to the establishment of a common economic system; it may be the leaven from which may grow a wider and deeper community between countries long opposed to one another by sanguinary divisions. By pooling basic production and by instituting a new higher authority, whose decisions will bind France, Germany, and other member countries, this proposal will lead to the realisation of the first concrete foundation of a European federation indispensable to the preservation of peace.

> Robert Schuman, *The Schuman Declaration. Fondation Robert Schuman*
> (http://www.robert-schuman.eu/en/declaration-of-9-may-1950).

Two things in the excerpt from Schuman's speech merit attention. First, the plan was innovative because it proposed the institution of an impartial body – the High Authority – that would be empowered to monitor and execute the agreement between the member states. This feature would give the ECSC the characteristics of a **supranational organization**: member states handed over part of their sovereignty to a third, neutral party that would supervise the execution of the terms of the treaty. In Schuman's plan the High Authority was authorized to make decisions that were needed to execute the agreements laid down in the treaty. And in those cases where member states and the High Authority disagreed, they would be able to bring their dispute to a court that would be authorized to issue a binding judgment. The supranational formula differentiated the organization from all the other organizations which had been set up so far: these had been **intergovernmental organizations**.

> **Supranational organizations:** organizations in which countries pool their sovereignty on certain matters to allow joint decision-making.

> **Intergovernmental organizations:** organizations in which member states work together on policies of common concern but retain their full sovereignty.

A second important feature of the plan was its limited scope. Cooperation would start on a small basis by first trying to manage the common market for coal and steel. It was a deliberate decision to do this, because it was absolutely clear that the time was not ripe yet for a fully fledged federal state. In such a federal state member states should have been willing to cease to be independent and become part of a United States of Europe. Although at the time this was of course a bridge too far, there were many federalists that actively promoted these ideals and strived for a development of integration in this direction. In their view the supranational model acted as a halfway house on the road to a truly federal state. Small and concrete steps would provide the foundations for an eventual transfer of sovereignty to a new centre.

Schuman's plan needed to be turned into a treaty between the countries that wanted to take part in this experiment. In addition to France, five countries joined the negotiations. Germany was very happy to accept France's invitation. It was the first time that it would be treated on an equal footing and it made possible the abolition of the Ruhr Authority. The countries of the Benelux (Belgium, the Netherlands, Luxembourg) simply had to join because their economies depended very much on those of France and Germany. Italy joined the negotiations for both political and economic reasons. Just like Germany it wanted to regain respectability after the war. It also felt its industry would benefit from being part of the common market for coal and steel.

Negotiations on the treaty took almost a year. Opinions differed on the amount of power that should be given to the High Authority and the ways in which it could and should be controlled. The Dutch and the Germans successfully insisted on a solution that would make it possible for the member states to supervise the High Authority. The result was an additional body in the form of the Council of Ministers that would represent the governments of the member states. The Council constituted an intergovernmental institution that would act as a counterweight to the supranational High Authority.

On 18 April 1951 the six countries signed the Treaty of Paris which formally established the European Coal and Steel Community. The Community's four main institutions were:

- a Council of Ministers, representing the member state governments, to co-decide on policies not provided for in the Treaty;
- a High Authority, consisting of independent appointees, acting as a daily executive making decisions on the basis of the Treaty provisions;
- a Court of Justice, consisting of independent judges, to interpret the Treaty and adjudicate conflicts between member states and the High Authority;
- a Common Assembly, drawn from members of national parliaments, to monitor the activities of the High Authority.

The initial institutional design of the ECSC proved to be quite resilient. It is still clearly visible in the institutional make-up of the EU today and it provided the template for organizing the other Communities that were set up in the decades to come.

■ A brief historical survey of European integration

In order to better capture the historical developments it is useful to look at three different questions that help explain the steps that were taken over the decades.

- In which areas did member states decide to cooperate? This question looks at the *policies* that member states agreed upon. The first way to chart the history of integration is by tracing the incorporation of new policy areas over time.
- How did the member states organize their cooperative efforts? This second question looks at the *institutional framework* they put in place to make these policies. It examines the institutions that were set up, their powers and the way they arrive at decisions.

- Which countries became members? This question looks at the developments in the organization's *membership*. The process of enlargement charts this third element of European integration.

When surveying the EU's history, it is useful to keep the above distinctions in mind. In addition to the historical overview below, the book's website (www. navigatingthe.eu) contains a timeline that gives an overview of the main events with respect to these three questions.

In a formal sense steps in integration are characterized by the adoption of treaties in which member states agree to cooperate in certain areas as well as by subsequent amendments to such treaties. Table 1.1 lists the four founding treaties: the European Coal and Steel Community, the European Economic Community, the European Atomic Energy Community and the European Union. The founding treaties have been amended frequently in order to incorp-orate changes in policies, the institutions and membership. The table therefore also lists the most important amending treaties. Note that in 2002 the ECSC treaty expired whilst the EEC treaty was renamed twice, and is now known as the Treaty on the Functioning of the European Union.

The 1950s: from one to three Communities

After the six founding members had **ratified** the Treaty of Paris, the ECSC started operation in July 1952, with Jean Monnet as the first President of the High Authority. In the meantime new integrative steps were underway. The Korean War, between communist North Korea and capitalist South Korea, heightened concerns about the global threat of communism. The USA therefore pressed

> **Ratification:** procedure through which a member state formally commits itself to a treaty, in most countries via a majority vote by its parliament.

for a rearmament of the FRG that would bolster the defensive capabilities of Western Europe and defend the West German border against a possible attack from the east. For the French in particular the prospect of an independent Germany with its own army was unacceptable, however. A solution was found in following the ECSC model: West German troops would be brought under a supranational command. In April 1952 the member states agreed on a Euro-pean Defence Community (EDC) that would establish such a structure. Soon thereafter another treaty – European Political Community (EPC) – was drafted in order to provide for an appropriate institutional framework that would give political guidance to the activities of the EDC. The initial plans that were proposed by a constitutional committee drawn from the ECSC parliamentary assembly consisted of setting up a quasi-federal legislature consisting of a Chamber of the Peoples, elected by direct suffrage, and a European Senate appointed by national parliaments.

The pace of integration was remarkable: only three years after the Treaty of Paris, the ECSC members were on the brink of taking major steps both in terms of policies and in terms of the accompanying institutional structures.

Table 1.1 An overview of the major treaties. (Founding treaties in bold)

Treaty name	Year signed	Entry into force	Type	Treaty establishing
Treaty of Paris	1951	1952	Founding	**European Coal and Steel Community (ECSC)**
Treaties of Rome	1957	1958	Founding	**European Economic Community (EEC)** / **European Atomic Energy Community (Euratom)**
Single European Act	1986	1987	Amending	
Treaty of Maastricht	1992	1993	Amending/ Founding	**European Union (EU)**
Treaty of Amsterdam	1997	1999	Amending	
Treaty of Nice	2001	2003	Amending	
Treaty of Lisbon	2007	2009	Amending	

ECSC: Expired 2002 merged with TEC

EEC → Treaty on European Community (TEC) → Treaty on Functioning of European Union (TFEU)

Euratom → Treaty establishing the European Atomic Energy Community (Euratom)

European Union (EU) → Treaty on European Union (TEU)

Indeed the plans proved to be too ambitious. Plans for the EDC divided French society and politics to such an extent that in the end the French parliament decided not to debate the proposal further. This then also obviated the need to further discuss the plans for EPC. In the end the move towards supranational cooperation in these areas was clearly a bridge too far.

Despite the failure of the EDC and EPC, new initiatives to increase cooperation were launched soon thereafter, albeit in areas that were less sensitive. Jean Monnet, disillusioned by the lack of progress in European cooperation, resigned as President of the High Authority. He further pursued his federalist ideals by setting up the Action Committee for the United States of Europe. Monnet pressed for broadening cooperation in the field of energy by proposing a European Atomic Energy Community. Around the same time Dutch Foreign Minister Beyen came up with proposals for a common market that would cover all types of economic activity.

Representatives of the founding member states discussed these different proposals in a series of meetings that started in the Italian city of Messina. In the end the governments agreed on the establishment of two new Communities that were laid down in the Treaties of Rome. The European Atomic Energy Community (Euratom) would strive for the development of nuclear energy, whilst the European Economic Community (EEC) would focus on establishing the free movement of goods, services, workers and capital between the member states.

The agreement on abolishing barriers to trade was accompanied by worries about the effects this might have on specific groups. Hence some provisions were made that would make it possible to alleviate such negative side-effects. The French, for example, successfully lobbied for the inclusion of a common agricultural policy that would enable measures to support farmers. In a similar vein the Italian government demanded measures that would reduce differences in prosperity between the regions in Europe. In this manner Italy hoped to secure funds that would be targeted at the extremely poor southern regions of the country. The treaty therefore also enabled the setting up of a European Social Fund. Although it would take several years before they actually were implemented, the treaty already provided the legal possibilities to develop these policies.

The institutional set-up of Euratom and the EEC was roughly similar to that of the ECSC, with one exception. The powers of the supranational executive in the EEC and Euratom – called the Commission – were significantly less than those in the ECSC. The Commission was granted the right to make legislative proposals for what came to be known as Community legislation, but all these proposals needed to be approved by the Council of Ministers.

The 1960s: progress and setbacks

Of the three Communities the EEC turned out to be the most energetic. Progress on the elimination of **customs duties** was ahead of schedule

Customs duties or tariffs are charges levied on imports or exports, resulting in higher prices for consumers buying those products.

and the Commission managed to complete this three years earlier than planned.

Three other developments signalled the EEC's success in cooperating on the economic front. In 1963 the member states signed the Yaoundé agreement, a **preferential trade agreement** with the EEC's former colonies. And in 1965 the Commission represented the six member states in negotiations for the Kennedy round of the General Agreement on Tariffs and Trade (GATT), the negotiating framework for liberalizing trade in the world. Finally, in 1962 the Council agreed on the organizational features of the Common Agricultural Policy (CAP): it established a system of guaranteed minimum prices for specific agricultural products. In 1967 the first common markets (for cereals, pig meat, poultry meat and oilseeds) started operating. The CAP was different from the other policies because it liberalized trade within the Community but at the same time provided measures to protect European farmers by guaranteeing them minimum prices and levying import duties on products from outside of the Community.

In a **preferential trade agreement** countries agree on lowering the tariffs they charge for importing goods.

The early 1960s also were marked by two key rulings of the Court of Justice (CJ) that made a lasting imprint on the legal order of the Community. In its rulings the Court argued that the new legal framework of the Community amounted to more than an ordinary international treaty and formed an integral part of the legal order of the member states. As a result individuals could invoke European legislation directly (**direct effect**) and European legislation assumed precedence over national legislation (**supremacy**) (see Briefing 1.2).

Direct effect: a major legal principle in EU law holding that individuals can directly invoke EU legislation in cases before national courts.

Supremacy: a major legal principle in EU law holding that if national legislation is in conflict with EU law, EU law overrides national legislation.

Judicial activism: type of judicial behaviour where judges take a broad and active view of their role as interpreters of the law.

Several member states and their national courts initially objected to the Court's interpretation of the status of European law. The Court's rulings were seen by many as part of a deliberate strategy to increase its own powers through **judicial activism**. The decades to come would witness numerous other rulings of the Court that fostered integrative steps. Member states nevertheless accepted the Court's ruling, albeit reluctantly.

The success of the EEC did not go unnoticed in neighbouring countries. Hence, the UK, Ireland, Denmark and Norway made applications for membership. In 1963 French President Charles de Gaulle vetoed the UK's application, much to the dismay of the other member states. De Gaulle considered the British to be too strongly aligned to the United States. He also feared a loss of influence for France as a result of the possible entry of such a large country. As a result negotiations with all four candidates were aborted. De Gaulle would again veto the UK's application in 1967. Negotiations were resumed only after he had stepped down as president of France and was replaced by Georges Pompidou in 1969.

Briefing 1.2

Excerpts from the Court's rulings establishing direct effect and supremacy

Direct effect: In the case *Van Gend en Loos* v. *Nederlandse Administratie der Belastingen* (1963) the Dutch transport company Van Gend en Loos challenged an increased import duty it had to pay to the Dutch authorities on the ground that it violated Article 12 of the EEC Treaty, which expressly forbade introducing new duties. The Dutch court referred the matter to the Court because it was unsure whether individuals had the right to directly invoke Community law in a national court case. In its ruling the Court argued that:

> this Treaty is more than an agreement which merely creates mutual obligations between the contracting states. [...] Independently of the legislation of member states, Community law therefore not only imposes obligations upon individuals but is also intended to confer upon them rights which become part of their legal heritage. [...] According to the spirit, the general scheme and the wording of the Treaty, Article 12 must be interpreted as producing direct effects and creating individual rights which national Courts must protect.

Supremacy: In the case *Costa* v. *ENEL* (1964), an Italian citizen, Flaminio Costa, brought a case before an Italian court claiming that plans to nationalize the electricity company ENEL violated Community law. The Italian court referred the case to the Court of Justice which clarified the status of European law as follows:

> By contrast with ordinary international treaties, the EEC Treaty has created its own legal system which, on the entry into force of the Treaty, became an integral part of the legal systems of the member states and which their Courts are bound to apply. By creating a Community of unlimited duration, having its own institutions, its own personality, its own legal capacity and capacity of representation on the international plane and, more particularly, real powers stemming from a limitation of sovereignty or a transfer of powers from the states to the community, the member states have limited their sovereign rights, albeit within limited fields, and have thus created a body of law which binds both their nationals and themselves.

Source: Court of Justice of the European Communities, *Reports of Cases before the Court* (Luxembourg, 1963 and 1964).

De Gaulle's vetoes were part of a larger legacy of events that seriously slowed down the pace of integration. The most important of these was the empty chair crisis. In 1965 the Commission proposed to the Council a different way of financing the Common Agricultural Policy. Because it would give the European Parliamentary Assembly and not the Council the right to decide upon the budget, de Gaulle felt that this undermined the power of member states. Tensions further increased when de Gaulle objected to a scheduled change in decision-making rules in the Council that would introduce a new rule for making decisions, called **qualified majority voting** (QMV). This

Qualified majority voting: Decision-making rule in the Council which requires a majority that is substantially larger than a simple majority of (50%+1), but does not require unanimity.

would eliminate the possibility for a member state to veto proposals in some policy areas.

The French president decided to withdraw his ministers from participation in the meetings of the Council. This paralysed decision-making for half a year, because the remaining members did not want to make any drastic decisions until France returned. It did so after the member states agreed on a declaration that came to be known as the **Luxembourg Compromise**. The declaration provided for a safeguard clause that would give every member state a veto to block decisions considered to be a matter of vital national interest. While the compromise was never formalized into a provision in any of the treaties, it had a real effect on decision-making in the Council. It necessitated finding a consensus even in those instances where the formal rules would allow decisions on the basis of majority voting. The crisis also forced the Commission to be more cautious in advancing its plans. This obviously slowed down decision-making and the process of integration in the years to come.

> **Luxembourg Compromise:** agreement allowing a member state to block a decision in the Council if it declares the matter to be of 'vital national interest'.

The 1970s: moving out of gridlock, slowly

The early years of the 1970s were difficult, not least because of the economic crisis. Eurosclerosis held the member states in its grip: a relatively inflexible labour market coupled with a system of generous unemployment benefits made their economies inflexible and economic recovery difficult. The economic setbacks seemed to generate a retreat from European cooperation with member states unwilling to move ahead with integrative steps. The Council had accumulated a backlog of no fewer than 1,000 Commission proposals that it was unable to decide upon because member states were blocking decision-making with a reference to the Luxembourg Compromise. This in turn demotivated the Commission. It would take until the end of the 1970s before pessimism gave way to renewed confidence.

Despite this general mood of pessimism, a couple of small developments would provide the foundation for more significant integrative steps in the decades to come. First, in 1970 the Treaty of Luxembourg was signed. Its significance lay in granting the Community its own resources and giving the European Parliament the right to approve part of the budget (its powers were extended in 1975 through a second budgetary treaty). The position of the Parliament was further strengthened by the decision to directly elect its members from 1979 on.

Negotiations with the aspiring four members were also concluded in the early 1970s. In 1973 the UK, Ireland and Denmark finally joined. Norway, however, stayed out after its citizens rejected membership in a referendum.

The 1970s also witnessed the rise of a new body that would eventually develop into one of the EU's most important institutions: the European Council. From 1969 on the political leaders of the member states – the so-called Heads of State and Government – had started meeting informally to discuss the most urgent problems. In 1974 these meetings were formalized through the establishment of the European Council (not to be confused with the Council of Europe). The first role of the European Council would be to provide political guidance to the activities of the Community. It did so by identifying new areas of cooperation and surveying the possibilities for developing policies in these domains. In 1970, for example, the Werner Report recommended measures to coordinate economic and monetary policies. This provided the basis for several agreements to dampen currency fluctuations in the early 1970s. In 1978 the European Council made the decision to set up the European Monetary System (EMS), which fixed exchange rates between the participating countries.

A second important role of the European Council would be to discuss and tackle the major problems the Community faced. A notable early example was the UK's problem with the budget. In 1979 Prime Minister Margaret Thatcher complained about the UK's status as a net contributor: 'What we are asking is for a very large amount of our own money back, over and above what we contribute to the Community.' Five years later the European Council finally agreed on a formula that would give the UK a substantial rebate on its contribution. The rebate is still in force today.

In the second half of the 1970s Greece, Portugal and Spain applied for membership. The three countries had each suffered under dictatorships. The end of their autocratic regimes provided an opportunity for these countries to consolidate democracy and boost their economic development by joining the Community.

A major impediment to the further development of the Community had been the continued existence of all kinds of **non-tariff barriers** to trade. Even if on paper enterprises were allowed to import and export goods without any restrictions, in practice national laws and regulations often prevented this.

> **Non-tariff barriers** are all kinds of conditions, restrictions or regulations that do not consist of tariffs, but still make the import or export of products difficult or impossible.

Firms very often brought cases to court to address such barriers. One case involved a German importer who was not allowed to sell a French liqueur in Germany because the alcohol percentage was below what German law prescribed. In the 1979 *Cassis de Dijon* ruling the Court of Justice concluded that the German law violated the principle of the freedom of movement of goods and was hence incompatible with European law. The ruling established the principle of mutual recognition which is further explained in Chapter 8 (see Briefing 8.1).

In 1979 the first direct elections for the members of the European Parliament (EP) – the new name for what was originally known as the Common Assembly – were held. While at this stage the EP's powers were still limited, its direct mandate would make it more assertive in the years to come.

The 1980s: moves towards a single market

The Court's *Cassis* ruling made clear that there was a wide gulf between the principles and the practice of the Community's free trade area. Customs duties might have been abolished, but there were so many other barriers that a truly single market did not exist yet. In 1985 a new Commission took office under the leadership of Jacques Delors, who made the completion of the single market one of its key ambitions. At the request of the European Council the Commission made a proposal in which it sketched a timeline that would remove all barriers by 1992. To realize this goal it was deemed necessary to facilitate decision-making in all policy areas relating to the single market. This necessitated a revision of the treaties, which was achieved via the Single European Act (SEA). The SEA – signed in 1986 – included measures to advance the single market project and further broadened the EU's sphere of activity by including environmental policies, social policy and measures to increase economic and social cohesion between the member states. The Act also formalized some forms of cooperation which had already been developed outside of the treaties: Economic and Monetary Union (EMU) and Foreign and Security Policy.

The Act also contained a number of significant institutional changes. Decision-making on the single market was facilitated and the EP was granted new powers through the introduction of two new decision-making procedures. It was given the right of assent for enlargement and association agreements and also acquired some say over a limited number of policies through the cooperation procedure.

After Greece had joined the Community in 1981, Portugal and Spain joined in 1986. The accession of these countries was not unproblematic. Greece was economically very backward, but the solid support of Germany and France ensured its entry, despite reservations on the part of the Commission. The entry of Spain and Portugal met with resistance from France and Italy who feared a flooding of cheap agricultural products as well as an influx of guest workers. These worries were handled by agreeing to a transition period that would put limits on exporting certain products as well as quotas, limiting the amounts to be exported.

In 1987 both Turkey and Morocco applied for membership. Morocco's application was immediately turned down because it was not considered to be a European country. The Turkish application would be the start of a very long accession process that is still under way.

The 1990s: the road towards European Union

The project of completing the single market proved to be quite successful and led to renewed attention to achieving further integration in the fields of economic and monetary policies. In 1989 Commission President Jacques Delors brought out a report on achieving Economic and Monetary Union, once again at the request of European Council. Delors proposed a timetable consisting of three different stages that would ultimately result in a single monetary policy and a replacement of national currencies by a single currency.

The same year witnessed the fall of the Berlin wall which would bring to an end a four-decade era of communism in the Central and Eastern European

Countries (CEECs). The events necessitated further reflections on the political future of the Community. A new treaty revision was needed to incorporate these developments.

The Treaty of Maastricht broadened the areas that would be part of Community policies, including a timetable to introduce a single currency, the Euro. All member states committed themselves to joining the Eurozone once their economies would meet all requirements. The UK and Denmark negotiated **opt-outs** and hence were enabled to keep their own currency. Sweden managed to escape the obligation by not joining the Exchange Rate Mechanism, which is a prerequisite for being able to adopt the Euro. 'Maastricht' further expanded cooperation in the fields of foreign policy through establishing a Common Foreign and Security Policy (CFSP). Under the heading of Justice and Home Affairs (JHA) it launched agreements on asylum and immigration policies as well as judicial and police cooperation. In terms of institutional changes the Treaty of Maastricht further increased the EP's legislative powers through the introduction of co-decision. For a limited number of policy areas this new decision-making procedure allowed the EP to modify legislative proposals before approving them. (The procedure would eventually become the most common form of decision-making and hence is called **ordinary legislative procedure** today).

> **Opt-outs:** specific exceptions that are granted to a member state when it is unwilling or unable to fully accept all provisions of a treaty or a law.

> **Ordinary legislative procedure:** decision-making procedure that is most commonly used in the EU for adopting legislation, giving equal powers to the European Parliament and the Council.

The institutional structure for these different policies was quite complex and captured by referring to three different pillars. The first supranational or Community pillar consisted of all policies that were part of the three founding treaties and their respective amendments (ECSC, EEC and Euratom). The second pillar and third pillar represented CFSP and JHA, respectively: these two pillars were referred to as intergovernmental, because they granted most decision power to the Council and the member states represented there (we explain these different decision-making procedures in Chapter 4).

To still suggest some modicum of coherence the term 'European Union' was coined to refer to the overall structure that was supported by these three different pillars. Hence the EU was built on a very uneven foundation, which reflected the divergent views on levels of cooperation for different policy areas. Still, one other ingredient was added to symbolize unity: the Treaty also introduced the concept of European Union citizenship. Although initially this decision was seen as a highly symbolic move, it would achieve real significance through several Court rulings that granted rights to European citizens living in another member state.

The 1990s witnessed important developments in terms of enlargement. During the decades of the Cold War Austria, Sweden and Finland had decided not to apply for membership because they wanted to maintain their neutrality. With the fall of the Berlin wall this was no longer needed. Given the affluence and the level of democracy in each of these countries, their applications were warmly welcomed. In fact, accession negotiations for this fifth enlargement proved to be somewhat of a mirror image of the previous two. Instead of member states demanding guarantees to alleviate worries about negative effects of new members, this time the candidates expressed worries about the possible negative effects of joining the Community for certain sectors.

Several deals were struck with each of these countries, such as measures to protect farmers in Finland and Austria that went well beyond those mandated by existing Community policies. The three countries joined the EU in 1995.

While the German Democratic Republic (GDR) had already joined the EU via the reunification of Germany, between 1994 and 1996 ten other CEECs submitted an application for membership. Given the radically different background of these countries, the European Council formulated some additional rules that would guide the admission process (the **Copenhagen criteria**, see Briefing 1.3).

Copenhagen criteria: fundamental conditions regarding institutions, human rights and economic readiness aspiring member states have to meet before being able to join the EU.

Together with the earlier applications of Malta and Cyprus this made for twelve potential new members. The prospect of these significant enlargements necessitated further treaty revisions. The first of these resulted in the Treaty of Amsterdam, but many decisions were in the end forestalled. Nevertheless, the Treaty further increased the use of co-decision and hence the power of the EP. It also provided for further coordination in the area of CFSP. Also immigration policies and related topics such as procedures on issuing visas were moved to the first, Community pillar.

In the meantime a core group of twelve countries had steadily moved towards achieving monetary union following the timetable that was proposed by Delors. In 1998 the European Central Bank started operations and in 1999 the third and final stage of EMU was reached. From 1 January 2000 exchange rates were fixed and national currencies of were replaced by the Euro. Two years later Euro coins and notes were brought into circulation and replaced the national coins and notes within half a year.

The 2000s: further enlargements, difficult treaty revisions and the beginning of a financial crisis

Although there were large disparities in the readiness of different CEECs for membership, political considerations made it desirable to arrange for a timetable that would result in allowing as many countries as possible to join at the same time. Eight of the ten CEEC countries succeeded in qualifying together for membership and in May 2004 they became members, together with Cyprus and Malta. Bulgaria and Romania followed suit in 2007.

In 2004 Croatia became a candidate member of the EU, and – after almost ten years of negotiations – became the EU's twenty-eighth member state in 2013. Accession negotiations with other candidate countries were less successful. Those with Turkey started in 2005 but proved to be difficult with respect to its relations with Cyprus, issues of freedom of speech and judicial reform.

Briefing 1.3

How to become a member of the EU

Article 49 of the Treaty on European Union states that any European state which respects and promotes the basic values of the EU can apply for membership. Countries have to submit this application to the Council of Ministers. On the basis of advice from the Commission the Council will have to accept the application unanimously. Negotiations take place between the member states and the candidate country and can only start if the country meets the so-called Copenhagen criteria, drawn up at a meeting of the European Council in 1993:

• stable political institutions that foster democracy and respect human rights;
• a well-functioning market economy;
• the institutional capacity to work towards political, economic and monetary union.

Once these conditions have been satisfied the Commission starts a process called *screening* in which it outlines the *acquis communautaire*, or *acquis*, the body of legislation and policies that every aspiring member has to incorporate as a condition for membership. The *acquis* is divided into thirty-five chapters that each deal with a separate policy area. Member states negotiate with the candidate country on a chapter by chapter basis, and are updated on the status of progress by the Commission. If candidates have satisfied all conditions, a chapter can be closed and new chapters can be opened. When all conditions have been satisfied a draft accession treaty is drawn up which needs to be approved by the Council, Commission and EP and signed by the member states and the candidate member. Membership comes into effect after each member state has ratified this treaty according to its own national procedures (usually approval by parliament).

The EU helps potential candidates meet the Copenhagen criteria by giving financial support aimed at strengthening democratic institutions, reforming the economy and training civil servants. The road to membership is long. Many of the countries that were part of the 2004 enlargement took about ten years to complete the full trajectory, while Turkey's journey continues to be tortuous. After applying in 1987, it took until 1999 before the EU accepted the application. It took another six years before the start of accession negotiations in 2005 and progress on the different chapters is very slow.

Source: European Commission, enlargement website (www.ec.europa.eu/enlargement).

Iceland gained candidate status in 2010, but the Icelandic government put the negotiations on hold in 2013 because no agreement could be reached on important dossiers such as those concerning fisheries and financial supervision.

Table 1.2 EU member states, waves of enlargement and key characteristics

Member state	Date joined	Population in millions	GDP as % of total EU GDP	GDP in Purchasing Power Standards	Unemployment as % of the labour force	Euro as currency
Belgium	1951	11.2	2.9	120.4	8.4	X
France	" "	65.6	15.8	108.6	10.3	X
Germany	" "	80.5	20.9	123.5	5.3	X
Italy	" "	59.7	11.9	100.4	12.2	X
Luxembourg	" "	0.5	0.3	263.1	5.8	X
Netherlands	" "	16.8	4.6	127.8	6.7	X
Denmark	1973	5.6	1.9	125.9	7.0	
Ireland	" "	4.6	1.3	129.0	13.1	X
United Kingdom	" "	63.9	14.5	104.3	7.5	
Greece	1981	11.1	1.4	76.5	27.3	X
Portugal	1986	10.5	1.3	76.1	16.4	X
Spain	" "	46.7	7.8	95.7	26.1	X
Austria	1995	8.5	2.4	129.8	4.9	X
Finland	" "	5.4	1.5	115.3	8.2	X
Sweden	" "	9.6	3.2	126.3	8.0	
Cyprus	2004	0.9	0.1	91.8	15.9	X
Czech Republic	" "	10.5	1.1	81.2	7.0	
Estonia	" "	1.3	0.1	71.4	8.6	X
Hungary	" "	9.9	0.7	66.7	10.2	
Latvia	" "	2.0	0.2	64.3	11.9	X
Lithuania	" "	2.9	0.3	71.8	11.8	X
Malta	" "	0.4	0.1	86.3	6.4	X
Poland	" "	38.5	3.0	67.1	10.3	
Slovakia	" "	5.4	0.6	76.1	14.2	X
Slovenia	" "	2.1	0.3	83.9	10.1	X
Bulgaria	2007	7.3	0.3	47.5	13.0	
Romania	" "	20.0	1.1	52.9	7.3	
Croatia	2013	4.3	0.3	61.2	17.2	
EU-28		505.7	100.0	100.0	10.8	

Source: Eurostat. All figures 2013, except for GDP (2012).

Table 1.2 gives some core characteristics for the current members and ranks them in the order of joining the EU. In some older documents and analyses a distinction is often made between what is called the EU-15, consisting of the 'old' member states, and the new member states, which after the 'Big Bang' enlargement were termed the EU-12. The distinction is made because of the significant differences between these countries in terms of their length of membership, political background and economic development. The level of affluence in the new member states is substantially lower than that of the EU-15. Also the size of the economies of the newer member states is very small, making up no more than 7.3% of the Union's gross domestic product (GDP). The willingness of the EU-15 countries to accept these countries into the EU was therefore mixed, and was largely framed in terms of the need to consolidate democracy and ensure peace and stability in a wider Europe.

The first decade of 2010 was also characterized by a lengthy period of revision of the treaties. The Treaty of Amsterdam had left many issues unresolved and necessitated a new round of modifications that resulted in the Treaty of Nice in 2001. It reassigned the voting weights of the member states in the Council and the number of seats for the members of the EP, but only after long and protracted battles between the member states. As a result of all these struggles there was a widespread feeling among the leaders of many member states that the institutional architecture of the EU needed a major overhaul. How could the EU be made more democratic, transparent and effective? Instead of calling for a new **Intergovernmental Conference** (IGC), in which member states would debate

Intergovernmental Conference: meeting of the member states to discuss and decide a revision of treaties. As its name indicates an IGC is a purely intergovernmental affair that only involves representatives of the member state governments.

these issues, they agreed on establishing a convention – with a much broader membership than an ordinary IGC – that would examine these questions. Its recommendations would then provide input to the IGC.

The convention consisted of 207 delegates drawn from national parliaments, the European Parliament, the Commission and the governments of member states. After numerous plenary sessions and group meetings over the course of sixteen months, its chair – former French President Giscard d'Estaing – succeeded in presenting a single text on which all delegates could agree. *The Draft Treaty establishing a Constitution for Europe* would do away with the patchwork of amending treaties that had made for such a complex institutional set-up of the EU. Although very lengthy, it greatly simplified the legal structure of the EU by putting things in the right place and providing a clear overview of the Union's competences. The document was of course remarkable in another sense: the Convention delegates dared to characterize the Treaty as a constitutional document. With the benefit of hindsight this might have been the element that triggered most opposition.

The IGC that examined the draft treaty adopted nearly 90% of its contents and succeeded in agreeing on a final text a year later. The Constitutional Treaty streamlined decision-making further by bringing almost all decisions under the *ordinary legislative procedure* thus making the EP a co-legislator in almost all policy areas. It also introduced a semi-permanent President for the European Council and a High Representative for CFSP who would represent the EU in foreign policy matters.

Many member states felt that this major revision of the EU's treaty base necessitated the consent of their citizens. As a result, several member states decided to hold a consultative referendum, even if they were not required to do so. Fuelled by the prospect of these referendums public debates surfaced on the pros and cons of European integration. Signs were hopeful when Spanish voters kicked off the referendum practice and approved the treaty with an overwhelming majority of 76%. Only three months later, however, on 29 May and 1 June 2005, respectively, French and Dutch voters rejected the treaty. Although the outcomes of both referendums were only consultative and could have been ignored by their governments, the EU member states decided to take the signals seriously and suspend the ratification process.

After a period of reflection the European Council decided to redraft the treaty into an ordinary amending treaty. Although much of the content of the treaty survived, some changes were made to accommodate the worries that had surfaced through the outcomes of the referendums. At the request of the Dutch government, references to the constitutional character and official symbols and anthem of the EU were removed. The French successfully pleaded for removing the phrase 'free and undistorted competition' as one of the objectives of the Union. In December 2007 the Treaty of Lisbon was signed.

Wary about the possibility of new no's in referendums all member states decided to ratify this treaty by parliamentary approval and not call referendums. The Irish, however, were constitutionally obliged to submit the treaty to a referendum. The Irish voted no, causing a great deal of frustration among all the member states. The European Council made additional guarantees to the Irish. The most important concession was to refrain from reducing the size of the European Commission, in order to enable every member state to appoint its own commissioner. The guarantees and the impending economic crisis successfully turned around public opinion and in a second referendum the Irish voters approved the Treaty. After all the member states had ratified the text, the Treaty of Lisbon came into effect on 1 December 2009, no less than eight years after initial deliberations on revising the Nice Treaty had started. Treaty modification and ratification had proven to be very complex in a Union of no fewer than twenty-seven member states.

Following the bursting of the housing bubble in the United States in the course of 2008, a global financial crisis evolved that would keep the EU in its grip for several years. The crisis essentially consisted of two interrelated problems. First, a banking crisis affected many so-called systemic banks in the Eurozone, necessitating large support packages from national governments or an outright nationalization of these banks to keep them afloat. Second, in what was known as a sovereign debt crisis the public budgets of many Eurozone governments faced increasing debts and deficits – partly because of the activities to rescue banks. This made it more

Map 1.1 Member states of the EU as of 1 January 2015

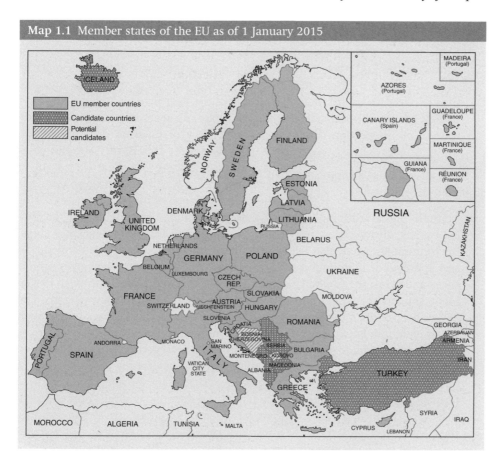

and more likely that countries would not be able to meet their debt obligations.

Greece was the first country so overburdened with debt that it ran the risk of defaulting on its debt payments and having to leave the Eurozone. The Eurozone countries and the International Monetary Fund (IMF) agreed on several rescue packages on condition of severe austerity measures. Later that year Ireland was bailed out with a €70 billion aid package. In the course of 2011 Portugal also received support in order to avoid bankruptcy, and later on Cyprus and Spain as well. In the countries affected this generated widespread domestic protest, with citizens repeatedly taking to the streets to challenge the austerity policies their governments were forced to adopt.

The banking and the sovereign debt crisis revealed that current regulatory frameworks were insufficient to monitor and control the financial system and that the public finances of the member states needed to be subject to stronger controls as well. In Chapter 8 we will outline the different measures the EU took in order to address these challenges.

◼ What history teaches us about EU politics today

The overview of the major steps in the history of the EU tells us a lot about politics in the EU today. While we tend to regard them as historical events by now, they were political decisions at the time they were made. The insights thus derived are useful in analysing EU politics as it is made today.

First, while a superficial look at the course of events may suggest a steady process of integration, every step along the way involved difficult negoti-ations. The reason for this is very simple: polit-icians very often disagree on what they want to achieve. Member states have diverging opinions on the pace and scope of integration: the UK, for example, has traditionally been a **Eurosceptic** member state, whilst Luxem-bourg has always been a staunch supporter of further integrative steps. Decision-making has also been difficult because it required the cooperation and approval of many different actors – each of them with their own prefer-ences and ideas: the Council, Commission, European Council, European Parlia-ment, the member states and – in the case of referendums – their citizens. The EU has been deliberately designed to make decisions in this fashion. In this book we provide a detailed overview of decision-making procedures and practices enabling the reader to understand the complexities of getting to a final decision.

Eurosceptic: term used for people, member states or political parties that have been highly critical of European integration.

Second, while major steps have been made via the drafting and amending of formal treaties, other decisions have been as significant for integration as these formal steps. Think, for example, about the three key rulings of the Court of Justice that were outlined above. The Court has been much more active than member states ever expected it to be. As a result integrative steps have been fostered and accelerated to a large extent by the Court's judgments. The decisions of the Euro-pean Council provide another example. Although it does not have many formal powers, it exerts an enormous influence because it brings together the political leaders of the member states. In the chapters to come we therefore pay as much attention to the informal side of decision-making as to the formal aspects of it.

Third, decision-making on policies, institutions and members is very often related. Every debate about a new policy is accompanied by discussions on the role of different institutions and the rules that are used to make decisions. In the EU a major point of debate concerns the relative role of the intergovern-mental institutions – the European Council and Council – and supranational institutions – the Commission, Court and European Parliament. Should legis-lative decisions only be made by the Council, representing the member states, or should the EP as the representative of the citizens have a say as well? Is it sufficient to have a majority of the member states in favour of a proposal, or should unanimity be required? Every major inclusion of a new policy automat-ically generated a debate on these types of questions. When studying the current political decisions in the EU, it is important to keep this in mind: how do the different interests try to safeguard their position and how is this translated in agreements on the nature and scope of policies?

Controversy 1.1

How large should the EU become?

Ever since the fall of the Berlin wall there has been a steady eastward expansion of membership, with many countries currently in the process of becoming members. The accession of these new members is not undisputed, however. Critics point out that the current size of the EU already makes it too big to be able to make swift decisions. This complexity is not only the result of having too many members, but also a consequence of the increased diversity of the EU. Take Turkey, for example. For many critics, Turkey's membership is seen as a bridge too far, because the country does not share the Christian heritage of the other EU members. In addition critics point out that the country is very poor while at the same time so populous that it would wield a big influence in the Council. Supporters of the entry of Turkey point out that the EU will only benefit from Turkey's accession by virtue of its size and the markets this will open. Its membership will encourage the country to bring its democratic and human rights up to the level of EU members. Finally, incorporating Turkey into the EU will improve its position as a strategic buffer between Europe and the Middle East. Take a look at any of the other aspiring members and make a similar overview of the arguments in favour and against accepting that particular country as a member of the EU.

■ Summary

- The aftermath of the Second World War led to several initiatives for European cooperation on the military, political and economic fronts. The major challenge facing Europe was how to rebuild Europe and ensure a peaceful recovery of Germany as an independent country.
- While most of the organizations that were set up were intergovernmental in nature, France proposed an innovative scheme by introducing a plan for a supranational community in which a High Authority would be authorized to manage the common market of coal and steel.
- The French proposal resulted in the establishment of the European Coal and Steel Community through the Treaty of Paris in 1951 with six founding members: France, Germany, Italy and the Benelux countries. In 1957 the Treaties of Rome established the European Economic Community (EEC) and the European Atomic Energy Community (Euratom).
- The basic institutional structure of the early Communities consisted of a Commission entrusted to oversee the execution of policies, a Council of Ministers representing the member states, a Court of Justice to adjudicate conflict and a European Parliament representing the citizens of the member states. From the mid-1970s the European Council – bringing together the Heads of State and Government of the member states – emerged as the institution providing further political direction to the EU's activities.

- Since the 1950s European integration has consisted of a gradual incorporation of new policy areas, the establishment of new institutions and the inclusion of new member states. The integration process was marked as much by progress as it was by setbacks. While treaty changes provided the clearest indications of further integrative steps, other events such as the rulings of the Court of Justice or decisions of the European Council have been at least as significant for integration as well.
- The political struggles that were fought over the course of the EU's history tell us a lot about politics in the EU today. A major issue facing every integrative step is what the adoption or change of policies will mean for the powers of the different institutions and the possibilities to safeguard the interests they represent.

Further reading

A well-known account of the early days of European integration is Alan Milward, *The Reconstruction of Western Europe* (Routledge, 1987). Luuk van Middelaar's *The Passage to Europe* (Yale, 2013) provides a captivating account of key defining moments in the EU's history, while Desmond Dinan's *Origins and Evolution of the European Union* (Oxford, 2014) provides a diverse set of historical essays.

Websites

- The Virtual Resource Centre for Knowledge about Europe – CVCE – is host to the European Navigator, a multimedial portal with fact files, documents, pictures and films on European Integration: www.cvce.lu
- The EU itself hosts an informative timeline on European integration that connects steps in integration to the political events of the day. Not surprisingly it tends to emphasize the successes: http://europa.eu/abc/history

Navigating the EU

On the website www.navigatingthe.eu you will find online exercises for this chapter.

2   Analysing the EU

■ Introduction

Defining what kind of organization the European Union is has always been a challenge. In fact even those people who worked in its heart have had great difficulty pinpointing its essence. Jean Monnet, the first President of the High Authority, called the European Coal and Steel Community 'a new political form'. Given the nascent status of European integration in those days we could forgive him for being so vague. Three decades later, Jacques Delors, a two-term President of the European Commission, could do no better, describing the European Community as a UPO, an *unidentified political object*. After sixty years, José Barroso, another two-term President of the Commission, was only a little more precise, when he characterized the EU as a 'non-imperial empire'. There is probably a very simple explanation for these rather vague and disappointing definitions. Trying to capture the EU in a single definition is simply impossible if one does not know what exactly one wants to say about it. In other words, before being able to characterize something, one has to know what one wants to explain. This applies as much to politicians who work for the EU as to political scientists who want to study it. If we want to understand what the EU is, we first have to decide *what* we want to find out and *how* we are going to do that. This chapter will do this by answering the following questions:

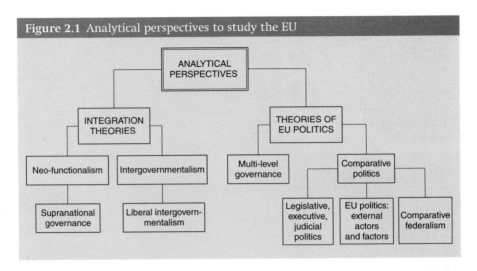

Figure 2.1 Analytical perspectives to study the EU

- What are the main theories that have been developed to understand and explain European integration and to explain policy-making in the EU?
- What major insights can be drawn from these different theories?
- What are the major features of the comparative politics approach to studying the EU?

After reading this chapter you will have found out that there are two major approaches to studying the EU. Figure 2.1 depicts the different theories that are discussed in this chapter. Integration theories seek to understand how the EU has come about and which factors have made it what it is today. Theories of EU politics, the second group of approaches, focus on the actual functioning of the EU: how does political decision-making work in the EU? Which actors and factors affect these decisions? What are the effects of the policies? Each of these perspectives, and the different approaches within them, offers useful insights into understanding what the EU is. There is in fact no best way of studying the EU. The theories we discuss differ because they ask different questions and use different methods to answer them. Each of them contributes to our understanding in its own way. Still, in this chapter we will pay more attention to the comparative politics approach, simply because it is the approach that we find most useful to understand the EU and accordingly use in this book.

■ Explaining integration

The first and oldest group of approaches to studying the EU finds its origin in the study of international relations. The study of international relations (IR) seeks to understand how sovereign states interact with each other and what forms of conflict and collaboration may be the result of this. In its beginnings, the EU obviously looked like just another form of international cooperation between such states, albeit with interesting features – such as the Commission as a supranational body – that had not been seen in other forms of cooperation yet. Hence it was quite natural that the first group of scholars to deal with the EU came from the study of IR. Below we discuss the two major approaches and their spin-offs.

Neo-functionalism and supranational governance

Neo-functionalism was developed at the end of the 1950s by Ernst B. Haas, a German-born political scientist who at the age of fourteen had fled Nazi Germany and found refuge in the United States. After obtaining his Ph.D. in political science in New York, Haas moved to the University of California where he published his major work *The Uniting of Europe* in 1958. The book provides a detailed account of the early stages of European integration (from 1950 to 1957) by studying the actions and motives of the key players at the national level (member states, parliaments, political parties, trade unions and employers) and the supranational level (the High Authority, the Parliamentary Assembly, supranational interest groups, etc.).

> **Neo-functionalism:** integration theory which states that member states will work together to reap economic benefits, setting in motion a process in which ever more tasks are delegated to the supranational level.

Haas' approach is rooted in the pluralist school which at that time was the dominant paradigm of political science in the USA. Pluralists consider politics to be a group-based activity and believe that all interests will eventually organize to affect decision-making. This pluralist conception of politics is reflected in Haas' definition of integration:

> The process whereby political actors in several distinct national settings are persuaded to shift their loyalties, expectations and political activities toward a new centre, where institutions possess and demand jurisdiction over the pre-existing national states. The end result of a process of political integration is a new political community, superimposed on the pre-existing ones.
>
> Ernst B. Haas, The Uniting of Europe: Political, Social, and Economic Forces, 1950–1957 *(University of Notre Dame Press, 2004: 18).*

According to pluralists politics amounts to nothing less than a clash of different interests, with every group trying to lobby the government for as much political support as possible. The process of integration and its results reflect the relative success of different groups in advancing their interests. Haas shows that in the case of European integration this means that groups are not restricted to the boundaries of their country but can forge **transnational** alliances with like-minded groups in other countries in order to further advance their interests.

> An organization is called **transnational** if it connects subnational levels of governments or brings together any other type of organization (businesses, civil society groups) from different countries.

Finally, and also in line with the pluralist conception of politics, Haas deliberately focuses upon activities of **political elites** (spokesmen, lobbyists, politicians, high-level civil servants). He claims that European integration was primarily an

> **Political elites** consist of the relatively small number of people at the top of a political system who exercise disproportionate influence or power over political decisions.

elite-driven process and shows that ordinary people were not very well informed or concerned about it.

Why did these sovereign nations decide to start working together? Haas identifies four subsequent steps which drive integration:

1. Recognizing the possibility of mutual economic gains, governments decide to start cooperation in a specific policy area. They set up a supranational body which is responsible for administering and implementing their arrangement.
2. After the arrangement has been put in place, all parties realize that further economic gains can only be arrived at if adjacent sectors are integrated as well, spurring additional integrative steps. The result is what Haas calls a *spillover* of integration into other fields (see *functional spillover* below).
3. The creation of a new centre of authority fosters the emergence of new transnational interests that put additional pressure on governments to move towards further integration. This process is advanced by the new supranational institutions – such as the Commission – as well, who are eager to take up new responsibilities in order to advance their status as policy-makers.
4. The increased complexity of several functional arrangements will lead to a further institutionalization at the supranational level in order to coordinate policy-making. The result is a peculiar form of policy-making somewhere in between that of a purely intergovernmental organization and a fully fledged federal state.

Spillover

As the steps outlined above indicate, economic motives start the process of integration only to take more and more policy areas on board once it is moving ahead. Neo-functionalism thus understands integration as a self-perpetuating process, once the first integrative steps have been taken. A central role in this process is played by the concept of **spillover**. Spillover is the major driver of integration. It exists in three varieties – functional, political and cultivated – which we discuss below:

> **Spillover** refers to 'the way in which the creation and deepening of integration in one economic sector creates pressures for further economic integration within and beyond that sector and greater authoritative capacity at the European level' (Ben Rosamond, *Theories of European Integration*, Palgrave Macmillan, 2000: 60).

- *Functional spillover*. This type of spillover is technical in nature and based upon the insight that the full benefits of integrative steps can only be attained if further moves in neighbouring fields are made. Haas himself points out that the first integrative step of building a common market for coal and steel 'had run up against its own topical boundaries' and 'that economic integration in the long run can not rest on supranational rules and institutions for one sector alone'. The result is that neighbouring sectors will be integrated as well. Haas pointed to the emergence of Euratom and the EEC as a proof of such integrative steps.

Briefing 2.1

Functionalism as a precursor to neo-functionalism

As its name suggests neo-functionalism has its roots in an earlier theory of integration called functionalism. In integration theory functionalism is most clearly associated with the work of David Mitrany, an academic born in Romania who was struck by the cruelties of the First and Second World Wars. In 1943 he published *A Working Peace System* which aimed at setting up a form of world organization that would do away with the evils that were caused by conflicts between nation-states. Instead of the nation-state formula of organizing government on a territorial basis, Mitrany proposed the organization of tasks on the basis of functional interests which would advance human welfare. Form would follow function. Organizational arrangements should be tailored to the types of tasks that needed to be carried out. The result would be a proliferation of overlapping international and transnational organizations, each of them specifically designed to optimally serve its purposes. Mitrany believed citizens would gradually shift their loyalties to these new organizational arrangements and thereby reduce nationalistic tendencies which had so often resulted in conflicts between states. Hence world peace would be the result of this functional organization of governmental tasks. Note, however, that Mitrany was strongly opposed to a comprehensive regional or federal organization of government, as this would simply reproduce nationalistic tendencies at a higher level. Mitrany's ideas of functionally organizing governmental tasks were further developed in theories of neo-functionalists.

A well-known example from economics concerns the creation of a single market: the abolition of tariffs between the member states will increase trade between them but only to some extent. Exchange rate fluctuations may constitute a further barrier. Hence functional pressures will develop in favour of moving towards the stabilization of exchange rates. This will eventually lead to pleas for a single monetary policy and single currency which will further bring down the transaction costs of international trade.

- *Political spillover*. This second type of spillover is the result of deliberate pressure exerted by national interests because they expect to benefit from further integrative steps. A much-cited example of this type of spillover concerns the activities of the European Round Table of Industrialists, a lobby group of major industrial corporations. These multinational businesses had a great stake in the creation of a single market as this would make it much easier for them to produce and sell their products in the different member states. Hence, they were particularly active in lobbying governments and the Commission to create the single market and pass the Single European Act (SEA). They also were very much in favour of the accession of the Central and East European states as this would open up new markets and production possibilities to industrial companies.

- *Cultivated spillover*. This type of spillover points to the role of supranational actors such as the Commission, EP and Court of Justice. In this conception supranational institutions are not simply implementing and administering the agreements between the member states, but play an active role in fostering (hence: cultivating) further integration. They can do this by using their formal powers (such as the authority to issue court rulings) as well as informal means. The Commission, for example, can act as a **policy entrepreneur** and in this capacity successfully rally support for further integrative steps. The Commission garnered support for the SEA by convincing industrial corporations in the member states to press their governments for a further liberalization of the energy market, thus breaking the resistance of the national energy conglomerates who still monopolized the energy markets. As this last example shows, the different types of spillover may often work in tandem in creating subsequent integrative steps.

> The Commission acts as a **policy entrepreneur** when it successfully influences decisions made by others, by skilfully mobilizing support, building coalitions and proposing solutions in the direction of an outcome close to its own preferences.

Neo-functionalist spin-off: supranational governance

The main point of criticism levelled at neo-functionalism is its understanding of integration as a linear and self-sustaining process. Critics can easily point out that instead integration has moved in fits and starts. The empty chair crisis showed that it was possible for integrative steps to come to a halt and even reverse. Thus towards the end of the 1970s – a period of little progress – Haas himself considered his theory a failure and declared it obsolete. However, when integrative steps picked up again at the end of the 1980s a revived interest in the ideas of neo-functionalism emerged. Just as interest had waned in the wake of the slowdown of further integrative moves, now the theory regained its attractiveness, as a new wave of cooperation emerged.

This also revived interest in the neo-functionalist framework. One of the most important spin-offs of neo-functionalist theory is the theory of supranational governance which has been developed by Alec Stone Sweet and Wayne Sandholtz. Rather than formulating an across-the-board theory, they point out that some policy sectors are more prone to integrative steps than others. Integrative moves are more likely in those sectors where there is a considerable amount of trade between member states. In those areas trade interests will demand further integrative steps and lobby their national government as well as seek support for these from supranational actors which will be happy to respond to those demands. The result is a differentiated picture with a continuum which runs from a purely intergovernmental mode of policy-making in areas such as foreign policy to a purely supranational mode of policy-making in areas such as the internal market (we further outline these different modes of decision-making in Chapter 4).

In line with neo-functionalist ideas (and contrary to the intergovernmentalist viewpoints we discuss below) Stone Sweet and Sandholtz point out that member states can oversee integrative steps only to a limited extent. Once a policy area has been integrated, moves by supranational actors such as court rulings by the Court of Justice may give the integration process a dynamic of its own that generates further steps which can no longer be contained by the member states. Take, for example, the Court's judgments in the area of patient rights. Invoking the four fundamental freedoms several patients successfully brought cases before the Court demanding coverage of medical treatment which they had received abroad. These rulings now necessitate new European legislation requiring insurers to provide such coverage.

Haas lived long enough to witness this renewed interest in his theories. In the preface to a new edition of his *Uniting of Europe* he was very happy to renounce his earlier declaration of obsolescence: neo-functionalism had a 'new lease on life'.

Intergovernmentalism

Intergovernmentalism constitutes the second important branch of integration theory. For a long time its position was most eloquently defended by Stanley Hoffmann. Hoffmann was born in Austria and raised in France during the Second World War. He too moved to the United States and became a well-known historian at Harvard University. Hoffmann's ideas on European integration appeared in a number of important essays which he published over the course of several decades.

> **Intergovernmentalism:** integration theory which holds that member states are fully in charge of cooperative steps they take and only collaborate with a view to their direct self-interest.

Intergovernmentalist theory has its roots in the realist approach of international relations theory which posits that issues of sovereignty and security are dominant in explaining the behaviour of countries. Governments are the sole players in the international political arena and do so with a view to maintaining the vital stakes of the nation-state, which are political rather than economic. Contrary to neo-functionalists, intergovernmentalists do not accept the idea that non-governmental groups are able to exert a strong influence on the preferences and activities of governments.

This then results in a much more sceptical assessment of the willingness of governments to actually transfer sovereignty to a new centre. In his best-known essay – published in 1966 – Hoffmann calls the nation-state 'a factor of non-integration':

> Thus the nation-state survives, preserved by the resilience of national political systems, by the interaction between separate nations and a single international system, and by leaders who believe in the primacy of 'high politics' over managerial politics and in the primacy of the nation.
>
> Stanley Hoffmann, 'Obstinate or Obsolete? France, European Integration and the Fate of the Nation-State'. *In:* The European Sisyphus: Essays on Europe 1964–1994 *(Westview, 1995: 96).*

Briefing 2.2

Social constructivism and the eastward expansion of the EU

At the end of the 1990s social constructivism came to the fore as a third approach to understanding integration. Social constructivists emphasize the interconnectedness between the actions, ideas and values of political actors, on the one hand, and the norms and structures that they have created through their interactions, on the other hand. Whilst liberal intergovernmentalists see actors as autonomous entities with fixed and set preferences aimed at maximizing self-interest, social constructivists point out that these preferences are at least partly shaped by the social and institutional settings in which politicians interact and the language and discourse they use when discussing politics. A good example of social constructivism at work is Frank Schimmelfennig's explanation of the Eastern enlargement of the EU. The eastward expansion of the EU ran directly counter to the immediate economic interests of several old member states, whilst the geopolitical situation did not require anything more than a mere association agreement. What then made these countries nevertheless agree? Schimmelfennig claims the supporters of Eastern enlargement made use of 'rhetorical action' to convince the opponents. They underlined the EU's commitment to the fundamental norms that shaped the EU, such as liberal democracy, a market-based economy and respect for human rights. By showing the commitment of the new member states to these norms, the supporters of enlargement were able to argue that enlargement would allow for a further consolidation and expansion of the core values of the EU. These arguments 'entrapped' the opponents as it would be hard for them to openly oppose these core democratic values. As a result even countries that materially would not benefit from Eastern enlargement in the end supported eastward expansion.

Source: Frank Schimmelfennig, 'The Community Trap: Liberal Norms, Rhetorical Action and the Eastern Enlargement of the European Union', *International Organization*, 55, 1, 2001: 47–80.

A key element in Hoffmann's theory concerns the distinction between low politics (such as economics) and high politics (such as territorial security and sovereignty). While the former is governed by a *logic of integration* and may indeed lead to collaboration because nations share the same interests, the latter is governed by a *logic of diversity* which expresses itself in the diverging preferences of the different countries with respect to issues of high politics. In such cases nations 'prefer the self-controlled uncertainty of national self-reliance to the uncontrolled uncertainty of the blending process' – the term he uses to characterize integration.

In line with his emphasis on the power of the nation-state Hoffmann also rejects the idea that supranational actors would be able to further integration beyond the limits set by the member states. He likens the process of integration to a grinder that comes to a halt as soon as the member states stop providing it with something to grind.

Spin-off: liberal intergovernmentalism

Hoffmann's theory has been further developed by one of his students, Andrew Moravcsik, who examined the negotiations of the major treaties signed between 1952 and 1992. Moravcsik's close reading of the positions, preferences and activities of Germany, France, Britain and the Commission (the actors he analysed in depth) generates the following conclusions:

- The preferences of member states are not formed autonomously but are the result of the influence of different domestic interests on their respective governments.
- Economic considerations are always a major consideration, while geopolitical considerations only play a role in half of the cases examined.
- The outcomes of negotiations are the result of bargaining between the member states, with those standing to win the most willing to grant concessions to those not perceiving the deal to be in their interest. The role of policy entrepreneurs such as the Commission has been minimal, but not completely absent.
- The institutional arrangements to put these deals into effect should be seen as means to ensure the credible commitment of each of the member states. While this may involve the delegation of tasks to supranational institutions such as the Commission or the Court of Justice, member states have organized this delegation in such a fashion that these institutions cannot go beyond their mandate.

Compared to Hoffmann, Moravcsik pays more attention to the role of domestic, economic influences on the positions of national governments in international negotiations and organizations. These national governments are still the key players in these contexts, however, with minimal influence of supranational actors such as the Commission.

Moravcsik's theory was not left uncriticized. The main point of criticism is his focus on major treaty negotiations as the cases for his study. Many commentators have pointed out that member states are by definition the key players in these processes. Hence his finding that they had most influence on the outcomes is not surprising at all. Moravcsik has countered this criticism by pointing out that his theory not only applies to these major decision-making events, but in fact also helps explain day-to-day decision-making in intergovernmental decision-making bodies such as the Council of Ministers. For example: while member states can formally rely on majority voting in the Council, they rather seek consensus and strive for unanimity. He therefore argues that actual decision-making thus reflects a classic intergovernmental context in which each member state interest is maximally protected.

Insights

Integration theories have provided valuable insights into the functioning of the EU. And although intergovernmentalists and supranationalists may differently weigh the role of various actors, they do agree on the following two points:

- Member state preferences and activities are not fully autonomous, but partly the result of domestic circumstances, most importantly the activities of interest groups that try to lobby their governments. Hence, a better understanding of member state positions in negotiations requires knowledge of the domestic forces that shaped those positions.
- The roles and influence of actors depend upon the type of decision and the policy area studied. What may be true in some policy areas does not have to hold in other ones.

The debate between neo-functionalism/supranationalism and (liberal) inter-governmentalism has been heavily influenced by actual developments in European integration, with periods of EU deepening providing support for the former and periods of stagnation bolstering the latter. In the late 1980s, the debate was revived with the adoption of the Single European Act. Controversy 2.1 outlines the issues at stake in that debate and the points brought forward by both parties.

■ Explaining EU politics

Just as the EU evolved over the decades and took on more and more tasks, the analysis of the EU broadened. Scholars started asking different questions by analysing the actual functioning of the EU as a political system, rather than seeking to explain how it came about in the first place. These analyses start where integration theories end. Whilst the primary concern of IR theories is to understand the EU as the result of the interaction between states as well as the institutions that they created, theories of EU politics approach the EU as a political system in its own right and examine its functioning. The first way in which the theories below differ from integration theories, then, is that they ask different questions.

The theories below also differ in another respect, however. Scholars started to employ a more diverse set of perspectives to answer these questions. The analysis of integration was traditionally dominated by so-called actor-centred approaches. Neo-functionalists and intergovernmentalists paid most attention to the preferences and actions of member states, the Commission, and so on, but they showed relatively little concern for contextual factors (rules, trad-itions, cultures) that shape their behaviour. Many analysts argued that greater insights in the behaviour of actors could be obtained by paying more attention to these factors. Under the banner of the *new institutionalism* several approaches have emerged that study this effect (see Briefing 2.3 for an overview of the different schools). Hence, theories of EU politics employ a wide and diverse set of research angles in which more attention is paid to the role of these insti-tutions and their impact on the behaviour of politicians, civil servants, pres-sure groups and citizens.

The above developments have resulted in an extremely rich and diverse body of studies examining EU politics. Below we discuss the two major

Controversy 2.1

The debate over the Single European Act

As we saw in Chapter 1, the 1986 Single European Act (SEA) was an important step in the development of the European Union. It revived the project of creating one internal market between the member states and provided new impetus to an organization that had been characterized by stagnation in the years before.

Among EU scholars, the SEA incited a fierce debate on what explained this major step forward. In an article published in 1989, Wayne Sandholtz and John Zysman argued that the adoption of the Single European Act was the result of activism by supranational actors, in particular the European Commission supported by a coalition of transnational business groups ('1992: Recasting the European Bargain', *World Politics*, 42: 95–121). These supranational actors provided the political leadership that produced the SEA proposals and convinced member state governments to agree to them. Unlike 'traditional' neo-functionalists, Sandholtz and Zysman did not think that functional spillovers were important but like neo-functionalists they stressed the importance of supranational actors in the integration process.

In a 1991 article Andrew Moravcsik took issue with this explanation ('Negotiating the Single European Act: National Interests and Conventional Statecraft in the European Community', *International Organization*, 45, 1: 19–56). Against the supranational explanation of Sandholtz and Zysman, he pitted an intergovernmental one that argued for the importance of the interests and power of (large) member states in bringing about the SEA. According to Moravcsik, the SEA can most fruitfully be explained as a bargain between the three largest and most powerful member states: Germany, France and the UK. The elements included in the SEA conform to those issues on which the preferences of these three member states converged, while it excluded issues that ran against their interests. Supranational actors may have facilitated the process leading up to the SEA but they did not initiate it and only marginally affected the outcomes.

Since then, both sides have further developed their arguments, publishing more fine-grained analyses that include a wider range of cases than just the SEA. Yet, the fundamental controversy on the role and importance of supranational actors has never been resolved and continues to inform much of the scholarly debate on integration theories.

branches: the first, *multi-level governance*, argues that the EU in many respects is a one-of-a-kind political system that has organized its policy-making process in a unique fashion. The second, the *comparative politics approach*, argues that the EU in fact shares many of the features of national political systems and therefore can best be studied using the tools that have been developed for that purpose.

Briefing 2.3

Three types of institutionalism

- *Rational choice institutionalism* assumes that actors try to maximize their self-interest. Institutions are important because they define the 'rules of the game'. In that way, they determine how decisions are made and what strategies actors can and cannot use. Institutions are therefore important as constraints on the behaviour of actors. Rational choice institutionalism defines institutions in a narrow sense as formal rules, such as laws and procedures. A real-life example concerns decision-making on fisheries quotas in the European Union. These quotas are often set at a much higher level than the level proposed by scientific advisers and the European Commission. This can be explained by looking at the institutional rules that govern decision-making on quotas. Fisheries quotas are ultimately determined by the Council of Ministers, in which each member state is primarily concerned with its own interests. Because member states with a large fisheries sector can block a decision, decision-making tends to inflate the quotas proposed by the Commission.

- According to *sociological institutionalism*, institutions do not merely define the rules of the game but shape the way actors perceive the world as well as their own preferences and identities. As a result, actors do not merely attempt to maximize their self-interests but are searching for the outcome that is most legitimate in terms of the institutional values within which they have been socialized. Sociological institutionalism also takes a broader perspective on institutions, including informal conventions, norms and traditions. We can illustrate this by returning to the example of EU fisheries quotas. Instead of focusing on rational strategic bargaining within a given institutional context, sociological institutionalism would point out that EU fisheries policies are founded on three fundamental objectives: protecting fish stocks, protecting the economic viability of the fisheries sector, and protecting vulnerable communities dependent on fisheries. People working within fisheries policy have been socialized into this paradigm, and are therefore likely to seek a balance between these objectives rather than give precedence to one of them. This may explain why quotas are set at a higher level than those proposed by scientists, who look exclusively at ecological aspects.

- *Historical institutionalism* includes elements of both rational choice institutionalism and sociological institutionalism. Its distinctive feature is the focus on sequences of decisions. The central idea behind historical institutionalism is that past choices exert an influence over current choices by making some alternatives more attractive than others. This is called 'path dependency'. Once it is decided to pursue a certain course of action, it becomes increasingly difficult radically to depart from that course later on. This is so both because such a change would require large investments (e.g. in new technologies) and because the status quo is often seen as 'the right way' to do things. An example of this in EU fisheries policies is the division of quotas among member states. During the

1980s, it was decided to use a fixed formula for dividing the overall EU quota among the member states. This principle of 'relative stability' guides EU fisheries policy to this day and it is nearly impossible to change this pre-set formula. Therefore, the division of fisheries quotas among member states is highly path dependent: it can only be understood by looking at earlier decisions that have effectively 'locked in' EU policies.

Multi-level governance

Multi-level governance (MLG) emerged as a new perspective for analysing EU politics at the beginning of the 1990s. Many scholars were unhappy with the rather crude conceptualization of the integration debate which pitted member states against supranational actors such as the Commission and the EP. They pointed out that processes of integration are far more complex and varied than the simple transfer of sovereignty from member states to the supranational level. This coincided with a more general trend in politics during the 1980s: the emergence of a different mode of policy-making known as **governance**.

Governance: term used to refer to a mode of governing characterized by collaborative and networked forms of policy-making.

The development of the governance approach in the context of the EU is most closely associated with the work of political scientists Liesbet Hooghe and Gary Marks. Their analyses of EU cohesion policies revealed that policy-making in this area developed in a highly fragmented and diverse manner and seriously challenged the dominance of the national governments. Three key insights emerged from their case study:

1. Decision-making authority has been dispersed over several levels of government and is no longer confined to national governments. It also includes subnational levels (regions) and supranational levels (Commission).
2. The national level of government depends upon the resources (information, money, expertise) of other levels of government in order to prepare and implement these policies.
3. Subnational levels of government are directly involved in making cohesion policies and do not have to rely on the willingness of their national government to press their case in Brussels.

Hence, all these developments amount to the emergence of a system of multi-level governance in which national governments are no longer the dominant players in EU policy-making but rather act alongside subnational and supranational actors. Subnational actors (cities, regions, provinces) have found direct ways to access EU decision-making processes, alone and in tandem with others through building transnational coalitions. At the same time supranational actors have been able to seriously constrain the room for manoeuvre of member states, be it the Commission with its right to initiate legislation and set the agenda, the EP with its increase in legislative powers or the Court through its court rulings.

> Multi-level governance does not confront the sovereignty of states directly. Instead of being explicitly challenged, states in the EU are being melded gently into a multilevel polity by their leaders and the actions of numerous subnational and supranational actors.
> *Liesbet Hooghe and Gary Marks,* Multi-Level Governance and European Integration *(Rowman & Littlefield, 2001: 27).*

These insights necessitate a new perspective on policy-making in the EU. Instead of seeing the EU as a new level of government that stands at the pinnacle of a hierarchy, MLG scholars speak about 'interconnected arenas', in which local, regional, national and supranational levels of government depend upon each other. In such a constellation policy-making does not follow classic command and control patterns where a higher level of government simply prescribes what lower levels should do. Instead policy-making is characterized by negotiation and deliberation between these different levels of government.

According to MLG scholars the EU is unique in the extent to which it relies on these newer modes of decision-making. One example concerns the Open Method of Coordination (OMC) which has emerged as an alternative mode of policy-making to the hard legislation of regulations and directives. In OMC policies member states voluntarily agree to work towards common goals by using benchmarks, targets and mutual learning, instead of being forced to reach a certain policy objective by a certain date as would be the case if ordinary legislation were used (see Chapter 4 for further explanation of OMC).

If one subscribes to this view on EU policy-making, it becomes clear that understanding the EU's functioning is impossible if one only studies governmental actors at the national and the supranational level and their interactions. It is necessary also to analyse the activities of local and regional levels of governments. In addition one should be aware of the emergence of new policy-making communities that may emerge in the shadow of the EU's main institutions. For example, much of the operational details of policy-making are decided upon and coordinated in any of the numerous comitology committees (see Chapter 11) in which civil servants from the ministries of member states discuss and deliberate the most feasible way of implementing these policies.

In short, in the eyes of MLG scholars the functioning of the EU can best be appreciated by paying attention to those features that make it a unique political system, which cannot be easily compared to any other form of political organization, be it an intergovernmental organization or a nation-state. MLG scholars thus tend to highlight those aspects that make the EU so special. Below we discuss an approach that takes the exact opposite position as its starting point.

Comparative politics approaches to the EU

Adherents of the comparative politics approach claim that the best way to understand EU politics is to compare the EU with national political systems.

While the EU's nature and character fall short of that of sovereign nation-states, it nevertheless can be considered a political system in its own right. Just like national political systems the EU makes binding decisions in a way that is very similar to how national democratic systems operate. Its institutions perform legislative, executive and judicial tasks and are structured in a quite similar fashion to that of national political systems.

As a result, all the questions we can ask about the functioning of national political systems can be asked about the EU as well. Comparativists point out that this has two advantages:

- First, by building upon the insights from comparative politics it is possible to use an established body of theories that guides research questions and employs well-developed methodological tools to answer them. Instead of having to start from scratch, comparative scholars can make profitable use of these earlier insights.
- Second, the insights thus obtained can be put into perspective by comparing them to findings from studies of national political systems. This makes it much easier to interpret and understand EU policies than if one were to treat and study the EU as a unique case.

In many respects, then, the comparative approach is very modest in its ambitions. It essentially tries as much as possible to integrate the analysis of the EU into the established body of knowledge on the functioning of political systems in general. It does so by answering the same type of questions about the EU as we would ask of any political system. How are legislative and executive powers organized? How is legislation passed? What is the authority of the Court of Justice? To what extent do citizens support and trust the EU? What determines people's voting behaviour at EP elections? How do interest groups try to influence decision-making in the EU?

What should be clear is that comparativists do not claim that the answers to these questions will be similar. There are obvious differences in the way the EU, for example, organizes its legislative process, compared to that of a country such as Germany. However, this is not much different from what you would find if comparing two national political systems. A comparison of legislative processes in Germany with those of the USA would yield at least as many differences as comparing Germany with the EU. Still, it is exactly through these comparisons that it becomes possible to better understand the functioning of any political system. The comparative school of analysing the EU is very diverse. Below we outline three major groups that in turn are home to a wide range of specialized approaches.

Studying the EU polity: legislative, executive and judicial politics
A first group of studies examines the three governmental functions of the EU through looking at the role of the different institutions – such as the European Commission, Council, European Parliament and Court of Justice – in

legislative, executive and judicial policy-making. Such studies focus both on the internal functioning of these institutions and on the relations between them:

- Studies of *legislative politics* examine everything that has to do with passing EU legislation. Scholars in this field, for example, examine the voting behaviour of the members of the European Parliament. To what extent do members of the same political group all vote in a similar fashion? Do they vote more according to ideological differences or according to nationality? Other studies focus on decision-making in the Council. Which countries tend to vote in a similar fashion? How much voting power do different countries have under different decision-making rules? Another important area of research concerns the analysis of *legislative bargaining* between the different institutions. What are the relative powers of the Commission, Council and the European Parliament in the ordinary legislative procedure? Has the EP gained influence since the old rules for co-decision were replaced by new ones as a result of the Maastricht Treaty?
- Studies of *executive politics* focus on the role of the European Commission as an executive. An important strand of research examines the room for manoeuvre or policy discretion the Commission has in implementing policies which have been decided upon by the Council and the EP. Other studies look at other executive actors such as the European Central Bank (see Chapter 11 for a further overview).
- Analyses of *judicial politics* study the adjudication of conflicts at the EU level through its judicial system. Scholars in this field look at the way the European Commission, member states and other interested parties invoke EU law and are involved in legal procedures before the Court of Justice. The behaviour of the Court itself is an important focal point. Do its rulings favour integration or does it more often side with the member states? Does it yield more often to the pleas of larger member states or are all member states treated in an equal manner?

Many of the above studies employ rational choice institutionalism (see Briefing 2.3) to explain policy-making. In this perspective each of the actors seeks to maximize its self-interest by pursuing a strategy that is most likely to be successful. Hence legislative bargaining is interpreted as a strategic game and its outcome is determined by the preferences of the actors and the decision-making rules. Outcomes will change if either preferences or rules change.

Studying EU politics: citizens, political parties and interest groups

As a complement to those studies that focus on the EU polity itself, another batch of studies concerns itself with examining the activities and strategies of what we might term external actors and factors. Comparative politics by now contains a mixed bag of subdisciplines that each examines part of this puzzle: these look at the role of public opinion, interest groups, the media and political parties in the EU political process. There is great methodological diversity to the approaches to these topics in EU studies, reflecting the many parent disciplines upon which EU scholars build.

The starting point of any of these studies is to assume that in principle the role of these factors and actors will be similar to that in national political systems, unless one can identify clear differences. Take the study of interest groups in the EU, for example. Many studies have shown that the behaviour of interest groups follows patterns that are roughly similar to the patterns found in national political systems. Interest groups, for example, try to lobby as early as possible in the political process in order to influence legislation as effectively as possible – that is, when it is still being drafted. While in the national context this means that they will seek access to civil servants in ministries, in the EU context it means that the Commission is one of the most favoured points of entry for them. And just as in national political systems, interest groups will shift their attention to different points of entry if they fail to get their way initially.

Still, interest group activity is also different from what we find in national political systems. One modification is the possibility of interest groups to both directly lobby EU actors as well as to seek to influence decision-making indirectly by targeting their national governments. Another reason for modification concerns the possibility of forming alliances across borders and hence employing a highly varied set of strategies when trying to influence policies compared to those that are available at the national level (see Chapter 6).

While early studies of the EU made profitable use of theories and methods from the study of national political systems, EU scholars by now have generated insights that are useful in analysing national political systems as well. Hence a fruitful exchange of ideas is taking place between comparativists studying national political systems and those studying the EU. One of the best examples is that of second-order elections, which refers to all those elections that are less important than the first-order elections, such as those for the national parliament (we further explain what they are in Chapter 5). The concept of second-order elections was first developed by two EU scholars, Karl-Heinz Reif and Hermann Schmitt, to explain people's voting behaviour for the first elections for the European Parliament. Because there is less at stake at these second-order elections, turnout for these elections will be lower. In addition, many voters will not so much care about the positions of the parties in that race, but rather use their vote to evaluate national politics. This is of course a phenomenon that can also be witnessed during elections at local, regional and provincial level. Hence, the concept of second-order elections is now widespread amongst analyses of any non-national election.

Comparative federalism

Comparative federalism constitutes the third group of studies within the comparative approach. This group of scholars seeks to gain insights into the functioning of the EU by comparing it to federal states such as the USA, Canada or India. Federal states share the following three characteristics which according to federalists can also be found in the EU:

- First, a federal system is a political system in which sovereign states have set up a higher, federal level of government to which they have delegated certain policy-making tasks. In this federal conception the EU has a two-tier system, with the member states forming the constituent states, and the supranational level constituting the federal level.
- Second, in federal systems the autonomy of the member states is constitutionally guaranteed via the explicit enumeration of competences. In the EU the Treaty of Lisbon contains such an enumeration. It makes a distinction between exclusive competences for the EU and areas where the EU and the member states share competences, leaving all other unnamed policy areas to the member states.
- Third, federal systems are characterized by a judicial system in which legislation at the federal level has precedence over lower level legislation and rulings of the federal court take precedence over those of lower level courts. In the EU the doctrines of direct effect and supremacy guarantee that EU law has such a status in those domains where the EU is competent.

One could say that comparative federalists try to make the comparison of the EU with national political systems as realistic as possible by not simply comparing it to any national political system, but only the subclass of federal states.

An important focal point of this approach is fiscal federalism. This studies the optimal allocation of policy competences between two levels of government – for example, when it comes to regulatory, fiscal or monetary policies. The actual allocation in the EU is then compared to that of other federal states to analyse and explain differences. A second strand of federalism studies takes a closer look at the way federations organize democratic representation. The issue here is how different types of interests – those of citizens, territories and other categories – are represented at the two levels of government and how democratic and effective the resulting policies can be considered to be.

■ Questions asked in this book

The overview in this chapter has shown that there are many questions to be asked about the EU and many ways to answer them. Hence, asking what the EU is, is indeed a mission impossible, and we should not be disappointed by the odd characterizations of the three Commission Presidents in the introduction to this chapter. The old proverb 'Where you stand, depends on where you sit' is as relevant for politics itself as it is for analysing EU politics. Choosing one of the approaches depends very much on one's interests. In the remainder of this book we make use of the comparative politics approach because we believe it is the best way to get acquainted with the EU.

The next ten chapters will do so in the following way. We first outline the EU's polity by outlining its institutional hardware. Chapter 3 introduces its major decision-making institutions, while Chapter 4 outlines the formal procedures for legislation and decision-making. We then move on to examining different actors and factors that affect politics: public opinion and political participation (Chapter 5), interest groups (Chapter 6) and, lastly, political parties and their relation to the EP (Chapter 7).

With these building blocks in place we examine actual decision-making in the next four chapters. We first give an overview of the different areas of EU policy-making in Chapter 8. We then outline three important stages of decision-making: agenda-setting (Chapter 9), decision-making (Chapter 10) and implementation (Chapter 11). In Chapter 12 we look at the major internal and external challenges for the EU in the future and examine how the approach in this book can help us identify these.

■ Summary

- Understanding the EU involves making a decision on the type of questions you are interested in and the way in which you want to answer them.
- The most important distinction between different approaches to the EU is between theories of integration and theories explaining EU politics.
- Neo-functionalism and intergovernmentalism are the two major approaches in integration studies. Intergovernmentalists claim that the EU is best seen and studied as a classic international organization, to which member states have delegated a limited number of tasks. Neo-functionalists, on the other hand, argue that the initial delegation of tasks to the supranational level has generated an integrative dynamic of its own, leading to spillover of tasks into other policy domains.
- Theories of EU politics seek to understand the actual functioning of the EU as a political system, rather than explain how the EU came about in the first place. Multi-level governance and the comparative politics approach are the two major strands of research in this area.
- Multi-level governance scholars consider the EU to be a one-of-a-kind political system in which the old, hierarchical way of doing politics between member states has been replaced by a new, networked form of government where different levels of government (local, regional, national and supranational) have become mutually dependent for realizing their policy objectives.
- Comparative politics scholars try to understand the EU by asking the same type of questions they ask when examining nation-states. It is exactly by comparing the EU to national political systems that it becomes possible to find out how and why the EU operates differently compared to its member states.

Further reading

Ben Rosamond's *Theories of European Integration* (Palgrave Macmillan, 2000) provides the best and shortest summary of integration theory. Antje Wiener and Thomas Diez's *European Integration Theory* (Oxford University Press, 2009) gives the floor to the major authors of each approach and lets them explain and defend their take on integration. Brent Nelsen and Alexander Stubb provide a collection of classic texts on integration as well as seminal documents marking key moments in integration in *The European Union: Readings on the Theory and Practice of European Integration* (Palgrave Macmillan, 2014). Useful essays employing the federal comparison can be found in Anand Menon and Martin A. Schain (eds), *Comparative Federalism: The European Union and the United States in Comparative Perspective* (Oxford University Press, 2006).

Websites

- Some well-known journals that publish a lot of academic work on EU integration and EU politics are the *Journal of Common Market Studies*, *International Organization*, *European Union Politics*, *Journal of European Public Policy*, *European Journal of International Relations* and the *Journal of European Integration*. Much of the work employing the comparative politics approach appears in general political science journals. Some of those that publish a lot about EU-related research are the *British Journal of Political Science*, *European Journal for Political Research*, *Comparative Political Studies*, *Comparative European Politics* and *West European Politics*.
- Many European think tanks publish useful reviews and recommendations for policies. A useful overview can be found at www.eu.thinktankdirectory. org/
- Much of the research on EU politics is first published in the form of papers. A good starting point to find these papers is the European Research Papers Archive: http://eiop.or.at/erpa/

Navigating the EU

On the website www.navigatingthe.eu you will find online exercises for this chapter as well as a list with links to the most relevant journals covering the EU.

3   The institutional framework

■ Introduction

For a long time many observers have lamented the lack of a clear personification of the EU. Take, for example, the European Council – the institution that brings together the Heads of State and Government of the member states. It traditionally made use of a rotating chairman, who came from the member state that happened to hold the Presidency of the EU, a responsibility which lasted for only six months. Because this chairman was the face of the EU when it came to meeting heads of state of other countries, someone like the president of the USA would have to deal with no fewer than eight different EU 'Presidents' during his or her four years in office. The Lisbon Treaty tackled this problem by creating the more permanent post of President of the European Council. This new position ensures more continuity in chairing this institution and facilitates more lasting relations with other countries.

In 2014 the European Council had to appoint a successor to its first president, Herman Van Rompuy, who would be stepping down in December after completing his two terms in office. Already over the summer Van Rompuy started extensive consultations with all the members in order to find a candidate that would have the support of all. In the end the members of the European Council agreed on appointing Donald Tusk, the prime minister of Poland, as their new president. Apart from the fact that Tusk had successfully led two subsequent coalition governments and was a much respected leader, it certainly helped that he came from a 'new' member state. After the presidency of the Belgian Van Rompuy, there was general agreement that it was long overdue to now let a candidate from one of these countries occupy this post.

This chapter will show that the appointment of Tusk tells us a lot about the character and nature of the EU's institutions. The choice of Tusk was a deliberate one to counterbalance the dominance of candidates from the old member states in key positions. And although he could have been elected through a majority vote, the outgoing President Van Rompuy deliberately strived for a unanimous choice. In this chapter we show how the EU's institutional design fosters this type of decision-making by answering the following questions:

- Which interests do the EU institutions represent and how are executive, legislative and judicial powers allocated to them?
- What are the tasks of each of the institutions and how do they organize their work?
- How should we evaluate the EU's institutional framework in terms of its capacity, on the one hand, to represent interests and, on the other hand, to act effectively?

The primary purpose of the EU's institutional set-up is to make sure that all relevant interests – those of member states, citizens and the EU as a whole – are represented in key phases of decision-making. This set-up ensures that decisions are made in a consensual manner and can rely upon the support of all interested parties.

◼ The EU institutional framework

Table 3.1 outlines the EU's institutional framework following Article 13 of the Treaty on European Union (TEU). We can see that there are no fewer than seven official institutions that form the backbone of the EU's decision-making apparatus. (The table does not list two other bodies that you may run across from time to time: the European Economic and Social Committee (EESC) and the Committee of the Regions (CoR). These are advisory bodies that we discuss further in Chapter 6.) Some institutional names sound very much like those found in national political systems (Parliament, Court of Justice), whilst others have rather unique names that we do not find anywhere else (Commission, Council). All in all this results in a rather peculiar institutional constellation that cannot be readily compared to those of national political systems (nor to that of international organizations).

Despite the fact that there is no one-on-one relation, these institutions perform tasks which are very similar to those of national political institutions. We can understand their role by answering two questions:

- Which interests do the different institutions represent and protect?
- How are the different governmental functions – executive, legislative and judicial – allocated over the different institutions?

Table 3.1 The institutions of the EU as outlined in Article 13 TEU

Name	Role	Representing
European Council	Executive	Member states
Council	Executive/Legislative	Member states
European Commission	Executive	Union
European Parliament	Legislative	Citizens
Court of Justice of the European Union	Judicial	Union
European Central Bank	Executive	Union
Court of Auditors	Control	Union

The ordering of these questions is deliberate. The institutional framework of the EU has been designed in the first place to balance different interests. It is this overriding concern which has subsequently resulted in a rather complex organization of the powers of the institutions, in particular when it comes to legislative and executive powers. Instead of locating executive and legislative power in clearly separated branches of government and basing them on popular sovereignty, the EU has several sources of power and distributes these tasks over multiple bodies.

Representation of interests

Let us first look at the way the institutions seek to incorporate different interests. Ensuring the representation of relevant interests is a major characteristic of democratic political systems. In national political systems this is achieved by making sure citizens can directly affect the composition of the parliament and – in the case of presidential systems – the head of government as well. Such an arrangement follows the principle of popular sovereignty: citizens determine the composition of the legislative and executive branch.

The EU does not neatly follow this principle of popular sovereignty, however. Although it makes sure that citizens can directly affect the composition of one of its institutions – the European Parliament – it seeks to incorporate a much wider range of interests:

- Citizens are represented by the European Parliament, whose members are chosen via direct popular elections in each of the member states.
- Member states are represented in the European Council – bringing together the Heads of State and Government of the member states – and the Council of Ministers – consisting of representatives at ministerial level of the member states.
- The interests of the European Union as a whole are represented and protected by all other institutions: Commission, Court of Justice, Court of Auditors and European Central Bank. Officeholders in each of these

institutions are to act independently and without instructions from any government or other institution.

In Chapter 1 we already noted that those institutions that represent the member states (the European Council and the Council) are labelled as **intergovernmental institutions**, while those representing the Union as a whole are considered to be **supranational institutions**. Note, however, that the European Parliament is also considered to be a supranational institution. The reason for this is that its members represent the EU's citizens not so much on the basis of their nationality, but on the basis of ideology, creating a body that in practice very often wants different things than the Council wants.

> **Intergovernmental institutions:** EU institutions that represent the member states: European Council and Council.

> **Supranational institutions:** all those EU institutions that represent the general interest of the EU (Commission, Court of Justice, European Central Bank and Court of Auditors) as well as the European Parliament.

According to political scientist Giandomenico Majone, the EU's set-up can best be compared to that of 'mixed government'. This is a form of government that was employed in seventeenth-century England. In that context it sought to balance the interests of territorial rulers and those of 'estates' who represented social and political interests. Such a balance can also be found in the EU. While in contemporary democracies the executive and legislative powers are ultimately rooted in one clear sovereign (the people), the EU has several sources of power which are represented by different institutions.

Allocation of powers

Having outlined the various interests and their institutions, we can now examine their role in governing the EU, by showing how executive, legislative and judicial powers are allocated:

- *Executive tasks* consist of giving political direction, implementing policies and externally representing the EU. In the EU these tasks are distributed over four different institutions:
  - The European Council *provides political direction* and *represents* the EU externally in its relations with other countries and international organizations.
  - The Council's executive role consists of the *implementation* of policies.
  - The Commission fulfils all three executive roles. It *initiates* legislation, it *implements* policies (such as in the area of competition) and it *represents* the EU externally with respect to specific policies for which the Commission bears responsibility.
  - The European Central Bank has an executive role in terms of *implementing* monetary policy in the member states that have the Euro as their currency.
- *Legislative tasks* consist of examining, modifying and adopting legislative measures which provide the basis for EU policies. In the EU the European

Parliament and the Council share legislative powers. This arrangement can somewhat be likened to the organization of a **bicameral legislature** in federal systems. If we analyse the EU in such federal terms, the European Parliament represents the citizens and the Council the member states. The EP and Council, however, lack an important power that is present in national political systems: they do not have the formal right to initiate legislative proposals. This right belongs to the Commission, which has the monopoly on initiating legislation.

> **Bicameral legislature:** legislature consisting of two houses or chambers. In federal systems one house represents the national population, whilst the other house represents regional populations by province, state or canton.

- *Judicial tasks* consist of the interpretation of EU law as well as the adjudication of conflicts involving EU institutions, member states and all other parties that may be involved (citizens, corporations). These tasks are in the hands of the Court of Justice.
- Providing additional supportive tasks, the Court of Auditors examines the EU's revenues and expenses. Its reports and observations are used by the European Parliament and Council in exercising their powers to control the EU's budget.

Below we outline the EU's six major institutions. We start with the most political, intergovernmental institution, the European Council, and then examine its older cousin, the Council. We then turn our attention to the supranational institutions: the Commission, the EP, Court of Justice and the European Central Bank. Finally, we reflect upon the nature and purpose of the EU's institutional framework.

■ The European Council

The European Council may be one of the younger institutions of the EU but easily qualifies as its most important. Founded in 1974 it brings together the heads of government (prime ministers) and heads of state (this applies in particular to France, who will be represented by the French president, and not the prime minister). By bringing together the government leaders of the EU member states, the European Council is capable of committing all the member states at its highest level and hence has enormous political clout. As a result European Council meetings are one of the most closely watched events, easily drawing 1,500 journalists to Brussels to cover its deliberations and outcomes.

In addition to the prime ministers or presidents of the member states the European Council has three other members, who are, however, not allowed to vote:

- The President of the European Council. He or she chairs the meetings, prepares the agenda and represents the Council externally. The members of the European Council elect their president for a renewable term of two and a half years.
- The High Representative of the Union for Foreign Affairs and Security Policy (High Representative). This person is responsible for executing the

EU's foreign policies and in charge of the External Action Service, the EU's *corps diplomatique*. The High Representative is also responsible for the EU's developmental policies and humanitarian aid operations. The High Representative is also a member of the Commission ensuring coordination of the work of the Council with that of the Commission.

- The President of the Commission represents the Commission and his or her presence at European Council meetings ensures coordination with the activities of the Commission.

Tasks

Although the European Council is one of the EU's most important institutions, its formal powers are surprisingly limited. For one thing, the Treaty on European Union explicitly states that it does not have legislative powers. Still, the European Council is able to affect policy-making to an enormous extent because it represents the governments of the member states at the highest and most general level. Hence its powers are derived from its political status and the leverage of each of its members over the actions of their respective governments. In practice the European Council is concerned with the following four tasks:

- *Providing political direction.* The European Council sets the long-term strategic agenda of the EU both with respect to internal policies and the Common Foreign and Security Policy (CFSP). This agenda-setting role is formulated in Article 15 of the TEU which states that 'it shall provide the Union with the necessary impetus for its development and shall define the general political directions and priorities thereof'. Large projects such as the road to the Single Market or the establishment of European Monetary Union or the EU's climate strategy all have first received their 'blessings' from the European Council. It is then up to the other institutions to develop concrete policies and adopt necessary legislation. On a regular basis the European Council reviews major policy developments concerning the EU's economic development, foreign relations and security issues. Finally the European Council gives authoritative guidance on opening up, progress and finalizing of accession negotiations with aspiring member states (formal decisions on these are taken by the Council).

- *Problem solver and ultimate arbiter.* In this second capacity, the European Council acts as the ultimate intergovernmental decision-making body for issues that cannot be resolved by the Council. For example, the European Council handled the UK's problem with its financial contribution to the EU budget and arranged and approved a special rebate. It also managed the difficult revision of the Constitutional Treaty, by first calling a period of reflection and then negotiating the major terms for its revision into the Lisbon Treaty. The European Council also was the centre of gravity in the midst of the financial crisis, where it took several ad hoc emergency decisions in order to avoid the collapse of the Euro.

Briefing 3.1

Revising the EU treaties

The procedures for amending a treaty as outlined in Article 48 of the TEU provide a good illustration of the way different interests are taken into account when making decisions in the EU. In the *ordinary revision procedure* any member state, the European Parliament or Commission can submit proposals for revision to the Council, which will subsequently forward this request to the European Council. The European Council then decides by a simple majority on convening an Intergovernmental Conference (IGC) where member states have to agree unanimously on the proposed changes. These changes finally need to be approved by all the member states using their own proper ratification procedures. The EU can also make use of two different *simplified revision procedures*, which do not require the convening of an IGC. In the first of these the EP, Commission or any member state can request a change to any of the EU's internal policies as long as it does not imply an increase in the EU's competences. The European Council decides on this on the basis of unanimity, after consulting the Commission, EP and – in the case of monetary affairs – the ECB. The decision then has to be approved by all the parliaments in the member states. In 2011 the European Council for the first time made use of this procedure to enable the establishment of a financial stability mechanism for the Eurozone countries. The European Council can also use a simplified revision procedure when it wants to change decision procedures in the Council from unanimity to qualified majority voting or from the special legislative procedure to the ordinary legislative procedure (see Chapter 4 for further information about these procedures). The European Council adopts these proposals by unanimity after they have been approved by a majority of the EP. National parliaments are informed of this decision and if one or more of these voice objections to it within a period of six months, the decision is not adopted.

- *Treaty revisions.* The European Council has a formal role in revising the treaties. In the *ordinary revision procedure* it decides by a simple majority vote to convene an Intergovernmental Conference (IGC) where representatives of the member states will discuss treaty changes. For so-called *simplified revision procedures* it needs to unanimously agree on changing the EU's policies or decision-making procedures. (See Briefing 3.1 for further information about treaty revisions.)
- *Appointments.* The European Council is involved in a range of key appointments. It appoints its own president. It moreover appoints the President of the Commission and the Union's High Representative. Because these two functionaries are also members of the Commission, their appointments need to be confirmed by the EP. Finally it appoints the members of the executive board of the European Central Bank.

Organization and decision-making

The European Council meets four times a year in Brussels and can if necessary meet for additional extraordinary or informal sessions. A normal meeting lasts for two days, but in fact does not take up more than twenty-four hours. This obviously necessitates elaborate preparations on the part of the president. The agenda, draft decisions and conclusions are as much as possible prepared by the General Affairs Council – one of the configurations of the Council of Ministers (see below). The president will also engage in bilateral contacts to explore member states' positions on issues and early on identify areas of agreement and contention. In the early days it was customary to visit all member state capitals as part of this preparation, but with twenty-eight member states this is not feasible anymore.

Day one starts in the afternoon with a meeting with the President of the European Parliament, who will inform the European Council of the most pressing issues. This is followed by a first working session which is usually devoted to discussing general issues. The session is adjourned for the 'family photo' and followed by a dinner which is used for further bilateral discussions and deliberations on outstanding issues. During the night the president will finalize the draft decisions and conclusions which will be discussed on the second day. This day starts with a second working session which is devoted to discussing foreign policy issues and finalizing these conclusions. After the meeting is over, the president will call a press conference, as will the member states who meet with journalists in their press rooms in the Council building.

To keep the meetings as effective and informal as possible, deliberations take place behind closed doors and attendance is limited to the Heads of State and Government only. Only if the issue at hand necessitates may they be joined by one additional member of their government, such as a foreign minister or minister of finance. Member state delegations are briefed on the proceedings every twenty minutes by a member of the Council secretariat which summarizes the main points to the so-called Antici group, consisting of the personal assistants of the permanent representatives of the member states. They will subsequently communicate this information to the other members of their delegation.

Article 15.4 TEU states that decisions are made by consensus, except when the Treaty provides differently. One of those exceptions is the appointment of its president which does not require unanimity. Still, as we saw in the introduction to this chapter, the heads of government strived for a consensus and did not vote on the appointment of Tusk. This is characteristic of decision-making in the European Council. All in all formal votes are rarely taken.

■ The Council

The Council (also known as Council of Ministers) is the older cousin of the European Council and has been around from the start of the EU as the

Table 3.2 Council configurations and average number of meetings per year, 2009–14

Council configuration	Number of meetings
Foreign Affairs	13
General Affairs	11
Economic and Financial Affairs (ECOFIN)	11
Agriculture and Fisheries	10
Transport, Telecommunications and Energy	6
Cooperation in the fields of Justice and Home Affairs (JHA)	6
Competitiveness	5
Employment, Social Policy, Health and Consumer Affairs	4
Environment	4
Education, Youth and Culture and Sport	3

Source: Council agendas as reported on the Council website (www.consilium.europa.eu).

institution representing the member states at the European level. The European Council may attract much more media attention than the Council meetings, but the Council in fact does most of the actual work and meets much more often. It essentially has a say over all of the EU's policies, and is the major policy-making organ when it comes to the CFSP. Whilst in an institutional sense the Council operates as a singular entity, it is in practice a multifaceted organ. It operates in different configurations which focus upon specific policy areas (see Table 3.2). Member states themselves can determine who they send to a specific meeting as long as it is someone 'at ministerial level who may commit the government of the Member State in question and cast its vote' (Article 16.2 TEU). This gives governments some flexibility in choosing their delegate: they can also send one of their **permanent representatives** to attend the meeting.

> **Permanent representatives:** member states' ambassadors to the EU who reside in Brussels and prepare much of the work of the European Council and Council.

Tasks

The Council's nature has frequently been characterized as chameleonic. This not only applies to its capacity to operate in different configurations but also to the fact that it has both legislative and executive tasks.

- First, with respect to all of the internal policies of the EU the Council acts as a legislator. In most of these areas it is co-legislator together with the European Parliament, and can be considered as one of the EU's two legislative chambers, with the EP acting as the representative of the EU's citizens and the Council representing the interests of the member states. The Council also concludes international agreements with third countries and international bodies in the areas of Common Commercial Policy, Development Aid and Humanitarian Operations.

- Second, in its executive role the Council is responsible for the EU's external relations through the CFSP. The Council adopts conclusions, recommendations, decisions and sanctions on a wide range of issues such as armed conflicts, human rights issues, terrorism and the proliferation of nuclear weapons. The Council is also able to take operational measures in this area via its European Security and Defence Policy. It can send civilian, police and military missions to contribute to peacekeeping, state-building and the rule of law in countries with an unstable political climate. The Union's High Representative for Foreign Affairs and Security Policy is responsible for implementing these policies. He or she is in charge of the European External Action Service, the EU's own *corps diplomatique*. Finally, the Council also makes the key formal decisions in the accession procedure of new member states by officially declaring countries as candidate members and deciding upon their accession process following the Copenhagen criteria.

One of the consequences of this double role of having both executive and legislative powers is that Council meetings are only partly public. In its executive role the Council deliberates behind closed doors, while in its role as legislator the proceedings are public and transmitted via the EU's audiovisual services.

Organization

There are currently ten different configurations in which the Council meets (see Table 3.2). The most important consists of the General Affairs Council which meets monthly and is responsible for the overall coordination of the Council's work. This includes acting as a transmission belt to the European Council. It prepares the meetings of the European Council and is responsible for following up on decisions being made there. The Foreign Affairs Council discusses all matters relating to the EU's foreign relations. Other important Councils are those on Economic and Financial Affairs (ECOFIN) and the Agriculture and Fisheries Council.

In line with the intergovernmental nature of the Council, member states take turns in presiding over Council meetings for a period of six months. In this period the country assumes the so-called *Presidency* of the European Union. The member state in question chairs all the Council meetings and those of the bodies that prepare them. The only exception is the Foreign Affairs Council which is always chaired by the Union's High Representative.

Member states can use the presidency to set the agenda of the Council and focus on specific priorities, but their room for manoeuvre is limited. First, most of the work of the Council consists of debating and deciding on legislation in progress, the workload of which is largely decided by the Commission, which initiates most legislation. Second, external events – such as a global financial crisis – may seriously upset any new initiatives a member state might want to launch. Third, experience shows successful Presidencies are those where member states have sought to facilitate rather than dominate Council meetings, because such an attitude will usually lead to concrete results. This underlines the EU's decision-making culture which values small, incremental steps over far-reaching and too ambitious plans that will never be able to take root in the mere six months of a country's presidency.

Just as is the case in national political systems, most of the Council's work is prepared at the administrative level by civil servants who debate, discuss, negotiate and decide upon the bulk of issues on the basis of mandates from their governments. There is an elaborate system of around 250 working parties in which specialists from the member states hammer out every detail of a proposed policy.

It is only after deliberations in these forums that proposals find their way to the **Committee of Permanent Representatives (Coreper)**. The EU's permanent representatives meet in Coreper II and discuss all political, financial and foreign policy issues. More technical matters in specific policy areas are discussed in Coreper I, which is attended by the deputy permanent representatives of the member states. Finally, in some policy areas the meetings of the Council are prepared by special committees, such as the Special Committee on Agriculture (SCA) or the Political and Security Committee (known by its French acronym COPS).

Coreper: Committee of Permanent Representatives. Highest preparatory body for meetings of the Council and European Council.

The myriad system of preparatory bodies and groups helps resolve the bulk of decision-making issues that are on the table. As a result, in Council meetings about 80% of the decisions are so-called A-points that do not require any further deliberation and can be rubber-stamped by the ministers. This enables the Council to spend the rest of its time on so-called B points, for which agreement needs to be found at the highest level before definite decisions can be taken.

The Council's meetings involve more than deciding upon legislation. On the one hand, it is involved in thinking and deliberating about issues which might at some point in time become the subject of legislation; on the other hand, it takes executive decisions – for example, on extending sanctions against a certain country or on the continuation of external missions.

■ The Commission

The Commission is the third institution with executive tasks. It is different from the European Council and the Council because instead of representing member state interests it 'shall promote the general interest of the Union and take appropriate initiatives to that end' (Article 17 TEU). For this reason commissioners are supposed to do their work independently.

The Commission is headed by a College of Commissioners, which currently consists of twenty-eight members, including its president. They need to swear an oath before the Court of Justice promising 'neither to seek nor to take instructions from any government or from any other body' and to work in the 'general interest of the Community'.

The oath in Luxembourg rounds off a long process which involves all of the EU's major institutions as well as the member state governments. This process starts with the nomination of a President of the Commission by the European Council, 'taking into account the elections to the European Parliament and after having held appropriate consultations'. This clause, which was added to the Lisbon Treaty, enabled the EP to actively nominate the candidate for Commission President in 2014 EP elections by having all major political groups nominate their own *Spitzenkandidat*, and agreeing to propose the candidate of the largest political group to the European Council. Following the formal nomination by the European Council, the EP subsequently needs to approve this candidate with a simple majority. After the president has been elected, each of the member states nominates a commissioner in consultation with the president-elect, who is in charge of allocating the portfolios amongst these nominees. The Council formally nominates the other members of the Commission, after which the European Parliament has to formally approve of the Commission as a whole. Having secured the approval of the EP, the European Council finally appoints the Commission on the basis of a qualified majority vote.

Tasks

The Commission is responsible for preparing, coordinating, managing and implementing EU policies. Its tasks fall into four categories:

- *Preparing and initiating legislation*. In all areas – except CFSP and some policies regarding police cooperation – the Commission has the monopoly to initiate legislation and send legislative proposals to the Council and EP. In order to properly carry out this task the Commission spends a considerable amount of time preparing legislative texts on the basis of evaluations of existing policies and via different types of consultations. Once the Commission has sent legislative proposals to the Council and EP it is responsible for managing the legislative process and negotiating adjustments with these two institutions.
- *Implementing policies*. The Commission's tasks as a daily executive involve administering the EU's budget and keeping track of revenues and expenses. It also manages programmes – for example, in the area of development aid. The Commission is authorized to make executive decisions in order to implement Community legislation, ranging from determining the warning texts on cigarette packaging to approving mergers between two companies on the basis of EU competition law.
- *External representation*. In many policy areas the Commission is the external representative for the EU. For example, in trade negotiations the EU is represented by the Commissioner for Trade who negotiates on behalf of the member states.

- *Guardian of the treaties*. The Commission monitors the correct application of Community law in the EU and the correct implementation of policies by the member states and private actors such as corporations. It can enforce a correct implementation of these laws by sending warnings, imposing fines or bringing a case before the Court of Justice (see Chapter 11 for further information on these actions).

Hence if we review the tasks of the Commission we see two different roles. The first three tasks – initiating, implementation and representation – are similar to those of any executive in governmental systems. The fourth task, however, is peculiar to the EU's unique institutional set-up. The Commission monitors the obligations of the member states and all other actors that are under the influence of EU law and is empowered to take legal action if they fail to live up to these obligations. Given all these tasks it is not surprising that many think the Commission is very powerful. Still, as Briefing 3.2 shows, the Commission is, just like any other EU institution, dependent upon other institutions to exercise many of these powers.

Organization

The structure of the Commission follows the classic hierarchical pattern of government bureaucracies. At the top of the hierarchy the College of Commissioners acts as the highest decision-making body and is politically accountable for its decisions to the European Parliament. It is chaired by a president who is responsible for the overall policy coordination and who is assisted in this by several commissioners acting as vice-presidents. The president also allocates the portfolios amongst the commissioners (with the exception of the CFSP portfolio which is reserved for the High Representative of the Union for Foreign Affairs and Security Policies). Most commissioners bring with them extensive experience as former (prime) ministers in their home countries. The weight and relevance of portfolios they get differs considerably, however. Highly coveted portfolios include the areas of competition, trade, internal market and agriculture, because on these terrains the EU has considerable powers. Concerns about the effectiveness of the Commission have kept pace with the increase in the number of member states and hence the number of commissioners. Over time this has resulted in giving the Commission president a greater say over the work of individual commissioners and empowering him or her to demand that commissioners resign if they fail in their duties. Moreover, in 2014 Jean-Claude Juncker, the new Commission president, decided to elevate the status of the Commission's vice-presidents and make them responsible for broad policy areas in an attempt to better coordinate policy-making.

Every commissioner has a small support staff in the form of a cabinet with around six members. The cabinet is responsible for managing the relations with fellow commissioners and with the administrative apparatus of the Commission. The Commission meets every Wednesday

Briefing 3.2

The power of the Commission

'The Commission is often attributed powers of mythic proportions, a bureaucratic monster whose sole purpose is to force its poor, unsuspecting citizens into a straitjacket of uniformity. [. . .] In reality this view greatly overestimates the power of the Princess's 22,500 loyal servants. They are by no means in control of everything and are frequently overwhelmed by the sheer magnitude of their task. Their motto is "enough is enough" and "too much" is definitely to be avoided at all costs. They have neither an army, nor a police force at their disposal and live in a world made exclusively of paper. True, they do have considerable influence on a number of economic and political matters, allowing them to affect the daily comings and goings of some 500 million European citizens. But they can rarely dictate binding legislation.

The Princess opens the dance, moving gracefully to the centre of the floor, in the hope that her Ministers and her Members of Parliament will follow. Sadly, this is not always the case. More often than not, the Princess trips over their out-stretched feet. She assumes the general public admires her unreservedly, but in this she is gravely mistaken. Her aim is the unification of Europe, whether the public wants it or not. And often, the public does not want it at all! For this reason, she sometimes dreams of a more grateful public, and she despairs when she realises that this is never going to happen.'

Source: Derk-Jan Eppink, *Life of a European Mandarin: Inside the Commission* (Lannoo, 2007: 11–12).

morning and deliberates behind closed doors. The Wednesday meetings of the Commission are prepared on Mondays by the heads of the cabinets of the commissioners (so-called chefs' meetings), enabling the commissioners to focus on those topics that cannot be resolved there. Decisions are usually made on the basis of consensus, but any commissioner can ask for a vote in which case a simple majority suffices to adopt a decision. Only about 2% of Commission decisions are actually made during these meetings. Others are made through a written procedure or delegated to individual commissioners.

The Commission bureaucracy consists of forty departments in the form of directorates-general which focus on specific policy areas (environment, competition) and services (communication, translation, budget). The departments are led by a director-general who oversees the activities of several directorates which are further subdivided into units. All in all the Commission staff numbers around 25,000 employees. Commission officials are selected via a highly competitive procedure (the *concours*) consisting of several examinations. When successful the candidates will be placed on a reserve list, from which the departments select their personnel.

Briefing 3.3

A handful of presidents

The EU abounds with presidents. In fact all of the EU's institutions are chaired by a president. The European Council, the EP, the Court, the ECB: all of them have a president who heads their respective institution. In addition to these presidents, institutions such as the Commission and the EP are also very generous in appointing a string of vice-presidents. Finally, to make life even more complicated there is also the figure of the *Presidency* of the Union, which is the rotating chairmanship of the Council by the member states.

With all these presidents around it should not be surprising that major events in the EU usually feature several of them. Take, for example, the formal taking up of the presidency by a member state every half year. By now such an event features the President of the European Council, the President of the Commission as well as the prime minister of the country assuming the Presidency of the Union. With such a crowded stage it is often difficult to address general questions from the media. Out of respect for the other's presidential status, none of them wants to be the first to answer, often resulting in a comedy of mutual deferrals until at last one of the presidents dares to pick up the tab.

■ The European Parliament

On its website the European Parliament prides itself as the 'only supranational institution whose members are democratically elected by direct universal suffrage'. Its 751 members are elected for a fixed term of five years in nationally administered elections. The number of seats per member state is related to the population using a so-called degressively proportional formula, with a guaranteed minimum of six seats for the smallest member state (Malta, one seat per 70,000 inhabitants) and a maximum of ninety-six for the largest member state (Germany, one seat per 840,000 inhabitants).

European Parliament elections are essentially fought between national parties in each of the member states and are often dominated by national issues (something which we discuss in detail in Chapter 5). Hence political parties in the EP are organized not according to nationality but along ideological lines. In the EP members of different national parties sit together in political groups on the basis of these ideological affinities. Currently there are seven political groups representing the major ideological viewpoints such as the Christian Democrats, Social Democrats and Liberals (these groups are discussed in detail in Chapter 7).

Member states have considerable leeway in organizing and administering the elections as long as they use a system of proportional representation in allocating the seats. As a result, national idiosyncrasies find their way into the

EP elections as well, resulting, for example, in different minimum age require-ments for candidates (from eighteen in most member states to twenty-five in Italy), nomination requirements (by political parties, or by a specified number of individual citizens) and the day of election (weekdays in the Netherlands and the UK, Sundays in other countries).

Powers

The powers of the EP can be divided into four categories:

- budgetary powers;
- legislative powers;
- scrutiny of the executive;
- appointment and dismissal of the Commission.

Budgetary powers

While the Treaty of Rome already involved the EP in drawing up the Commu-nity's budget, it would be 1970 before it received the right to approve it. For a long time the EP only had a say on a limited number of budget categories, but since the Lisbon Treaty it has been able to modify any expenditures as long as it stays within the bounds of the so-called multi-annual framework. The EP also discharges the Commission on a yearly basis for its management of the budget.

Legislative powers

Ever since the beginning of the ECSC, the Parliamentary Assembly – as the EP's precursor was called – had been given advisory powers on legislative issues. The launch of the Single European Act in 1985 for the first time granted the EP real legislative powers through the introduction of the *assent procedure* (giving it only the right to approve or reject a proposal) and the *cooperation procedure* (allowing it to suggest modifications before the Council cast a definitive vote). The 1992 Treaty of Maastricht set the EP on an equal footing with the Council by introducing co-decision.

In a co-decision procedure both the Council and the EP need to agree on legislation proposed by the Commission. Both the Council and the EP can propose amendments to the proposal. Co-decision initially applied to fifteen policy fields (such as internal market, services, environment), and was grad-ually extended to cover more and more areas. Under the Lisbon Treaty the procedure now covers eighty-five legal bases and applies to more than 95% of Community legislation. For this reason it is now called the *ordinary legislative procedure*. It will be further explained in Chapter 4.

The EP does not have the right to initiate legislation – something which is the Commission's prerogative. However, through the adoption of its own initiative reports, motions for resolutions and written declarations it can press the Commission to take action on a certain policy issue. Since the Treaty of Maastricht the EP has also obtained the right to formally demand that the

Commission submit legislative proposals 'on matters on which it considers that a union act is required for the purpose of implementing the treaties' (Article 225 TFEU). The Commission does not have the obligation to yield to those demands, but if it does not do so, it has to provide an explanation.

Scrutiny of the executive

The EP has several means to scrutinize the behaviour of the EU's executive institutions. First, the EP has the right to ask for and receive information, by submitting written or oral questions to the Commission, Council and European Council. The right to ask for information thus provides a first way to keep these executive bodies accountable and is used quite frequently. In 2013 the EP submitted more than 12,000 written questions to the Commission and the other institutions, a number that has been steadily rising over the years.

A second tool of scrutiny concerns the EP's right to set up temporary commissions of inquiry to investigate 'contraventions or maladministration in the implementation of Union law' (Article 226 TFEU). These committees work as fact-finding missions in all those cases where the EP feels that it has been insufficiently informed about certain developments. The EP has set up such committees to investigate things as diverse as the existence of the espionage network ECHELON, and organized crime, corruption and money laundering in the EU. While the Commission, Council and member states are to provide all relevant information upon request, the EP ultimately depends upon the willingness of these actors to cooperate. Information may be withheld because of considerations of secrecy or national security and witnesses cannot be forced to appear at hearings.

Third, the EP is able to submit cases to the Court of Justice. The EP can challenge decisions when it believes that they have been made on the wrong legal basis. In 2006 the EP challenged a Council decision on providing guarantees to the European Investment Bank, because its treaty basis – economic cooperation – only gave the EP a consultative role. The EP successfully argued that the decision also involved development cooperation, and hence required a co-decision procedure, giving it a much larger say in the decision-making process. In 2010 the EP challenged the legality of a unilateral decision by the Council on allowing the use of force as part of the surveillance of the EU's external sea borders, resulting in its annulment by the Court in 2012. The Court agreed with the EP that the Council should have involved the EP as a co-legislator on this issue.

Appointment and dismissal of the Commission

Above we outlined that the EP has the right to approve the President of the Commission and needs to approve the full Commission before they can take office. Over time the EP has become more assertive in the way it has used these rights. Since 1995 it has made use of public hearings to scrutinize the candidates, whilst from 1999 onwards the terms of the Commission were aligned with those of the EP, enabling it to hold these hearings right after the EP elections. In the run-up to these hearings candidates have to submit testimonials on their professional experience, their outlook on the EU and on their portfolio. The hearings for the Barroso I Commission in 2004 were the first to lead to the replacement of one of the candidate commissioners, as a result of closer scrutiny by the EP. The EP committee on Justice and Liberty disapproved of the candidature of the designated Commissioner for Justice, Freedom and Security – the Italian Rocco Buttiglione – because of his views on homosexuality. After it became clear that the EP would withhold its vote of consent, Italy was forced to come up with another candidate. The replacement of Buttiglione was accompanied by a reshuffling of some of the portfolios to achieve a better match between commissioners and their policy responsibilities. This pattern was repeated during the hearings of subsequent Commissions, in 2009 and 2014: in both instances one of the candidates did not survive parliamentary scrutiny and had to be replaced.

In the run-up to the 2014 EP elections the EP became also more assertive in the selection of the candidate for Commission president, by having each political group put forward a candidate and agreeing to nominate the candidate of the winning political group as the preferred Commission president. This arrangement was the result of a rather expansive reading of the treaty provision that requires the European Council to take account of the outcome of the EP elections when nominating the Commission president. It was only after the EP elections that the government leaders discovered that by agreeing to this course of action, they in fact had given the EP the power to actively propose the candidate for Commission president.

In addition to having the power to approve the College of Commissioners, the EP also has the ability to dismiss the College. The procedure to do this is quite demanding. First, a motion of censure needs to be tabled, after which at least three days need to pass before it can be voted upon. The adoption of the motion requires at least two-thirds of the votes, and the votes in favour of dismissal need to represent at least half of the members of the EP. Hence a double majority is required to dismiss the full Commission.

Aside from these procedural hurdles, the most important hurdle for dismissal of the Commission is the fact that the EP has to send away the full Commission. This means that in practice only a severely malfunctioning Commission will be disapproved of to such an extent that a double majority will be obtained. It should not be a surprise that only seven motions of censure have been tabled since 1972 and none of them has been adopted. Still, one of these motions succeeded in getting the Commission to resign. In 1999 the Santer Commission stepped down following allegations of financial mismanagement. When it became clear that the motion of censure would obtain the double majority if tabled, the College did not await the actual vote but resigned beforehand. This event is another indication of the EP's assertiveness in making the most of its powers to appoint and dismiss the Commission.

Controversy 3.1

Should the European Parliament elect all the members of the Commission?
While the EP has some impact on appointing the Commission, its influence is not comparable to that of legislatures in most of its member states which have a parliamentary system. In these systems the government emerges from parliament and is fully and solely dependent upon its support to stay in power. The advantage of this model is that this allows citizens to indirectly affect the composition of the executive via its votes in parliamentary elections. As a result the political preferences of voters will ultimately be reflected in the composition of the cabinet.

Some scholars such as British political scientist Simon Hix have suggested that the EU should follow this model when it comes to the composition of its core executive: the Commission. Hence, they applaud the increased involvement of the EP in selecting the Commission president and the de facto right of the EP to veto any candidates it finds unsuitable for the job. As a next step, one could envision giving the EP the possibility to nominate all commissioners as well as empower it to dismiss them, just as national parliaments can send away individual ministers. What are the advantages and disadvantages of this increased dependence of the Commission on the EP? How would it affect the institutional balance that we have outlined in this chapter?

Source: Simon Hix, *What's Wrong with the European Union and How to Fix It* (Polity, 2009).

In order to better grasp the role of the EP in the institutional framework Table 3.3 summarizes its tasks and compares it to those of national parliaments. In other words: how do the EP's powers compare to those of a typical parliament (in the case of bicameral systems, the lower house) in one of the member states? (Obviously there may be slight deviations from the table in some countries, but it gives the most common features of the practices in the EU member states.)

The table reveals that the EP's powers are similar to, but in all cases less extensive than, those of national parliaments. There are two critical differences. First, unlike national parliaments the EP does not have the right to initiate legislation. Second, the EU executive is not fully accountable to the EP because the Council and European Council have an independent existence.

Organization

The EP is autonomous in organizing its work and has established its own Rules of Procedure which provide a detailed overview of its organizational structure

Table 3.3 Comparing the powers of the EP and national parliaments

	European Parliament	Lower house in parliamentary systems
Legislative and budgetary powers	• No right to initiate legislation • Can modify Community legislation	• Right to initiate legislation • Can modify all legislation
Scrutiny of the executive	• Has limited say over treaty revisions • Can submit oral and written questions • Can conduct investigations but has no legal means to enforce cooperation	• Needs to approve changes to the constitution • Can submit oral and written questions • Can conduct parliamentary enquiries and summon witnesses to be heard under oath
Appointment and dismissal of the executive	• Elects the Commission president on proposal of the European Council and approves the College of Commissioners as a whole. Does not determine the composition of the Council or European Council • Can dismiss the College of Commissioners (not individual commissioners) requiring a two-thirds majority of the votes. Cannot dismiss the Council or European Council	• Cabinet emerges from parliament and depends upon parliamentary support • Can dismiss the government and individual cabinet members through a simple majority vote

and its *modus operandi*. Its internal organization strongly resembles that of national parliaments. A paramount feature of this is the division of labour and specialization via specialized **parliamentary committees**. In addition to meeting in plenary, subgroups of the EP meet on a much more regular basis in one of these committees. Hence, while the media tend to favour pictures of the plenary chambers of the EP in Brussels or Strasbourg, most of the work of the EP is actually done in one of the countless smaller meeting rooms that are rarely featured in newscasts.

Parliamentary committee: subdivision of Parliament dealing with specific policy areas. Prepares and debates proposals before sending them to the full, plenary Parliament for final decision-making.

Currently the EP has twenty standing committees each focusing on a specific policy area and which are identified by their French acronyms – such as PECH for fisheries and JURI for legal affairs. The committees bear primary responsibility for all the legislative groundwork in their respective policy areas. Committees range in size between twenty-five and seventy-one members and their political composition should reflect that of the plenary Parliament, with chairmanships being distributed according to the size of the political groups.

Briefing 3.4

Draft agenda of the EP Committee on Foreign Affairs
Committee on Foreign Affairs (AFET)
Meeting Monday 31 March 2014, 15.00–19.30
Tuesday 1 April 2014, 9.00–12.30
Brussels

1. Adoption of agenda
2. Chair's announcements
3. Approval of minutes of meetings of 10–11 February 2014, 17 February 2014, 27 February, 2014, 3 March 2014, 10 March 2014, and 17–18 March 2014
4. Analysis on the Egyptian constitution, the constitutional processes in Egypt and Tunisia and of the constitution development in Libya
5. Exchange of views with Fathallah Sijilmassi, Secretary General of the Union for the Mediterranean.
   *** *Electronic vote* ***
6. EU – Albania: Protocol to the Stabilisation and Association Agreement (accession of the Republic of Croatia) *Rapporteur: Nikola Vuljanić (GUE/NGL) Responsible: AFET – Opinions: INTA, AGRI*
7. Framework Agreement between the EU and its Member States, of the one part, and the Republic of Korea, of the other part *Rapporteur: Norica Nicolai (ALDE) Responsible: AFET – Opinions: INTA – Robert Sturdy (ECR)*
8. EU strategy towards Iran *Rapporteur: María Muñiz De Urquiza (S&D) Responsible: AFET*
9. EU foreign policy in a world of cultural and religious differences *Rapporteur: Marietta Giannakou (PPE) Responsible: AFET*
   *** *End of electronic vote* ***
10. Exchange of views with a delegation from the Eerste Kamer of the Kingdom of the Netherlands on EU-Russia relations and the Eastern Partnership
11. Exchange of views with Štefan Füle, European Commissioner for Enlargement and European Neighbourhood Policy, on the state of play of the ENP and on the progress reports
12. Public hearing on the political and economic situation in Belarus (see separate programme)
13. Exchange of views with Nabil Fahmi, Minister of Foreign Affairs of Egypt, on the current situation in Egypt
14. Exchange of views with Greek Foreign Minister Evangelos Venizelos on maritime security (to be confirmed)
15. Presentation of the final report on the monitoring of journalists trials in Turkey by the ad-hoc delegation of the European Parliament
16. Any other business
17. Date of next meeting

Briefing 3.4 shows a draft agenda of one committee and underlines that the first and foremost of the committee's activities consists of debating legislative proposals. Depending upon the type of legislation such debates may in fact involve several committees. For every piece of legislation one of the committee's members is appointed as a **rapporteur**. Obviously some legislative dossiers are much more prestigious and important than others. Securing those rapporteurships is one of the most challenging tasks of the different political groups and often generates enormous strife between and within them. In order to distribute these positions fairly each political group is allocated a number of points based upon its size in the EP. In a kind of auction the rapporteurships are awarded to the group willing to bid the highest number of points.

Rapporteur: Member of Parliament responsible for summarizing a committee's opinion and its modification proposals on a specific piece of legislation.

The rapporteur's task is to summarize the committee's opinion and consolidate all the possible amendments in a draft report. In case legislation touches upon the work of different committees, one committee will be assigned the leading role and incorporate the opinions of other committees in its final report. It is only after the committee has agreed on the rapporteur's draft report that it is submitted to the plenary Parliament and votes are taken on all the amendments.

As Briefing 3.4 attests there is more to committee work than debating legislation, however. In principle committees can discuss and deliberate on any issue they deem to be important for their policy area. Such debates may involve hearing representatives of the Council, Commission or any other experts as the sample agenda shows. In addition to being members of committees, Members of the European Parliament (MEPs) may also be part of one or more of the EP's delegations. These delegations maintain contacts with the parliaments of other countries, including those of candidate member states.

The EP is the only parliament in the world that has multiple seats. Its official seat is in Strasbourg where it has to meet in plenary session twelve times a year. Most of its work is done in Brussels, however, where it holds additional plenary sessions, and MEPs meet in committees and political groups. While the Parliament itself favours Brussels as its sole location, both France – hosting the EP's seat in Strasbourg – and Luxembourg – which hosts the Parliament's secretariat – have vetoed such a move for obvious reasons. The location of the Strasbourg seat is now enshrined in the Treaty and it is unlikely that France will ever accept a treaty revision that would abolish it. The result is a monthly travelling circus of members, support staff and translators, costing the EU an estimated €200 million a year.

■ The Court of Justice

While the EU's executive and legislative powers are spread over different institutions, judicial powers in the EU are clearly allocated to one institution: the Court of Justice (CJ). In that sense the Court – which in everyday parlance is often also called the European Court of Justice (ECJ) – can be considered as the EU's judicial branch. Like any court in a democratic political system, the Court and its judges enjoy full independence in order to properly carry out their work. The Court's judges are 'appointed by common accord of the governments of the Member States' (Article 19 TEU). All candidates are reviewed by a panel consisting of judges from the Court as well as legal experts from the member states. Judges normally have considerable judicial experience in their member state, including their country's highest court, or are highly regarded legal scholars with an excellent track record in academia. They are appointed for a renewable term of six years.

Tasks

While the Court concerns itself with a quite diverse set of tasks, there are three main areas of jurisdiction that form the core of its activities:

- *Reviewing the legality of acts*. The Court is allowed to assess whether the activities of the EU's institutions have been based on the proper judicial basis and carried out using the appropriate procedures (Article 261 TFEU). This is one of the classic tasks of any court. Member states, EP, Council and Commission are all allowed to bring cases before the Court – called **actions for annulment** – if they believe any of the

  Action for annulment: case brought before the Court of Justice in which an interested party asks the Court to declare a decision by any of the EU's institutions to be void.

  institutions has not acted in accordance with EU law (the section on the EP above gives two examples of these types of cases). Natural (citizens) or legal persons (corporations, associations) are also allowed to submit cases but they have to show that they have a direct interest in the case (*locus standi*).
- *Establishing infringements*. If member states fail 'to fulfil an obligation under the Treaties' (Article 258 TFEU) the Commission is allowed to bring a case before the Court. The Commission will ask the Court to formally establish that a member state has not acted in accordance with EU law. If the Court agrees, it will rule that the member state has to remedy the error. If the member state does not follow up on the Court's ruling, another case can be brought before the Court and fines may be imposed. Member states are also allowed to start these

  Infringement procedure: legal procedure set in motion against a member state if it does not comply with EU legislation.

  infringement procedures against other member states (see Chapter 11 for a detailed overview of this procedure).
- *Giving preliminary rulings*. The third task of the Court is to advise courts in the member states on cases which touch upon EU law. The principles of supremacy and direct effect require courts in the member states to apply EU law in all relevant cases. In those cases where they feel uncertain about the precise interpretation of EU law they can submit their case to the Court

Preliminary ruling: binding interpretation on a matter of EU law delivered by the Court of Justice at the request of a member state court.

and ask it to give a **preliminary ruling** on the matter (Article 267 TFEU). The ruling is preliminary because the referring court will make the final judgment and has to incorporate the Court's opinion in its ruling. Obviously, if it fails to do so, interested parties can appeal the ruling in higher level national courts or – if it concerns a ruling of the highest national court – start a case before the Court.

As far as EU law is concerned, the Court by now can be said to stand at the pinnacle of the EU's judicial order. Accordingly some scholars have compared its role to that of the US Supreme Court. There are, however, important limitations on the Court's powers. The Court has been excluded from some areas of EU policy-making. It cannot rule on acts issued in the area of CFSP, except when it concerns reviewing the legality of sanctions against persons or organizations. It also has limited jurisdiction in the areas of judicial cooperation in criminal matters and police cooperation.

Organization

The Court actually consists of three different courts:

- The Court of Justice forms the highest court. It deals with all references for preliminary rulings as well as infringement proceedings initiated by the Commission. It decides upon actions for annulment brought by member states against the EP or the Council. It rules in those very rare instances where any high-level EU appointee (commissioners, European Ombudsman, fellow judges) might have seriously breached their obligations. The Court also acts as an appeal court for cases on which the General Court (below) has ruled. The Court has twenty-eight judges (one per member state) and eleven advocates-general who assist the Court in its proceedings. These advocates-general, who are appointed in a similar manner to the judges, prepare the ground for the judges in cases that are particularly difficult. Their opinions are meant to provide the judges with a first take on the case at hand and are usually guiding for the final ruling.
- The General Court deals with direct actions brought by natural or legal persons seeking the annulment of acts as well as cases brought by member states against the Commission. It also handles issues of intellectual property and decides on a range of other cases. (Until the entry into force of the Treaty of Lisbon it was called Court of First Instance.) There are at least twenty-eight judges (one per member state).
- The Civil Service Tribunal deals with labour disputes between EU civil servants and their employer, the EU. The seven judges in this court issue rulings on all kinds of employment-related conflicts regarding salaries, promotions or lay-offs.

Court cases consist of a written and an oral part. The oral part of the procedure is open to the public. Deliberations of the judges take place behind closed doors. If necessary, the uneven number of judges in each chamber ensures that it is always possible to take a definite vote on a ruling. The Court is located in Luxembourg where it employs some 2,100 people. As is the case with all of the EU's institutions, many employees are concerned with providing translations of documents.

■ The European Central Bank

In political systems central banks serve a variety of purposes: to issue a country's currency, act as a lender of last resort and implement monetary policies. The adoption of the Euro as the EU's single currency required the setting up of an EU-wide central bank that would take care of these tasks for the Eurozone. In 1998, one year before the introduction of the Euro, the European Central Bank (ECB) was established in order to serve this function. Together with the central banks of the Eurozone countries, the ECB constitutes the European System of Central Banks (ESCB).

> The **Eurozone** consists of all member states that have adopted the Euro as their currency. The ministers of finance of the Eurozone countries form the **Eurogroup**, whilst the ECB and the national banks of the countries that have adopted the Euro are called the **Eurosystem**.

Tasks

- *Conducting the EU's monetary policy*. As the central bank for the Eurozone, the ECB has the monopoly to issue the Euro currency and decides on the Eurozone's monetary policy. Article 282 of the TFEU states that the primary objective of the ECB's monetary policy is to maintain price stability, while its policies should also support the general economic policies of the Union. Setting the interest rates at which commercial banks can borrow and deposit money at the ECB is the main tool for this.
- *Maintaining the financial stability of the Eurozone system*. As a result of its responsibility to provide for a smooth operation of payment systems, the ECB keeps track of the financial health of the Eurozone and its banks and other financial institutions. Together with the central banks of the member states it analyses the assets of the commercial banks and their capacity to withstand financial shocks. On the basis of this it can demand banks to take measures to remedy any unacceptable risks.
- *Conducting foreign exchange operations and maintaining the Eurozone's foreign reserves*. To ensure the liquidity and the stability of the Eurozone, the ECB may buy or sell foreign reserves. Most of these reserves are in the hands of the Eurozone members, but the ECB manages these in close coordination with national central banks.

Organization

The ECB's main decision-making body is the Governing Council, which consists of the members of the ECB's executive board and the governors of the banks of the Eurozone countries. The president and the five members of the executive board are elected by the European Council for a non-renewable term of eight years. Just like the judges of the Court of Justice, these members are selected on the basis of their competence and expertise and are required to act independently.

The bank's governing council meets twice a month and decides every month on the key interest rates at which commercial banks can deposit or borrow money. The decision is always watched closely by financial markets as it guides all the interest rates that commercial parties will set in the money market. Decision-making takes place by simple majority vote, but most decisions are actually taken by consensus. Since the accession of Lithuania as the eighteenth Eurozone member, the voting rights of the bank governors have rotated on a monthly basis, with the countries with the five largest economies sharing four votes and the remaining countries sharing eleven votes. The secrecy of decision-making is highly prized because any sign of disagreement among the bank's board members would be likely to cause instability in the financial system. The advent of the financial crisis has increased the bank's role as a policy-maker and policy adviser, not only with respect to the management of the financial system, but also with respect to supervising the fiscal policies of the member states (see also Chapter 8). The president of the ECB participates in the meetings of the Eurogroup, comprised of the ministers of finance of the Eurozone countries. In addition to the powers with respect to monetary policies, it has a strong advisory role in determining the EU's budgetary and economic policies. The ECB is based in Frankfurt, Germany, and employs around 1,750 people.

■ Making sense of the institutional framework

At the start of this chapter we showed that the EU's institutional hardware is somewhat different to that of national political systems. This applies in particular to executive and legislative functions which are both *shared* between the different institutions. This means that the core policy-making functions in the EU are not in the hands of one institutional actor, but require cooperation and collaboration between different bodies that represent different interests. This complicated arrangement is very different from those found in national states which make use of presidential and parliamentary systems. Let us briefly point out why the EU does not fit either of these models.

On the one hand, the EU clearly is not organized along the lines of a presidential system. In these systems, such as the USA, executive power is vested in a single, unitary executive (the president), which derives its democratic legitimation via direct popular election. In the EU, however, executive tasks are distributed over the European Council, Council, and Commission, and none of them is directly elected.

The EU does not qualify as a parliamentary system either. In those systems, the executive emerges from the legislature, via the composition of a cabinet that rests on majority support of parliament (this is the principle of parliamentary sovereignty). The executive can be forced to step down via a vote of no confidence.

It is clear that this constellation does not apply to the EU either. Two of the executive powers (European Council and Council) do not emerge from Parliament nor can they be dismissed by it. The third, the Commission, emerges as a result of a complex nomination process which involves not only the EP but also many other actors. This is clearly different from the principle of parliamentary sovereignty, which ultimately boils down to the idea that the legislature determines the composition of the executive. And while Parliament can send away the Commission, this is a difficult and demanding procedure that is not comparable to the one available to national parliaments.

Still, it is possible to characterize the EU's organizational philosophy using models that have been put forward to typify national political systems. Political scientist Arend Lijphart has pointed out that all democratic political systems essentially boil down to two different models of democracy. *Majoritarian* political systems seek to concentrate executive power and put relatively few constraints on its exercise. As the term indicates, these political systems value the ability to actually govern over the need to secure the consent of all interested parties. Hence, such systems give all executive power to the party that simply has the majority of votes, even if it is only a bare majority. The United Kingdom provides the most clear-cut example of such a political system.

Consensual political systems are based on a different philosophy. In these systems the institutions have been designed in such a way that they disperse power and restrain its use. For example, this is achieved by using a system of proportional representation which results in election outcomes where none of the political parties has a majority of the seats. Accordingly, the government will most of the time consist of coalitions that usually command a sizeable majority of the seats in parliament. Consensual systems put a strong emphasis on ensuring broad support for policies. Such systems usually also allow courts to review the legality of acts in order to further restrain the exercise of power. Consensual models are especially appropriate in political systems that are heterogeneous in terms of ethnicity, religion and language. Switzerland, with its many religions and languages, provides a good example.

If we have to characterize the EU it is clear that its system fits into the category of consensual political systems. This explains the EU's emphasis on balancing all relevant interests when making decisions. As we have outlined in this chapter the EU has an institutional configuration in which almost no decision can be taken by one institution on its own, but always needs to be approved by, confirmed by or negotiated with other institutions. A further restraint on the powers of the executive is achieved via the power of the Court to review these executive and legislative decisions.

In the next chapter we will gain further insight into this consensual nature of decision-making in the EU. As we will see there, many decisions not only require the assent of multiple institutions, but decision-making within institutions often requires qualified majorities or even unanimity in order to protect the interests of all actors. And even if formal rules only prescribe a simple majority – such as was the case with the appointment of the EU president – actors will in many cases nevertheless strive for unanimity, and as such respect the culture of consensus which permeates the EU's institutional framework.

■ Summary

- The EU's institutional framework consists of seven institutions, each of which represents different interests and has been allocated executive, legislative, judicial and other powers (see Table 3.1 for an overview).
- Executive powers are exercised by the European Council and Council, which represent the member states, and the Commission and ECB, which represent the general interest of the Union. Legislative powers are in the hands of the Council, representing the member states, and the European Parliament, representing the citizens. Judicial powers are in the hands of the Court of Justice.
- The organizational structure of the EU's executive and legislative institutions is characterized by a horizontal and vertical division of labour. The Council, Commission and EP have organized themselves according to different policy sectors. In addition each of these institutions prepares and discusses policies at lower levels (in committees), allowing the top level to rubber-stamp most of the decisions and concentrate on unresolved issues.
- The division of labour between these different institutions cannot be readily compared to those of national political systems. The EU does not have a presidential or a parliamentary system because legislative and executive powers do not emanate solely from the people. Instead it can be better characterized as 'mixed government' or as 'a polity with many principals'.
- While the institutional hardware of the EU is unique, it is based upon a common model for organizing democratic systems: that of consensualism. It aims to disperse power and constrain the use of it.

Further reading

A good overall source on institutions is John Peterson and Michael Shackleton, *The Institutions of the European Union* (Oxford University Press, 2012). Further and more detailed insights on individual institutions can be found in Uwe Puetter, *The European Council and the Council: New Intergovernmentalism and Institutional Change* (Oxford, 2014), Richard Corbett, Francis Jacobs and Michael Shackleton, *The European Parliament* (John Harper, 2014) and Takis Tridimas, *The European Court of Justice and the EU Constitutional Order* (Hart, 2014). A highly recommended reflection on the EU's institutional evolution is Jan Zielonka, *Europe as Empire: The Nature of the Enlarged European Union* (Oxford, 2007).

Websites

- A useful gateway to all of the EU's institutions can be found at http:// europa.eu/about-eu/institutions-bodies
- For a full overview of the organization and tasks of the different institutions it is indispensable to take a look at Title III of the Treaty on European Union as well as Part VI of the Treaty on the Functioning of the European Union. Both of them can be found at http://europa.eu/ lisbon_treaty

Navigating the EU

On the website www.navigatingthe.eu you will find online exercises for this chapter.

4   Legislation and decision-making: putting the institutional puzzle together

▣ Introduction

In December 2012, the European Commission presented a proposal for a revision of the Tobacco Products Directive (TPD), a piece of legislation that regulates the production, sale and packaging of tobacco products in the EU. The old directive from 2001 needed to be replaced because in 2005 the EU had become party to the WHO Framework Convention on Tobacco Control, requiring stronger rules to discourage people from smoking. A new directive was also necessary to deal with new developments such as the emergence of e-cigarettes as a new product that had so far escaped regulation.

After its release, the proposal went to the Council of Ministers and the European Parliament for decision-making. Within the Council, it was discussed in the 'Employment, Social Policy, Health, and Consumer Affairs Council', which includes the ministers of health of the member states. Within the European Parliament, the responsible committee was the Committee on Environment, Public Health and Food Safety. The proposal was also discussed in four other parliamentary committees. While the proposal was being discussed in the Council and the EP, formal opinions were issued by two advisory bodies: the Economic and Social Committee and the Committee of the Regions. The

Commission also received opinions from seventeen national parliaments, seven of which raised severe objections against the need to regulate this at the EU level.

In June 2013 the health ministers in the Council reached a 'political agreement' after making several changes to the proposal from the Commission – for example, by asking it to not ban menthol cigarettes. Soon thereafter the European Parliament debated the proposal and indicated which amendments it wanted to see adopted in order to make the proposal acceptable. It gave its rapporteur, Linda McAvan, a mandate to negotiate on its behalf with the Council and the Commission. After a series of informal meetings representatives from the EP, the Council and the Commission reached agreement in December 2013. The EP approved this agreement in its session in February 2014, whilst the Council approved it one month later, thereby formally adopting the proposal. The speed at which the EU managed to adopt this piece of legislation was remarkable. Despite the complexity of the issues on the table and the many changes that were suggested by member states and MEPs, it had taken only fifteen months to get the new TPD adopted.

The TPD proposal followed a procedure that is known as the 'ordinary' legislative procedure. As its name implies this is by now the most commonly used way to adopt legislation in the EU. In this chapter we will outline the formal rules of this decision-making procedure as well as those of the 'special' legislative procedures. We will also show how the EU institutions interact alongside these formal procedures through various negotiating arrangements in order to facilitate and accelerate finding agreement. In so doing, this chapter will address the following questions:

- What types of decisions are taken within the EU?
- What types of decision-making procedures exist in the EU and what role do the various institutions play in this?
- How does qualified majority voting in the Council of Ministers work and to what extent do member states actually vote on legislative proposals?
- What role do national parliaments play in the legislative process?
- How do alternative forms of decision-making such as the Open Method of Coordination and Enhanced Cooperation work?

This chapter builds on the institutional sketch given in Chapter 3. There, we discussed each of the EU's institutions. In this chapter, we will explain how these institutions work together to make decisions. Together, the two chapters provide an overview of the formal backbone of the EU: its institutions and the procedures governing decision-making.

The central question underlying the entire chapter is: why are EU decision-making procedures the way they are? Like the EU's institutional set-up, its decision-making procedures seek to find a balance between competing objectives: fostering EU-wide approaches to issues, protecting the sovereignty of its member states and installing an element of democracy in the way decisions are made in the EU. If you understand the logic behind this balancing act, the complex and diverse world of legal instruments and decision-making procedures in the EU becomes much easier to navigate.

■ Types of decisions in the EU

Decision-making results in decisions. Hence, it is important to understand the type of decisions that can be adopted in the EU. In this chapter we focus on those major decisions that as a rule require the involvement of the three major institutions: Council, European Parliament and European Commission.

The treaties define a range of different types of legal instruments, and stipulate which types can be used for which issues. Because the legal instruments differ in the degree to which they are binding upon the member states, they allow for variation in the balance between EU obligations and member state sovereignty. Therefore, the types of decisions available in the EU themselves reflect a highly political trade-off between competing objectives and interests.

Legal instruments in the EU

The Treaty on the Functioning of the European Union defines four basic legal instruments: Regulations, Directives, Decisions, and Recommendations and Opinions. Fact file 4.1 gives an overview of these instruments. They form the legal 'tool kit' that the European Union can make use of.

Each of these types of instrument serves a different purpose. The first two, Regulations and Directives, constitute the EU's legislative acts. They are used to lay down general and binding norms. Decisions concern individual cases. Recommendations and Opinions, finally, contain non-binding norms. The Treaty on the Functioning of the European Union determines which instrument(s) can be used for which issues.

In some areas all types of instruments are available – for instance, when it comes to the establishment of the internal market, a core task of the EU. In other areas, some instruments cannot be used. For instance, in the field of

Fact file 4.1

Legal instruments of the European Union
Article 288 of the Treaty on the Functioning of the European Union gives an overview of the 'legal acts' of the EU. It discerns four such acts. In the words of the Treaty itself:

- A regulation shall have general application. It shall be binding in its entirety and directly applicable in all Member States.
- A directive shall be binding, as to the result to be achieved, upon each Member State to which it is addressed, but shall leave to the national authorities the choice of form and methods.
- A decision shall be binding in its entirety. A decision which specifies those to whom it is addressed shall be binding only on them.
- Recommendations and opinions shall have no binding force.

social policy the EU can adopt Directives, but not Regulations. For some specific issues in this policy area, including 'combating social exclusion' and 'the modernization of social protection systems', no EU legislation is allowed at all. This is no coincidence. Social policy is, politically speaking, a sensitive area, in which member state governments have been reluctant to cede power to the EU. This explains why the use of Regulations, which have a direct impact within the member states, is precluded. It also explains why in the most sensitive areas of social policy (i.e. those relating to poverty and social protection) the EU cannot adopt any (binding) legislation at all.

When no binding decisions are allowed, recourse can be had to non-binding instruments, such as Recommendations and Opinions. These instruments also appear under other names. For example, in the field of economic policies, the Council can adopt 'broad guidelines', which are formally adopted as a Recommendation. The term 'broad guidelines' is deliberately left vague: what exactly are 'guidelines'? To what extent do they 'guide' member state action? And what is the difference between 'guidelines' and '*broad* guidelines'? The reason for these ambiguities is that the terminology is the result of compromises between member state governments during treaty negotiations. On the one hand, these terms suggest a degree of EU action in these fields while, on the other hand, they make it clear that the EU cannot force its member states to do (or abstain from doing) something. In this way, they find a middle ground between those member state governments that want the EU to play a larger role in economic policy-making and those member state governments that are opposed to EU 'interference' in their domestic economic policies.

Directives and Regulations

Above, we saw that the EU has two types of legislation: Regulations and Directives. The difference between the two relates to the way they become operational within the legal systems of the member states. The EU uses **Regulations** for two purposes: it adopts Regulations to organize its own work – for example, when it needs to set up a new agency or adopt rules on the way it hires and pays its staff. Regulations are also used to adopt those EU-wide policies that require legal provisions that are the same in every member state. As the official definition in Fact file 4.1 says, a Regulation is 'binding in its entirety and directly applicable in all Member States'. This means that a Regulation automatically has force of law within every member state, without the need for any further activity on the part of member state governments. This is different for **Directives**. When a Directive is adopted, each of the EU member states needs to adopt a (domestic) law that conforms to that Directive. This is what is meant by the phrase that a Directive is 'binding as to the result to be achieved' but that it 'leave[s] to the national authorities the choice of form and

> A **Regulation** is a type of EU legislation that is directly applicable in the EU and in all member states.

> A **Directive** is a type of EU legislation that needs to be transposed into national law by the member state governments.

methods'. Hence, a Directive needs to be 'transposed' by the member states, whereas a Regulation does not. Each Directive itself specifies the date before which transposition needs to have taken place.

The reason for the distinction between Regulations and Directives is that they can be used for different purposes. Regulations lay down a single set of standards for the entire European Union that comes into force simultaneously in all member states. As a result, it is particularly suited for situations in which EU policy-makers want to create a fixed legal framework without differentiation between member states.

Because Directives need to be transposed, they allow for variation between member states. In fact, this is exactly what they are supposed to do. By laying down a set of more general common European norms and leaving the specification of those norms to the member states, it is possible to achieve a degree of convergence among the member states while allowing at the same time for adaptations to national circumstances. This is useful because there are vast differences between member states in terms of natural conditions, legal systems, cultures and social conditions. It is also a way to overcome political disagreements. In many cases, it is not possible to agree upon a 'one size fits all' approach for the entire EU. Directives provide for a degree of flexibility in this regard that may allow member states with diverging ideas and interests to at least agree upon a common set of standards. The TPD, for example, allows member states to exempt tobacco products that have a very small market share from the stringent labelling requirements.

Over time, the formal distinction between Regulations and Directives has become blurred as Directives are often so detailed and specific that they leave little room for variation between member states. Briefing 4.1 takes a look at an example of a Directive in order to show how this works.

Other types of instruments

Although Regulations, Directives, Decisions, Opinions and Recommendations are the main types of legal instruments in the EU, they cannot be used in all circumstances. As we saw above, specific types of instruments cannot be used in certain policy areas. In addition, some areas have their own legal instruments, which differ from the four main ones defined in Fact file 4.1. The best example is the EU's Common Foreign and Security Policy (CFSP), in which member states cooperate on issues of foreign policy. Article 25 of the Treaty on European Union defines a different set of instruments for use only in the CFSP. Apart from 'general guidelines', the EU can adopt 'decisions', which may define 'actions to be undertaken by the Union', 'positions to be taken by the Union', and 'arrangements for the implementation' of those actions and positions.

The choice to use a different set of instruments for the CFSP reflects the special position that this policy area has within the EU. Foreign policy and military issues are among the prerogatives most zealously guarded by member

Briefing 4.1

The level of detail in a Directive

In theory, Directives define 'the results to be achieved', while leaving 'the choice of forms and methods' to the member states. In practice, however, Directives are often quite specific and leave little room for different 'forms and methods'. The Tobacco Products Directive is no exception to this.

Article 9, paragraph 1 of the Directive requires each unit packet of tobacco products to carry one of the following warnings: 'Smoking kills – quit now' or 'Smoking kills', leaving member states just the choice between prescribing one of these two statements to be used in their country. Paragraph 3 of the article subsequently states that 'For cigarette packets and roll-your-own tobacco in cuboid packets the general warning shall appear on the bottom part of one of the lateral surfaces of the unit packets, and the information message shall appear on the bottom part of the other lateral surface. These health warnings shall have a width of not less than 20 mm.' Paragraph 2 of Article 14 of the Directive states that a packet of cigarettes 'shall not have an opening that can be re-closed or re-sealed after it is first opened, other than the flip-top lid and shoulder box with a hinged lid. For packets with a flip-top lid and hinged lid, the lid shall be hinged only at the back of the unit packet.'

Hence, although formally speaking the Tobacco Products Directive only contains the 'results to be achieved', leaving 'form and methods' to national authorities, the articles above show that these rules are very detailed. In practice, this often goes so far as to make the difference between Directives and Regulations all but imperceptible.

state governments. By defining a different set of instruments, it is made clear that the normal EU instruments (including its legislative instruments) do not apply to the CFSP. One difference is that the CFSP instruments only have legal effects between the member states and not within the member states. Furthermore, unlike Regulations, Directives and 'regular' decisions, the Court of Justice (CJ) does not have the competence to review CFSP decisions. This guarantees that the interpretation of CFSP decisions remains a matter for member state governments and cannot be imposed on them by the CJ. The only exception to this rule concerns restrictive measures against natural or legal persons, such as when the EU decides on sanctions against persons or organizations. The affected persons can in these cases ask the CJ to review the legality of the Council decision also in the light of the EU Charter of Fundamental Rights.

■ Decision-making procedures in the EU

Above we saw how the various types of decisions that are taken in the EU allow for variation in the balance between common EU policies and the powers of the member states. The same balance can also be found in the different types of decision-making procedures. Some procedures give a greater role to the EU's supranational institutions, while others allow the member state governments to exert greater control over the outcome of the process. In addition, democratic legitimation, through the European Parliament, plays a greater role in some EU decision-making procedures than in others. As a result, decision-making procedures differ in three regards:

- the role of the European Commission (exclusive right of initiative or not);
- the role of the European Parliament (consent required or not);
- the decision rule in the Council of Ministers (unanimity or a 'qualified majority').

At one end of the spectrum is the decision-making procedure that gives an exclusive right of initiative to the European Commission, gives the EP full powers of amendment and consent, and allows for Council decision-making with a qualified majority. This procedure used to be known as 'co-decision' but since the Treaty of Lisbon it has been called the 'ordinary legislative procedure'. It is associated with what is called the **'Community method'** of decision-making.

The **Community method** is a way of making decisions in which the EU's supranational institutions (Commission, EP) play an important role.

At the other end of the spectrum are procedures in which the Commission has to share its right of initiative with member state governments, the EP has (at best) an advisory role, and the Council decides by unanimity. There is no one such procedure but a variety of

The **intergovernmental method** is a way of making decisions in which member state governments play a central role.

procedures that, to a greater or lesser extent, conform to this model. In the EU treaties, they are referred to as 'special legislative procedures'. These procedures conform to what is known as the **intergovernmental method**.

Since 2000, in a number of policy areas the so-called 'Open Method of Coordination' (OMC) has been used. Under the OMC, no binding legislation is adopted but coordination of policies between the member states is attempted through a process of benchmarking and policy learning. Because member state governments are firmly in the driving seat and cannot be bound by EU legislation, the OMC is also strongly intergovernmental in nature.

As its name implies, the ordinary legislative procedure is now the most common way of making decisions in the EU. This is especially the case since the coming into force of the Lisbon Treaty in 2009. Whilst in the parliamentary term 2004–9 49% of all legislative proposals were decided in that fashion, this had risen to 89% of all dossiers in the 2009–14 parliamentary term. Below, we will therefore devote most attention to the organization and actual functioning of this procedure.

■ The ordinary legislative procedure

The ordinary legislative procedure seeks to find a balance between the various institutions involved in EU decision-making (Commission, EP, Council) by giving each institution a specific role in the procedure. The consent of each of these institutions is needed to arrive at a decision. In addition, decision-making within the Council of Ministers takes place with a qualified majority, which means that a proposal can be adopted even though individual member states are opposed to it. Below, we will explain how the ordinary legislative procedure works. First, we will discuss the roles of the various institutions in the ordinary legislative procedure. Then, we will outline the steps taken in the formal procedure. Finally, we will discuss the ways in which the various institutions interact during the decision-making process outside of these formal steps.

The logic behind the ordinary legislative procedure

The formal roles of the institutions in the ordinary legislative procedure are strictly defined in the Treaty on the Functioning of the European Union:

- The European Commission has the exclusive (or, in EU terminology: 'sole') right of initiative. The Commission can also modify or withdraw its proposal during the decision-making process.
- The EP has to agree to the proposal before it can be adopted. Moreover, it can adopt amendments to the proposal.
- The Council of Ministers also has to agree to the proposal and it can adopt amendments as well.

From this brief outline, two points immediately become clear. First, the division of roles in the ordinary legislative procedure is such that the consent of all three institutions is necessary to reach a decision. Without the Commission, there can be no proposal, and without the Council or the EP that proposal cannot be adopted. Second, as a corollary to the first point, the ordinary legislative procedure has a great potential for deadlock, exactly because no institution can single-handedly force a decision. Not only do the EP and the Council both have to agree with a proposal, but both can also make amendments to the proposal. Since these amendments may not be the same (indeed, they most likely are not), it may happen that the two institutions end up drafting different versions of the same proposal. Yet, they need to agree to identical versions for a proposal to be adopted.

Therefore, the ordinary legislative procedure has been structured in such a way that, on the one hand, the balance between the different institutions involved in the process is maintained while, on the other, mechanisms are built in for reaching a conclusion (and thus breaking a potential deadlock). To that end, decision-making takes place in three rounds, which are called 'readings'. Let us go through the procedure step by step, illustrating each step with reference to the process leading up to the adoption of the TPD that we presented in the introduction to this chapter. An

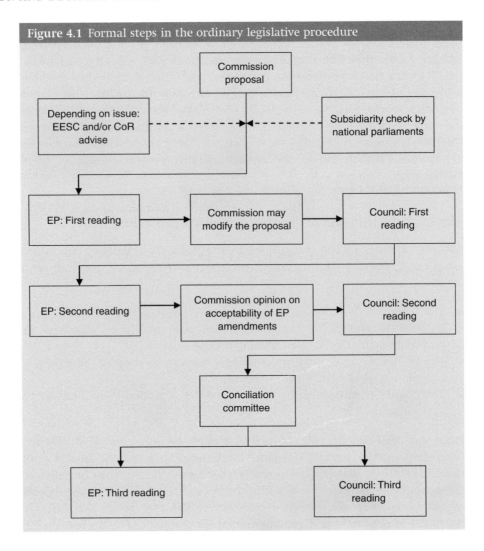

Figure 4.1 Formal steps in the ordinary legislative procedure

overview of the formal steps in the ordinary legislative procedure is provided in Figure 4.1.

Commission proposal and advisory bodies

The ordinary legislative procedure starts with a proposal from the European Commission. In this procedure, the Commission is the only actor that can make a formal proposal. Member states or (members of) the European Parliament cannot put forward a proposal (although they can put pressure on the Commission to do so – see Chapter 9 on agenda-setting). The only exception to this rule applies to proposals relating to judicial cooperation in criminal matters or police cooperation, which can be initiated either by the Commission or by at least a quarter of the member states, even when the ordinary legislative procedure is used to adopt the proposal.

Once the proposal is released, it goes to the European Parliament and the Council of Ministers. In some cases, the proposal also needs to go to the European Economic and Social Committee (EESC) and/or the Committee of the Regions (CoR). This is not a general feature of the ordinary legislative procedure, but depends on the issue at stake. If that issue relates to the remit of the EESC and/or CoR, the Commission is required to consult one or both of these bodies. For each issue area, this has been specified in the Treaty on the Functioning of the European Union.

After it is released, the Commission proposal is also sent to member state parliaments for a 'subsidiarity check'. Within eight weeks, national parliaments can raise objections if they believe the proposal violates the **subsidiarity principle**. We will explain how that procedure works below.

> The **subsidiarity principle** states that the EU is only allowed to act if the objectives of that action can be better reached at EU level than at member state level.

The first reading

The first reading in the EP

In the first reading, the European Parliament adopts a so-called 'opinion'. In order to do so, the proposal is assigned to one of the EP's parliamentary committees. If a proposal touches upon the remit of several committees, it is debated in each but one committee is assigned as the main responsible committee. In the TPD proposal, the Environment, Public Health and Food Safety Committee was the lead committee because the major purpose of the proposal was to reduce the harmful effects of smoking for public health. In addition four other committees provided opinions: the Industry Committee (because the proposal had a major potential impact on tobacco industries), the Internal Market Committee (because it touched upon the internal market for tobacco products), the Agriculture Committee (because in some member states tobacco is grown) as well as the Legal Affairs Committee. In the end, the Environment Committee put together a draft opinion for the European Parliament to adopt.

As we already outlined in Chapter 3, within the responsible committee one MEP – the rapporteur – is assigned the task of drafting that opinion. It is the rapporteur's task to chart political sensitivities and come up with a compromise text that a majority of the EP will support. The rapporteur is also the person that in between the formal procedural steps conducts negotiations with the Council and the Commission in order to reach agreement. In complex dossiers the rapporteur may be accompanied by so-called shadow rapporteurs that monitor the negotiations on behalf of other political groups. For the TPD proposal, the rapporteur was Linda McAvan, a British MEP for the Socialist party group.

In terms of its opinion, there are three options for the EP:

- It may agree with the Commission proposal without amendments.
- It may disagree with the Commission proposal without amendments.
- It may agree with the Commission proposal but include amendments.

The first two options are rarely used. Only seldom will the EP agree fully and in every detail with a Commission proposal, whereas a proposal that meets with such fundamental opposition from the EP that not even extensive amendments can remedy it will not even be released by the Commission. Normally, then, the EP will adopt an opinion that includes amendments. In doing so, the EP does not simply vote on the rapporteur's full text but needs to approve each proposed amendment separately. The number of amendments in the EP opinion depends on the extensiveness and controversiality of the proposal. In the first reading, the EP decides on its opinion with a 'simple majority' – that is, a majority of the members that cast a vote. If some or many MEPs are absent from the vote, the simple majority may be less than a majority of all elected MEPs. After the EP has adopted its opinion, the European Commission may change its proposal to include some or all of the EP's amendments, but this need not happen.

The first reading in the Council
Next, the Council can do two things:

- It can approve the EP's opinion including all amendments, if the EP has included any in its opinion. In that case, the proposal as amended by the EP is adopted as the final legislative act, and the procedure ends here. In the case of TPD this is what in formal terms happened, making this a first reading agreement. The Council was able to agree with the EP's opinion, because this opinion itself was the result of negotiations with the Commission and the EP, allowing a compromise between these three institutions. We further explain these negotiations below.
- Alternatively, if the Council does not agree fully with the EP opinion, it can adopt a **common position**, which may or may not include some of the EP's amendments. In addition, the Council can include its own amendments. Because in this case the Council's common position and EP's opinion are not identical, the procedure then goes to the second reading. The European

In first reading the Council adopts a **common position** when its viewpoint on a proposal differs from the EP's opinion and/or the Commission's modified proposal.

Commission plays a crucial role in determining the voting rule that applies within the Council. The Council can adopt the Commission proposal with a qualified majority, which roughly conforms to a majority of at least 55% of all member states representing 65% of the EU population. Below we will explain in greater detail what this voting rule entails. If the Commission has changed its proposal after the EP opinion to include some or all of the EP's amendments, those amendments can also be adopted in the Council by qualified majority. However, if the Council wants to adopt EP amendments that have not been included in the modified Commission proposal, it can only do so by unanimity (that is, with the consent of all its members). Likewise, the Council's common position is adopted with a qualified majority of votes in the Council but if it contains amendments that are not included in the Commission proposal, those amendments require unanimity. In this way, the Commission can increase the threshold for the adoption of amendments that it does not agree to.

The second reading

Differences between the first and the second reading
If the EP and the Council do not agree on an identical text in the first reading, the proposal goes to the second reading. In principle the second reading follows the same course as the first reading, with the proposal first going to the EP and then to the Council, and the Commission intervening to declare amendments either acceptable or not acceptable. At the same time, pressure is stepped up in order to force the institutions to come to a conclusion. This pressure results from several differences between the first and second readings:

- In the first reading, no time limits apply. The EP and the Council can take as long as they like to reach their decisions. In the second reading, time limits apply to both institutions. After receiving the Council's common position in first reading, the EP has three months to decide. If not, the Council's common position will become law. Similarly, the Council has three months to decide after receiving the EP's amendments in second reading. This time limit can be extended by one month, but no more.
- In the second reading, the European Parliament cannot adopt completely new amendments. Rather, it can only adopt amendments that (1) were already adopted by the EP in the first reading but not included in the Council's common position, (2) address elements in the Council's common position that did not appear in the Commission proposal (and therefore were not discussed in the EP in the first reading) or (3) are aimed at reconciling differences of opinion between the EP and the Council. In this way, the EP is forced to make 'constructive' use of its right of amendment in the second reading.
- The voting rule in the EP is different in the second than in the first reading. Whereas in the first reading a simple majority is sufficient to adopt the opinion including amendments, the EP needs an absolute majority (that is, a majority of all its elected members, not just those present at the vote) to adopt amendments in the second reading or to reject the proposal altogether. This raises the threshold for making changes to the proposal or rejecting it.

The EP in the second reading
This results in the following sequence of steps in the second reading. After the adoption of the Council's common position, it is up to the EP to make a move

again. The starting point for EP deliberations in the second reading is no longer the Commission proposal, but the Council's common position from the first reading. It can do three things with that common position:

- Adopt the Council's common position from the first reading as it is. For this, a simple majority suffices. Then the legislative act is adopted according to the common position. It is also the outcome if the EP fails to take a decision in the second reading within the specified time limit.
- Reject the Council's common position. For this, an absolute majority is needed. Then, the process ends without a legislative act being adopted.
- Adopt amendments to the Council's common position, whereby the restrictions outlined above apply.

The Commission in the second reading

If the EP has adopted amendments in the second reading, the Commission presents an opinion in which it declares for each amendment whether it finds that amendment acceptable or unacceptable. This opinion is important for decision-making in the Council. If an amendment is acceptable to the Commission, the Council can adopt it with a qualified majority, but if it is not acceptable to the Commission the Council needs unanimity to adopt it. The logic behind this is similar to the role of the Commission in the first reading, where it could raise the bar for EP amendments by not including them in its modified proposal.

The Council in the second reading

The Council in the second reading has two options:

- It approves all of the EP's amendments, either with a qualified majority or by unanimity, depending on the Commission's position. In that case, the legislative act is adopted with all of the EP's amendments in the second reading.
- It does not approve all of the EP's amendments. In that case, the procedure goes to the third reading.

Conciliation and the third reading

If the EP and the Council do not agree to the same amendments in the second reading, a special mechanism applies, called 'conciliation'. It is similar to the mechanism that is used in the US Congress when the Senate and the House of Representatives have adopted different versions of the same bill. The idea behind conciliation is that representatives of the EP and the Council, together with representatives of the European Commission, meet in a **conciliation committee**. The task of the conciliation committee

A **conciliation committee** consists of representatives of the Council and the EP, assisted by representatives of the Commission. Its task is to produce a compromise text if the Council and the EP have not reached an agreement after the second reading of the ordinary legislative procedure.

is to formulate a compromise text that reconciles the differences of opinion between the institutions.

This compromise text then goes back to the EP and the Council for a simple 'up and down vote' in a third reading. This means that both institutions only have the options of either adopting or rejecting the compromise text. They cannot make any new amendments. In so doing, the EP decides by simple majority and the Council by qualified majority. If both institutions adopt the compromise text that has come out of reconciliation, that text becomes law. If one or both of the institutions rejects the compromise text, the procedure ends without a legislative act.

Strict deadlines apply to the conciliation procedure. The conciliation committee needs to be convened no later than six weeks after the Council has come to its decision in the second reading. Subsequently, the conciliation committee has six weeks to propose a compromise text. The Council and the EP have six weeks to adopt that text. Each of these deadlines can be extended by two weeks at most. If one of these deadlines is not met, the proposal is deemed to have been rejected.

All in all, what we see in the ordinary legislative procedure is a fine-grained specification of the balance that the procedure seeks to maintain between the three institutions. At the same time, the procedure presents a 'funnel', in which the three institutions are increasingly pushed towards a conclusion (be it adoption or rejection) by setting strict deadlines, raising voting thresholds and not allowing new amendments to be introduced beyond a certain stage.

Informal processes under the ordinary legislative procedure

Above, we outlined the formal steps taken in the ordinary legislative procedure. These steps prescribe a clear sequence of activities: first the Commission releases a proposal, then the EP moves, then the Council, then the Commission again, and so on. In reality, decision-making does not follow this neat separation of steps and roles. Within the limits set by the formal procedure, the three institutions also act and interact in ways that do not follow directly from the formal procedure (although they are sometimes laid down in **interinstitutional agreements** between them). These actions and interactions are important for understanding how the procedure works, and they complement the formal steps in that procedure. As a result, the actual activities of institutions overlap to a much greater extent than the formal description of the procedure would suggest.

> An **interinstitutional agreement** is a binding agreement between the Commission, the Council and/or the EP, in which the institutions define arrangements for their cooperation.

Two practices facilitate this process. First, both the Council and EP have found ways to take a position on a proposal outside of the formal steps that the procedure prescribes. Second, the institutions have developed practices where they meet to discuss their positions in between the formal legislative steps. We discuss both practices in turn. First, institutions may decide to deliberate on a proposal and make their viewpoint clear, without taking the accompanying formal decision that the ordinary legislative procedure prescribes. Above we showed that officially the Council has to wait before adopting its common position until the EP has adopted an opinion in first reading. In reality the Council will often start discussing a legislative proposal as soon as it has received it from the Commission. During these discussions, the contentious issues are determined and compromises are explored. In the end, this may result in the adoption of a **political agreement**. As a result the Council's viewpoint is already known before it has adopted its common position. In the case of the TPD the Council reached such a political agreement in June 2013, several months before the EP debated the dossier in its plenary session. This way it could make clear to the EP which provisions in the proposal it would like to see changed. A somewhat similar practice can be seen in the EP when it has to decide on adopting its formal opinion on a legislative proposal. In the first reading the EP needs to do this by taking a so-called final vote on the complete dossier. The EP may, however, decide to vote on all amendments but postpone this final vote. The matter is then referred back to the committee and the rapporteur is given the mandate to negotiate the proposal with the Commission and the Council. By doing this, the proposal remains in the first reading of the procedure. This is what happened with the TPD proposal. In October 2013 the EP adopted 114 of the 171 amendments proposed. It deliberately postponed the final vote and instead decided to give its rapporteur a mandate to start negotiations with the Commission and Council.

> **Political agreement** refers to the situation where the Council already communicates its views on a proposal before the EP has formally adopted its opinion.

These negotiations between the institutions are the second leg of informal processes in decision-making. In the case of the TPD the Lithuanian presidency of the Council had already approached the rapporteur and shadow rapporteurs in the EP to discuss the political agreement in the Council before the EP debated it in its plenary session. After the EP had voted on the amendments negotiations were continued in the form of **trilogues**. Trilogues link together the formally separate decision-making processes and make it easier to reach agreement in a faster way than when the formal steps would be followed.

> **Trilogues** are regular meetings of representatives of the three institutions (Commission, EP and Council) that are convened in order to identify points of agreement and differences, and find a compromise on a legislative text.

In the TPD dossier the Commission, Council and EP reached agreement after several trilogue meetings on 18 December 2013. Once this compromise had been reached the EP adopted the compromise package as its opinion on 26 February 2014, and the Council adopted the same proposal on 14 March 2014.

Figure 4.2 shows that over the years more and more decisions have been concluded in first reading and that only very few dossiers make it all the way to the formal conciliation process in third reading. This is in fact achieved by engaging in a kind of conciliation at earlier stages of the procedure, through the system of trilogue meetings. Because so many first

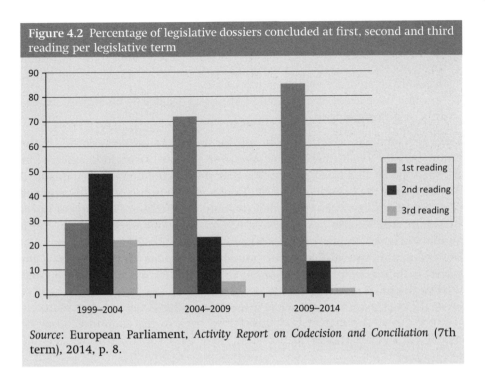

Figure 4.2 Percentage of legislative dossiers concluded at first, second and third reading per legislative term

Source: European Parliament, *Activity Report on Codecision and Conciliation* (7th term), 2014, p. 8.

reading procedures are now accompanied by extensive informal concili-ations, the average length to complete a dossier in first reading has gone up from eleven months in the 1999–2004 parliamentary term to seventeen months in 2009–14. Nevertheless, the average length to complete legislative dossiers has gone down from twenty-two months to nineteen months. This suggests that the increased use of informal procedures has speeded up decision-making considerably.

■ Other decision-making procedures

The ordinary legislative procedure is used for most issue areas in the EU. However, there is still a range of areas in which it does not apply. In those areas, there is not one single alternative procedure but a variety of procedures in which the balance between the institutions and the applicable voting rules in the Council is defined in different ways. In this section, we will show some of this variety and, crucially, explain the background to it.

The special legislative procedures

In the EU treaties, the ordinary legislative procedure is distinguished from the 'special legislative procedures'. These procedures differ from the ordinary legislative procedure because they depart in one or more respects from the balance between the three institutions that characterizes the ordinary legislative procedure:

- In some issue areas, the European Parliament cannot adopt amendments, has only an advisory role or no role at all.
- In some issue areas, the Council of Ministers decides by unanimity instead of a qualified majority.

Different combinations of a smaller role for the EP and the decision rule in the Council are used in different issue areas. For instance, association agreements between the EU and third countries are adopted by the Council by a qualified majority with the consent of the EP. Hence, the EP is only involved after the draft agreement has been concluded and only has the choice to adopt or reject that draft. The EP also has a consent role in the adoption of the EU's multi-annual financial framework, but then the Council decides by unanimity. However, most special legislative procedures combine an advisory role for the EP with unanimity in the Council. This is true, for instance, for proposals relating to spatial planning, family law, passports and residence cards, the EU's revenues, social security and social protection, and indirect taxes.

The European Council as an 'appeal body'

In some areas, the Council of Ministers can refer a decision to the European Council if vital national interests are at stake. In most legislative procedures, the European Council has no formal role, although political agreements are sometimes forged in the European Council in order to break a deadlock in the Council of Ministers. In some specific areas, however, the European Council has a formal role as a kind of 'appeal body' for the Council. This is the case, in particular, for sensitive issues relating to criminal matters (such as the definition of criminal offences and sanctions or the rights of suspects). In those cases, if a member of the Council finds that a proposal affects 'fundamental aspects of its criminal justice system', it may refer the issue to the European Council, which will decide by unanimity whether or not to proceed.

Decision-making under the CFSP

The role of the EP is the smallest in the EU's Common Foreign and Security Policy (CFSP). Here, the EP is only consulted on 'the main aspects and the basic choices' of the policy. It has no role in the adoption of decisions, except in decisions relating to the EU diplomatic service, where it is consulted. Likewise, the Commission has no exclusive right of initiative in this area; this right is exercised by any member state and by the High Representative for Foreign Affairs and Security Policy.

Strictly speaking, these are not 'special legislative procedures' because, as we saw above, no legislation can be adopted under the CFSP. The decisions that can be adopted are taken by the Council of Ministers and/or the European Council, normally acting by unanimity. In some cases, the Council may decide by qualified majority. However, in a number of those cases, any member of the Council may demand the use of unanimity if vital national interests are at stake, introducing yet another safety valve for individual member states in this area.

Navigating the maze of EU decision-making

One could easily lose one's way in this maze of procedures, with exceptions and special procedures for specific issues and issue areas. Still, it becomes much easier to navigate the maze if one reflects on the logic behind this variation. As a general rule, the closer an issue is to elements of national sovereignty that member state governments hold dear, the smaller the role for the EP (and the Commission) and the more likely it is that unanimity is used in the Council. Both EP involvement and qualified majority voting represent a risk for individual member states: the risk that a decision will be adopted that they do not agree with. For issues that are not that politically salient and do not touch upon vital interests, this is less of a problem. Here, the benefits of easier agreement in the Council and democratic legitimation through the EP outweigh the potential risk of being outvoted. However, for issues that are close to the vital interests of member state governments, those governments want to take fewer chances. As a result, for those issues, they have hung on to the power to veto a decision (hence requiring unanimity) and/or have diminished the role of the EP and even the Commission.

Although examples of such sensitive issues can be found in many policy areas, three broad areas stand out in this regard:

- Proposals relating to taxation and the budget often require unanimity, because taxation is a core element of national sovereignty and the member states that are net contributors to the EU budget are wary of being outvoted on budgetary matters.
- Issues of judicial and police cooperation are also sensitive because they touch upon member state governments' internal sovereignty. Hence, they can be referred to the European Council if a member of the Council so wishes. Moreover, as we already saw above, the European Commission does not have the exclusive right of initiative in these areas, as proposals can also be initiated by a quarter of the member states.
- Foreign policy is probably the most sensitive prerogative for member state governments. As a result, the main decisions under the CFSP are all taken by unanimity, the European Council plays an important role in decision-making, the EP has hardly any role to play in this area, while the Commission has to share its right of initiative with member states and acts through the High Representative for Foreign Affairs and Security Policy.

In these areas, the ordinary legislative procedure is replaced by another procedure or is complemented with additional safety valves that protect individual member states. In the end, EU decision-making procedures are the outcome of

Controversy 4.1

Simplifying legislative procedures in the EU?

Over the years, what is now called the 'ordinary legislative procedure' has been applied to an ever-increasing number of issue areas. Still, as we have seen in this chapter, important exceptions remain. In these areas, special legislative procedures are used. This stands in contrast to the practice in domestic political systems, where normally one basic procedure is used for all types of legislative decisions. Moreover, even the ordinary legislative procedure is quite complex, with differences between the various readings and different voting rules within the procedure.

Therefore, it has been argued that EU decision-making would benefit from a simplification of procedures. To begin with, the ordinary legislative procedure could be applied to all issue areas. This would give the European Parliament the same powers that national parliaments have in most of the EU member states. In addition, the procedure could be simplified, by saying no more than that the EP and the Council have the right to amend proposals and both need to approve a proposal before it becomes law. The relationship between the EP and the Council would then resemble that between the House of Representatives and the Senate in the US Congress.

Do you agree? Should the ordinary legislative procedure be used in all issue areas and should it be simplified? If so, what specific benefits do you expect from this change? If not, what disadvantages do you see?

treaty negotiations between member state governments. It is no surprise, then, that the protection of their interests should play such an important role in the types and diversity of procedures.

Nevertheless, there have been repeated calls for simplification of the EU's legislative procedures. Controversy 4.1 takes a further look at this issue.

■ Decision-making in the Council

The delicate balancing of member state interests that we explained above can also be observed in the way the Council of Ministers takes decisions. As we have seen, the Council plays an important role in all legislative decision-making procedures. Whereas the role of the Commission and the EP varies between issue areas, no legislation can be adopted without the consent of the Council. At the same time, decision-making within the Council does vary between issue areas. In the descriptions of the ordinary legislative procedure and the special legislative procedures, we already alluded to the two main decision rules used in the Council: unanimity and qualified majority voting. As we saw, the basic voting rule in the Council during the ordinary legislative procedure is qualified majority voting (known as QMV in EU parlance), with unanimity needed to adopt amendments that have not been endorsed by the Commission. In special legislative procedures and under the CFSP, unanimity is often (though not always) the rule. Unanimity is a straightforward decision rule: all member states need to agree in order for a proposal to be adopted. This rule gives a veto to each single member state. QMV is a more complicated decision rule that requires more explanation, because it reflects yet another balance to be struck within the EU: that between larger and smaller member states.

How qualified majority voting works

Two decisions need to be made in devising a voting rule in the Council: how votes are distributed among the member states, and how many votes are necessary for a decision to be adopted.

To illustrate the trade-off inherent in assigning votes to member states, consider two extreme possibilities. At one extreme, one could envisage a voting rule according to which each member state would have one vote. Such a voting rule would give equal voting power to, say, Germany and Malta. For that reason, it would not be acceptable to the larger member states, which could be outvoted by a coalition of small member states. The other extreme would be to give each member state a vote for each of its citizens. This solution would be unacceptable to the small member states since their votes would practically become irrelevant given the huge differences in population between the member states.

As to the number of votes needed to adopt a decision, various possibilities present themselves as well. On the one hand, one could simply define a majority as 50% of the votes plus one. This is the rule used for regular decision-making in national parliaments and in the EP. For member states, such a rule increases the risk of being outvoted. On the other hand, one could require a supermajority close to 100%. In that case, qualified majority voting would in practice almost amount to unanimity.

QMV is an attempt to find a middle ground between these extremes and reconcile the interests of large and small member states. As a result, QMV is quite a complex compromise. Moreover, the situation is complicated by the fact that the EU recently changed the rules for arriving at a qualified majority. Below we compare the two regimes in order to assess its effect on the relative voting power of every member state.

The old regime of qualified majority voting which was in place until 31 October 2014 allocated a total of 352 votes to the member states. The number of votes roughly reflected a member state's population, with the largest countries such as Germany and Italy each receiving the maximum number of twenty-nine votes and Malta, the smallest country, receiving three votes. Under these rules qualified majority is achieved when a so-called triple majority is reached, consisting of:

- a minimum of 260 out of the 352 votes (74%);
- a simple majority of member states (currently fifteen out of twenty-eight);
- at least 62% of the EU population being represented by those member states.

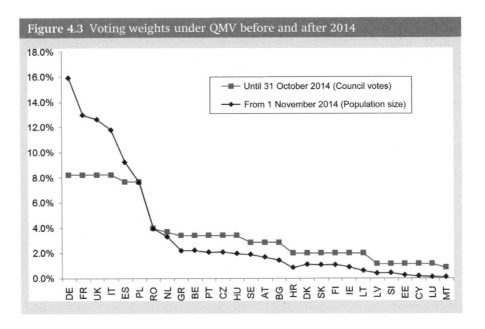

Figure 4.3 Voting weights under QMV before and after 2014

In the Treaty of Lisbon, a new regime was adopted with two considerations in mind: making it easier for the Council to adopt decisions under QMV as well as ensuring a stronger relation between a country's population size and its voting power. Under this regime, a qualified majority is reached if two conditions are met:

- A proposal is supported by at least 55% of the member states (sixteen of the twenty-eight).
- This majority represents at least 65% of the EU population.
- In order to block a decision at least four member states must vote against and represent at least 35% of the EU population.

As a result of the change, Germany saw its voting weight almost double to 16%, while, for example, Ireland's voting weight was halved from 2% to less than 1%. At the same time, while the relative voting power of member states changes on the basis of their populations, the need to obtain the support of at least 55% of the member states still protects smaller member states from being overruled by the larger countries, as does the rule that a 'blocking minority' needs to consist of at least four member states.

Because the population of the member states now directly affects the voting weight of every member state, the Council updates these every year on the basis of the population statistics of Eurostat, the statistical office of the EU. Figure 4.3 shows the implications of this change for the relative voting weights of each member state. The new regime for QMV came into effect as of 1 November 2014. This delay in application of the new rules was necessary to make the change acceptable to member states that stood to lose from the change. As a further compromise, between 1 November 2014 and 31 March 2017, each member state may request that the old regime of QMV is applied instead of the new regime, so that the new voting rules for QMV will only fully come into effect as of 1 April 2017. These elaborate manoeuvres around QMV show the political nature of the compromises that make up the voting rules in the Council.

Voting and consensus in the Council

The above discussion of voting rules should not obscure the fact that in reality voting does not take place that often in the Council. The president summarizes the proposal and asks whether the decision can be considered adopted. If no member state objects, the adoption of the proposal is recorded and all member states are supposed to have voted in favour. As a result about two thirds of decisions requiring QMV are in fact taken unanimously. Still, the bargaining position of member states is largely determined by their capability to contribute to a blocking minority. In that sense, the distribution of votes always plays a role in the background of negotiations in the Council, even if in the end a proposal is adopted without a formal vote.

There are, however, instances where member states are unable to support a proposal. In these cases a member state has two options: to abstain from voting or to cast a vote against. Under QMV both abstentions and no votes count when calculating the required majority: as a result both operate as a vote against. Of all the member states the United Kingdom most often either abstains or votes against proposals (in about 10% of the votes), whilst Germany, Denmark and the Netherlands also from time to time do this. As an alternative to abstaining or voting against, member states may also show their discontent by making a formal statement following the adoption of the vote, thereby not obstructing the adoption of the act. In the TPD case Poland, the Czech Republic, Romania and Bulgaria had earlier on showed their opposition to the political agreement that the Council had reached. In the end, however, only Poland voted against, whilst Hungary and Sweden both made a statement expressing concern about certain provisions of the proposal. An important reason for the lack of open voting is the 'consensus culture' that permeates the Council. Even when a qualified majority is reached and a decision can be taken, the member states in the majority will try to accommodate reasonable demands by the member states in the opposing minority. If these demands are not met, a member state may decide to signal its discontent by casting a vote against. Still, because it is certain that it will be outvoted by the others, it is often wiser to vote along with the majority and thus build up some political credit with the other member states with a view to decisions in the future. Another reason for the high degree of consensual decision-making is that much legislation in the end will have to be implemented by the member states themselves. Doing this might be more difficult for a government if it were to come out that in fact it had opposed the decision in the Council.

■ Member state parliaments and the subsidiarity check

With the conclusion of the Treaty of Lisbon, the role of national parliaments in EU decision-making has been strengthened. Before the Treaty of Lisbon, national parliaments were only involved indirectly in EU decision-making procedures, through their power to hold the minister representing their member state in the Council to account. Since national parliaments played no role at the EU level themselves, this was not a very effective power. Often, they would find themselves confronted with decisions taken within the EU for which they could hold their national minister accountable after the fact, but which they could not change.

The Treaty of Lisbon introduced several provisions that increased the involvement of national parliaments in legislative decision-making, by allowing them to check the subsidiarity and **proportionality** of legislative proposals. As a result all legislative proposals are sent to the national parliaments where they can be debated and discussed in the relevant parliamentary committees. On the basis of these deliberations national parliaments can ask the Commission for further clarification and information on the proposal and express their views through sending opinions as well as 'reasoned opinions'. This reasoned opinion constitutes an official statement in which the member state parliament declares the proposal to be in violation of the principle of subsidiarity. Every chamber of a national parliament has the ability to issue a 'reasoned opinion', allowing, for example, both the UK House of Commons and the House of Lords to voice objections. Every reasoned opinion that is cast can thus be considered a vote of one of the chambers of a parliament against the proposal. In order to give every parliament an equal voice, the reasoned opinion of a unicameral parliament is therefore counted as two votes. Depending on the number of reasoned opinions thus counted two things can happen:

> The **principle of proportionality** states that the burden to implement legislation should be minimized and commensurate with the objective to be achieved.

- If the number of votes is at least a third, the actor that initiated the proposal (usually the Commission) must review it. If the proposal relates to issues of judicial cooperation in criminal matters or police cooperation, this should already happen if the number is a quarter or more. The outcome of the review is not predetermined: the initiator of the proposal may withdraw it, amend it or maintain it, but is required to explain that decision. This is known as the 'yellow card' procedure, since the national parliaments give a warning to the EU legislators that they are about to violate the subsidiarity principle.
- If more than half the number of votes is reached, a more elaborate procedure is put in motion. Again, the initiator needs to review the

proposal and may decide to withdraw, modify or maintain it, explaining its decision in a reasoned opinion. Subsequently, the Council and the EP are required to consider the reasoned opinions of both the national parliaments and the Commission with a view to determining the compatibility of the proposal with the subsidiarity principle. This needs to be done before the end of the first reading. If 55% of the member states in the Council or a simple majority in the European Parliament find that the proposal violates the subsidiarity principle, it is withdrawn. This is known as the 'orange card' procedure, because it is more demanding than the yellow card procedure but still does not allow national parliaments to force the withdrawal of an EU proposal (which would be a 'red card').

In its first five years of existence a total of 312 reasoned opinions were issued, with the Swedish and Dutch parliaments most active and accounting for fifty and thirty-seven statements of subsidiarity concerns, respectively. In the TPD case nineteen legislative chambers made use of the opportunity to give their opinion on the legislative proposal, providing the Commission often with detailed suggestions on what parts of the directives would need to be changed. Seven of these constituted reasoned opinion, a number insufficient to generate a yellow card.

In two cases so far national parliaments have amassed a sufficient number of opinions to generate a yellow card. In 2012 the parliaments objected to a legislative proposal that would set certain EU-wide limits on the right to strike. The Commission decided to withdraw the proposal following these objections. The second yellow card was drawn in 2013 and resulted from the objection of fifteen chambers in eleven member states to the plans to establish a European Public Prosecutor's Office. In this case the Commission decided not to drop its proposal and published a communication in which it set out in detail why the proposal did not violate the principle of subsidiarity. This could be a risky strategy, because it is very likely that the objecting parliaments will use the leverage they have over their member states' ministers to force a blockade in the Council, once the proposal arrives there.

Although in its first five years only two yellow cards were actually drawn, the political relevance of involving national parliaments in the legislative process should not be underestimated. The yellow cards can be seen as the tip of an iceberg that consists of a by now intensive exchange of views between national parliaments and the Commission. In fact, only 14% of the opinions that the legislative chambers send are reasoned opinions. Most of the exchanges happen through the sending of ordinary opinions and through political dialogues where parliamentary chambers ask the Commission to clarify their legislative proposals. All in all for the Commission the system thus generates a wealth of useful information on the viability of its legislative proposals and the possible problems it may face when member states have to implement it.

■ The Open Method of Coordination

How the Open Method of Coordination works

The **Open Method of Coordination** (OMC) is a relative newcomer in EU policy-making. It was introduced in March 2000 as part of the Lisbon Strategy (not to be confused with the Treaty of Lisbon, which was adopted much later) and was meant to bring about a degree of policy coordination in social-economic policies. This fitted into the stated objective of the Lisbon Strategy to reinvigorate

> The **Open Method of Coordination** is a mechanism which aims at convergence of member state policies through a process of benchmarking and policy learning.

the European economy and make the EU the most competitive economy by the year 2010. In this area, member states did not want to be bound by EU legislation. At the same time, they acknowledged that the economic ambitions of the Lisbon Strategy required some kind of coordination of economic policies. The OMC was invented to fill that gap by creating an institutionalized 'learning process' between member states. Since its inception, the concept and approach of the OMC have been applied to a range of other policy areas, such as pensions, health care and education.

OMC works in four steps:

- The Council determines the objectives to be achieved in an area.
- Indicators are established for measuring the attainment of those objectives.
- Each member state formulates an action plan for reaching the objectives.
- Based on those indicators, the performance of each member state is 'benchmarked' (that is, it is assessed and compared to the performance of other member states).

The OMC is largely driven by the member states themselves, assembled in the Council. It is the Council that determines the objectives and indicators, and it is in the Council that the results of the benchmarking exercise are discussed. Nevertheless, the Commission does play a role, since it monitors the performance of member states and draws up the reports that are discussed in the Council.

The outcome of the OMC is non-binding. It is entirely up to the member state governments to decide what to do with this benchmarking exercise, and there are no penalties for those member states that perform badly. The idea is that 'peer pressure' (being exposed as an underachiever in the presence of one's colleagues from other member states) will form an incentive to perform better.

Why the Open Method of Coordination is used

The creation and rise of OMC can be understood along the same lines that were sketched above when we explained differences between decision-making procedures. In areas where member states are reluctant to accept binding legislation, because of cultural concerns (education) and/or the high budgetary stakes

Table 4.1 Instruments and procedures in EU social policy

	Legislation allowed?	Procedure
Occupational safety and health	Yes	Ordinary
Working conditions	Yes	Ordinary
Information and consultation of workers	Yes	Ordinary
Equality between male and female workers	Yes	Ordinary
Integration of persons excluded from the labour market	Yes	Ordinary
Employment conditions for immigrants from outside the EU	Yes	Special
Collective representation of workers and employers	Yes	Special
Employment protection	Yes	Special
Social security and social protection	Yes	Special
Combating social exclusion	No	OMC
Modernization of social protection	No	OMC

involved (economic policy, health), the OMC offers a way to discuss policies without actually being forced to change anything.

The use of various types of policy instruments and decision-making procedures can be nicely illustrated by looking at EU social policy. Table 4.1 shows different issue areas within this policy field and lists whether binding legislation (in this field only Directives) can be adopted in them and what procedure applies.

Binding legislation is not allowed in two areas that carry significant financial implications (social exclusion and social protection). Legislation is allowed in four other issue areas that touch upon either politically sensitive (employment of immigrants from outside the EU and collective bargaining) or economically significant (employment protection and social security) areas, but it requires a special legislative procedure in which the Council decides by unanimity and the EP is only consulted. In five other issue areas, finally, legislation can be adopted using the ordinary legislative procedure. These include areas such as the information and consultation of workers, equal working conditions for men and women, and occupational health and safety that are regulatory in nature and have been subject to EU legislation for quite a long time now. Hence, the type of issue at stake determines the instruments and procedures that can be used.

■ Towards a Europe of multiple speeds?

Examples of 'multi-speed Europe'

So far, we have discussed decision-making in 'the EU', taken as a whole. Indeed, many policies are adopted for the entire EU and apply to all member states. Still, in some areas policies have been adopted that only apply to a subset of all member states. In EU parlance, this is known variously as 'multi-speed Europe', 'variable geometry', 'Europe à la carte' and, the terminology used in the EU treaties, 'enhanced cooperation'. Examples of policies that apply only to part of the member states can be found in several areas:

- When it was introduced, the Euro was adopted by twelve of the then fifteen EU member states. Denmark, Sweden and the UK chose to retain their own currencies. Since the enlargements with countries of Central and Eastern Europe, new member states have had to qualify for adoption of the Euro by fulfilling certain macroeconomic requirements. As a result, some EU member states use the Euro but others do not.
- In the field of defence policy, cooperation has typically relied on the willingness of groups of member states to move forward. A good example is the creation of EU battle groups, 1,500-person strong military groups that can be deployed in military operations across the globe. Although the concept and creation of battle groups was approved by all member states, actual participation in battle groups remains contingent upon the willingness of individual member states to contribute. Similarly, EU operations in the field of the Common Foreign and Security Policy have relied on variable coalitions of member states that are willing (and able) to participate.
- In the field of justice and home affairs, groups of member states have concluded treaties on closer cooperation outside the EU framework. These treaties have subsequently become part of the EU proper. Examples include the Schengen Treaty on the free movement of persons across borders, and the Treaty of Prüm on the exchange of information between law enforcement authorities in different countries.

Since the 1997 Treaty of Amsterdam, these types of **enhanced cooperation** between groups of member states have been officially made possible within the EU. At the same time, the EU treaties specify a number of conditions for and procedures to be followed during the establishment of enhanced cooperation. Fact file 4.2 gives an overview of these conditions and procedures. The procedure was used for the first time in the summer of 2010, when the EP and the Council of Ministers allowed fourteen member states to move forward with a Regulation on divorce procedures that involve spouses from different member states. In 2012 enhanced cooperation was used in adopting EU patent legislation that allows patent holders to get EU-wide protection on the basis of a single application in one of the member states. Because Italy and Spain did not want to proceed, the other member states decided to use the enhanced cooperation procedure in order to adopt this legislation.

> **Enhanced cooperation** is a procedure through which a group of EU member states can adopt legislation (or a decision under the CFSP) that only applies to them and not to the other member states.

The arguments for and against enhanced cooperation

The conditions and procedures for establishing enhanced cooperation that we discussed above seek to ensure that agreements between a subset of member

Fact file 4.2

Conditions and procedures for establishing enhanced cooperation

Article 20 of the Treaty on European Union and Articles 326–34 of the Treaty on the Functioning of the European Union contain the conditions and procedures for establishing 'enhanced cooperation' between groups of member states.

Enhanced cooperation should respect the following conditions:

- It should include at least nine member states.
- Participation should be open to all member states, both at the time when a form of enhanced cooperation is created and after it has been established.
- It may not undermine the internal market or economic, social and territorial cohesion between the member states. It may also not introduce trade barriers or distort competition between member states.
- It should fall within one of the EU's competences. However, enhanced cooperation cannot be established in areas that fall under the exclusive competence of the European Union.

In addition, the Treaties include a procedure for establishing enhanced cooperation:

- For enhanced cooperation in policy areas outside the Common Foreign and Security Policy, the European Commission has the exclusive right to submit a proposal, upon request by a group of member states. The proposal has to be adopted by the Council of Ministers and consented to by the EP.
- For enhanced cooperation in the field of the Common Foreign and Security Policy, a group of member states can submit a proposal to the Council of Ministers. The Commission and the High Representative for Foreign Affairs and Security Policy may give their opinion. The EP is merely informed.
- In the Council of Ministers, all member states may participate in the deliberations, but only member states that will become part of the enhanced cooperation have the right to vote on the proposal.

states do not pose a threat to the EU as a whole, other (non-participating) member states or the EU's supranational institutions. Nevertheless, enhanced cooperation remains a controversial issue within the EU.

Its proponents argue that it is necessary in order to prevent European integration from slowing down and to allow a degree of flexibility in the type and extent of cooperation between member states. With the steady enlargement of the EU, the diversity of ideas, concerns and interests in the EU has also become greater. As a result, it is increasingly difficult to reach agreement on policies that cover the entire EU. Indeed, in many cases it makes little sense to adopt policies that are to be imposed from France to Bulgaria and from Spain to Sweden, since the kind of challenges EU member states have to cope with and the policies they can realistically aspire to implement vary widely. Why, then, should groups of member states not be allowed to proceed when they see scope for further cooperation, without burdening other member states with policies they do not want or are not yet ready for? Moreover, enhanced cooperation may act as a laboratory for new policy initiatives that can subsequently be integrated into the EU framework at large, as has been done with the Schengen and Prüm Treaties. If policies can only be adopted by and for the EU as a whole, these types of policy initiatives may well never materialize.

Opponents, by contrast, warn against the negative consequences of a 'variable geometry' of European integration. Enhanced cooperation undermines the solidarity and uniformity characteristic of the EU. This may lead to a 'first class' and a 'second class' EU, differentiating member states that are in the 'elite' of front-runners and member states that lag behind. Moreover, enhanced cooperation may result in a patchwork of policies from which each member state chooses what it likes while opting out of policies that are inconvenient. Yet, many policies are only effective to the extent that they apply to all member states, including those for whom they are not convenient. Finally, enhanced cooperation may be a way for small groups of countries to create a *fait accompli* for the others. As happened with the Schengen and Prüm Treaties, under enhanced cooperation a limited number of member states defines the contents of a policy. Once that policy is established, other member states face the choice of going along or staying apart, but they can no longer change the outlines of the existing policy. This, so the critics say, is hardly democratic and could be used as a deliberate strategy by (groups of) member states to circumvent established policy-making procedures in the EU.

The conditions and procedures for enhanced cooperation that are now laid down in the EU treaties seek to find a balance between the arguments pro and contra. While facilitating cooperation between small groups of member states, they also ensure a role for the European Commission and the EP and they stress the right of each member state to participate in any initiative to arrive at enhanced cooperation. As was shown above, multi-speed Europe is already a reality in several areas. Depending on the use that is made of the provisions on enhanced cooperation in the EU treaties, it may become even more important in the future. Depending on one's perspective, this will be a motor for further integration or a threat to the integrity of the EU. Yet, whatever one's perspective, member states still have the option to cooperate outside of the EU, either directly with each other or in the framework of other international organizations. The Schengen and Prüm Treaties, for instance, were concluded outside the EU. Rejecting on principled grounds forms of enhanced cooperation within the EU may lead to a rise of such initiatives outside the EU.

■ Summary

This chapter has looked at decision-making in the European Union. It has argued that:

- There are four 'regular' types of legal instruments: Regulations, Directives, Decisions, and Recommendations and Opinions.

- Regulations and Directives are the two legislative instruments that have general application, and Decisions are used for individual cases. Regulations are directly applicable in the member states once they are adopted at EU level, whilst Directives first need to be transposed by the member states into domestic legislation.

- Recommendations and Opinions are non-binding instruments. Non-binding instruments also occur under other names, such as 'Guidelines'.

- The EU's Common Foreign and Security Policy uses a different set of legal instruments, which have no legal effects within the member states.

- Decision-making procedures in the EU differ along three main dimensions: the involvement of the Commission, the involvement of the European Parliament, and the voting rule used in the Council of Ministers. The more politically sensitive an issue is or the closer to member state governments' vital interests, the smaller the role of the Commission and the EP in the associated decision-making procedure will be and the more likely the Council will be to decide by unanimity.

- The ordinary legislative procedure seeks to define a balance between the Commission, the Council and the EP. In this procedure, the European Commission has the exclusive right of initiative, and both the Council and the EP have to approve a proposal and can amend it. Decision-making in the Council takes place by qualified majority.

- Special legislative procedures differ from the ordinary legislative procedure because the EP cannot amend proposals or is only consulted and/or voting in the Council takes place by unanimity. Under the Common Foreign and Security Policy, the Commission and the EP have even smaller roles than under the special legislative procedures, and the European Council takes important decisions alongside the Council of Ministers.

- Qualified majority voting (QMV) is a voting rule that seeks to balance the interests of small and large member states. As a result, it requires double (or even triple) majorities in the Council.

- Although QMV is important in the background of Council decision-making, formal votes are often avoided in the Council and the member states try to find consensus before resorting to a vote.

- Member state parliaments can raise objections to a legislative proposal if they feel the proposal violates the subsidiarity principle. If enough national parliaments do so, the initiator of the proposal needs to review the proposal and justify any revisions made (or not made).

- The Open Method of Coordination (OMC) is a policy-making procedure that does not yield any binding decisions but attempts to bring about policy coordination through a process of benchmarking and learning.

- 'Enhanced cooperation' has been presented as a way to overcome the wide variety of interests and local circumstances in the EU. At the same time, it has been criticized for leading to a fragmented Europe of 'first rate' and 'second rate' member states.

Further reading

A good introduction to different forms of policy-making in the EU is the chapter by Helen Wallace and Christine Reh on 'Institutional Anatomy and Five Policy Modes' in Helen Wallace, Mark Pollack and Alasdair Young (eds), *Policy-making in the European Union* (Oxford University Press, 6th edn, 2014). Legal specifics of instruments and decision-making procedures can be found in any good textbook on EU law, such as Paul Craig and Gráinne de Búrca, *EU Law: Text, Cases, and Materials* (Oxford University Press, 5th edn, 2011). An in-depth analysis of the actual functioning of co-decision can be found in a special issue of the *Journal of European Public Policy* on 'Twenty Years of Legislative Co-decision in the European Union', 20, 7, 2013.

Websites

- The European Parliament's 'legislative observatory' is an excellent tool for tracking decision-making processes that involve the EP. It reproduces all steps in decision-making processes (including steps taken by other institutions), gives summaries of what happened at each step as well as links to underlying documents: www.europarl.europa.eu/oeil/
- The steps taken in decision-making procedures that involve the Commission can also be traced through Pre-Lex, with links to underlying documents: http://ec.europa.eu/prelex/apcnet.cfm?CL=en
- The results of votes taken in the Council of Ministers can be found on the Council's website: www.consilium.europa.eu
- All legislation that is adopted in the EU can be found on EUR-LEX, the EU's legal database: http://eur-lex.europa.eu/en/index.htm

Navigating the EU

On the website www.navigatingthe.eu you will find online exercises for this chapter.

PART II

Key actors in EU politics: citizens, interest groups and political parties

5   Public opinion and political participation

■ Introduction

In May 2014 the citizens of the twenty-eight EU member states headed to the polls to elect their representatives for the European Parliament. In the run-up to the elections the EP made every effort to mobilize as many voters as possible. Using the slogan 'This time it's different' it highlighted the fact that the political groups for the first time had put forward candidates for the post of Commission president. The winning political group would be allowed to nominate their candidate. For the first time citizens thus were able to influence the choice of the new Commission president, thereby making the elections more important and interesting to the voters.

These expectations were not fulfilled. With only 42.5% of the voters going to the polls, turnout was even lower than the previous all-time low of 43% that had been reached at the 2009 elections. Moreover, those people that made the effort to vote did not seem to be interested at all in electing the new Commission president. While the mainstream political parties still succeeded in holding on to a large majority of the seats, Eurosceptical parties on both the left and the right made important gains. Some of them, such as the UK Independence Party, the French National Front and the Greek Coalition of the Radical Left, actually won the elections, causing the BBC to qualify the outcome as a 'Eurosceptic earthquake'.

The facts outlined above pose important questions about people's opinions on the EU as well as their behaviour in EP elections:

- How do citizens evaluate the EU and how have their opinions changed over the years?
- Which factors explain citizen evaluations of the EU?
- How have citizens voted in EP elections and referendums on European integration and how can we explain their voting behaviour?
- What do these developments tell us about the possibilities for further integration?

In this chapter we show that the EU has, for much of its existence, not figured very prominently in the minds of many citizens. This lack of saliency – not being prominent in people's minds – allowed the member state governments and their politicians to move on with European integration without worrying too much about citizen opinions. The introduction of direct elections for the European Parliament did not make the EU more important in the views of voters. For a long time EP elections were therefore dominated by national issues and did not reflect voters' views on EU politics. In recent years, however, things seem to be changing. People are still reluctant to vote in EP elections, but a larger number of citizens are more critical of the EU, including those that go and vote. As a result further integrative steps cannot rely anymore on the implicit support of EU citizens, but may generate more and more resistance.

■ Public opinion, political participation and politics

Public opinion and **political participation** are two key concepts for understanding the relation between citizens and the political system. Public opinion refers to people's attitudes towards a given subject. In

Political participation: all activities that are aimed at influencing policies and/or the selection of politicians.

the case of EU politics these opinions may cover a wide range of questions: How interested are citizens in the EU? Do they think European integration is a good thing? Which problems should be tackled at the European level? How trustworthy are the members of the European Parliament? Do citizens support a further enlargement of the EU?

While public opinion is about everything that people *think*, political participation focuses on what citizens actually *do*. In principle citizens have the same opportunities to be active in EU politics as in their own national politics. First, there is a full range of forms of *non-electoral participation* stretching from contacting the European Parliament or Commission, sending letters to the European Ombudsman and signing petitions, to joining a national protest or even attending one in Brussels. While there is an almost infinite number of possibilities to do this, only a small minority of citizens actually engage them. At the EU level these activities are mostly undertaken by organized groups rather than individual citizens (see Chapter 6). In this chapter we therefore focus on the two forms of *electoral participation*: voting in elections for the

European Parliament and in national referendums on some aspect of European integration.

Public opinion and political participation are important for democracies because they connect citizens to the political system. If politicians are able to translate people's demands into policies and if they successfully tackle the most important problems this will most likely increase the **legitimacy** of the political system. Studying public opinion

> **Legitimacy:** the condition of being in accordance with the norms and values of the people.

and political participation is crucial to find out to what extent people support their political system and how they try to affect policy-making.

■ Public opinion

Interest in the public's opinion on some kind of cooperation between the nation-states of Europe dates back as far as the Second World War, which witnessed a proliferation of ideas on cementing the nation-states together (see Chapter 1). Political leaders had to be very careful in their plans for seeking new forms of cooperation between the nation-states. If there were to be some kind of cooperation between the different European countries, it was essential to find out to what extent the citizens of these countries supported such moves.

Support for such steps was surprisingly high. Scattered surveys held in the 1950s showed that:

- Between 55% and 75% of the citizens of founding members like France, the Federal Republic of Germany and Italy were in favour 'of making efforts towards uniting Europe'.
- Only a small minority was opposed to such efforts.
- Between 20% and 30% had no opinion on the issue.

In 1962, five years after the Treaties of Rome were signed, a Gallup poll concluded that there was 'very widespread support for the idea of European unification' amongst the citizens of the six member states. These general levels of support were accompanied by large majorities of citizens in favour of specific policies. When probed on specific themes a sizeable majority of citizens professed to be in favour of the elimination of tariffs (81%), equalizing social benefits (77%) and a common agricultural policy (69%).

But what to make of the answers to these questions? For a long time public opinion surveys on Europe have been haunted by the problem of **non-attitudes**. In one of the most influential

> A **non-attitude** is an expression of opinion which is not rooted in strongly held beliefs and hence can be very volatile.

early studies on public opinion, the authors summarized their results as follows:

> While large majorities of the mass publics in all member countries are generally supportive of the Community and its works, few people have seen its immediate

relevance to their daily lives. By and large they do not think about it very often, cannot answer simple questions about it, and do not list European issues per se as very salient ones.

Leon N. Lindberg and Stuart A. Scheingold, Europe's Would-be Polity: Patterns of Change in the European Community *(Prentice Hall, 1970: 257).*

For most people Europe and the European institutions were so distant that questions on European integration were rather novel to them and did not tap well-developed opinions. All in all, Lindberg and Scheingold characterized the public's mood towards the European project as a 'permissive consensus': permissive because the mood was supportive, and consensual because this was shared by a very large part of the population. The consensus enabled political elites to proceed with the integration project relatively unrestrained.

Briefing 5.1

Gauging public opinion in the EU: Eurobarometer

Since 1974 the European Commission has systematically monitored public opinion on Europe through its Eurobarometer surveys. They followed up on a 1972 report by the European Parliament (the Schuijt report) which pressed for a more active and effective information policy on the part of the European Commission in order to educate the public about Europe.

Every spring and autumn surveys are carried out in all member states amongst 1,000 randomly selected citizens from the age of fifteen upwards. This makes it possible to analyse and compare developments in public opinion across the member states as well as over time. The bulk of the questions focus on evaluating the EU: their country's membership, the speed of the integration process, attachment to the European Union, trust in the different EU institutions, citizen knowledge of and interest in EU affairs and their attitudes towards further expanding the EU. To put these into perspective more general questions on people's personal situation and their evaluation of policies in general are included as well.

The standard Eurobarometer is supplemented by special Eurobarometers which are held at the request of specific directorates of the Commission to gauge public opinion on issues as diverse as animal welfare, the Euro, radioactive waste or the Common Agricultural Policy. Results of these surveys often find their way into official policy documents of the Commission and speeches by European Commissioners, usually in order to signal support for a specific policy or indicate the need to further develop policies. Most of the standard Eurobarometer data as well as the reports are made public after a small embargo period. Academic scholars frequently use the data in all kinds of scholarly publications on the EU.

More information can be found at http://ec.europa.eu/public_opinion/index_en.htm

In the early 1970s three of the member states which had applied for admission – Denmark, Ireland and Norway – submitted their application to a popular vote by means of a referendum in order to get popular approval for membership. In order to monitor the public's mood and predict their behaviour the European Commission started polling public opinion in these countries in the run-up to those referendums. It did not take long before such surveys were to be conducted on a regular basis in each of the member states: the Eurobarometer studies were born (see Briefing 5.1).

One question which was included from the start of the Eurobarometer survey series asks citizens whether they consider their country's membership a good thing, a bad thing or neither good nor bad. The question has become one of the most prominent tools to assess the public's mood on European integration over time. Figure 5.1 charts this support up until 2012, the last year in which this question was asked. The figure also depicts the percentage of people that 'tend to trust' the EU. This question has been asked since 2001 and its trend roughly follows that of the other support question, allowing us to monitor the most recent developments in support for the EU. The figure shows a number of things:

- For the EU as a whole support steadily increases in the 1970s and 1980s and declines at the beginning of the 1990s. At the beginning of the 2000s support increases and peaks in 2007, after which it declines substantially to the lowest trust levels measured so far.
- Important EU-related events such as the accession of new member states or the outcomes of the 2005 referendums do not suggest a clear impact on approval rates.
- Important external events such as the oil crisis in 1973 or the fall of the Iron Curtain also do not seem to have affected approval rates. However, the 2008 financial crisis seems to have clearly impacted levels of support.

Figure 5.2 displays the trust levels in 2014 amongst the citizens of the different member states. Citizens from some of the new member states such as Romania, Lithuania and Bulgaria express the highest levels of trust in the EU, whilst those in countries such as Greece, Italy, Spain and the UK show very low trust levels. The findings above provide an important first insight into the nature of public opinion formation in the EU. Opinions on the EU are predominantly formed within national contexts. It is therefore hard to talk about *the* public opinion in the EU. It varies considerably between the member states and it may be strongly affected by country-specific events and circumstances.

We can see the same amount of variation when we look at people's opinions on the types of policies the EU should deal with. Table 5.1 lists different policy areas and the percentage of citizens that want some EU involvement in this.

At the top of the list of topics that should jointly be decided by the EU and member states are those with a clear cross-border dimension such as fighting terrorism, defence and foreign affairs, and the protection of the environment. Least support for joint policies can be found in those areas that involve a

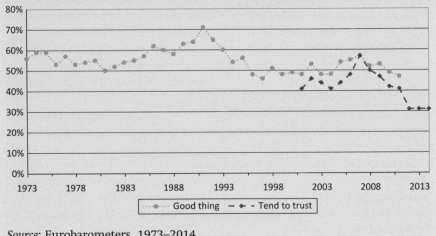

Figure 5.1 Public support for the EU. The lines represent the percentage of voters considering their country's membership to be 'a good thing' (1973–2012) and the percentage of citizens that 'tend to trust' the EU (2001–14).

Source: Eurobarometers, 1973–2014.

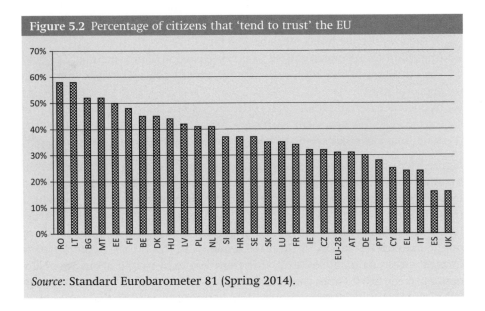

Figure 5.2 Percentage of citizens that 'tend to trust' the EU

Source: Standard Eurobarometer 81 (Spring 2014).

considerable transfer of money between citizens such as pensions, taxation, and health and social welfare. The second and third column of the table show the range of support by listing the countries where support for these policies is highest and lowest. Differences between countries can be as large as 50 percentage points. For example, whereas less than a third of the Finnish citizens believe the EU should be involved in decisions on immigration, almost 80%

Table 5.1 Support for the involvement of the EU in different policy areas

Policy area	Percentage in favour of decisions being made jointly		
	Average	Highest score	Lowest score
Fighting terrorism	78	92 (DK/LU)	62 (UK)
Scientific and technological research	73	92 (CY)	61 (UK)
Protecting the environment	68	86 (DE)	48 (MT)
Energy	66	86 (CY)	49 (UK)
Defence and foreign affairs	65	80 (LU)	23 (FI)
Fighting crime	62	81 (SK)	34 (UK)
Immigration	60	79 (MT)	28 (FI)
Competition	59	72 (CY)	41 (UK)
Reform and supervision of the financial sector	59	73 (BE/DE)	34 (UK)
Economic growth	57	75 (LT)	37 (UK)
Fighting inflation	56	73 (DE)	32 (UK)
Support for regions facing economic difficulties	56	80 (MT)	43 (UK)
Consumer protection	52	73 (CY)	33 (UK)
Transport	51	73 (BE)	26 (UK)
Agriculture and fishery	49	70 (CY)	22 (FI)
Reducing public debt	44	62 (LV)	17 (SE)
Tackling unemployment	39	59 (SK)	20 (UK)
Health	38	77 (CY)	14 (FI)
The education system	34	54 (LV)	14 (FI)
Social welfare	29	56 (CY)	11 (DK/FI/SE)
Taxation	28	43 (LT/PT)	8 (DK/FI)
Pensions	24	45 (PT)	5 (FI)

Percentage of respondents answering 'jointly' to the following question: 'For each of the following areas, do you think that decisions should be made by the [Nationality] Government or made jointly within the EU?'
Source: Eurobarometers 72 (2009), 74.2 (2010) and 76.3 (2011).

of Maltese citizens believe so. The table thus once again underlines the great amount of variation in public opinion when we compare citizens from different member states. This is not the only source of variation, however. Within every member state there are important differences between citizens as well. We explain these in the next section.

■ Explaining public opinion

In order to explain differences between citizen opinions on the EU it is useful to build upon our knowledge about people's evaluations of national politics. Many of the factors that determine someone's support for national politics also determine support for the EU. This applies by and large to all the aspects of integration we just discussed: the general evaluation of a country's membership, trust in the EU and the EU's involvement in different policy areas. Three groups of factors play a role: socio-demographic factors, general political evaluations and, finally, a group of EU-specific factors.

Socio-demographic factors
- *Education*: people with higher levels of education are more supportive of the EU.
- *Occupational class*: people in professional and managerial jobs are more supportive of the EU than manual workers or unemployed people. An important explanation for this is that those highly skilled workers benefit more from integration compared to those other categories.
- *Income*: support for the EU tends to be higher among people with higher disposable incomes.
- *Religion*: Catholics are more supportive than Protestants. While Catholicism has always been characterized by a strong transnational and internationalist tradition which sought to unite its followers, Protestantism developed in an opposite way and puts a strong emphasis on national sovereignty.

General political evaluations
- *Interest in politics*: people who are more interested in politics and who follow politics more actively in the media are more supportive of the EU than those with lower levels of political interest.
- *Political trust*: people who are more trusting of political institutions, such as their parliament, government, the police and the courts, are more supportive of the EU.
- *Support for government in office*: people who have voted for parties which are currently in their national government tend to be more supportive of the EU than those who voted for opposition parties.
- *Left–right*: after having taken into account the above factors, the impact of being conservative or progressive is relatively limited and differs from country to country. In some countries voters on the left and right are less supportive than those in the middle, while in others support is stronger among leftists or among rightist voters. This all depends on the position national political parties take towards the EU: voters take cues from their parties in order to determine what to think about the EU (see Briefing 5.2).

EU-specific factors
- *Knowledge and interest*: higher levels of knowledge of the EU and its institutions and more interest in the EU's affairs are related to higher levels of support.

Briefing 5.2

Cues

Many citizens do not make the costly and time-consuming effort to process all the information on the pros and cons of European integration, but rather rely on cues to make up their minds and decide what to think of certain issues. Cues are cognitive short-cuts which may be provided by trusted third parties such as political parties (party cue) or the media (media cue). They are especially important in the context of the EU given the complex, distant and abstract nature of many issues. The role of cues can be illustrated by looking at the behaviour of French voters in the referendum on the Constitutional Treaty. The table below shows the position of the different French political parties and the percentage of voters who voted in favour of the Treaty in the referendum. In those cases where the party line was clear, a clear majority of party supporters voted accordingly. The picture is different for the Socialist Party and the Greens. While officially in favour, these two parties faced strong internal division on the issue. As a result, voters were also mixed on the issue. These figures teach us an important lesson on the effect of cues: strong and unambiguous cues have a greater impact than those containing mixed messages.

Party	Party stance	% voters in favour
UMP	In favour	80
UDF	In favour	76
Socialist Party	Mixed	44
Greens	Mixed	40
MPF	Against	25
Front National	Against	7
Far Left	Against	6
Communist Party	Against	2

Source: Henry Milner, '"YES to the Europe I want; NO to this one": Some Reflections on France's Rejection of the EU Constitution'. *PSOnline.* April 2006 (www.apsanet.org/imgtest/PSApr06Milner.pdf).

- *Economic benefits*: if people believe the EU yields economic benefits, they are more supportive. This applies both to personal economic benefits from EU membership (so called 'egocentric' evaluations) and to evaluations of the benefit for the country as a whole ('sociotropic' evaluations).
- *Identity*: if people exclusively identify with their own country and do not consider themselves to be 'European', they are less supportive of the EU. The role of identity in shaping attitudes towards the EU is also reflected in people's evaluation of the further expansion of the EU. People tend to be more opposed to the membership of new countries if they believe that such

countries threaten their culture and their way of life. We further discuss this role of identity at the end of this chapter, because its impact has increased over time.

All in all, then, public opinion on the EU in a very large part is driven by the same factors as those factors that determine opinions towards the national government. This so-called 'logic of extrapolation' underlines the importance of national contexts for explaining public opinion about the EU. Rather than evaluating the EU as a separate entity, people assess it in close relation to their general evaluation of politics. Consequently, the recent decline in trust in the EU that we noted in Figure 5.1 is accompanied by a similar decline of people's trust in their national government.

◼ A gap between citizens and elites

In the introduction we pointed out that democracies should strive to translate the preferences of citizens into policies. In representative democracies citizens do not make policies themselves, however. Most of the decisions are taken by political elites, such as members of parliament, senior civil servants, business and labour leaders and media leaders. By comparing the viewpoints of political elites with those of citizens, it is possible to see to what extent they have a similar evaluation of the EU as a political system.

Figure 5.3 presents data from a study that compares the general public with these elites. While at the level of citizens we witness considerable variation between the member states, we notice a consistently high support at the elite level. More than 80% of the elite respondents – drawn from the groups listed above – think their country's membership of the EU is a 'good thing'. In many countries, then, there is a considerable gap between the elites and the general public.

The differences are also visible in the different types of policies that citizens and elites would like to see taken care of at the European level, although somewhat less pronounced. Neither citizens nor elites like to see a great amount of EU involvement in areas that involve a lot of spending. Elites, however, are to a much greater extent in favour of policies for which there is a clear functionalist logic (currency, immigration), while citizens tend to attach more importance to policies that cushion the effect of the single market: social policies, employment policies and environmental policies.

The gap between citizens and elites is also visible when we compare the positions of citizens with those of political parties. By and large political parties and their candidates are much more pro-integrationist than citizens. In fact in many member states all of the mainstream parties for a very long time have been fully supportive of European integration. However, since the beginning of the 1990s we have witnessed the emergence of Eurosceptic parties: some of these have specifically organized to oppose further European integration, while others are primarily nationalistic in focus and as a result are also critical about the EU (Chapter 7 further discusses the role of political parties).

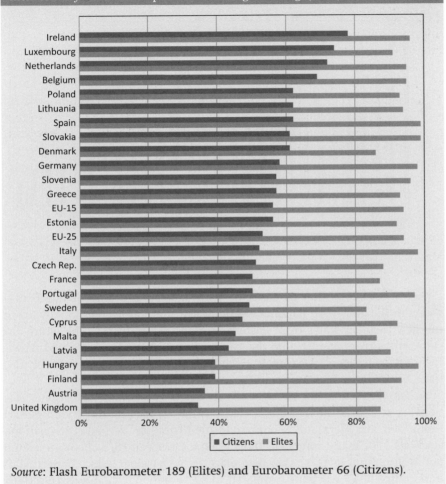

Figure 5.3 Percentage of citizens and elites agreeing with the statement that their country's membership of the EU is a 'good thing' (2006).

Source: Flash Eurobarometer 189 (Elites) and Eurobarometer 66 (Citizens).

■ Elections

Voting in the elections for the European Parliament remains by far the most common form of political participation for ordinary citizens. Every five years citizens in all the member states have the opportunity to elect a member of the European Parliament. As we saw in Chapter 3, parliamentary seats are allocated in elections conducted in all member states, rather than in a Europe-wide election on one and the same day. We therefore first compare turnout for EP elections with that for national elections in each of the member states.

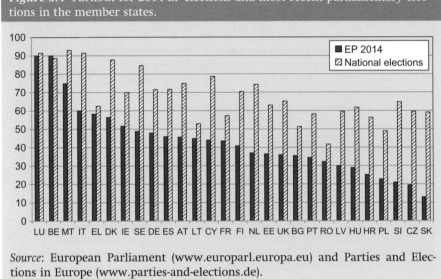

Figure 5.4 Turnout for 2014 EP elections and most recent parliamentary elections in the member states.

Source: European Parliament (www.europarl.europa.eu) and Parties and Elections in Europe (www.parties-and-elections.de).

Figure 5.4 shows that EP elections draw substantially smaller numbers of voters to the polls than national elections. Turnout has been especially low in the new member states from Eastern Europe and in the UK. The figure also shows that turnout rates for the two types of elections are related. Lower turnouts in national elections translate into lower turnouts for the EP elections, with rates which are typically 20–30% lower.

So why is turnout for EP elections so much lower than for national elections? A year after the first direct elections for the EP, political scientists Karl-Heinz Reif and Hermann Schmitt classified these as 'second-order national elections'. For many voters elections for the European Parliament are simply not as important as those that take place at the national level. The secondary importance of EP elections compared to these national 'first-order elections' has significant consequences for the behaviour of voters:

- First, because many voters consider EP elections much less important than national elections, turnout is usually lower than for parliamentary or presidential elections at home, as can be seen in Figure 5.4 (the only exceptions to this rule are Belgium and Luxembourg which have compulsory voting).
- Second, many who do vote in EP elections use them to evaluate national politics rather than European affairs. In this sense, voters use European elections to say something about the performance of their national governments. Consequently, governing parties will tend to lose votes in EP elections.
- Third, because voters feel there is not much at stake at EP elections, they are more inclined to vote with their 'hearts' instead of their 'minds'. They are more willing to vote for the smaller parties that they ignore in national elections because they feel they would be wasting their vote.

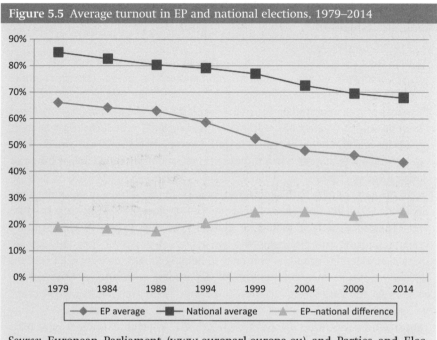

Figure 5.5 Average turnout in EP and national elections, 1979–2014

Source: European Parliament (www.europarl.europa.eu) and Parties and Elections in Europe (www.parties-and-elections.eu).

EP elections, then, are as much evaluations of national politics as they are of the EU. The fates and fortunes of political parties in EP elections are therefore to a large extent determined by developments 'back home'. Eurosceptic parties may benefit from this by offering voters a way to signal their discontent. These parties have been aware of the gap between citizens and the traditional elites regarding their attitudes towards the EU. Hence, they have strategically positioned themselves as critical of European integration.

There is, however, a large variety in the types of parties that express a Eurosceptic position: it ranges from extreme right populist parties such as the Hungarian Jobbik party to left-wing parties such as the Greek Coalition of the Radical Left. The extent to which voters are willing to cast a vote for these parties depends thus not only on the availability of Eurosceptic options but also on their political profile.

In some member states Eurosceptic positions are only expressed by a single, extremist party, making citizens reluctant to vote for them, even if they agree with their viewpoints on Europe. In countries such as the UK, Sweden, Denmark and Poland there is a greater variety of positions towards the EU, with more mainstream parties also expressing Eurosceptic viewpoints. This offers voters a better choice in finding a political party that matches their political views.

Figure 5.5 shows that while in 1979 the average turnout for the nine member states stood at 66%, it had gone down to a mere 42.5% for all twenty-eight member states in 2014. Although there are occasional increases

Controversy 5.1

A European public sphere?

An important issue in discussions about the relation between citizens and the EU focuses on the perceived lack of information and debate on the EU in the member states. According to many observers citizens are not interested in the EU because they are not well informed on the major issues that are debated in Brussels. News coverage around EP elections is relatively limited, tends to be focused on national politicians and is generally negative in tone. This results in the second-order effects we outline in this chapter: a low turnout at EP elections and vote choices based on national considerations.

An obvious solution to this problem would be to invest more in reporting news about the EU. In the end this should result in a truly European public sphere: in this ideal constellation there would be EU-wide debates on the EU with citizens reading, thinking and discussing the same themes wherever they live. The EU invests considerable amounts of money in helping to inform citizens. Each of the institutions has its own communications department with fancy websites, glossy magazines and easy-to-use fact files. The Commission even has its own YouTube website. Do you think the lack of a European public sphere is indeed the major cause of the low citizen involvement in the EU? Which measures do you think would be effective to better engage citizens? Is it only a matter of better communication or would it require something else?

in turnout in some member states, the overall trend is clearly downward: of all the elections held since 1979 in the different member states, two-thirds have witnessed a lower turnout rate compared to the previous election.

The decline in turnout for elections is not unique to the EP. In most member states turnout for parliamentary elections has also declined over the past decades, but not to the same extent as for the EP. Apparently EP elections are still not salient enough for most voters: not enough seems to be at stake and in some countries parties are aligned to such an extent that there does not seem to be much to choose between them. One factor that may explain the 'second-order' nature of EP elections, and the fragmentation of public opinion along national lines in general, is the lack of a 'European public sphere'. Rather than an integrated European public sphere, where public debate takes place and public opinion is formed, most of the public debate and public opinion formation takes place in domestic public spheres. Controversy 5.1 takes up this issue and the attempts by the EU institutions to create such a European public sphere.

■ Referendums on European integration

While elections focus on selecting candidates for public office, citizens can be given a more direct say in decision-making via referendums. Referendums are an example of direct democracy and give citizens the opportunity to vote on certain policy decisions. Membership of the EU obviously constitutes such a major decision as it involves the transfer of sovereignty to a new supranational body. Getting the explicit support of a country's citizenry provides a direct and explicit legitimation of such a decision and commits them to the European project. This is exactly what French President Charles de Gaulle had in mind when he dreamed of a pan-European referendum in the 1960s:

> Europe will be born on the day on which the different peoples fundamentally decide to join. It will not suffice for members of parliaments to vote for ratification. It will require popular referendums, preferably held on the same day in all the countries concerned.
>
> *Quoted in Bruno Kaufman, 'Initiatives and Referendums: Bringing in the People'.*
> *In Council of Europe,* Reflections on the Future of Democracy in Europe
> *(Council of Europe, 2005: 132).*

De Gaulle's dream has not yet materialized. Still, many individual countries have put important decisions on their country's relation with the EU to a popular vote: most of the referendums on European integration have either been about the fundamental decision to join the EU (membership referendums) or the approval of new treaties (treaty referendum) (see Fact file 5.1 for an overview).

The referendum practice was kicked off in 1972 when French President Georges Pompidou used his constitutional powers to let French citizens vote on the accession of Denmark, Norway, Ireland and the UK. After approval by the French voters, Denmark, Ireland and Norway conducted accession referendums in the same year. The UK initially decided to join the EC without conducting a referendum, but it asked its citizens to approve the continuation of EC membership in 1975, which they did.

While most referendums yielded outcomes supportive of integration, several times voters rejected further integrative steps. In 1992 Danish voters rejected the Maastricht Treaty by a very small margin and in 2001 the Treaty of Nice was rejected by Irish voters. In both cases voters eventually approved the treaties after their governments secured modifications or opt-outs. Danish and Swedish voters decided to stay out of the Eurozone in referendums in 2000 and 2003, respectively. As a result, both countries still have their own currency. As we showed in Chapter 1, the negative outcomes of the French, Dutch and Irish referendums forced the member states to make changes to the Constitutional Treaty and the Lisbon Treaty. The real effect of these referendums is somewhat unclear, however. While some modifications were made, the Treaty of Lisbon maintained most of the provisions of the Constitutional Treaty.

According to an extensive study of referendums by political scientist Sara Hobolt, three factors play a role in determining people's voting behaviour in referendums:

Fact file 5.1

Referendums on the EU

- Referendums may be either required by law (as is the case in Ireland and sometimes in Denmark) or voluntarily initiated by parliament or government.
- The outcome of a referendum may be binding on the parliament and government (Denmark, Ireland) or only constitute a recommendation, in which case it is called consultative referendum (France, Norway, UK). In practice, governments take the outcomes of consultative referendums as seriously as those of binding referendums.
- Since 1972 more than forty referendums on European integration have taken place.
- Most of the referendums have asked voters to approve either their country's accession to the EU or a new treaty. All but six of the countries which joined the EU after 1972 have had their membership approved via a referendum, including all countries that were part of the 2004 'big bang' enlargement.
- Belgium, Germany, Greece, Portugal, Bulgaria and Romania are the only six member states that have never conducted any referendum on the EU.
- Norway's citizens are alone in rejecting their country's accession to the EU and did so twice in referendums in 1972 and 1994.
- While no member state has ever left the EU, the citizens of Greenland opted out after their territory was granted home rule by the Danish government in 1979. In a 1982 consultative referendum 53% voted against the continuation of Greenland's membership. Greenland formally left the EU on 1 January 1985.
- Ireland and Denmark have held the largest number of referendums because their respective constitutions oblige them to hold binding referendums in all cases where there is a transfer of sovereignty.
- Although Switzerland is not a member of the EU, its citizens approved tighter economic bonds in several referendums as well as Swiss membership of the Schengen area. Two popular initiatives to start accession talks for formal membership were, however, rejected by large majorities in 1997 and 2001.

- Attitudes towards European integration are the most important factor in determining a yes or no vote. The stronger voters are in favour of European integration the higher the chance they will say yes to their country's membership or the ratification of a treaty.
- Voters who do not have very strong pro- or anti-European attitudes are more affected by second-order considerations. The chance of those moderate voters voting in favour of integrative steps increases when they are more supportive of the current government in office.
- Voters without strong opinions on the EU are more likely to follow the position of the party they voted for in the last election. Such voters make use of so called 'party cues' in order to make up their mind (see Briefing 5.2).

Voters in general turn out in larger numbers for referendums than for elections for the European Parliament. There are two good reasons for this. First, most referendums focus on one single issue and give voters a clear choice. Second, the outcomes of referendums are generally respected by their governments. Hence, citizens will generally feel that a vote in a referendum has a greater impact than a vote in EP elections.

Referendums thus seem to do a better job in connecting citizens to EU politics. Still, also in this case it is important to note that debates take place in national contexts and can focus on wholly different topics even when the same decision is at stake.

Take, for example, the French and Dutch no's to the Constitutional Treaty. While in both countries the percentage of no-voters was highest on the extreme right and the extreme left of the political spectrum, the reasons for these votes were different and inspired by different considerations. In France voters on the left were worried about the social dimension of Europe. Their concerns focused on the possible implications of the Services Directives, with fears of Polish plumbers taking over the jobs of French people. Voters on the right in France were mobilized by their parties on the issue of France's declining sovereignty as a result of further integration.

In the Netherlands concerns revolved in the first place around the lack of economic benefits of European integration. The issue gained enormous attention in the campaign after the president of the Dutch central bank conceded that the guilder had been undervalued when it was converted into the Euro. Dutch voters were also worried about the possible threats to Dutch identity as a result of further enlargements, including the possibility of Turkey joining the EU. The issue of Turkey gained prominence when it was successfully mobilized by a Member of Parliament (Geert Wilders) who had just been forced out of the Dutch liberal-conservative party (VVD), because of his stance against Turkey's membership of the EU. He used it successfully to mobilize support for his new party-list and in the course of doing this heavily influenced the campaign debate.

■ The shift from a permissive consensus to a constraining dissensus

The preceding paragraphs have made clear that recent developments indicate cracks in the permissive consensus identified forty years ago. These cracks have most likely been caused by the steady evolution of integration in the direction of the 'ever closer union' which was already dreamed about in the Treaty of Rome. In fact, when writing in the 1970s Scheingold and Lindberg themselves foresaw this: 'Only if the Community were to broaden its scope or increase its institutional capacities markedly would there be reason to suspect that the level of support or its relationship to the political process would be significantly altered.'

This is exactly what has happened. General support for the EU has shown a significant decrease, turnout remains very low and those people that do turn out increasingly vote for Eurosceptic parties.

Recent analyses of the attitudes of citizens show that issues of identity have become more prominent in determining people's stance towards politics, both at the national and at the European level. The more critical stance of EU citizens towards European integration can be seen as one of the expressions of this concern about identity. The Eurosceptical attitude that is witnessed in the behaviour of voters in EP elections and referendums has not emerged in isolation, but can be seen as one of the expressions of a concern to preserve national identities. This then also explains why nationalist parties – which tend to emphasize the importance of preserving national identity and culture – have been so successful both at the national and at the European level.

All in all, the permissive consensus which facilitated integrative steps for so long has by now been replaced by a 'constraining dissensus' – a term coined by political scientists Liesbet Hooghe and Gary Marks to mark the new constellation in which European integration takes place. While the signals of citizens may at times be erratic, their overall message is clearly in the direction of a more prudent approach to integration in the coming years.

■ Summary

- The EU does not figure prominently in citizens' minds. Most are not opposed to European integration, but their opinion on the topic is not well developed and can be unstable. For a long time a permissive consensus allowed political elites to proceed with integration in a relatively unrestrained manner.
- Over time support for the EU has risen and fallen, with a clear drop in trust in the EU being visible since the onset of the economic crisis. There are large differences in the levels of support between citizens from different member states.
- At the individual level the most important determinants of EU support are education, income, support for one's national government and knowledge of and interest in EU affairs.
- Elections for the European Parliament can be characterized as second-order elections. Voters turn out in smaller numbers than at national elections and use EP elections to evaluate their national governments. Turnout for the EP elections has gone down over the years.
- Citizens turn out in higher rates for referendums than for EP elections. While relatively few referendums have resulted in a 'no' to further integration, these no's have generally been taken seriously by the governments affected.
- Developments in electoral behaviour show that the permissive consensus has been replaced by a constraining dissensus.

Further reading
The thesis on the 'constraining dissensus' is developed in Liesbet Hooghe and Gary Marks, 'A Postfunctionalist Theory of European Integration: From Permissive Consensus to Constraining Dissensus', *British Journal of Political Science*, 1, 2009: 1–23, which is followed by a number of insightful comments by other scholars. A comprehensive analysis of the way citizens evaluate the EU can be found in Sarah Hobolt and James Tilley, *Blaming Europe? Responsibility Without Accountability in the European Union* (Oxford University Press, 2015). A diverse set of essays exploring the nature of the European sphere can be found in Thomas Risse (ed.), *European Public Spheres: Politics is Back* (Cambridge University Press, 2015).

Websites
- The Eurobarometer website contains numerous overviews and analyses on public opinion: http://ec.europa.eu/public_opinion/
- The Eurobarometer data files can be accessed at Gesis–Leibniz Institute for the Social Sciences. After free registration it is also possible to carry out some online analyses: www.gesis.org/en/services/data/survey-data/eurobarometer-data-service/
- Specific information on the behaviour of voters in European elections can be found on the website of the European Elections Studies, which contains data sets and an overview of publications using those data: www.ees-homepage.net

Navigating the EU
On the website www.navigatingthe.eu you will find online exercises for this chapter.

6   Interest groups and interest representation

■ Introduction

On 17 June 2013, European Commission President José Manuel Barroso and US President Barack Obama announced the start of negotiations on a Transatlantic Trade and Investment Partnership (TTIP). The negotiations were meant to lead to a comprehensive treaty, which would further liberalize trade and investment between the EU and the US and thereby foster economic growth. It covered not just import tariffs and other direct trade barriers, but also targeted domestic regulations that could hinder trade or impair investments.

The conclusion of the TTIP was strongly supported by large firms and business groups on both sides of the Atlantic, which stood to gain from increased trade and investment opportunities. They pushed for an ambitious and quick agreement and made their views known to European and US policy-makers by publishing position papers and organizing meetings and conferences that were attended by business representatives and government officials from the EU and the US.

A wide range of non-governmental organizations (NGOs) opposed the TTIP, arguing that it would undermine health, safety, consumer and environmental standards in the EU. Moreover, they criticized the 'intransparent' and 'undemocratic' character of TTIP negotiations, which they claimed were dominated by business interests, to the exclusion of NGOs and elected representatives. In letters to European Trade Commissioner Karel de Gucht, they voiced their concern and called for a public debate.

In their attack on the TTIP, NGOs sought to involve European citizens and mobilize public opinion. They were helped by the fact that, in the course of 2014, draft negotiating texts were leaked to the press. On 11 October 2014, a range of NGOs organized a 'European Day of Action' against the TTIP and two other trade agreements, with different types of protest, such as marches, seminars, flash mobs and concerts, scheduled in twenty-two countries throughout Europe.

In this way, a heated and highly polarized debate between proponents and opponents developed, in which the two sides used different approaches in attempts to influence the negotiating process and the ensuing agreement. This raises a number of important questions about interest group activity in the European Union:

- How many interest groups are there and whom do they represent?
- How is interest representation organized at the EU level?
- What strategies do interest groups use to affect EU policies?
- What impact do interest groups have in the EU?
- How democratic are the role and influence of interest groups?

We will see that a large number and wide variety of interest groups are active at the EU level. Although they cover a broad array of interests, most groups represent business interests. As the example of the TTIP shows, interest groups use different strategies to influence policy-making, from public protests to direct contacts with decision-makers. Because of the limited role of public opinion in EU politics and the difficulties of organizing cross-border protests, seeking direct contacts is a much more common strategy at the EU level than staging protests. Reflecting the EU's multi-level set-up, many interest groups seek these contacts on multiple levels, lobbying not just the EU institutions but also member state authorities. In the end, lobbying is meant to affect policy-making. Although it is difficult to make an overall assessment of interest group influence, the impact specific groups have depends crucially on the resources they command, the way the decision-making process is organized and the type of issue at stake.

■ Interest groups and lobbyists: who are they?

The number of interest groups in the EU

Lobbying has become an important activity in the EU. Estimates of the number of individual **lobbyists** in Brussels range from 10,000 to 30,000, with 15,000 probably the most reasonable figure. The number of **interest groups** lies between 3,500 and 4,000, with some authors quoting figures of up to 5,000 groups. The reason why it is so difficult to come up with a precise number of lobbyists or interest groups is that the definition of either is

> A **lobbyist** is an individual engaged in attempts to influence governmental decision-making on behalf of an interest group.

> An **interest group** is a group of people that share certain preferences regarding the outcomes of governmental decision-making and organize in order to influence those outcomes, without seeking elected office.

not clear-cut. Of course, there are many obvious cases of interest groups with established offices in Brussels that make it their daily job to influence EU policy-making. But there are also groups that occasionally engage in lobbying activities, even though their main focus is on other types of activities. Moreover, not all groups that lobby the EU necessarily have an office in Brussels. Some lobbyists fly in and out of Brussels to lobby the EU institutions but operate from another location. All this makes it difficult to pinpoint exactly how many lobbyists and interest groups there are.

Nevertheless, even when we only take into account the clear cases the number of lobbyists and interest groups is impressive and has been rising over the past decades. This goes to show at least two things. First, it shows that the EU has become an important policy-making institution in many areas. Otherwise, interest groups would not bother to spend time and money in attempts to influence EU policy-making. Second, apparently interest groups believe they can in fact make a difference and influence EU policy-making. Later in this chapter, we will look at the ways in which they try to do so and the extent to which they are successful in that regard. Before we do so, however, it is important to take a further look at the types of groups and lobbyists that are active in Brussels.

Types of interest groups in the EU

Table 6.1 gives an overview of the different types of interest groups in Brussels, based on a comprehensive analysis of the interest group population in the EU (see Jan Beyers *et al.*, 'The INTEREURO Project: Logic and Structure', *Interest Groups and Advocacy*, 3, 2, 2014: 126–40).

The largest group in this overview is individual *firms*. This category includes (large) companies that have an interest in EU regulation or subsidies, such as car manufacturers or banks. It also includes consultancy firms that specialize

Table 6.1 Types of interest groups in Brussels

Type of interest group	Share of total (%)
Firms	31
Business associations	25
Governmental organizations	11
Citizen groups	11
Non-profit organizations	10
Professional associations	4
Research institutes	3
Trade unions	1
Unknown/other	3

Percentages do not add up to 100 due to rounding.
Source: Joost Berkhout, Jan Beyers, Caelesta Braun, Marcel Hanegraaff and David Lowery, *Making Inference across Mobilization and Influence Research: Comparing Top-Down and Bottom-Up Mapping of Interest Systems*, Unpublished manuscript.

in lobbying for others. Known as 'public affairs' consultants, they do not represent one (type of) interest but make it their job to lobby on behalf of their clients. Hiring a commercial consultant is particularly useful if clients do not want to invest in setting up a lobby office and network in Brussels – for instance, because they only need to lobby the EU occasionally. Professional consultants may also have expertise and contacts that clients find valuable in a specific lobbying effort. Together, firms account for some 31% of all EU interest groups.

Business associations are umbrella organizations that represent firms. Some represent a specific type of industry. For instance, the European Chemical Industry Council (CEFIC) represents the European chemical industry. Its members include both national business associations (such as the Hungarian Chemical Industry Association and the French Union des Industries Chimiques) and individual chemical companies (such as AkzoNobel and Procter & Gamble). This category also includes 'peak business associations', which represent firms in all sectors of the economy. The prime example in the EU is BusinessEurope, which has as its members national peak organizations, such as the Italian Confindustria and the Confederation of Swedish Enterprise. National business associations (either sectoral or peak) are usually also directly represented in Brussels themselves. In all, business associations make up around 25% of all EU interest groups.

Large firms often both lobby directly in Brussels and are members of business associations. This offers them the opportunity to use different channels for different purposes: they can work together with other firms through their business association, but they can also directly contact EU officials if they want to convey a specific message. Likewise, national business associations are usually members of a European association, but also lobby in Brussels themselves. They will do so if a specific national issue is at stake or if they feel that their interests are not sufficiently well represented by the European business association.

The third-largest group is *governmental organizations* from the member states. These include local and regional governments, such as the German Länder, Spanish autonomous regions and large cities, but also national regulatory agencies. These governmental actors often have a lot to gain (or lose) from EU policies. For instance, local and regional governments are the main beneficiaries of the EU's structural funds, which are meant to support poorer regions in Europe (see Chapter 8). Also, governmental organizations in the member states often have to implement or are affected by EU legislation. In order to make sure their voice is heard in EU decision-making, many governmental organizations from the member states are therefore actively lobbying the EU or have even opened their own office in Brussels. They form some 11% of all EU interest groups.

Citizen groups are also called NGOs ('non-governmental organizations') or 'public interest groups'. These groups do not represent an industry or a profession but some kind of public interest that they believe in. Well-known examples are Amnesty International (for human rights) and Greenpeace (for the environment). European NGOs come in different forms. Some are single organizations that operate at the EU level (such as Greenpeace). Others resemble the structure of European business associations, bringing together national umbrella organizations and NGOs. For instance, the Association of European Cancer Leagues represents national organizations in the field of the fight against cancer, such as the Irish Cancer Society and the League against Cancer in Slovakia. Citizen groups form around 11% of all interest groups in the EU.

Non-profit organizations include, for instance, churches, hospitals, foundations and charities. They, too, may be affected by EU legislation or benefit from EU subsidies. For those reasons, they actively lobby in Brussels and make up around 10% of all interest groups.

Finally, three smaller categories, in terms of numbers of interest groups, complete Table 6.1. *Professional associations* represent a specific profession. An example is the Standing Committee of European Doctors (CPME), which represents medical doctors. *Research institutes* receive considerable funding from the EU. This category also includes think tanks, which try to initiate debates on issues they find important. Finally, *trade unions* are organizations of employees. Several trade unions from member states are active in Brussels. In addition, there are umbrella associations of trade unions at EU level. The most important of these is the European Trade Union Confederation (ETUC), which has as its members eighty-eight national trade unions.

All in all, a wide range of interests are active at the EU level: from private to public and from businesses to NGOs. Still, business interests account for the vast majority of interest groups in Brussels. In comparison, citizen groups are a much smaller group. This is a pattern that is also found in domestic political systems. One reason for this may be that it is more difficult for citizen groups to organize and find financing. After all, business groups represent relatively limited numbers of firms that all have a distinct (financial) stake in lobbying the EU. Thus, they will find it easy to come together and fund EU lobbyists. Citizen groups, by contrast, represent some diffuse interest that does not yield concrete benefits to specific organizations or individuals. Briefing 6.1 takes a closer look at this issue.

Lobbying through different channels

The discussion above shows that one and the same organization can be represented at the EU level in different ways. The organization can lobby in Brussels itself, it can hire a commercial consultant, and it can work through a national or a European association. Moreover, one and the same organization can be a member of more than one European association, depending on the issues it finds important. Finally, lobbying efforts can be aimed directly at the EU institutions or they can target national governments, which then take the message with them to Brussels. This mix of channels offers opportunities to

Briefing 6.1

Interest groups and the logic of collective action

It is a general tendency in political systems that concentrated interests organize more easily than diffuse interests. The mechanism behind this has been clarified by Mancur Olson in his classic book *The Logic of Collective Action: Public Goods and the Theory of Groups*, which appeared in 1965. According to Olson, interest groups provide collective goods for their members. If, for instance, a consumer group succeeds in improving consumer protection, all consumers profit from that effort, whether they are members of that consumer group or not. Moreover, there are so many consumers that the contribution of one additional member makes no discernible difference to the effectiveness of the group.

As a consequence, it is always more profitable for a consumer not to become a member of the consumer group. After all, if the group has a sufficient number of members, the consumer will benefit from the group's successes anyway and may as well avoid the membership fee. If, on the contrary, the group is not large enough to have an impact, one additional member is not going to make any difference, so the consumer would also do well not to pay the membership fee.

This basic dilemma applies to all interest groups. However, it is stronger for groups representing diffuse interests than for groups representing concentrated interests. To begin with, the number of potential members is much smaller when concentrated interests are at stake. Hence, these potential members are easier to reach and organize. Second, when concentrated interests are at stake, the potential gains of collective action are much larger than when the interests are diffuse. This leads to a stronger incentive for potential members to organize.

Take the example of the EU's Common Agricultural Policy (CAP). Under this policy, farmers are financially supported by the EU. This support is paid for out of tax contributions by citizens. Even though the overall benefits for farmers are equal to the overall costs for citizens, the benefits per farmer are much higher than the costs per citizen, since the number of farmers is much smaller than the number of taxpayers. Hence, the benefits of the CAP are concentrated, whereas the costs are diffuse. As a result, farmers have a much greater incentive to organize in support of the CAP than taxpayers have to organize against it. This may explain why farmers are among the best-organized interests in the EU while organized opposition against the CAP has remained weak.

organizations to make their message heard in various ways and to choose different channels for different issues. This is illustrated in Figure 6.1.

For instance, when a company does not agree with the position taken by its European business association, it can choose to lobby the Commission itself. The same is true when the issue at stake is of specific concern to one company but not important enough to be taken up by the European business association. At the same time, it should be stressed that this type of strategic 'hopping'

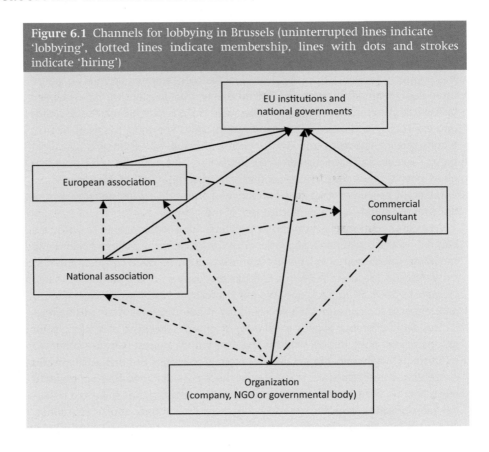

Figure 6.1 Channels for lobbying in Brussels (uninterrupted lines indicate 'lobbying', dotted lines indicate membership, lines with dots and strokes indicate 'hiring')

between channels of interest representation is only a realistic option for larger companies and NGOs. The vast majority of firms and other organizations in Europe have neither the resources nor the incentive actively to work through several channels of interest representation at the same time.

■ Organizing interest representation: between pluralism and corporatism

Systems of interest representation

Interest groups exist in all political systems. Whenever there are groups of people that try to influence government policy, there are interest groups. In Western democracies, in particular, interest groups have always played an important role in politics. However, the way in which the relationships between interest groups and government are structured differs greatly between political systems. In some countries, certain interest groups have a formal position in the policy-making process, whereas in others they do not. In some countries, there are a few large and powerful interest groups that deal with a wide range of issues, while in others there are many smaller and more specialized groups. These differences can be described in terms of different systems of interest representation. The two most important systems are 'corporatism' and 'pluralism'.

A **corporatist** system is characterized by the fact that a limited number of interest groups have a privileged position in policy-making. This means that some groups have special rights, for instance, to be consulted by government before a policy is adopted or, in an even more extreme form, to approve certain policies. In such a system, there are regular and formalized discussions between government and interest groups. Interest groups have become, as it were, part of government. Interest groups and government do not operate in opposition to each other (even though they may disagree on important issues) but they seek to cooperate in order to find consensus. The quintessential example of a corporatist system is Austria, but corporatist arrangements are also common in Germany, Belgium, the Netherlands and the Scandinavian countries. In these countries, the major labour unions and employers' organizations have an important role to play in formulating and approving social and economic policies. To this end, government consults with them on a regular basis. The position of these groups is privileged, and the number of groups involved is limited, because this role is only played by groups that are officially recognized as representative of broad constituencies.

> **Corporatism** is a system of interest representation in which a limited number of interest groups has privileged access to governmental decision-making.

A **pluralist** system is quite the opposite. In a pluralist system there are many interest groups, none of which has a privileged position in policy-making. As a result, groups are engaged in a continuous struggle to gain access to decision-makers. They cannot rely on any formalized discussions but have to vie for attention with competing interest groups. As a result, relations among interest groups and between interest groups and government tend to be more antagonistic than they are in a corporatist system. Whereas corporatism is typified by consensus-seeking among elites, pluralism is characterized by a constant struggle between groups for government attention and influence. The best examples of pluralist systems of interest representation are the United States and the United Kingdom.

> **Pluralism** is a system of interest representation in which large numbers of interest groups compete with each other for access to governmental decision-making.

The two systems have very different consequences for the way interest groups operate. In a corporatist system, access to government is limited but once a group has gained access it can have a lot of influence. After all, it only has to deal with a limited number of other interest groups and its privileged position in policy-making ensures that it will be listened to. In a pluralist system, by contrast, any group can in principle gain access to government. However, even if access is obtained there is no guarantee of success because many other groups have access as well. In a corporatist system there are a few powerful interest groups, while in a pluralist system there are many, but less powerful, interest groups.

Pluralism and corporatism in the EU

Given the existence of these two systems, scholars of EU interest representation have tried also to characterize the EU in these terms. In doing so, they have tended to conclude that the EU is predominantly pluralist. That is, there are many interest groups, and it is easy for them to gain access to EU policy-making but they have to share this access with a range of other groups. In short, the EU is a relatively open system of interest representation, which is typical of pluralism.

At the same time, elements of corporatism can be found in various parts of the EU. With the creation of the EEC in 1957, the European Economic and Social Committee (EESC) was established as a way to involve social and economic interest groups in policy-making, The EESC currently consists of representatives of employers' organizations and labour unions (the two traditional strongholds of corporatist systems) together with representatives from other interest groups, such as environmental groups and consumer groups. In a range of policy areas, the European Commission is obliged to ask the EESC for an opinion when it presents a proposal. In addition, the EP can ask the EESC for an opinion and the EESC can issue opinions on its own initiative on issues it deems important.

In 1994, a similar body was established to create a platform for regional and local governments: the Committee of the Regions (CoR). The members of the CoR are elected politicians in local or regional governments in the EU member states. Like the EESC, the CoR needs to be consulted on proposals that potentially affect its members and it can issue own-initiative opinions.

During the 1980s, an attempt was made to introduce a more far-reaching type of corporatism in the form of the Social Dialogue. The Social Dialogue includes a total of six organizations: three employers' organizations, led by BusinessEurope, the overarching EU business group, and three organizations of employees, the most important one being the European Trade Union Confederation (ETUC), the federation of European labour unions. The Social Dialogue is a platform for discussing social and economic issues among the main 'social partners'. This may lead to joint opinions as well as agreements between them. If the social partners wish so, these agreements are subsequently formalized into EU legislation by the Council. An example of where that happened was the agreement on parental leave, which was reached within the Social Dialogue in 1995 and adopted as a Council Directive in 1996.

The EESC, the CoR and the Social Dialogue are examples of corporatist forms of interest representation because they grant certain rights to a limited number of groups that are deemed to be representative of broad interests in Europe. At the same time, their practical meaning has remained limited. The EESC and the CoR are large bodies that need quite some time to reach compromises among their members. This dilutes the impact of their opinions on decision-making. Moreover, they are usually consulted only after a Commission proposal has been published, while most influence for interest groups is to be had when a formal proposal is still being developed. The Social Dialogue is a much smaller platform, which, through the conclusion of agreements among the social partners, can also take more far-reaching initiatives than the EESC and the CoR. In practice, however, the number of agreements reached has remained limited, mainly because employers' organizations have been reluctant to bind themselves to European-level agreements. As a result, these bodies have not achieved the level of corporatism that can be found in some EU member states.

Another policy area that shows elements of corporatism is agriculture. From the early 1960s onwards, the EU has had an extensive Common Agricultural Policy (CAP) with heavy subsidies for farmers. Policy-making on agricultural matters always included representatives of farmers' groups, joined at the EU level in COPA/COGECA. COPA/COGECA would be routinely involved in policy debates with the European Commission's DG Agriculture and the Council of Agricultural Ministers. Since the early 1990s, however, the stronghold of farmers has diminished, as new interests have become active in this area, including environmental groups and consumer groups. Although COPA/COGECA is still a powerful interest group in Brussels, it now has to compete with other groups, leading to a more pluralist constellation than used to be the case.

Designed pluralism in the EU

All in all, interest representation in the EU is more pluralist than corporatist in nature. It is very open to interest groups and groups tend to focus on one specific issue (area) or sector of industry. This is one of the reasons why, as we saw above, so many interest groups are active at the EU level. At the same time, the variety of interest groups in the EU is also a result of attempts by the European Commission actively to stimulate the creation and activities of certain groups. On an annual basis, the Commission spends some €1 billion on supporting EU-level interest groups. This money goes primarily to NGOs, which, as we saw above in Briefing 6.1, suffer most from the 'logic of collective action'. Controversy 6.1 invites you to think further about the pros and cons of Commission support for EU interest groups.

For the European Commission, supporting EU-level interest groups has been a way to increase the legitimacy of EU initiatives. This perspective was voiced in the *White Paper on Governance*, a Commission document published in 2001. According to the White Paper, interest groups form a European 'civil society', which 'plays an important role in giving voice to the concerns of citizens and delivering services that meet people's needs'. As a result, so the Commission argues, civil society offers 'a chance to get citizens more actively involved in achieving the Union's objectives and to offer them a structured channel for feedback, criticism and protest' (European Commission, *White Paper on Governance*, COM (2001) 428, 25 July 2001, p. 14 and p. 15, respectively).

At the same time, Commission support for EU-level interest groups is not merely a matter of creating 'fair' competition between them. It has also been a

Controversy 6.1

Financial support for NGOs

In order to redress the imbalance between business interests and NGOs, many NGOs are subsidized by the European Commission. In some cases, the European Commission has even actively sought to create a European NGO in an area it deemed important. All in all, the Commission is estimated to spend around €1 billion in subsidies for NGOs per year.

The Commission's argument for this type of support is that it achieves a more balanced representation of interests at the EU level. Critics point out, however, that these subsidies bias interest representation by artificially strengthening certain (types of) interest groups. What do you think of these arguments? Do you think the Commission should continue supporting NGOs (or perhaps even step up its effort) or would you argue for a reduction or even the full abolition of financial support?

way to develop a European 'constituency' that the Commission can mobilize in support of its initiatives. For the Commission, it is a great benefit if it can tell member state governments and the European Parliament that its proposal is supported by a wide range of European interest groups. As a result, the Commission has shown a clear preference for interest groups that are willing to support its causes and take a constructive (as opposed to confrontational) stance in influencing EU policy-making. Interest groups that fit into these categories have often enjoyed easier and more extensive access to the Commission than other groups. In that sense, although the EU represents a pluralist system of interest representation, it is a form of designed pluralism, shaped by the preferences and financial incentives of the European Commission.

■ Interest group strategies

As we saw above, the EU has attracted a wide variety of interest groups. The purpose of these groups is to influence policies. But what do they actually do to achieve this? In this section, we will discuss a number of strategies that interest groups can pursue. As we will see, the variety of interests is matched by the variety of strategies that groups employ. This variety poses a number of strategic choices (sometimes even dilemmas) for groups. Below, we will survey the menu of options available to groups and indicate what reasons groups have to choose one strategy rather than another.

Inside lobbying and outside lobbying

If an interest group seeks to influence policy-making, what it wants to achieve is to change the minds of the people who decide on a given issue. In so doing, the group can use two basic types of strategies, which rely on different logics of political influence. These strategies are called 'inside lobbying' and 'outside lobbying'.

To begin with, interest groups can try to talk directly with decision-makers. They can phone them, arrange meetings to discuss policies, respond to consultations from the Commission or the Parliament, or become part of a committee or forum that advises EU institutions on a given issue (see Chapter 9 for a closer look at how EU proposals are developed). This was the strategy used by firms and business associations in their lobby over the TTIP, the example with which we started this chapter. What they tried was to become part of the debates among policy-makers and influence policy-making from within. Put simply, they want to sit at the same table as the decision-makers in order to affect their decisions. That is why this strategy is called **inside lobbying** – after all, lobbying takes place *inside* policy-making institutions.

> **Inside lobbying** is a strategy in which interest groups seek to influence policies through direct contact with policy-makers.

Alternatively, or in addition, an interest group can try to mobilize public opinion by organizing strikes and demonstrations, or attracting media attention to its cause. Think, for instance, of the 'European Day of Action' against the TTIP that was organized by NGOs. Other examples are the confrontations between activists and whaling vessels that Greenpeace uses to draw attention to the whale hunt, and the general strikes organized in recent years by labour unions in countries such as Spain, Greece and Portugal in opposition to austerity measures and economic reforms by their governments. When they use this strategy, interest groups hope to affect decision-makers by showing how much public support they have. Rather than influencing policy-making from within, they seek to put pressure on decision-makers by mobilizing groups and citizens *outside* the decision-making institutions. That is why this strategy is called **outside lobbying**. In the literature on interest representation, inside lobbying and outside lobbying have often been linked to specific types of groups. Briefing 6.2 discusses the definitions put forward in this literature.

> **Outside lobbying** is a strategy in which interest groups seek to put pressure on policy-makers by mobilizing public opinion.

The choice of strategy by interest groups

When choosing between these two strategies, interest groups can rely on one strategy or on a combination of the two. However, some groups typically rely more on inside lobbying while other groups make greater use of outside lobbying. This depends on a number of factors:

- *The target of the lobby.* Outside lobbying works best when the decision-maker that is targeted is sensitive to public opinion. For instance, elected politicians depend more on public opinion than civil servants, because they rely on public opinion for their re-election. Therefore, if an interest group wants to influence the EP, outside lobbying is more likely to be successful than when it wants to influence the European Commission.

Briefing 6.2

Interest groups and social movements

The political science literature often makes a distinction between interest groups and social movements. *Interest groups* are formally structured organizations that seek to influence government policies through inside lobbying. *Social movements* are more or less unstructured groups that engage in political protest, such as strikes, demonstrations and blockades (what we here call outside lobbying). These definitions identify certain types of political activity with certain types of groups.

In reality, however, the two forms often overlap. Some formal, well-structured groups (such as trade unions) engage in both inside and outside lobbying. Likewise, social movements are often structured around a (formal) social movement organization that is central to organizing political protest and seeks to establish 'inside lobbying' contacts with policy-makers. These overlaps make it increasingly difficult to make a clear-cut distinction between types of groups. An alternative approach is therefore to see inside lobbying and outside lobbying as two potential strategies for all groups that try to influence EU policy-making – even if some groups tend to rely more on one type of strategy and other groups rely on the other.

- *The organization and identity of the interest group.* Inside lobbying and outside lobbying require very different skills. For inside lobbying, a group needs to establish and maintain contacts with policy-makers, and be able to gather and present information in a way that ties in with the policy debates in a given field. For outside lobbying, a group needs to have a sufficiently large network of members and volunteers to organize large-scale events and relay those events to the media. These capabilities cannot be built up overnight. They are often the result of long experience and carefully developed networks. As a result, interest groups tend to rely on the time-tested strategies that they are familiar with.
- *The issue at stake.* Some issues appeal to public sentiments more easily than others. Thus, it is difficult to conceive of a large-scale demonstration being organized against a proposal on accounting standards. However, people can more easily be mobilized for things that they feel are close to their interests (such as the protection of their jobs and wages or environmental pollution in their neighbourhood) or that have great symbolic value (like the protection of whales). As a result, outside lobbying will typically be used only for the latter types of issues.

As a result of these factors, some groups specialize in a certain strategy. Interest groups that represent firms and industries or local governments rely almost completely on inside lobbying. By contrast, other groups mix the two strategies. Labour unions organize demonstrations and strikes, but they also engage in inside lobbying with decision-makers in the EU institutions. Likewise, farmers' groups are part of consultations on agricultural policy and often meet with Commission officials (inside lobbying), but once in a while they also organize large-scale demonstrations and blockades in Brussels to show the determination of their members (outside lobbying). Groups that rely (almost) completely on outside lobbying are scarce at the EU level.

Inside lobbying and outside lobbying in the EU

The fact that few EU interest groups only rely on outside lobbying reflects a more general pattern in EU interest representation. Compared to outside lobbying, inside lobbying is much more prevalent at the EU level. Outside lobbying is also remarkably less common at the EU level than within its member states. This has been studied systematically by Doug Imig and Sydney Tarrow, two scholars of social movements and political protest (Doug Imig and Sydney Tarrow, 'Political Contention in a Europeanising Polity', *West European Politics*, 23, 4, 2000: 73–93). They counted the number and types of political protest within the EU (including its member states) in order to find out how often EU-related protests take place and what form they take. For the period 1984–97, they found that EU-related political protest only formed about 5% of all protests staged within the EU member states. The remaining 95% were related to domestic issues. This figure of 5% is lower than what one would expect on the basis of the scope and impact of the EU's policies. Moreover, of these 5%, only some 20% (hence, 1% of all political protest taking place) were genuine 'collective European protests' – that is, cross-border protests organized at the EU level and aimed at the EU institutions. The European Day of Action against the TTIP falls into this category but was in fact exceptional.

The remaining 80% of EU-related protests were aimed at member state governments. Examples include French farmers protesting to the French government against reform of the EU's Common Agricultural Policy, and Spanish fishermen urging the Spanish government to defend their interests against French fishermen in the EU's Common Fisheries Policy. This is what Imig and Tarrow call 'domesticated political protest': related to EU policies, but aimed at domestic decision-makers. A more recent study found a similar pattern for the period 1997–2007 (Katrin Uba and Fredrik Uggla, 'Protest Actions against the European Union, 1992–2007', *West European Politics*, 34, 2, 2011: 384–93).

Why do we find so little EU-related political protest and why is it so often aimed at domestic governments? Imig and Tarrow explain this by pointing at the unfavourable **political opportunity structure** for political protests at the EU level and the organizational constraints that many groups face. The political opportunity structure determines whether decision-makers are receptive to certain claims and strategies. As we explained above, outside lobbying (which is just another word for political protest) tries to

> The **political opportunity structure** is the institutional and political context within which an interest group operates and that determines the receptiveness of decision-makers to the claims of that group.

put pressure on decision-makers from the outside by mobilizing public opinion. This strategy will only work if decision-makers are sensitive to public opinion. At the EU level, however, this is much less the case than in most of its member states (see Chapter 5 for a more extensive discussion). The European Commission is not directly elected. Unlike governments in parliamentary systems, it also does not rely on a governing coalition in the European Parliament. The EP itself is elected, but as we saw in Chapter 5 EP elections are normally decided on domestic not European issues. Finally, the Council of Ministers as a whole is not dependent on public opinion, and much of its deliberation is confidential. Domestic politicians, by contrast, rely heavily on public opinion for re-election. As a result, they will take care not to provoke massive public protests against them. This is one reason why interest groups at the EU level tend to focus more on inside lobbying and why, if they do use outside lobbying, they target member state governments, which are more likely to listen.

In addition to the political opportunity structure, many groups find it *difficult to organize* political protests at a European scale. These protests involve coordinating the activities of large numbers of citizens in different countries, with different languages and each with their own newspapers and broadcasting systems. It is difficult to reach that many people and to mobilize them to fight for the same cause. This, too, is a reason why pan-European protest is scarce.

Finally, the *issues at stake* are partly different at the EU level than within the member states. Many of the issues that are closest to people's daily lives (such as economic policies, social benefits and moral issues) are still primarily dealt with by member state governments (see Chapter 8). Most of the issues dealt with by the EU are more remote from most citizens' daily lives and therefore less likely to arouse equally strong sentiments.

Having said this, the EU is not static and neither are the interest groups active in it. Over the decades, the EP has obtained a much stronger role in EU decision-making and the EU deals with a much wider array of policies and issues. As a result, EU-related political protest has been on the rise since the early and mid-1990s and so have truly collective European protests. As the EU's political opportunity structure has evolved and groups have learnt how to organize themselves at the European level, outside lobbying has become more important in EU politics. Nevertheless, inside lobbying remains the rule and outside lobbying the exception. This is why we will now take a closer look at inside lobbying.

Lobby routes and coalition formation

When interest groups use inside lobbying strategies, they face a number of important choices. One choice is whether to lobby at the EU level or at the member state level or both. This reflects the multi-level nature of EU decision-making which, as we saw in Chapter 4, involves both the EU institutions and the governments of the EU member states (through the Council of Ministers). An interest group is therefore confronted with a range of potential targets: the Commission, the EP and each of the EU's member state governments. Here, too, interest groups will make the decision based on which target they think will be most receptive to their cause, what influence that actor wields in the decision-making process and the organizational capabilities of the interest group itself.

Ideally, groups are active at several levels at the same time, talking to the Commission and MEPs in Brussels, and approaching politicians and government officials in member state capitals. Such a multi-level strategy corresponds well with the way many EU interest groups are organized. As we saw above, most groups take the form of a European federation, with an office in Brussels and members in the various member states. This leads to a natural division of tasks, whereby the Brussels office tries to influence the EU institutions and the group's members target their own national government.

Besides the choice between national and European routes, interest groups also have to decide whether to work alone or to join forces with other groups. The advantage of 'going alone' is that the demands and message of the group are not diluted by compromises with partner groups. The disadvantage, however, is that no group is capable of single-handedly influencing EU decision-making. Just remember the enormous number of interest groups and lobbyists active in Brussels today, each trying to get attention for their claims and arguments. The voice of one single group will not easily be heard in this cacophony. Moreover, decision-makers are much more likely to listen to a lobbyist if he or she can claim to speak for a wide range of groups than just for one group. Forging coalitions is therefore essential if an interest group wants to have any impact. Finding the right partners and coming up with joint positions is one of the crucial jobs of lobbyists in Brussels.

■ Do interest groups matter?

Above, we have seen that many interest groups and lobbyists try to influence EU policy-making. They would not take all this trouble if they did not believe their activities affected policies. However, this still leaves the question of exactly what influence they have. Does 'big business' rule Brussels? Or are interest groups a peripheral force next to member state governments?

The influence of interest groups in the EU

Determining the influence of interest groups is a notoriously difficult issue in political science. Ideally, what we want to know is whether a decision would have been different in the absence of interest groups or a specific interest group. If so, the difference between the decision that was taken and the decision that would have been taken in the absence of interest groups is the influence exerted by those interest groups. Although conceptually this is a straightforward way to determine interest group influence, in practice it is almost impossible to assess.

For instance, one way of assessing interest group influence is to take a policy proposal, see what the response of an interest group was, and then determine whether the policy proposal changed as a result of that response. Simple as it may seem, this approach is fraught with caveats. First, if we observe that a policy proposal has changed, how can we be sure that it was changed *because of* the response by the interest group? Maybe policy-makers disagreed among themselves and changed the proposal for that reason. One reason why it is difficult to determine whether interest group activity caused a change is that policy-makers often have a strategic interest in downplaying or emphasizing the role of interest groups. In most cases, policy-makers do not want to be seen as lackeys of interest groups, so they will claim they changed their position for reasons other than interest group pressure. In other cases, they want to pacify (the members of) some interest group by stating they responded to that group's demands, even if they had different reasons for changing their position.

Second, any policy proposal is subject to numerous pressures, from interest groups, member state governments, MEPs and governments from states outside of the EU. It is nearly impossible to isolate the effect of interest group activity (let alone of one interest group) in this plethora of activities.

Third, and most fundamentally, interest groups need not always do something in order to have an impact on policy-makers. If policy-makers know that a powerful interest group is likely to oppose some idea, they will think twice before they propose it. Influence can therefore also be exerted without doing anything. These *anticipation effects* are extremely difficult to uncover because we cannot link the position of policy-makers to observable interest group behaviour.

The most we can do, therefore, is to carefully analyse the various possible routes of influence that interest groups have in order to arrive at a reasonable estimate of their impact on policy-making. Even then, it is very difficult to determine the *overall* influence of interest groups. Yet, studies of interest group influence do tell us more about differences *between* interest groups, answering the question of which groups are more powerful than others (and why).

In general, the impact of interest groups in policy-making depends on three sets of factors:

- characteristics of the interest groups;
- characteristics of the political system;
- characteristics of the issue that is at stake.

We will discuss each in turn.

Resources and interest group characteristics

Interest groups differ greatly. Some represent millions of members, some only a handful. Some are rich, some are not. Some have an office in Brussels, some do not. It makes sense to assume that these differences affect the ability of interest groups to influence policy-making. For instance, if a group is rich, it can hire more (and presumably better) staff and it can spend more money in order to set up a campaign.

In a more general sense, lobbying can be seen as an example of a 'resource exchange': interest groups are able to influence policy-makers because they have something to offer that those policy-makers value. For instance, interest groups have a lot of information about the issues they deal with. Because the European Commission needs information in order to make policies, it is very interested in obtaining that information. This offers opportunities for interest groups to influence policy-making. Likewise, for the European Commission it is very helpful to be able to point at the support of certain interest groups. If the Commission can claim that its proposal is supported by the affected industry, or by most NGOs dealing with the issue, it can considerably strengthen its position vis-à-vis the EU member states and the European Parliament. As a result, the Commission will often make modifications to its proposals in order to obtain the support of important interest groups.

The two examples point at two important sources of interest group influence in the EU: expertise and political support. The more knowledgeable an interest group is, the more impact it will have on policy-making. As we saw above, the EU is characterized more by inside lobbying than by outside lobbying. In inside lobbying processes, expertise is crucial because interest groups need to engage directly with policy-makers and other experts in discussions on the content of policies. In addition, the wider the constituency of an interest group, the stronger its voice will be. It makes quite a difference whether an interest group represents a few firms in one member state or it can claim to represent the entire European industry in a given field. This is the reason why, at the EU level, interest groups normally strive to form broad coalitions – both geographically (including as many member states as possible) and functionally (including as many different types of groups and sectors as possible). This is the only way to stand out from the crowd of EU interest groups.

Characteristics of the political system

Even though resources are important for an interest group, they do not fully determine its success. Whether or not an interest group is able to influence policies also depends on the way the political system operates. For instance, it makes quite a difference whether the system is pluralist or corporatist in nature. Likewise, money is more important as a resource for US than for EU interest groups because of differences in the political systems. Because election campaigns are more important in US politics than at the EU level, and because candidates need to spend a lot of money to win an election, financial resources are crucial for US politicians. Hence, campaign contributions to politicians are an important way for interest groups to gain access to powerful decision-makers. Conversely, because elections play a much smaller role in the EU, other resources become important. As a result, interest groups that represent firms (and which, as a result, tend to have more financial resources) are relatively more successful in US politics than in EU politics, as Christine Mahoney showed in a comparison between lobbying in the EU and the USA (Christine Mahoney, 'Lobbying Success in the United States and the European Union', *Journal of Public Policy*, 27, 1, 2007: 35–56). These are circumstances that interest groups can hardly change, but that do affect their chances of making a difference in the policy-making process.

In addition, the 'multi-level' nature of the EU may affect the influence of interest groups. Exactly how it affects interest groups is subject to debate among political scientists. On the one hand, it can be argued that the EU strengthens interest groups by offering them various different access points. A group can choose whether to go to the EU level or to lobby a national government. As a result, the EU's multi-level nature multiplies the options interest groups have, which decreases their dependence on any one level of government. If a group is not successful 'back home', it can always try again in Brussels. And if it is set to lose at the EU level, it can always try to reverse its odds by targeting member state governments. In this way, its position vis-à-vis each level is strengthened. On the other hand, the EU has also increased the options for member state governments. When dealing with interest groups, they can now point at agreements made at the EU level or obligations flowing from EU law. This offers them new opportunities to resist demands from interest groups. In reality, both things may take place at the same time: interest groups can exploit new opportunities at different levels of government, while governments can use the EU to circumvent domestic interest groups. Which of the two is stronger will vary between countries and between interest groups. The EU's multi-level character strengthens groups that are in a relatively weak position domestically but face better chances in Brussels, while it weakens groups that are strong domestically but find it more difficult to operate at the EU level.

The importance of issues

Finally, the impact of interest groups depends crucially on characteristics of the issue at hand. Interest groups are most effective if they face little competition from other interests. This means, first of all, that a particular interest group is more effective when few or no other interest groups are involved in the policy-making process. In addition, the impact of interest groups as a whole depends on the scope or salience of an issue. Interest groups can exert the greatest influence when an issue is confined to a small circle of policy-makers. This is often the case when the issue is seen as relatively 'technical' and with limited impact beyond the immediate area it deals with. This is favourable for interest groups because it means that they can target their efforts on a limited number of policy-makers. Moreover, the policy-makers themselves are more likely to consider interest group claims when they do not have to worry about the repercussions of their decisions for other stakeholders.

All of this changes when an issue becomes subject to broader debates, involving a wider range of stakeholders and political actors at higher levels. In those situations, interest group demands have to compete with a host of other considerations. This is clearest for issues that are considered to be 'high politics'. High politics issues are dealt with at the highest level of government (in the EU: the European Council). Here, interest group demands are easily swamped by geopolitical or electoral considerations. These considerations may work to the advantage of some groups, but no group will be able to exert the kind of direct influence that can be had with more limited issues.

■ Lobbying and democracy

We have seen that interest groups play important roles in EU policy-making. Even if they are not always successful in reaching their objectives, there are many situations in which they do affect the policies adopted. This raises obvious issues of democracy. After all, in a democratic political system, decisions should ideally reflect the preferences of the full citizenry, not of specific interests. Moreover, decision-making should be more or less transparent, so that citizens are able to know how and why a decision was taken and can hold their elected representatives to account if they do not agree. Lobbying may undermine both qualities. By lobbying for specific interests, decisions may move away from what most citizens would prefer. In addition, lobbying (particularly inside lobbying) is almost by nature an informal activity that takes place outside of the public view. As a result, it detracts from the transparency of the policy-making process and makes it more difficult to assess why and how a decision was taken.

This, however, does not automatically make lobbying an undemocratic or even anti-democratic activity. In fact, an argument can also be made in favour of lobbying. To start with, lobbying can improve the quality of decision-making by giving new information and additional viewpoints to policy-makers. Often, interest groups are knowledgeable about the issue they are engaged in. That knowledge can add to the quality of deliberations in the policy-making process. In addition, lobbying can bring viewpoints to the attention of policy-makers that would otherwise be ignored. There is no reason to assume that, in the absence of interest groups and lobbying, policy-makers would automatically do what is 'in the best interest' of citizens or what is supported by the majority of them. By promoting alternative viewpoints, interest groups may represent points of view that are shared by many citizens but are not (yet) heard in the policy-making process.

However, all this relies crucially on two conditions. First, whether or not lobbying helps the representativeness of policy-making depends on the balance between interest groups. If only one interest group is represented in the policy-making process, the outcome is likely to be severely biased towards that group. In the EU, it is sometimes claimed that business interests play too great a role compared to other types of groups (such as environmental and consumer groups). In terms of numbers of groups, this claim certainly seems to have merit. As we saw above, the vast majority of EU interest groups represent business interests, which may lead to a bias in favour of business-oriented policies. At the same time, research into the impact of interest groups suggests that business interests have a greater impact in US politics than in the EU because business interests have greater financial leverage than NGOs and money plays a greater role in US than in EU politics. Moreover, the European Commission actively tries to support European NGOs in order to stimulate a more 'level playing field' among interests.

The second condition that determines whether lobbying helps or threatens democracy has to do with the way in which lobbying takes place. Some forms of lobbying, such as giving objective information in order to highlight certain consequences of proposed policies, can hardly be objected to. This becomes different when lobbyists deliberately distort information or studies in order to mislead decision-makers. In the extreme, bribing decision-makers is even a criminal activity. In terms of transparency, as well, there is a continuum from more or less open contacts between interest groups and policy-makers to secretive meetings that are deliberately hidden from the public eye. Thus, there is a continuum of lobbying activities, from those activities that do not harm and may actually help democratic policy-making to activities that undermine it. Therefore, it is impossible to pass judgement on lobbying and interest groups per se: much depends on how the lobbying is done. This is the reason why there has been much debate about rules and codes of conduct for lobbyists. The European Commission and the European Parliament operate a joint register for interest groups and individual lobbyists (the so-called Transparency Register). Once they have registered, they are supposed to comply with a Code of Conduct. Yet, the register does not show what types of contacts actually take place between lobbyists and policy-makers. Moreover, although interest groups and lobbyists are 'expected' to register, there are few sanctions for those who do not. Most concretely, registration is required if a lobbyist wants to obtain access to the Parliament buildings.

Whatever one's normative judgement on lobbying, it is also a fact of political life. As long as (groups of) people are affected by government decisions or passionate about their ideas, they will try to convince policy-makers of their point of view. In the EU, as well, lobbying is set to remain an important feature of its political process. Hence, understanding which groups are involved and how lobbying works is an important precondition for understanding EU politics in general.

■ Summary

This chapter has discussed interest groups and lobbying in the EU. It argues that:

- According to estimates some 15,000 lobbyists and more than 3,500 interest groups are active in Brussels.

- The vast majority of these groups represent business interests. This can be explained by the fact that business groups typically represent specific interests while NGOs represent diffuse interests.
- Interest groups can use different channels to lobby the EU: they can lobby themselves, hire a consultant, or lobby through national or European associations. In addition, groups can lobby the EU institutions or target national governments.
- Interest representation in the EU is more pluralist than corporatist in nature, although pockets of corporatism can be found in social policy and the EU's Common Agricultural Policy.
- The European Commission has actively sought to support the creation and activities of EU interest groups, in an attempt to integrate them into the EU policy-making process. For the Commission, this has been a way to achieve a more balanced representation of interests but also to create an EU-level constituency that it can engage in its initiatives.
- Interest groups can use two types of strategies: inside lobbying and outside lobbying. When groups rely on inside lobbying, they try to influence policy-making from within, by becoming part of deliberations on policies. When groups use outside lobbying, they try to put pressure on policy-makers from the outside, by staging public protests and involving the media.
- Interest groups may use combinations of these two strategies, but often they rely more on one or the other.
- In the EU, inside lobbying is much more prevalent than outside lobbying, because EU policy-makers are less vulnerable to public opinion, protests at a European scale are difficult to organize, and the types of issues the EU deals with are more remote from citizens' daily lives.
- The impact of interest groups depends on three things: characteristics of the interest groups themselves, characteristics of the political system they operate in, and characteristics of the issue they are active on.
- The most important interest group characteristics that affect their impact in the EU are expertise and political support.
- Because campaign financing is less important in the EU than in the USA, money plays a smaller role for interest groups in the EU than in the latter.
- The EU's multi-level character offers opportunities for interest groups to circumvent governments but also for governments to withstand interest group demands.
- Interest groups are most effective when an issue is confined to a limited set of participants and stakeholders.
- Whether or not lobbying helps or is a threat to democracy depends on the balance between interest groups and the way in which lobbying takes place.

Further reading

Good introductions to interest representation and lobbying in the EU are Justin Greenwood, *Interest Representation in the European Union* (Palgrave Macmillan, 3rd edn, 2011) and Rinus van Schendelen, *The Art of Lobbying the EU: More Machiavelli in Brussels* (Amsterdam University Press, revised edn, 2013). Christine Mahoney, *Brussels versus the Beltway: Advocacy in the United States and the European Union* (Georgetown University Press, 2008) presents one of the few systematic empirical comparisons between lobbying in the EU and the USA. A somewhat older but still outstanding analysis of political protest in the EU is presented in Doug Imig and Sydney Tarrow (eds), *Contentious Europeans: Protest and Politics in an Emerging Polity* (Rowman & Littlefield, 2001).

Websites

- European Commission and European Parliament's Transparency Register: http://ec.europa.eu/transparencyregister
- European Economic and Social Committee: http://www.eesc.europa.eu
- Committee of the Regions: www.cor.europa.eu
- European Public Affairs Consultancies' Association (EPACA): www.epaca.org
- Society of European Affairs Professionals (SEAP): www.seap.be

Navigating the EU

On the website www.navigatingthe.eu you will find online exercises for this chapter.

7   Political parties and the European Parliament

■ Introduction

In March 2009 David Cameron, the leader of the British Conservative Party, announced that the Conservatives would form a new political group in the European Parliament after the EP elections of June that year. In doing so, the Conservatives would break away from the Christian Democrat European People's Party (EPP), with which it had been allied in the EP for almost two decades.

The relationship between the Conservatives and the EPP had always been strained, as the Conservatives were much more Eurosceptical than the (traditionally strongly pro-EU) 'continental' conservative and Christian democratic parties assembled in the EPP. Before joining the EPP group, the Conservatives had cooperated with like-minded parties in the 'European Democrats' (ED) group. When the British Conservatives decided to join the EPP political group in 1992, they only did so as an 'associated party'. In 1999, this associated status was made more visible by adding 'ED' to the name of the EPP group in Parliament. Still, the British Conservatives continued to disagree with the EPP 'party line' on many important issues and frequently threatened to withdraw from the EPP-ED group altogether to form their own political group.

Cameron's decision to set up a new political group attracted a lot of criticism within his own party. Several Conservative Members of the European

Parliament (MEPs) voiced their discontent with the move, fearing that the Conservatives would lose influence in the EP. They were joined by former Conservative commissioners Leon Brittan and Chris Patten, as well as the (Christian Democratic) President of the European Commission, José Barroso. Nevertheless, on 22 June 2009, eight parties, including the Conservatives, presented their new political group under the name European Conservatives and Reformists (ECR). A few months later, they also created the Alliance of European Conservatives and Reformists (AECR), a political party at the European level.

The story of the Conservatives and the EPP raises a number of questions about the role of political parties in the EP and EU politics in general. Why did the Conservatives stay in the EPP political group for almost twenty years when there were so many differences of opinion? When Cameron did create a new group, why did a number of prominent party members voice their opposition? And what is the relationship between political groups in the EP and European political parties, such as the AECR?

In order to answer these questions, we need to take a closer look at what political parties do in the EU, both inside and outside of the EP. In this chapter, we will do so by looking at the following questions:

- What do we mean by the term 'political party' in the EU?
- Which political groups are active in the European Parliament?
- What are the benefits of forming a political group?
- What role do political groups play in the EP?
- What role do European political parties play outside of the EP?

We will see that political parties play an important role in the European Parliament. The EP's 'political groups' are instrumental in structuring the Parliament's work, and they tend to vote as cohesive blocks. In that sense, the EP is increasingly operating like domestic parliaments. Outside of the EP, by contrast, European political parties have been slow to develop and have only assumed a limited number of tasks. They remain confederations of domestic parties and lack the key tasks of recruiting candidates for political office and organizing the electorate. As a result, European political parties do not play the central and independent role in EU politics that domestic political parties play in domestic politics.

■ Political parties in the EU: three levels

A **political party** is a group of like-minded people who organize in order to influence politics through winning political office.

When we talk about **political parties** in the EU, it is important to note that the term can be used for three different types of entities, which need to be clearly distinguished:

- *Domestic political parties* play a role in the EU because they compete for seats in the European Parliament during the EP elections.

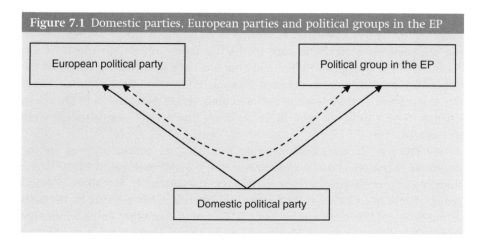

Figure 7.1 Domestic parties, European parties and political groups in the EP

- *Political groups* are coalitions between elected MEPs from different member states in the EP. They play important roles in the daily operation of the EP and structure the voting behaviour of MEPs.
- *European political parties* are associations between domestic political parties and operate outside of the EP.

The relationship between these three forms of 'political party' is shown in Figure 7.1.

Within the 'triangle' in Figure 7.1, domestic political parties play a central role. They are the ones that send MEPs to the European Parliament. Hence, they also decide which political groups to form or join. David Cameron's decision about the affiliation of the Conservative MEPs in the EP is a good illustration of this process. In addition, domestic political parties are the founders and members of European political parties, and are firmly in the driving seat when it comes to deciding about the activities of those European parties. As a result, there is no close, direct link between European political parties and the political groups in the EP. Any link that exists between European political parties and political groups runs via domestic parties. This is indicated by the curved, dashed line between them, as opposed to the straight full lines between domestic parties, on the one hand, and European political parties and political groups in the EP, on the other. Hence, domestic political parties play a pivotal role, organizing and controlling both political groups and European political parties.

■ Political groups in the European Parliament

The development of political groups in the EP

When the European Coal and Steel Community (ECSC) was created in 1951, it included a **Common Assembly** alongside the High Authority (the

> The **Common Assembly** was the predecessor of the European Parliament and was created as part of the ECSC in 1951.

precursor of the European Commission) and the Council of Ministers. The Common Assembly consisted of members from the national parliaments of the six member states who met to discuss issues related to the ECSC. In contrast to the European Parliament that we have now, the members of the Common Assembly were not elected directly, but combined the membership of the Assembly with their work as national members of parliament. As we saw in Chapter 5, this only changed in 1979, when direct elections to the EP were introduced.

Nevertheless, from 1953 onwards, the national representatives in the Common Assembly chose to organize on the basis of political ideology rather than country of origin. In these early days, the Assembly had three political groups: Socialists, Christian Democrats and Liberals. By organizing on the basis of political groups, the members of the Common Assembly emphasized that they primarily represented ideological cleavages in Europe and not different member states.

With the creation of the European Economic Community and Euratom in 1958, the tasks of the Common Assembly were extended to these communities, too, and it was officially renamed 'European Parliamentary Assembly'. In 1962, the Parliamentary Assembly decided to call itself the 'European Parliament'. This emphasized the role the Assembly saw for itself – not as a mere collection of national members of parliaments but as a European parliament in its own right, even if this name was only formalized in the 1986 Single European Act.

From the 78 members of the ECSC's Common Assembly, the European Parliament has grown to 751 MEPs. Most of these MEPs belong to one of the EP's seven political groups. Table 7.1 gives an overview of these groups. The seven groups vary widely in terms of their ideological underpinnings, level of ideological cohesiveness and level of organization. In the following sections, we will discuss these three elements in turn.

The ideological underpinning of the EP's political groups

An **ideology** is a more or less systematic and comprehensive set of ideas and beliefs about politics that guides the positions of politicians, political parties and/or citizens on specific political issues.

In terms of **ideological** underpinning, most of the political groups are defined in classic left/right terms, ranging from the (post-) Communists, the Greens and the Socialists on the left to the Christian Democrats, Liberals and Conservatives on the right. All in all, therefore, the political groups in the EP tend to reflect the political distinctions that also exist within the member states.

The main exception to this left/right scheme is the Europe of Freedom and Direct Democracy Group (EFDD), which is based on a Eurosceptic platform. Its uniting ideology consists of opposition to the EU as a threat to national sovereignty and identity. As we saw in the introduction to this chapter, the European Conservatives and Reformists Group was also founded on a Eurosceptic platform, based on its conservative ideology. However, in contrast to

Table 7.1 Political groups in the European Parliament (as of 1 July 2014)

Political group	Created in	Ideological orientation	Website
Group of the European People's Party (EPP)	1953 (as 'Christian Democrat Group')	Christian Democratic	www.eppgroup.eu
Group of the Progressive Alliance of Socialists and Democrats in the European Parliament (S&D)	1953 (as 'Group of the Socialists')	Social Democratic	www.socialistsanddemocrats.eu
Group of the Alliance of Liberals and Democrats for Europe (ALDE)	1953 (as 'Liberal Group')	Liberal	www.alde.eu
European Conservatives and Reformists Group (ECR)	2009	Conservative/Eurosceptic	www.ecrgroup.eu
Confederal Group of the European United Left-Nordic Green Left (EUL/NGL)	1973 (as 'Communist and Allies Group')	(Post-) Communist	www.guengl.eu
Group of the Greens/European Free Alliance (G/EFA)	1984 (as 'Rainbow Group')	Coalition of Greens and regionalists	www.greens-efa.eu
Europe of Freedom and Direct Democracy Group (EFDD)	1994 (as 'Europe of Nations')	Eurosceptic	www.efdgroup.eu

the EFDD, it does not oppose the existence of the EU as such but focuses on reform of the EU and is reluctant to concede new powers.

Ideological cohesiveness in the EP's political groups

The shared ideological underpinnings of the EP's political groups obscure important distinctions within each of these groups, which are reflected in their level of ideological cohesiveness. In the end, the political groups in the EP are collections of (elected representatives from) domestic parties. These domestic parties have all evolved within specific national contexts and political traditions. As a result, the British Labour Party has partly different positions and priorities than, say, the French Parti Socialiste (PS) or the Austrian Sozial-demokratische Partei Österreichs (SPÖ).

Still, some political groups include wider national differences than others. The three oldest political groups are those of the Christian Democrats, Social-ists and Liberals. These three political groups were the first to be established when the ECSC's Common Assembly decided to organize along party lines. Currently, they are the only groups that have members from (almost) all EU member states. This is not surprising, as Christian democracy, social democracy and liberalism have been the three defining political ideologies in Western Europe during the twentieth century. International cooperation among domes-tic parties from these ideologies often predates the creation of the ECSC. For instance, the first Congress of Christian People's Parties was held in 1925, while cooperation between socialist parties extends back as far as 1864, when the First International was established.

Nevertheless, there are also differences in cohesiveness between these three 'classic' political groups. Despite the differences between social democratic parties in the EU member states, each of these parties is based on a largely similar political ideology. This is helped by the fact that socialism and social democracy had from the outset an explicitly international outlook. The idea of international solidarity has always been important in socialist thinking; it is no accident that the First International was founded already in 1864. Since the 2009 EP elections, Social Democrats have formed the major part of the Progres-sive Alliance of Socialists and Democrats Group (S&D).

The group of the European People's Party (EPP) is a somewhat more mixed bag and is a good example of the difficulties of forming cohesive political groups on the basis of domestic political parties. Christian democracy shares a number of ideas in different countries, but these ideas were often developed in specific national contexts and not as part of an international political programme as with the Socialists. In fact, as conservatives, Christian Demo-crats put a high value on local and national traditions, which has led to quite distinct political profiles for each of the Christian democratic parties in Europe.

Moreover, Christian democratic parties do not exist in all European coun-tries. The EPP therefore also includes parties that are conservative but not explicitly Christian in character, such as the Spanish Partido Popular (PP) or the French Union pour un Mouvement Populaire (UMP). These parties have developed from specific national concerns. The UMP, for instance, builds on the French political tradition of 'Gaullism', a peculiarly French brand of political ideas that cannot be found in any other EU member state.

The Liberal group in the EP, nowadays named the Group of the Alliance of Liberals and Democrats for Europe (ALDE), also hosts a diverse set of political parties. Broadly speaking, two strands can be discerned in European liberalism. One strand, which is on the right of the political spectrum, stands for market liberalism and a minimal state. The other strand, which is more centrist or left-leaning, emphasizes equality of rights and social justice. As a result, Liberal parties in different member states take quite different positions in their political system. For example, the German Freie Demokratische Partei (FDP) has traditionally placed itself in between the Christian Democrats and the Social Democrats, participating in alternating coalitions with these two powerhouses of German politics. The British Liberal Democrats are seen as left-leaning in ideological terms. The Belgian Open Vlaamse Liberalen en Democraten (Open VLD), by contrast, is firmly on the right of the political spectrum and has placed greater emphasis on market liberalization and financial austerity. In some countries, such as the Netherlands, liberalism is represented by two parties: one of the market liberalism and one of the social liberalism variety. Although competitors on the domestic level, these parties work together in the ALDE group.

In the introduction we already saw the background to the creation of the European Conservatives and Reformists Group (ECR). The parties in this group are all 'conservative' and are united by a considerable degree of Euroscepticism, expressed in their opposition to 'Euro-federalism'. Under this broad umbrella, the ECR brings together twenty-two parties from fifteen member states, dominated by the British Conservatives, the Polish Law and Justice Party, and the Eurosceptic German party Alternative für Deutschland.

The Confederal Group of the European United Left–Nordic Green Left (EUL/ NGL) is a group consisting of far left parties, most of them of a communist or post-communist persuasion. Although communist representation in the European Parliament as a political group dates back to 1973, the fall of communism in Central and Eastern Europe has led to significant changes within this political group. It now also includes communist parties from the former communist countries in Central and Eastern Europe.

The rise of the Greens began in the 1980s, when Green parties, devoted to environmental protection and progressive social policies, sprang up in several European countries. The Greens started their life in the EP under the aegis of the Rainbow Group, a coalition with so-called 'stateless nations' or 'regionalists'. The latter include parties that represent minorities within certain EU member states, such as the Scottish National Party and the Republican Left of Catalonia. They are not Green parties but generally adhere to a progressive social agenda. After the Greens split off from the Rainbow Group in 1989 to form their own political group, the two groups were reunited in 1999 as the Greens–European Free Alliance.

The Europe of Freedom and Direct Democracy Group (EFDD) is not so easy to characterize in left/right terms. Its uniting ideology consists of opposition to European integration and an emphasis on the sovereignty of the member states vis-à-vis the EU. The British UK Independence Party (UKIP), the largest member of the group, even advocates the withdrawal of the UK from the EU. The second-largest member besides UKIP is Italy's Five Star Movement, a protest party founded by the comedian Beppe Grillo. In addition, the group includes members from a number of smaller right-wing parties.

Level of organization

Political groups differ not only in terms of ideology, but also in terms of the level of organization. Some political groups are ad hoc coalitions between like-minded MEPs that form after an EP election, while others are based on more enduring forms of cooperation. Examples of the former include the EFDD and EUL/NGL political groups. The members of these groups cooperate within the EP, but they do not have a common organization outside of the EP. Other groups are affiliated to a European political party, which provides a platform for cooperation apart from the political groups in the EP. Most European parties publish a party manifesto preceding the elections for the EP, which includes common positions on a range of issues related to the EU. The organization and role of European parties will be discussed more extensively below.

The benefits of forming a political group

Above, we surveyed the field of political groups in the EP. It turned out that there is a fair amount of variation among domestic parties, which makes it difficult to form one single group in the EP. Still, MEPs and parties that are represented in the EP find it very important to be part of a political group. This is why the British Conservatives only left the EPP political group when they had found enough partners to form a new political group. It also explains why the Conservatives remained part of the EPP-ED political group between 1992 and 2009, despite considerable differences in opinion on European integration. In turn, the other parties in the EPP-ED political group made great efforts to keep the Conservatives on board during this period. Why, then, is it so important to political parties to cooperate in political groups?

The answer to this question is twofold. Part has to do with the internal rules and procedures of the European Parliament. The other aspect has to do with the political advantages of being part of a (large) political group. The Rules of Procedure of the European Parliament greatly encourage the formation of political groups by granting them a range of specific powers and privileges. For instance, political groups receive subsidies and have guaranteed seats on parliamentary committees. The Conference of Presidents, which organizes the work of the EP, consists of the President of the EP plus the presidents of all political groups. Being on the Conference of Presidents is important because it decides on such things as the agenda for EP meetings and the composition of parliamentary committees. Also, political groups can table amendments to proposals that are being discussed in the EP or propose to reject a proposal altogether. Outside of political groups, only parliamentary committees and groups of at least forty MEPs can do so. To give a final example, when a conciliation committee is formed to discuss a compromise with the Council of Ministers under the ordinary legislative procedure (see Chapter 4), seats on the EP delegation to the committee are allocated according to the composition of the EP by political group. Hence, it is very unattractive for an individual MEP or domestic political party not to be a member of a political group.

In order to form a political group, three conditions have to be met. First, the group needs to consist of at least twenty-five MEPs. Second, these MEPs need to come from at least one-quarter of all EU member states. Currently, this implies the members should come from at least seven different member states. Third, the group should be formed 'according to political affinities', as the EP's Rules of Procedure state it. The latter condition is meant to prevent the creation of purely 'technical groups' of MEPs who work together to obtain the benefits of a political group without actually sharing a common political programme.

All in all, the EP's rules on political groups encourage organization along ideological lines. They almost force MEPs to form political groups across EU member states on the basis of a shared political programme. This, in turn, conditions many of the activities that take place within the Parliament.

In addition to these procedural incentives, there are also important political benefits in forming a political group. Figure 7.2 shows the distribution of seats in the EP between the twenty-eight member states. The EU's largest member state, Germany, occupies 96 seats out of a total of 751, or 12.8% of the total. All other member states have smaller numbers of seats. The largest single domestic party in the EP, Germany's Christian Democratic CDU/CSU, currently occupies thirty-four seats, or 4.5% of the total. Hence, in order to get things done in the EP, it is necessary to work together with MEPs from other member states. By forming a political group, MEPs can present a unified front that controls a substantial number of votes, which increases the chances of obtaining decisions that are favourable to that group.

Of course, working together in a political group also means that MEPs and domestic political parties represented in the EP need to compromise with their colleagues from other countries. This is made easier by the fact that the political groups are based on common ideological backgrounds, but as we saw above there can be substantial differences within a political group. MEPs and domestic political parties therefore face an important trade-off. On the one hand, by joining a political group they may have to compromise on some of their objectives. On the other hand, being part of a political group increases their chances of achieving results.

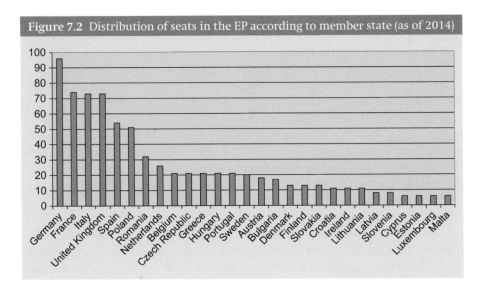

Figure 7.2 Distribution of seats in the EP according to member state (as of 2014)

This trade-off also characterized the relationship between the British Con-servatives and the EPP political group that we discussed in the introduction. To illustrate this further, take a look at Figure 7.3, which shows the size of the political groups in the EP.

In the 2014–19 European Parliament, the EPP political group is the largest, holding 221 of the EP's 751 seats. The S&D group is second, with 191 seats. For the British Conservatives, being a member of the EPP-ED political group was attractive because it made them part of the EP's largest political group. In comparison, the ECR group is much smaller with only 70 seats. The logic also worked for the other parties in the EPP. For them, having the Conservatives on board was an important asset, because the seats of the Conservatives, and those of some of the other parties that later joined the ECR, solidified the position of the Christian Democrats as the largest group in the EP. This calculus explains why both the Conservatives and the rest of the EPP political group for a long time went to great lengths to maintain their coalition, despite clear differences of opinion. This is also why some Conservative MEPs and former commission-ers opposed David Cameron's decision to start his own group, because it would diminish the influence of the Conservatives in the EP. Briefing 7.1 looks at this trade-off in greater depth, on the basis of insights from political science theories of coalition formation.

■ MEPs: between political group and member state

Above, we discussed the various political groups in the EP and the benefits of forming political groups. In this section, we turn to the question that is most important for an understanding of politics in the EP: do political groups

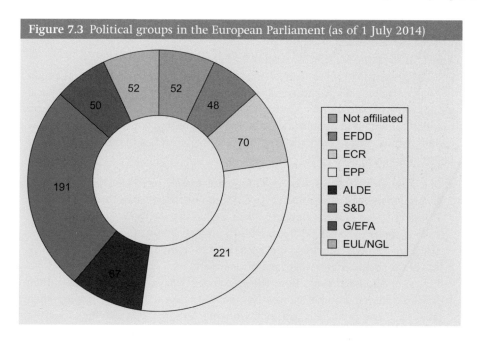

Figure 7.3 Political groups in the European Parliament (as of 1 July 2014)

matter? First, we discuss how often MEPs vote with or against their own political group. Only if political groups are able to 'bring out the vote' do they have any real political significance. Second, we ask to what extent political groups structure political conflict in the EP. In national politics, we are used to thinking of political parties as voting along certain lines, the 'left–right' dimension being the most relevant in most countries. Do similar conflict dimensions also exist within the EP and, if so, what do they look like? Finally, we look at coalitions between political groups in the EP. Since no political group has an absolute majority, they have to cooperate to achieve something. Does this lead to stable coalitions between political groups in the EP, similar to the coalitions that we find in national politics? And, if so, which groups tend to form coalitions?

Do political groups vote as blocks?

Political groups bring benefits to their members, both in terms of formal 'perks' and in terms of political power. However, for this political power to be actualized, political groups need to vote as a block. If individual MEPs or domestic parties within a political group do not vote with the overall party line, the potential for forming one block in the EP is severely diminished. This is not just a theoretical possibility. In fact, on the face of it, there are few reasons why MEPs would vote with their political group if it conflicts with domestic impera- tives. Of course, the two need not be in conflict. The formation of political groups on the basis of ideological affinities is meant to bring together parties

Briefing 7.1

Coalition formation in the European Parliament

Political groups in the European Parliament are in essence coalitions between (MEPs from) domestic political parties. In order to understand why certain political groups form, we can therefore make use of existing theories in political science on coalition formation in domestic politics. The key question in these theories is why certain parties elect to work together. Two main approaches to this question have been formulated:

- One approach assumes that politicians are mainly interested in maximizing power for its own sake. Power gives important benefits to those holding it, including status and the perks of office. Politicians are then said to be 'office-seeking'. Applied to the EP, this approach predicts that national political parties will strive for political groups that command as many seats as possible, regardless of the ideological background of their partners.
- The other approach starts from the idea that politicians want to have certain policies adopted. In other words, they want to make a difference through their policies. These politicians are 'policy-oriented'. As a result, coalitions will be formed among parties that take similar policy positions, even when this means losing some power.

In the EP, the same two considerations play a role in the formation of political groups. A group that wants to increase its power will opt for the inclusion of as many members as necessary without being too strict about the ideological background of those members. A group that cares mainly about ideology will only accept members that fit its profile, even if this implies a smaller group.

In reality, all political groups in the EP balance these two objectives; they are both 'office-seeking' and 'policy-oriented'. Still, some groups have leaned more towards increasing their membership while other groups have adhered more closely to a shared ideological background. For instance, in the early 1990s, the EPP decided to expand its membership in order to become the largest political group in the EP, even if this meant the inclusion of parties that did not have a Christian democratic background. As a result, after the 1999 elections the (then) EPP-ED group became the largest single political group for the first time since 1975, but with much greater internal diversity than before.

that share certain basic ideas about the way the EU should be run. Still, as we saw above, there is quite a lot of variety within political groups. Moreover, on some issues of EU politics, political parties from the left and the right within a certain country tend to agree, regardless of ideological background.

If this occurs, MEPs can hardly abandon the position of their constituency and political party 'back home'. To begin with, MEPs depend for their position on elections in their own country and they are selected as candidates by their domestic parties. Moreover, if MEPs have political ambitions beyond the EP (such as becoming a cabinet minister) they also rely on their domestic party. In comparison, the political leadership of the political group in the EP has little to offer, although it can determine which MEPs obtain rapporteurships for legislative proposals or chairmanships of parliamentary committees. As a result, in case of conflict between the two it is not at all obvious that the official position of the political group will prevail over domestic imperatives.

Nevertheless, political groups in the EP tend to vote relatively cohesively. Political scientists Simon Hix, Abdel Noury and Gérard Roland have studied the **cohesion** of political groups in the EP between 1979 and 2004 by analysing the extent to which MEPs vote with or against their political group in the EP (Simon Hix, Abdel Noury and Gérard Roland, *Democratic Politics in the European Parliament*, Cambridge University Press, 2007). They found that in the vast majority of cases, MEPs vote with their political group and not with their compatriots in other political groups. Moreover, political groups have become more cohesive over time, voting together more often. By contrast, the cohesion among MEPs from the same member state has decreased over time. More recent analyses have shown that this trend has continued since 2004 (www.votewatch.eu). Cohesion is generally strongest among the EPP, S&D, ALDE and Greens/EFA groups. Overall, the cohesion of these groups is still weaker than that of parties in national European parliaments but stronger than that of the two parties in the US Congress.

> **Cohesion** is the extent to which MEPs of the same political group vote together. If all MEPs from a political group vote exactly the same, cohesion is high. If some MEPs in a political group vote for a proposal or amendment while other MEPs from that same group vote against, cohesion is low.

Political groups have therefore become stronger as the EP has become more powerful. According to Hix, Noury and Roland, political groups have become stronger because domestic parties have realized that in order to operate effectively in the EP, they need to vote together, even if the position of the political group does not always conform with their own ideal position. This shows that political groups are important factors in the EP. If we want to understand how MEPs vote, we need to look first at the positions taken by their political groups.

Conflict dimensions in the EP

In the previous sections, we saw that the EP's political groups, with the exception of the EFDD group, can be ordered along the familiar left/right divide. The left/right divide is the best-known and most important so-called **political cleavage** in the domestic politics of most EU member states. Cleavages are based on social differences between groups of citizens that lead to different perspectives on the kind of policies that the government should pursue. Thus, 'leftists' think that the government should intervene in the economy in order to create greater equality while

> A **political cleavage** is a stable conflict dimension between political groups that is rooted in social differences between groups in society.

'rightists' believe that the economy works best if the government does not interfere with it too much. In addition to the left/right cleavage, there may also be other cleavages in a country – for instance, between different regions in a country or between cities and the countryside.

Cleavages structure politics because issues tend to be absorbed into existing cleavages. So, if the left/right cleavage is the only important cleavage in a country, all issues will typically be interpreted in left/right terms. In this way, cleavages lead to 'packages' of political positions that go together, so that a leftist position on unemployment benefits goes together with a leftist position on immigration policies and a leftist position on environmental protection. If an issue cannot be defined in such terms, the chances are that it will largely be ignored by existing political parties. By structuring politics, cleavages also lend a degree of predictability and stability to political systems. If cleavages are strong, you can easily predict the position of a political party on one issue from its position on another issue. After all, since cleavages lead to the 'packages' of political positions described above, if politicians support one part of the package they are forced also to adhere to the other parts.

Cleavages are important for understanding domestic politics, but are they also relevant in the European Parliament? Studies of voting behaviour in the European Parliament show that they are. As in most European states, the left/right cleavage is the most important conflict dimension in the European Parliament. This means that in most of the cases support for and opposition to proposals depends on where a political group stands in terms of left and right. It also means that politics in the EP is remarkably like domestic politics and you can understand quite a lot about the voting behaviour of political groups in the EP by looking at them in left/right terms.

In addition, voting patterns in the EP reveal a second, though less important, conflict dimension between groups that support further European integration and groups that are more reluctant to let the EU play a greater role vis-à-vis its member states. Above, where we reviewed the seven political groups in the EP, we already saw that opposition to the EU is a particularly important part of the platforms of the ECR and the EFDD. To some extent it also characterizes the positions taken by the EUL/NGL. The three large centrist groups (EPP, S&D and ALDE) as well as the Greens have generally been supportive of further integration. This conflict dimension is peculiar to the EU, although it is similar to the opposition to central governments by regional political parties in some EU member states, such as Italy, Spain and the UK.

Coalitions between political groups in the EP

A **coalition** is a set of parties that work together to achieve some political objective – for instance, to create a government (in parliamentary political systems) or to coordinate voting behaviour (in the EP).

Above, we saw that political groups are **coalitions** of domestic parties that work together in order to gain more clout in the EP. However, since no political group commands a majority of votes, each group needs the support of other groups to achieve something. In principle, this could take two forms. On the one hand, coalitions between political groups could form on each individual issue separately. Then, we would find different coalitions on different issues. On the other hand, political groups could agree to support each other on a range of issues. Then, they would form stable coalitions. The latter pattern is what we typically find in the domestic politics of EU member states, where parties in parliament form stable coalitions for certain periods of time.

Coalition formation in domestic politics is the result of the parliamentary system that exists in most EU member states. In a parliamentary system, the government can only operate if it is supported by a majority in parliament. Hence, parties form coalitions in order to form such a majority. In the EP, this type of coalition formation is not relevant. After all, the EU does not operate under a parliamentary system. Its 'government' (that is, the Commission) is not formed on the basis of the prevailing majority in the EP, so there is no need (or use) to create a governing coalition. Nevertheless, there can be benefits for political groups in agreeing to work together and hence win a greater proportion of votes.

Up until the mid-1990s, such coalitions indeed formed between the three largest political groups: the EPP, the Socialists and ALDE. These three groups often formed a triangle that voted together on major issues. For political parties outside this triangle, it was almost impossible to get anything done (unless they happened to agree with what the 'big three' wanted). This has led to the image of the EP as largely ruled by a grand coalition of Christian Democrats and Socialists, aided by Liberals.

This grand coalition still plays an important role in the EP. Since the mid-1990s, however, the Christian Democrats and the Socialists have voted against each other more often, leaving more scope for alternative coalitions (e.g. between left-wing or right-wing groups) or ad hoc coalitions around specific issues. These coalitions are primarily based on the congruence of the policy positions taken by political groups on a given issue. As a result, political groups tend to vote most often with the groups that are closest to them on a left/right scale. Yet, in contrast to the way parliaments work in most EU member states, political groups in the EP do not form longer-term coalitions in which they agree to support each other between two elections.

■ Political parties outside the European Parliament

The previous sections reviewed the role of political groups in the European Parliament. These political groups are the result of cooperation between (groups of) MEPs from different EU member states. In addition, domestic political parties from various EU member states may also cooperate outside the EP. Then they form European parties in order to coordinate their activities. Although European parties and political groups in the European Parliament sometimes have close links, they are not the same. Some political groups are affiliated with one single European party. A good example is the EPP group, which is directly linked to the European People's Party. Likewise, the vast majority of parties in the S&D group are members of the Party of European Socialists (PES). Other party groups are affiliated with two different parties. For instance, the Greens/European Free Alliance group has ties with both the European Green Party and the European Free Alliance. Still other political groups include members from domestic parties that belong to a European party alongside members from domestic parties that do not. Thus, the EUL/NGL group includes parties that are members of the European Left Party and members that are not affiliated to a European party.

In each of the EU member states, political parties are important players in politics. Their importance stems not only from the fact that they are represented in parliaments but also from their activities outside parliament. They have members who vote on candidates for elected office and party platforms, they actively recruit people to represent the party, and may organize debates and publish discussion papers in order to have an input into the political debate. In short, political parties are organized and have a role in politics independent from the elected representatives for those parties. An important question is whether European parties perform the same roles that parties within the member states do. To what extent are they a political force of their own in EU politics? That is the question this section will address.

The development of European political parties

Initially, the development of European political parties was closely linked to developments in the European Parliament. As we saw above, cooperation between Christian Democratic and Socialist parties in Europe was initiated well before the Second World War. These forms of cooperation remained rather loose. They presented opportunities for domestic political parties to meet and discuss informally, but did not go beyond that. The development of more strongly institutionalized European party federations started after the creation of the ECSC in 1951. It proceeded in four stages.

The early years

The first stage runs from the creation of the ECSC to the 1970s. After political groups had formed in the ECSC Common Assembly (and later the EEC's European Parliamentary Assembly), Christian Democratic, Socialist and Liberal parties started to cooperate at the European level. Socialist parties from the six EEC member states formed a 'liaison bureau' within the Socialist International in 1957. In 1965, the European Union of Christian Democrats was established. Liberal parties worked together in the Liberal International, which had been founded in 1947 and had a predominantly European membership. In this first period cooperation remained rather informal. These were not European parties, neither in practice nor even in name. Rather, they were platforms where representatives from various domestic parties could meet to discuss issues relating to the European Communities. There was little use for more intensive forms of cooperation, anyway, because the Common/Parliamentary Assembly consisted of representatives from national parliaments.

Direct elections to the EP

The formation of European party federations entered the second stage when it was decided that the EP would be elected directly by citizens in the member states. Election campaigns called for closer coordination – for instance, in the formulation of a common party manifesto. In the mid-1970s, the main political groups therefore created European party federations to replace the weak platforms existing until then. In 1974, Socialist parties formed the Union (also: Confederation) of Socialist Parties of the European Community. Christian Democratic parties followed in 1976 with the European People's Party. That same year, Liberal parties established the Federation of Liberal and Democratic Parties in the European Community. Each of these party federations drafted a party manifesto for the first direct elections to the EP, in 1979, but in the end election campaigns remained a matter for each of the domestic parties that were members of the federation.

Recognition of European political parties

Party formation at the EU level entered the third stage in 1992, when European political parties were mentioned for the first time in an official EU treaty. The Treaty of Maastricht included a provision which stated that '[p]olitical parties at European level are important as a factor for integration within the Union. They contribute to forming a European awareness and to expressing the political will of the citizens of the Union.' Although they had little practical effect, these words at least recognized the potential role to be played by political parties in the EU. Furthermore, the Treaty of Maastricht, and the earlier Single European Act of 1986, expanded the role of the European Parliament, which also implied a greater relevance for political parties. In response to these developments, several European party federations were strengthened or reincorporated. In 1993, the Confederation of Socialist Parties was renamed the Party of European Socialists (PES), while the Liberals continued under the name of European Liberal Democrat and Reform Party (ELDR). Moreover, the three traditional party federations were joined in 1993 by the European Federation of Green Parties, a party federation that succeeded the previously much looser cooperation between Green parties from several European countries. In 1994, the European Free Alliance was established as a European party federation, as a follow-up to earlier cooperation schemes between regionalist parties that had started in 1981.

The Party Regulation

The fourth stage was set in motion by the 2000 Treaty of Nice, which amended the provision on political parties included in the Treaty of Maastricht. Whereas the provision in the Treaty of Maastricht only expressed the sentiment that political parties had an important role to play without specifying any concrete rights or obligations, the amendment in the Treaty of Nice provided for the adoption of 'regulations governing political parties at European level and in particular the rules regarding their financing'. On the basis of this provision, a Regulation on the financing of European political parties was adopted in 2003. In 2014, a new Regulation was adopted, which will apply from 2017. Controversy 7.1 highlights the debate on the definition of a 'European political party' that surrounded both Regulations.

The 'Party Regulation' has had important practical implications. Until the adoption of the Regulation, European party federations had been closely tied to their political groups in the European Parliament. They received most of their funding from the budgets of the political groups, and it was common for the staff of European party federations to be seconded from the EP secretariat. The Party Regulation provides for a clear separation between political groups in the EP and European political parties. Political parties now receive their funding directly from the EU, while they are required to hire their own staff. In response to the Party Regulation, and in particular the funding opportunities attached to it, the Greens and the EFA further formalized their party structures. In addition, several new European political parties were recognized in the years following the adoption of the Regulation. The Alliance of European Conservatives and Reformists, which we met in the introduction to this chapter, was one of them.

The thirteen European political parties

As of 2014, there are thirteen official European political parties. These parties are listed in Table 7.2. These thirteen European political parties represent most of the major political families that have traditionally been present in the EU member states. This is further highlighted in Fact file 7.1. Exceptions are the agrarian parties, which are represented in a number of member states but are not organized in a separate EU-level political party.

Six out of the seven political groups in the European Parliament now have a counterpart European political party (or, in the case of ALDE and the Greens/ EFA group, two counterpart parties). Only the EFDD group has no link to a European political party, even though many of its views coincide with those of the European Union Democrats. The European Alliance for Freedom brings together representatives from several radical right-wing Eurosceptic parties, such as France's Front National, the Austrian Freiheitliche Partei Österreichs (FPÖ) and the Dutch Party for Freedom. These parties are represented in the EP and tried to form a political group after the 2014 elections, but they failed to reach the required membership threshold.

Controversy 7.1

What is a European political party?

The Party Regulation stipulates five criteria for an organization to be recognized as a 'European political party'. This recognition is required to receive financial support from the EU:

- It must have its seat in an EU member state.
- It must, either:
  - be represented, in at least one quarter of member states, by members of the European Parliament or in the national parliaments or regional parliaments or in the regional assemblies;
    or:
  - have received, in at least one quarter of the member states, at least 3% of the votes cast in each of those member states at the most recent European Parliament elections.
- It must observe the principles on which the European Union is founded. In the 2003 Regulation, these were specified as the principles of liberty, democracy, respect for human rights and fundamental freedoms, and the rule of law. The 2014 Regulation includes the values of respect for human dignity, freedom, democracy, equality, the rule of law and respect for human rights, including the rights of persons belonging to minorities. These are identical to the values that, according to Article 2 of the Treaty on European Union, the EU as a whole is founded on.
- It must have participated in elections to the European Parliament, or have expressed the intention to do so.
- It may not pursue profit goals.

This definition was the outcome of prolonged debate. Several issues were at stake in that debate. First, how 'transnational' should a European political party be? The Party Regulation sets the threshold at one-quarter of the member states, but earlier proposals referred to one-third of all member states. Apart from specific thresholds, more principled questions can be asked. Why should a party that focuses on the EU be excluded if it is active in only one member state? Or, by contrast, shouldn't we expect a European political party to aspire to be active in (almost) all member states rather than just one-quarter or one-third?

Second, should a party be required to subscribe to certain fundamental values? Some Eurosceptic political parties were afraid that the reference to 'the principles/values on which the European Union is founded' would exclude them. Similarly, extreme rightist groups could be denied funding on the basis of the principles included in the Regulation. Should EU democracy be protected against such parties or, rather, is it undemocratic to deny them funding on the basis of their beliefs? Do you think the new wording in the 2014 Regulation makes a difference compared to the terms used in the 2003 Regulation?

Table 7.2 The thirteen officially recognized European political parties (as of March 2014)

European political party	Party family	Affiliation with EP political group	Website
European People's Party (EPP)	Christian Democratic	EPP	www.epp.eu
Party of European Socialists (PES)	Socialist (social-democratic)	S&D	www.pes.eu
Alliance of Liberals and Democrats for Europe Party (ALDE)	Liberal	ALDE	www.aldeparty.eu
European Democratic Party (EDP)	Centrist (pro-EU)	ALDE	www.pde-edp.eu
Alliance of European Conservatives and Reformists (AECR)	Conservative	ECR	www.aecr.eu
Party of the European Left (EL)	Socialist (ex-communist)	EUL/NGL	www.european-left.org
European Green Party (EGP)	Green	Greens/EFA	www.europeangreens.eu
European Free Alliance (EFA)	Regionalist	Greens/EFA	www.e-f-a.org
European Alliance for Freedom (EAF)	Radical right-wing	None	www.eurallfree.org
Movement for a Europe of Liberties and Democracy (MELD)	Eurosceptic	None	www.meldeuropa.com
Alliance of European National Movements (AEMN)	Radical right-wing	None	www.aemn.info
Europeans United for Democracy (EUD)	Eurosceptic	None	www.europeansunitedfordemocracy.org
European Christian Political Movement (ECPM)	Orthodox Christian Democratic	None	www.ecpm.info

Fact file 7.1

Party families

Although political parties were created within individual countries, specific parties from different countries often show close ideological affinities. Therefore, parties from different countries can be grouped in 'party families', which share a common ideological background. In *Foundations of Comparative Politics* (2nd edn, Cambridge University Press, 2009), Kenneth Newton and Jan van Deth discern seven main party families:

- Socialist parties, including ex-communist, left-socialist and social democratic parties;
- Christian Democratic parties;
- Agrarian parties;
- Liberal parties;
- Conservative parties;
- Nationalist, regional and minority ethnic parties, including radical right-wing parties and (either right- or left-wing) regionalist parties;
- Green parties.

The roles and functions of European political parties

European political parties and the EP elections

Although European political parties are now more clearly separated from political groups in the European Parliament, their main activities remain linked to the EP. In fact, as we saw in Controversy 7.1, to be recognized a European political party should be active in EP elections or declare that it aspires to be. Historically, as well, the creation of European party federations was closely linked to the development of the European Parliament. In practice, however, the role of European political parties in relation to the EP and EP elections remains limited. After all, elections to the EP are contested by *domestic* parties in *national* elections for *national* shares of seats in the EP. This means that the selection of candidates is done by domestic parties, not by the European political party. Also, the election campaigns are organized and conducted by domestic parties, not the European political party. Most domestic political parties have been reluctant to cede a greater role to European political parties in these areas. In that regard, they guard their party's 'sovereignty' as jealously as many member state governments guard their state's sovereignty.

The most important role for European political parties with regard to EP elections is to coordinate the party positions of their members. Starting with the first direct elections to the EP in 1979, all major European political parties have presented party manifestos before each EP election. These party manifestos represent a consensus among the members of the European political party on the positions to be taken on important issues in the elections, but they only play a minor role in the actual election campaigns.

European political parties and the other EU institutions

Outside of EP elections, some European political parties have sought to become active in the other EU institutions. This makes sense if parties want to exert influence over EU policies. After all, in the EU's fragmented decision-making system, being active in the EP only brings one so far. It would vastly increase the power of a political party if it could also coordinate participants in the European Council, the Council of Ministers or even the European Commission. In each of these institutions, participants have a party-political background and their parties are usually members of one of the European political parties. This is also true of the Committee of the Regions, whose members are organized in political groups.

These opportunities for political coordination outside the EP are mainly relevant for the three largest party families in the EU (the Christian Democrats, the Socialists and the Liberals) because they tend to supply most ministers, heads of government and commissioners. The EPP, the PES and the ALDE organize meetings between the leaders of their member parties (whether or not they are currently in government in their country) on the eve of European Council meetings in order to discuss the issues on the agenda. In this way, they try to come to a joint 'Christian Democratic', 'Socialist' or 'Liberal' voice in the European Council.

Officially, the European Commission does not operate on a party-political basis. However, most commissioners are former national politicians with close links to a political party. Each of the larger European political parties now identifies 'its' commissioners on its website. These commissioners may even join the party leaders' meeting before a European Council meeting.

In the run-up to the 2014 EP elections, the largest European political parties designated their own candidates for Commission president. These candidates became known as the 'Spitzenkandidaten', after the German word for 'top candidate'. After the elections, when the EPP turned out to have won most seats, a majority in the EP was able to force member state governments to accept the EPP candidate, Jean-Claude Juncker, despite initial opposition from some heads of government. This was not only a new step in the relationship between the EP and the member states and the stakes involved in EP elections, but also marked a stronger role for European political parties.

Comparing European and domestic political parties

When we compare the roles and activities of European political parties with their counterparts in the EU member states, several important differences can be observed. One way of looking at these differences in a systematic way is to compare the functions that political parties perform at the domestic and European levels. Table 7.3 lists the five main functions of domestic political parties, and the extent to which European political parties perform them.

Domestic political parties perform each of the five functions listed in Table 7.3, although there may be differences in the extent to which they focus on one or the other. European political parties, by contrast, perform a much more limited set of functions. To start with the functions that are performed

Table 7.3 The functions of domestic and European political parties

Domestic political parties …	European political parties …
1. Structure the choice offered to voters by presenting a limited number of clear alternatives in elections and by organizing elected representatives in parliament.	Structure the choice offered to voters by organizing a wide range of domestic parties into a more limited set of European parties that will form political groups in the EP after the elections.
2. Aggregate interests by putting together more or less coherent packages of positions on a wide range of issues.	Aggregate interests by formulating joint party manifestos and by facilitating debate and exchange between domestic parties.
3. Recruit candidates for political office and socialize them into existing political routines.	Do *not* recruit or socialize candidates for political office.
4. Form governments.	Do *not* form the EU government.
5. Form a liaison between the state, on the one hand, and voters and civil society, on the other.	*Hardly* form direct liaisons between the EU institutions and citizens or civil society.

by both, domestic and European political parties structure the choice offered to voters. Without political parties, voters would face a potentially limitless array of possible vote options, each representing a different combination of policy positions. Like domestic political parties, European political parties offer a much more limited number of options by organizing domestic parties into broader European platforms.

Second, both domestic and European political parties aggregate interests by formulating more or less coherent 'packages' of policy positions, often based on a shared ideology. In the absence of parties, politics would revolve around a struggle between special-interest groups that are active on only one or a few related issues. Both domestic and European political parties bring together these separate interests by formulating overarching party programmes.

Yet, European political parties are much less active on the other three functions that domestic political parties usually perform. To begin with, with the notable exception of the 'Spitzenkandidaten', European political parties do not recruit or socialize candidates for political office. This is a key function of domestic political parties, and one that accounts for much of their importance in domestic politics. When it comes to the European level, however, most of the recruitment and socialization of candidates remains the exclusive responsibility of the domestic parties that are members of the European party.

Neither do European political parties form the EU government. Although the political profile of European Commissioners has become more pronounced over the years, the Commission as a whole does not have a clear party-political profile and it is not formed by political parties or the parliamentary majority after the EP elections.

Finally, because European political parties are confederations of domestic parties, they hardly form direct liaisons between the EU institutions and citizens or civil society. The core members of European political parties are domestic political parties. A number of European political parties also admit individual citizens as members alongside domestic parties. In order to establish links with citizens and civil society, some European parties have created organizations for specific groups of citizens, such as a youth association or a women's association. Moreover, several European political parties have created separate 'European political foundations', which act as a think tank for the party and a platform for debate with civil society. These initiatives notwithstanding, the role played by citizens in European parties is limited, and domestic parties remain firmly in the driving seat when it comes to determining the course and activities of European political parties.

All in all, then, European political parties are best seen as cooperation frameworks between domestic parties. They focus on bringing together, facilitating and coordinating member state political elites rather than organizing voters and citizens. Even at the elite level, some of the key functions of political parties (recruiting candidates for political office and forming governments) are carried out by domestic parties. As a result, European political parties are not (yet) fully fledged political parties but they have succeeded in establishing themselves as mediators between the various domestic parties at the EU level.

■ Summary

This chapter has dealt with the role of political parties in EU politics. It argues that:

- Three types of 'political party' play a role in EU politics: domestic political parties, political groups in the EP and European political parties. Among these three types, domestic political parties play the central role because they create and manage the other two.
- Since the early days of the ECSC, political groups in the European Parliament have formed around shared ideologies rather than nationality.
- The EP's rules of procedure stimulate the formation of transnational political groups by granting them specific rights and benefits.
- In addition, MEPs from different domestic parties have an incentive to work together in order to have more influence on EP decision-making.
- Nevertheless, tensions remain between the benefits of working together in transnational political groups and the need for domestic parties to give up some of their policy positions.
- Despite the tensions inherent in their formation, political groups in the EP tend to vote together in the vast majority of cases. As a result, they are remarkably cohesive.
- Politics in the EP is structured predominantly along a right/left dimension, with an additional dimension that revolves around support for and opposition to further European integration.

- Coalitions between political groups in the EP are not fixed but are formed on the basis of shared policy positions on certain issues.
- European political parties originated in response to developments in the European Parliament. However, they have become increasingly independent from the political groups in the EP.
- The existing European political parties reflect most of the main party families to be found in the EU member states.
- The largest European political parties now also try to organize their party members in the Council and the College of Commissioners.
- The functions performed by European political parties are more limited than those performed by domestic political parties. In particular, European political parties structure politics by limiting the number of choices and aggregate interests in more or less consistent policy programmes. At the same time, they do not recruit candidates for political office, do not form governments, and hardly form a link between rulers and ruled in the EU.

Further reading

A good collection of essays on the development of European parties, with contributions on each of the major parties, is Pascal Delwit, Erol Külahci and Cédric van de Walle (eds), *The Europarties: Organisation and Influence* (CEVIPOL, 2004). The most extensive study of party politics in the European Parliament is Simon Hix, Abdul Noury and Gérard Roland, *Democratic Politics in the European Parliament* (Cambridge University Press, 2007). Amie Kreppel, *The European Parliament and Supranational Party System* (Cambridge University Press, 2002) traces the development of political groups in the EP and the evolution of the EP as a legislature since 1957. A collection of studies on the role of political parties in the various EU institutions can be found in Björn Lindberg, Anne Rasmussen and Andreas Warntjen (eds), *The Role of Political Parties in the European Union* (Routledge, 2010). These contributions were also published as a special issue of the *Journal of European Public Policy*, 15, 8, 2008.

Websites

- European Parliament: www.europarl.europa.eu
- The site www.votewatch.eu contains the voting records of MEPs and political groups, as well as analysis and background information.
- For the websites of the political groups in the EP, see Table 7.1 above.
- For the websites of the thirteen European political parties, see Table 7.2 above.

Navigating the EU

On the website www.navigatingthe.eu you will find online exercises for this chapter.

PART III

EU policies: agenda-setting, decision-making and implementation

8　An overview of EU policy-making

■ Introduction

When you work in a factory, EU law is everywhere. To begin with, the European Union has set a wide range of standards in the field of working conditions. For instance, an EU directive specifies the safety standards for the equipment you work with. Another directive regulates safety and health signs at work. Depending on the type of industry and the type of work you do, you are protected by specific legislation relating to dangerous chemicals and exposure to noise or radiation. Your maximum number of hours at work is covered by the Working Time Directive. Moreover, if your company goes bankrupt, or if it is taken over by another company, your rights as an employee are protected by EU law.

At the same time, the EU's role in this field is largely confined to adopting legislation and setting standards. To begin with, the actual implementation of the policies is left to member state governments. Moreover, although the EU is very active in the field of regulatory policy (promulgating norms and standards), it is much less involved in distributive policies (financing facilities) and redistributive policies (affecting the distribution of income and wealth). EU legislation may protect safety at work, but if an accident occurs and you become disabled, your entitlement to a disability benefit is determined by national law. The EU plays no role in determining the eligibility criteria or the height and duration of the benefits. And if you receive a benefit, it is funded by the government or an insurance scheme in your country, not the EU.

Occupational health and safety is just one of many areas in which the EU is active. Yet, as we saw above, there are also areas in which the EU plays a much smaller role. This chapter seeks to sketch the broader picture within which the subsequent chapters on agenda-setting, decision-making and implementation of EU policies can be placed. After reading this chapter, you should know what types of policy the EU makes, in which areas it is important and in which areas it plays a smaller role, and how the role of the EU in policy-making has evolved over the past decade. Therefore, we will address the following questions:

- What policy areas is the EU involved in and why?
- What role does the EU play in (re-)distributive policies?
- What types of regulatory policy does the EU pursue?
- How much policy does the EU make?
- How has the EU's policy-making role evolved over the past decade?

In answering these questions, we will see that the EU plays a wide range of roles in policy-making: from strict European regulation of activities to looser forms of coordination between member states. In (re-)distributive policy, the EU's roles are even more lopsided, since the vast majority of the EU budget goes to only a few policy areas. For the final question, about the evolution of the EU's role, we will look at two areas that are at the 'frontier' of EU policy-making: Economic and Monetary Union (EMU) and EU foreign policy. These two areas have experienced significant developments in the EU's policy-making activities in recent years. This shows that the EU's role in policy-making is not fixed but changes over time. Moreover, the developments in EMU and foreign policy have not just been 'more of the same' but have involved types of policies that have the potential to change the relationship between the EU and its member states in fundamental ways. For those reasons, they merit closer attention.

■ What does the EU do?

Over the years, the EU has become active in a wide range of policy areas. As a result, it is increasingly difficult to name a policy area in which the EU plays no role at all. Nevertheless, there are vast differences in the degree of EU involvement in various areas. Table 8.1 gives an overview of policy areas ranging from policies that are (almost) completely determined at the EU level, through areas in which the EU has a strong and a weak involvement, respectively, to areas that are the (nearly) exclusive province of the member states.

Table 8.1 shows that only a few areas are fully dealt with at the EU level. This is the case for the 'classic' EU policies of external trade (that is, trade with countries outside of the EU), competition policy, agriculture and fisheries. In these areas, comprehensive EU policies have been developed and all major decisions are taken at the EU level. Since the introduction of the Euro,

Table 8.1 EU involvement in policy areas

(Almost) exclusively EU	Strong EU involvement	Weak EU involvement	(Almost) exclusively member states
Examples:	Examples:	Examples:	Examples:
• External trade	• Environment	• Social policy	• Primary and secondary
• Competition	• Regional policy	• Foreign	education
policy	• Occupational	policy	• Housing
• Agriculture	health and safety	• Defence	• Crime 'on the streets'
• Fisheries	• Internal market	• Taxation	• Culture
• Euro	• Tobacco control	• Health care	
	• Cross-border crime	• Spatial	
	• Development aid	planning	
	• Transport		
	• Research and		
	development		

decisions on monetary policy (for instance, setting interest rates) have also been taken at the EU level, but only for those member states that have adopted the Euro.

On the other side of the table are policy areas in which the EU plays no or hardly any role. These include some of the typical 'local' issues, such as housing, and crime that takes place 'on the streets' such as burglary, theft, domestic violence and disturbances of the public order. In addition, the EU plays a very small role when it comes to policy areas that are closely linked to the 'national identity' of the member states, such as primary and secondary education and cultural policy. These areas are almost exclusively dealt with by the member state governments themselves and in some federal member states even by regional governments.

In between are policy areas in which the EU does play a role, but to a greater or lesser extent. The EU plays an important role in areas such as environmental policy and occupational health and safety, where it has built up extensive bodies of legislation covering a wide range of issues and aspects. This is also true of specific issues within wider policy areas in which the EU plays a smaller role. For example, the EU plays an important role in tobacco control policies, although it is much less involved in health policies in general.

In addition, the EU plays a smaller, 'supportive' role in a range of policy areas that are still predominantly dealt with by member state governments. In some of these areas, the EU focuses specifically on cross-border issues. For example, the way health care is organized and financed is decided exclusively by member state governments. The EU has no say in this. But if you are from one EU member state and fall ill in another member state, EU legislation does specify your right to treatment in that other member state and who will pay the costs for this. Likewise, social insurance and pension policies are determined by (and vary widely between) the member states. Yet, the EU has adopted legislation for situations in which workers move between or are active in different member states. The EU also plays a smaller role in areas that are close to the 'core' of state sovereignty, such as foreign policy and defence policy. Here, member state governments have been extremely reluctant to allow a greater role for the EU, both because foreign and defence policies go to the core of what it means to be a 'sovereign' state and because foreign policy priorities and preferences differ widely between the EU member states. Therefore, for all policy areas in the 'weak involvement' category the EU is involved in a supportive role, leaving the key policy decisions firmly at the member state level.

■ The limits of (re-)distributive policies in the EU

Types of policy in the EU

In the previous section, we looked at the extent to which the EU plays a role in various policy areas. However, apart from the *extent* of EU involvement, it is also important to look at the *ways in which* the EU is involved. In 1964, American political scientist Theodore Lowi introduced a threefold typology of public policies that can help us understand the types of EU involvement (Theodore J. Lowi, 'American Business, Public Policy, Case-Studies, and Political Theory', *World Politics*, 16, 4, 1964: 677–715). According to Lowi, governments pursue three different types of public policy:

- Distributive policies, which serve a specific group in society. Examples are government investment in a road or a subsidy to a theatre company.
- Regulatory policies, which set general norms for certain types of activities. Examples include rules and regulations to prevent pollution or legislation on equal opportunities in the workplace.
- Redistributive policies, which transfer money from some groups to other groups. Examples of this category are unemployment benefits or policies of progressive taxation.

Modern governments engage in each of these three types of policy. The EU, by contrast, is overwhelmingly concerned with the second type of policy: regulation. The limited role of (re-)distribution in the EU can be seen by taking a look at the EU budget. Table 8.2 shows the total budget for the EU and for governments in a number of EU member states, both in Euros and as a percentage of that country's (or the EU's) **gross domestic product** (GDP).

Gross domestic product (GDP) is a measure of the size of an economy, which equals the total value of goods and services produced in a country in a given year.

As Table 8.2 shows, European governments typically spend almost half their country's GDP. To be sure, there are vast differences between member states. In Denmark, the EU member state where government spending relative to the entire economy is highest, government expenditures accounted for some 59% of GDP in 2012. In Lithuania, the member state with the lowest government

Table 8.2 Government spending in 2012 in the EU and selected member states

Member state/EU	Budget (billions of Euros)	As a percentage of GDP
Denmark	146	59.4
United Kingdom	925	48.1
Germany	1,191	44.7
Ireland	70	42.6
Lithuania	12	36.1
All EU member states	6,378	49.3
European Union	129	1.0

Sources: Eurostat, Annual Government Finance Statistics and European Union Budget for the Financial Year 2012.

spending, it was a bit over 36%. Still, the differences between member states are small compared to the difference with the EU. Whereas each member state government spends more than 30% of its country's GDP, the EU only spends around 1% of European GDP.

The difference becomes clear if you think of some of the things that member state governments spend money on, such as dispensing unemployment benefits, building hospitals, subsidizing housing or paying police staff. These are all things that the EU does not do. As we saw above, the EU is not responsible for social benefits, only for coordinating cross-border use of those benefits. Also, the EU does not finance health systems, it does not have an army, nor does it hire and pay police staff, fire service staff, doctors or nurses.

Where the EU gets its money from

The difference between the EU and member state governments can also be seen on the revenue side of the budget. The EU budget is financed from three main sources:

- customs and agricultural duties levied on imports into the EU (in EU parlance these are known as the 'Traditional Own Resources' or TOR);
- member state contributions based on the value added tax (VAT) levied;
- member state contributions based on their gross national income (GNI, a measure that is similar to the GDP).

Figure 8.1 shows the composition of the EU's revenues in terms of these sources.

Over time, member state contributions based on the size of their economy (that is, their GNI) have become more important. In 2014, they accounted for almost three-quarters of all EU revenues. Import duties and contributions based on member states' VAT revenues make up most of the remainder of the budget. Until the late 1980s, these two sources accounted for almost the entire EU budget, but since then they have gradually been replaced by

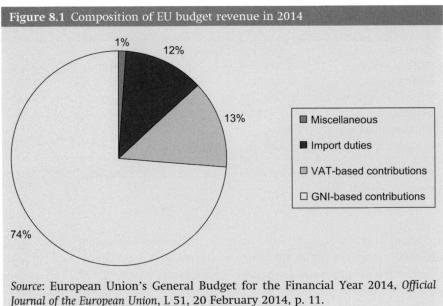

Figure 8.1 Composition of EU budget revenue in 2014

Source: European Union's General Budget for the Financial Year 2014, *Official Journal of the European Union*, L 51, 20 February 2014, p. 11.

contributions based on GNI. The relative importance of duties has diminished as the EU has liberalized its agricultural and trade policies. In addition, a shift has taken place from VAT-based to GNI-based contributions. The reason for this is that the GNI better reflects differences in affluence between member states than VAT revenues and hence member states' (economic) 'ability to pay'. In addition, it is much easier to calculate the GNI than to assess VAT revenues.

Compared to member state governments, the EU lacks two important sources of revenue:

- The EU does not impose its own taxes. There is no EU income tax or EU value added tax. Member states contribute to the EU budget partly on the basis of their VAT revenues but this is only a small part of those revenues.
- The EU does not borrow money. Member state governments can borrow money in order to cover budget deficits. However, the EU is not allowed to run a budget deficit.

These differences practically rule out a role for the EU in macroeconomic policies. Decisions on tax rates and budget deficits are important ways for governments to pursue economic and redistributive objectives. Think, for instance, of the huge rises in budget deficits following the financial crisis of 2008. For member state governments this was a way to cushion the effects of the crisis on the economy. This is something the EU cannot do, simply because it does not have the financial means to engage in large-scale economic policies. As a result, distributive and redistributive policies, which require vast amounts of money, are much less important for the EU than they are for member state

Controversy 8.1

What type of EU do we want?

On 23 January 2013, British Prime Minister David Cameron delivered a long-awaited speech, in which he set out his vision for the European Union. He started by arguing that the EU had contributed to securing peace in Europe, but added: '[T]oday, the main, over-riding purpose of the European Union is different: not to win peace, but to secure prosperity.'

He then defined three major challenges confronting the EU:

- the 'problems in the Eurozone';
- the 'crisis of European competitiveness';
- the 'gap between the EU and its citizens which has grown dramatically in recent years'.

To address these challenges, Cameron proposed a set of principles for 'a new European Union'. He argued that the completion of the single market (that is: free trade between the EU member states) should be the core task of the EU. In addition, he argued for a more central role of the member states in the EU, by allowing more flexibility (the 'enhanced cooperation' that was discussed in Chapter 4), the abolition of EU legislation in certain areas (such as working hours and parts of environmental, social and justice policies) and a greater role for national parliaments in EU decision-making.

Do you agree with David Cameron's diagnosis of the key challenges facing the EU? And do you think his proposals will help to solve these issues? If not, what alternative course of action would you envisage for the EU?

Source: David Cameron, *EU Speech at Bloomberg* (www.gov.uk/government/speeches/eu-speech-at-bloomberg).

governments. Some have argued that the EU should play a greater role in these areas, while others think the EU should focus on a limited number of activities. Controversy 8.1 presents one such proposal for further discussion.

What the EU spends its money on

Differences between the EU and its member states relate not just to the overall size of the budget and the sources of revenue but also to the composition of expenditures. Figure 8.2 shows how the EU has spent its money across a number of major budget categories between 1980 and 2015.

Two budget categories stand out: agriculture and structural funds. Together, these two policy areas alone account for some 75% of all EU spending. As a result, these are the only two policy areas in which the EU pursues substantive (re-)distributive policies. However, between these two categories, there has

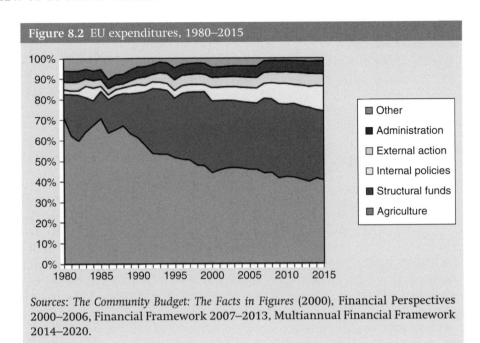

Figure 8.2 EU expenditures, 1980–2015

Sources: *The Community Budget: The Facts in Figures* (2000), Financial Perspectives 2000–2006, Financial Framework 2007–2013, Multiannual Financial Framework 2014–2020.

been a marked shift. Whereas agricultural policy took up more than 70% of the EU budget in 1980, this share had been reduced to a bit over 40% in 2015. During the same period, the structural funds have grown in size, from a little over 10% in 1980 to around 34% in 2015.

The **Common Agricultural Policy (CAP)** is the set of EU policies designed to regulate agricultural markets and provide financial support to farmers.

The EU's **Common Agricultural Policy** (CAP) was set up to provide farmers with a fixed income by guaranteeing minimum prices for their produce. As agricultural production in the EU soared, so did the amount of agricultural subsidies paid by the EU. Since the early 1990s, the EU has engaged in a series of reforms of the CAP meant to reduce the level of subsidies for farmers. This explains the decrease in the share of CAP spending noted above. Even then, the CAP remains the single most important item on the EU budget.

Cohesion policy is the set of EU policies designed to reduce economic disparities between regions by giving financial support to economically underdeveloped regions in the EU member states.

Structural funds are the financial part of the EU's regional policy (also called **cohesion policy**). They include three specific funds:

- The European Regional Development Fund (ERDF) is the largest of the three funds. It supports investments to stimulate economic development, so as to reduce economic disparities across the EU. ERDF funds go to regions in all EU member states, but the largest share is reserved for economically less well-developed regions. Under the heading of 'European territorial cooperation', ERDF funds are also used to support cooperation projects between regions in different member states.

- The European Social Fund (ESF) subsidizes projects aimed at reducing unemployment. This includes, for instance, initiatives to help entrepreneurs and small and medium-sized enterprises (SMEs) and training programmes for unemployed people.
- The Cohesion Fund is specifically focused on member states with a GNI per inhabitant of less than 90% of the EU average. This includes all member states in Central and Eastern Europe, plus Cyprus, Greece, Malta and Portugal. Money from the Cohesion Fund can be used for investments in transport infrastructure and environmental projects.

Other budget items are much smaller, but may still be important for the sectors concerned. As part of its internal policies, the EU spends quite a sizeable sum of money to subsidize research and development, which is related to the aim of making the European economy more competitive. Expenditures under the heading of 'external action' include first and foremost aid to developing countries, which the EU gives alongside its member states. Administrative costs (such as paying for personnel and office space) form only a small part of the overall EU budget.

All in all, (re-)distributive policies in the EU take a very specific form, as reflected in the size of the EU budget, the sources of revenue and the composition of expenditures. Only in two areas (agriculture and regional policy) does the EU play an important (re-)distributive role. In all other policy areas, the EU's role is predominantly regulatory in nature. We will turn to regulatory policies in the next section but first we will take a look at budgetary politics in the EU.

Budgetary politics in the EU

Although the EU budget is small compared to national government budgets, budgetary politics is among the most contentious issues in the EU. One reason for this is that the financial costs and benefits of the EU are much easier to quantify than the costs and benefits of regulatory policies or the increase in affluence and security that the EU offers. Most of the budgetary battles have focused on the contributions that member states pay to, and the revenues they receive from, the EU. The balance between contributions and receipts is known as the 'operating budgetary balance' of a member state. Table 8.3 gives an overview of the member states that are net contributors to and net recipients from the EU in terms of this operating budgetary balance, based on figures from the European Commission over 2012 (and therefore not yet including Croatia, which only joined the EU in 2013).

The operating budgetary balance of a member state is determined by two things: the size of its contributions to the EU and the amount of money it receives, in particular from the EU's agricultural and cohesion policies. It is no

Table 8.3 Net contributors and recipients in the EU in 2012 (figures in millions of Euros)

Member state	Net contribution	As % of national GNI	Member state	Net receipts	As % of national GNI
Sweden	1,925	0.46	Spain	3,999	0.39
Denmark	1,126	0.45	Ireland	671	0.50
Germany	11,954	0.44	Malta	71	1.14
France	8,298	0.40	Romania	2032	1.56
Belgium	1,494	0.39	Slovenia	572	1.63
Netherlands	2,365	0.39	Czech Republic	3,045	2.14
United Kingdom	7,366	0.39	Slovakia	1,597	2.28
Austria	1,073	0.35	Greece	4,545	2.33
Finland	659	0.34	Portugal	5,027	3.12
Italy	5,058	0.33	Poland	11,997	3.30
Luxembourg	80	0.25	Bulgaria	1,330	3.43
Cyprus	25	0.15	Hungary	3,280	3.59
			Latvia	956	4.29
			Lithuania	1,514	4.82
			Estonia	785	4.84

Source: European Commission, EU Budget 2012 Financial Report, p. 111.

surprise, then, that the list of net contributors (relative to GDP) is led by Sweden, an affluent member state with a relatively small agricultural sector. Although there are more net recipients than contributors (fifteen versus twelve, in 2012), the net receipts of member states benefiting from the EU tend to be higher relative to their economy than the net contributions of the EU's 'paymasters'. The reason for this is that the level of economic development varies greatly across the EU. Not only do the twelve net contributors include all large member states, but these member states are also among the most affluent in the EU. While in 2012 around 65% of the EU population lived in the twelve net contributors, the combined GDP of these member states was nearly 75% of the EU total. This difference can be illustrated by comparing the net contribution of Italy and the net receipts of Portugal in Table 8.3. In absolute terms (i.e. in Euros), the Italian contribution more or less equalled the Portuguese receipts, but relative to their economies the figure was more than nine times higher for Portugal.

Budgetary politics has been particularly important for a number of member states. Some net contributors with relatively high contributions and small agricultural sectors have demanded, and obtained, reductions on their EU contributions. Without these reductions, the Netherlands, Sweden and the UK would pay more to the EU than the figures in Table 8.3 indicate. Conversely, EU receipts have been important sources of revenue for some of the poorer member states in Southern Europe and, since their accession, for Central and Eastern European member states. These member states have often fought hard to maintain their share of EU funds and have made their support for the EU budget, treaty changes or other proposals contingent on the financial contributions they receive. Similarly, member states with large agricultural sectors, which benefit from the CAP, have often blocked attempts by other member states to scale down the size of the EU's agricultural expenditures.

◼ Regulatory policies in the EU: the internal market and beyond

As we saw in the previous section, the EU is primarily involved in regulatory policies. In this section, we will take a closer look at the types of regulatory policy that the EU is engaged in. In so doing, three types can be discerned, which also developed in the EU roughly in this order over time:

- regulation aimed at market integration;
- regulation aimed at mitigating the negative impacts of economic activity;
- regulation not (directly) related to economic activities.

Let us take a closer look at each of these three types.

Regulation aimed at market integration: negative integration and positive integration

In the 1950s, the EU started out as a market integration scheme. The aim of its member states was to form a common market (nowadays normally called 'internal market') to facilitate intra-European trade. In doing so, they adopted a dual strategy which has become known as 'negative integration' and 'positive integration'.

Negative integration
Negative integration consists of eliminating barriers to trade. It is called 'negative' because it stipulates what member state governments cannot do. A good example is the prohibition on levying customs duties on imports from other member states. In the EU, this is prohibited because customs duties are a barrier to trade. Likewise, member states are prohibited from setting quotas, which specify the maximum amount of a product that can be imported (or exported) in a given period. Yet, negative integration goes beyond such obvious things as customs duties. If a member state government adopts a law or a policy that (directly or indirectly) benefits domestic producers to the detriment of producers from other member states, this too constitutes a barrier to trade and is forbidden under EU law. A good example was the 'Buy Irish' campaign organized in the early 1980s by the Irish government, which was meant to encourage Irish consumers to buy Irish (rather than imported) products. Because this campaign sought

> **Negative integration** is the abolition of trade barriers that are imposed by member states.

189

actively to prevent consumers from buying products from other member states, it violated EU rules on free trade.

Often, a member state measure that (allegedly) distorts trade is much more subtle. An example of this was the case of Nicolas Decker, a Luxembourg citizen who had bought a pair of glasses in Belgium (on prescription from his Luxembourg doctor) and now claimed the costs from his (Luxembourgian) health insurance company. The health insurance company refused to reimburse the costs because Decker had not asked their permission before buying his glasses abroad, even though the health insurance regulations explicitly required him to do so. The issues raised by this case were much more complicated than those in the 'Buy Irish' case because the insurance company (and many member state governments with it) argued that authorization prior to buying medical equipment abroad was necessary to ensure the quality of health-care provision and keep the costs of the health-care system in check. Nevertheless, the Court of Justice concluded in this case, too, that the requirement to ask prior permission was an impermissible restriction on the free movement of goods between member states, and Decker should have his costs reimbursed.

Therefore, the central issue (often, dilemma) in negative integration is to distinguish member state measures that are meant to protect domestic producers by discouraging trade with other member states from member state measures that restrict trade but serve a legitimate purpose, such as protecting consumers, public health or the environment. The former are prohibited, the latter are allowed. The Court of Justice has developed an extensive and subtle case law to make this distinction. A key ruling in this regard has been the 1979 *Cassis de Dijon* case. It provides a good illustration of the steps that the Court takes in determining whether a member state measure is allowed. Briefing 8.1 shows how this works and explains the important principle of 'mutual recognition' that underlies the Court's case law in this area.

Positive integration

Negative integration can go a long way towards creating a common market by systematically eliminating barriers to trade. This, however, is a cumbersome procedure. Firms, member state governments or the European Commission need to go to the Court of Justice each time they believe that a member state imposes unjustified barriers to trade. Moreover, for some issues simply eliminating national laws may threaten other values, such as environmental or consumer protection. In those cases, an alternative to negative integration is to adopt EU legislation in order to create one set of norms and standards for the entire EU (for the applicable procedures, see Chapter 4). This is called **positive integration** because new (EU) laws substitute for existing member state laws: rather than saying what laws member states cannot adopt, they are told what laws they have to adopt.

Positive integration (also known as **harmonization** or the **approximation of laws**) is the adoption of EU laws to reduce the differences between member state laws in a given area.

Briefing 8.1

Mutual recognition and Cassis de Dijon

The CJ's 1979 *Cassis de Dijon* ruling (Case C-120/78) is a milestone in the Court's case law on negative integration. Cassis de Dijon (also known as Crème de Cassis) is a French fruit liqueur. In Germany, however, it could not be sold as 'liqueur' because it contained less than 25% alcohol. According to the German government, this minimum alcohol limit was necessary for two reasons. First, it was meant to discourage the marketing of low-alcohol drinks which, so the German government argued, would more easily 'induce a tolerance towards alcohol than more highly alcoholic drinks'. Second, consumers might be misled when they bought a drink sold as 'liqueur' that turned out to contain less alcohol than they expected. This would give an unfair advantage to producers of (cheaper) low-alcohol drinks.

In its ruling on the case, the Court of Justice carefully reviewed these lines of argument. Its line of reasoning proceeded in three steps, which are typical of the way the Court deals with free movement cases:

- In the first step, the Court assessed whether the prohibition to sell Cassis de Dijon as a 'liqueur' formed a barrier to trade. It concluded that it did because it had the effect of hindering trade between member states. As a result, the prohibition could only be justified if it served a legitimate purpose and if it was necessary for attaining that purpose.
- In the second step, the Court looked at the purpose of the German ban. It concluded that both the protection of public health and the protection of consumers are legitimate purposes for which member states may impose restrictions.
- In the third step, the German prohibition failed after all because requiring a minimum alcohol content in 'liqueur' was not necessary to attain either purpose. To begin with, the Court did not see how requiring liqueur to contain *more* alcohol would benefit public health. In addition, protecting consumers could be achieved by requiring the alcohol content to be put clearly on the label, a much less trade-restrictive measure with the same effect.

As a result, Germany could not prohibit the sale of Cassis de Dijon as 'liqueur'. The importance of the *Cassis de Dijon* ruling, and a series of similar rulings during the late 1970s, lay in the introduction of the principle of 'mutual recognition'. This principle states that member states cannot restrict the marketing of a product that is lawfully produced and marketed in another member state unless the restriction is needed to achieve some legitimate objective of public policy. This is the key principle underlying negative integration in the EU.

In many policy areas, this is how EU legislation started. For instance, EU legislation on the approval of new medicines is meant to prevent trade barriers between member states that would result from different national norms and standards, while at the same time guaranteeing a sound assessment of the quality of medicines. The same logic applied to much of the EU's earlier environmental legislation. Hence, positive integration is an instrument to facilitate market integration but in so doing it automatically leads to the consideration of other issues that may affect markets (such as the quality of medicines and the environment).

Regulation aimed at mitigating the negative impacts of economic activity

In addition to regulation aimed at market integration, the EU also adopts regulatory policies that are aimed at mitigating the negative impacts of economic activity. Above we mentioned the example of environmental policy, which partly started out as a way to ensure market integration. Since these beginnings in the 1970s, however, environmental issues have become independent concerns for the EU. This was formalized when the 1986 Single European Act introduced a separate legal basis for EU environmental legislation. This means that the EU can (and does) also adopt environmental measures simply for the sake of protecting the environment. The same is true of a number of other policy areas for which the EU has obtained an independent competence, such as the equal treatment of men and women and occupational health and safety.

Regulation aimed at mitigating the negative impacts of economic activity implies quite a significant broadening of the scope of the EU's remit and policies when compared to regulation that is aimed purely at market integration. Yet, it is still linked to economic activity in the sense that it seeks to mitigate the negative impacts of economic activity. After all, environmental pollution is the result of producing and consuming goods and services, while occupational health and safety is directly linked to the production of goods and services. This is different for the final type of EU regulatory policy.

Regulation not (directly) related to economic activities

Since the 1992 Maastricht Treaty, the EU has also been involved in issues that are not (directly) linked to economic activity, most notably foreign policy and justice and home affairs. This was an important step in the EU's development because it now firmly moved from being an 'economic' community to a 'political' one. In a broader sense, of course, foreign policy and justice and home affairs have links with economic issues, but the direct aims of these policies relate to other objectives: strengthening the role of the EU and its member states in global politics and preventing crime.

As in most other policy areas, the EU's role in these areas is predominantly regulatory in nature. The EU does not have its own army or police but it has adopted an increasing number of regulatory measures aimed at coordinating the policies and activities of member states. In particular since the early 2000s and the terrorist attacks of 9/11, the area of justice and home affairs has become a veritable growth market in EU policy-making. Developments in EU foreign policy have been slower but marked nonetheless. Later in this chapter, we will take a closer look at this gradual evolution of EU foreign policy over the past decade.

Over time, then, the EU has moved from a project aimed at market integration to a much broader union covering non-economic issues as well. In that regard, the EU has firmly moved 'beyond the internal market'. Still, the internal market and market integration remain key issue areas for the EU and make up much of its policy-making activities. In the next section, we will take a closer look at exactly what the EU's regulatory output entails.

■ The regulatory output of the European Union

When we want to understand what kind of regulatory policies the EU pursues, we should also look at its regulatory output: the numbers and types of Directives, Regulations and Decisions taken. Figure 8.3 shows the numbers of Directives, Regulations and Decisions adopted by the EU between 1975 and 2012.

In Chapter 4, we saw what types of decisions the EU can take. Figure 8.3 shows their relative importance in a quantitative sense. However, this is not the same as their qualitative importance. Regulations make up by far the largest proportion of EU regulatory output: more than two-thirds over the entire period 1975–2012. In comparison, Directives make up only a tiny proportion of the EU regulatory output: less than 4% over the same period. Still, in a qualitative sense, Directives are often seen as the most important type of EU legislation.

This paradox becomes more understandable when we look at the things Regulations and Directives are about. Fact file 8.1 gives some examples of Regulations, Directives, Decisions and Recommendations adopted in February and March 2014.

The examples show some typical features of each of these types of decision:

- Most Regulations are Commission Regulations, which specify more general provisions laid down in Directives and Regulations adopted by the Council (often together with the EP). Commission Regulations are used for two reasons: because they contain very specific, technical provisions and/or because they need to be updated regularly (see also the discussion of delegated and implementing acts in Chapter 11).
- Regulations are used most often in two policy areas: agriculture (including fisheries) and external trade. Fact file 8.1 gives examples of both. These are areas in which large numbers of specific rules need to be adopted on things

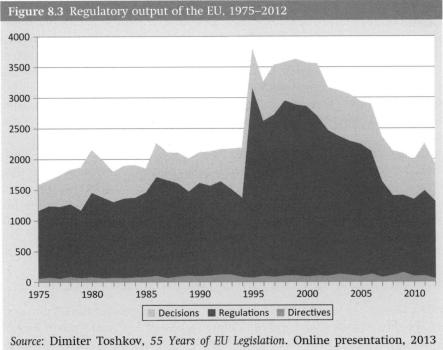

Figure 8.3 Regulatory output of the EU, 1975–2012

Source: Dimiter Toshkov, *55 Years of EU Legislation*. Online presentation, 2013 (www.dimiter.eu/Eurlex.html; data from EUR-Lex).

like minimum prices (agriculture), quotas (fisheries) and tariffs (external trade). Together, these policy areas account for more than two-thirds of all EU regulatory output over the past decades – in many years even making up more than 75% or 80% of the total.

- Directives tend to contain broader and more generally applicable rules applying to classes of products (such as lifts), groups of people (third-country nationals) or issues (taxation of savings income).

- Like Commission Regulations, Decisions often specify provisions in more general EU legislation. The difference is that Decisions relate to specific cases (e.g. measures to combat African swine fever in Poland). In addition, Decisions are used for such things as approving mergers of firms (as part of the EU's competition policy), making appointments to committees and concluding agreements with states outside the EU.

- Recommendations are used in policy areas where the EU has little or no formal competence and/or where member state governments do not want to be bound by formal legislation (which often amounts to the same thing). See in Fact file 8.1, for instance, the recommendation on a quality framework for traineeships, an area in which the EU is only weakly involved.

Fact file 8.1

Examples of Regulations, Directives, Decisions and Recommendations adopted in February and March 2014

Examples of Regulations:

- Commission Implementing Regulation (EU) No 180/2014 of 20 February 2014 laying down rules for the application of Regulation (EU) No 228/2013 of the European Parliament and of the Council laying down specific measures for agriculture in the outermost regions of the Union.
- Commission Regulation (EU) No 245/2014 of 13 March 2014 amending Commission Regulation (EU) No 1178/2011 of 3 November 2011 laying down technical requirements and administrative procedures related to civil aviation aircrew.
- Commission Implementing Regulation (EU) No 268/2014 of 14 March 2014 fixing the import duties in the cereals sector applicable from 16 March 2014.
- Regulation (EU) No 333/2014 of the European Parliament and of the Council of 11 March 2014 amending Regulation (EC) No 443/2009 to define the modalities for reaching the 2020 target to reduce CO_2 emissions from new passenger cars.

Examples of Directives:

- Directive 2014/36/EU of the European Parliament and of the Council of 26 February 2014 on the conditions of entry and stay of third-country nationals for the purpose of employment as seasonal workers.
- Council Directive 2014/48/EU of 24 March 2014 amending Directive 2003/48/EC on taxation of savings income in the form of interest payments.
- Directive 2014/33/EU of the European Parliament and of the Council of 26 February 2014 on the harmonisation of the laws of the Member States relating to lifts and safety components for lifts.

Examples of Decisions:

- Commission Decision of 3 March 2014 on setting up a Scientific Committee on Occupational Exposure Limits for Chemical Agents.
- Council Decision 2014/198/CFSP of 10 March 2014 on the signing and conclusion of the Agreement between the European Union and the United Republic of Tanzania on the conditions of transfer of suspected pirates and associated seized property from the European Union-led naval force to the United Republic of Tanzania.
- Council Decision of 11 March 2014 appointing four United Kingdom members of the Committee of the Regions.
- Commission Implementing Decision of 12 March 2014 concerning certain protective measures relating to African swine fever in Poland.

Examples of Recommendations:

- Commission Recommendation of 7 March 2014 on strengthening the principle of equal pay between men and women through transparency.
- Council Recommendation of 10 March 2014 on a quality framework for traineeships.

Source: EUR-Lex.

Hence, although the number of Regulations (and also of Decisions) is much higher than the number of Directives adopted in the EU, the use of these instruments also differs a lot, with Regulations and Decisions being used predominantly for the further specification of more general rules laid down elsewhere or for specific cases. This is why Directives are often seen as the main legislative instrument in the EU, even though their numbers are quite modest. Conversely, it is also important to bear in mind that in terms of what the EU does and what EU institutions are occupied with, Directives are only the tip of the iceberg. Like any modern government, the EU spends much of its effort and time on relatively detailed and technical regulatory issues that are necessary to put policies into practice.

■ Economic and Monetary Union

So far, we have sought to give an overview of the various areas in which the EU is active and the types of policy associated with these areas. It is important to keep in mind, however, that the scope of EU policy-making is not static. The remit of EU policy-making has expanded over time and continues to develop even today. In this and the next section, we will focus on two areas in which particularly important developments have taken place in recent years: the policies surrounding the Economic and Monetary Union and foreign policy. Both areas have seen an expansion of EU policies that challenges long-held 'truths' about the EU and have the potential to transform key elements in the relationship between the EU and its member states.

The creation of EMU

The introduction of a common currency was already on the EU agenda in the 1960s, when the European Commission published a plan for the introduction of an Economic and Monetary Union (EMU). In 1970, this was followed up by the so-called Werner Report, which sketched the road towards EMU (see also Chapter 1). The discussions in the Werner Report covered a wide range of policy areas, but the key point was to achieve a single currency for all EU member states, backed up by joint or at least coordinated economic policies.

The **Economic and Monetary Union (EMU)** includes the coordination of economic and fiscal policies, a common monetary policy and a common currency.

The Werner Report, and subsequent political debates about EMU, revealed two fundamentally opposed visions on the issue. The so-called 'economist' position argued that economic convergence among member states was a precondition for a common currency. Proponents of this position argued that large differences between member states – for instance, in their inflation levels, unemployment rates and balance of payments – would destabilize the common currency. When every country has its own currency, such differences put pressure on exchange rates but this can be solved by changing the exchange rates between currencies (through 'devaluation' and 'revaluation' of currencies). With one common currency, this is no longer possible. Therefore, these imbalances had to be eliminated before countries adopted a common currency.

The 'monetarist' position reversed this logic, arguing that the adoption of a common currency would automatically lead to economic convergence. According to the monetarist argument, under a common currency international markets would reduce differences between national economies. The policy implications of this position were diametrically opposed to those of the 'economists', as no prior economic convergence was needed before a common currency could be introduced.

Underlying these different views were high economic and political stakes. The economist position was supported by Northern European member states such as Germany and the Netherlands, which feared high inflations levels and a weak currency, if a common currency was introduced without economic convergence. The monetarist position, on the other hand, was supported by Southern European member states such as France, for which economic convergence would have implied vast (and painful) domestic policy reforms.

Crude as this brief exposition is, the controversy between these two positions and the compromises between them help us to understand many of the issues involved in the debates on the EMU that have taken place since 1970. In the 1992 Treaty of Maastricht, it was finally decided to introduce a common currency, the Euro. The approach towards creating a common currency was a compromise between the German and French positions. The most important German demand that was satisfied in the Treaty of Maastricht was the establishment of a strictly independent European Central Bank, modelled after the German Bundesbank, which had the task of preventing excessive inflation. In addition, the Treaty defined a number of criteria for a member state if it were to adopt the Euro. The best known of these were a government deficit of no more than 3% of GDP and a sovereign debt of no more than 60% of GDP. In addition, convergence criteria were defined for inflation rates, exchange rate stability and long-term interest rates. This was all very much like the 'economist' German position.

On the other hand, however, economic policy-making remained firmly in the hands of individual member states and enforcement of the criteria was defined rather loosely. This reflected the French preference for the introduction of a common currency over a prior economic union.

As a result, the 'economic and monetary' union showed two faces: *monetary policy* was centralized at the European level, while *economic policy* remained a task for member state governments. The 1996 Stability and Growth Pact (SGP), a package of additional norms governing member states in the Eurozone, was an attempt by the German financial elite to strengthen the regulatory framework laid down in the Treaty of Maastricht and hence make it more 'economist', but in practice it made little difference.

The weakness of economic policy coordination became apparent in 2001/2, when a number of member states violated the 3% norm for budget deficits. Two of these member states happened to be France and Germany, which successfully pressed for a postponement of the sanctions foreseen in the SGP and a relaxation of the SGP itself.

The creation of the Euro implies a number of important lessons. First, it shows the essentially political nature of bargaining and decision-making on this topic. The Euro is not primarily an economic project, but a political one. Second, it shows the dependence of economic policies on member state governments. Although a common currency was created, economic policy-making remained for member state governments to decide.

The Euro after 2008

Until 2008, fundamental changes in the governance of the Euro remained unthinkable. Member state governments were highly reluctant to submit to stricter norms and supervision at the EU level, as this would directly affect their room for manoeuvre in economic and fiscal policy-making. Coordination of economic policies took place through relatively informal mechanisms, which were based on benchmarking and the exchange of best practices. This started with the European Employment Strategy (EES) in the late 1990s, which evolved into the Open Method of Coordination (OMC) from 2000 onwards (see Chapter 4 for a description of the OMC).

Economic policy coordination was therefore largely non-binding. Moreover, the policies surrounding the Euro did not involve any expenditures or transfer of money at the EU level, apart from the already longer-existing expenditures under the EU budget.

All this changed after the EU was hit by the financial crisis. In the wake of this crisis, some member states came into severe budgetary difficulties, both because they had to bail out banks that were on the brink of collapse and because they had to pay increasingly high interest rates if they wanted to finance their budgetary deficits. In response, a number of initiatives were taken that meant a fundamental break with previous practice:

- The supervision of national economies was strengthened. The European Commission obtained a more central role in this supervisory system. One of the lessons of the crisis had been that it was necessary to detect and correct economic weaknesses ('economic imbalances', as they are called in EU parlance) before a member state got into trouble. Supervision has therefore become focused on the prevention of economic weaknesses, alongside the correction of weaknesses once they have arisen, which potentially vastly increases the scope of EU involvement in member state economic policy-making. This also includes the scrutiny of member state budgets by the European Commission before they are adopted by national parliaments.

- Vast amounts of money were devoted to preventing member states from collapsing financially. Initially, this happened under temporary financial arrangements, but in 2012 a permanent support structure was created under the name 'European Stability Mechanism' (ESM). The ESM has a maximum lending capacity of €500 billion, of which €80 billion is provided by the member states in the Eurozone. In this way, besides a regulatory regime, a vast financial capacity has been created at the EU level.
- The European Central Bank took an active role in the management of the financial crisis by buying up government bonds from member states in financial trouble. This was an important break with previous practice, as the ECB had not been involved in this type of operation before.
- In addition, supervision of financial markets and institutions was stepped up at the EU level. Strictly speaking, these policies fall outside of the EMU, but the two are closely connected since failures in these markets and institutions had precipitated the financial crisis. These steps, too, were for a long time unthinkable, as member states with large financial centres (most notably the UK and Germany) were reluctant to give up control over their financial sectors. As of 2011, however, the European financial sector is overseen by three new supervisory authorities, for banks, securities, and insurance and pension markets, respectively. Moreover, from November 2014 onwards, the European Central Bank was tasked with the supervision of banks.

The changes outlined above have resulted in a patchwork of new institutions and regulatory instruments, reflecting the complex relationship between the EU and EMU. For instance, since not all EU member states have adopted the Euro, the ESM was established under a separate treaty between the member states in the Eurozone. At the same time, the European Commission plays a central role in the management of financial support to member states by the ESM.

Other parts of the new regulatory framework have been adopted as Regulations and Directives under EU law and apply to all EU member states. The new system of economic and budgetary supervision is not confined to member states in the Eurozone but applies to all member states, although additional and more stringent requirements apply to member states within the Eurozone. Some of these additional requirements have been laid down again in a separate Treaty on Stability, Coordination and Governance, which was signed in 2012 by all EU member states except the Czech Republic and the UK.

The regulatory requirements imposed on banks and financial markets also apply to all member states. However, supervision by the ECB only covers banks in member states that have adopted the Euro (and in other EU member states if these member states choose so). Even within the Eurozone, the ECB shares its supervisory authority with member state authorities. Large, so-called 'significant' banks are supervised directly by the ECB, albeit in cooperation with authorities from the bank's member state. This includes 120 banks that together account for some 80% of banking capital in the Eurozone. Other, 'less significant' banks are still supervised by member state authorities, but then in cooperation with the ECB, which may intervene if necessary.

These examples go to show that even though the financial crisis proved an enormous push for further integration, the outcome is still the result of profoundly political deals, in which different, often contradictory interests needed to be reconciled. The end result is a complex system of rules and supervision, which seeks to reconcile the interests of Euro and non-Euro member states, as well as maintain a balance between supranational and member state authority.

The future of economic governance in the EU

The financial crisis has created an unprecedented impetus for institutional reform. Yet, fundamental and thorough as these changes look on paper, their real impact will only become clear in the future. A number of important questions remain for the (near) future:

- How will economic supervision work in practice? Despite the strengthened role of the European Commission, the main economic policy decisions are still made at the member state level. Supervision by the European Commission may effectively shift this balance to the European level, but much of this may also remain a paper tiger.
- Will financial sanctions prove to be an effective deterrent against non-compliance? The use of financial sanctions was already foreseen in the SGP and has been further formalized since the financial crisis. In the end, however, imposing financial sanctions remains a very unattractive option for the European Commission, since it entails a direct political confrontation with a member state and only worsens that member state's financial condition.
- Will the EU acquire independent powers to levy taxes? According to some observers, the EU needs a larger budget and an independent tax base if it is to be an effective stabilizing force in the EU economy, similar to the federal government in the US. The European Parliament tried to put this on the EU agenda, but member state governments firmly resisted this.
- Will financial markets be further regulated to prevent another crisis? One proposal in this regard has been to introduce a 'financial transaction tax' (FTT). The idea behind an FTT is that by taxing financial transactions, it would discourage short-term speculative money transfers. It would also be a way to let the financial sector pay a greater (proponents of an FTT would say 'fairer') share of tax revenues. An FTT could be levied by member states, but some would prefer the revenues to go directly to the EU itself. In either case, the idea is both hotly debated and highly controversial. In 2011, the European Commission introduced a proposal for an EU-wide FTT. Since this was unacceptable to a number of member states, in 2013, the Commission

launched a new proposal, this time under the 'enhanced cooperation' procedure (see Chapter 4).

For all these questions, too, the central lesson of the introduction of the Euro applies: governance of the Euro and supervision of member state economies remain essentially political processes. Too much is at stake for member state governments to let go of these prerogatives easily. For the time being, the EMU remains a hybrid construction, with one currency (at least for a part of the member states), an EU regulatory and supervisory framework, but with largely decentralised economic policy-making.

■ EU foreign policy

Another area in which the EU has expanded its policy-making activities over the past decades, although less visibly and more gradually than in the case of EMU, is foreign policy. In a broader sense, the EU has already for a long time played important roles vis-à-vis non-member countries in a number of ways:

- *External trade*. The EU forms a single trade bloc, with one integrated trade policy vis-à-vis third countries. If conceived of as one economic unit, the EU is among the world's largest economies, together with China and the US. This means the EU is a major player in global trade policies. It is a full member of the World Trade Organization (WTO), and it has a range of trade agreements with countries outside the EU.
- *Development aid*. The EU has its own development assistance policy, alongside those of its member states.
- *External regulatory issues*. International relations and global politics are not just about 'classic' international issues, such as international security and trade, but also about all kinds of regulatory issues, from human rights to environmental protection and from food safety to migration. For issues that are regulated at the EU level, the EU plays an important role in international debates and negotiations, often alongside its member states.

Yet, the EU's role has remained much more limited in the field of 'foreign policy' per se: policies relating to security issues or, put differently, 'matters of war and peace'. This is the area that, in national states, is typically covered by a Ministry of Foreign Affairs (or in the US: the Department of State).

The limited role of the EU in this field is not surprising for at least six reasons:

- Foreign policy goes to the core of (member) state sovereignty. The ability (and prerogative) to conduct diplomatic relations, raise an army and conduct military interventions are among the central elements of what it means to be a 'sovereign' state. Member state governments are not easily willing to shift these tasks to the EU level.
- Foreign policy priorities and preferences differ vastly among member states. Often, this is linked to historical experiences and geographical

differences. For instance, Poland and the Baltic states are much more sensitive to the threat of Russian domination and Russian military aggression than member states on the Atlantic coast. Likewise, former colonial ties often still play a role in defining political priorities, such as France's continued interest in Africa, Spanish ties to Latin America and the UK's 'special relationship' with the US.

- **'Strategic cultures'** differ greatly between member states: some member states have a tradition of armed intervention and see this as a viable option in international conflicts, while others tend to eschew the use of force and rely more on diplomatic and other non-military means.

> A country's **strategic culture** is the set of assumptions and values through which it typically interprets and reacts to international events.

- Member states differ vastly in their diplomatic status and military capabilities. Among EU member states, France and the UK have by far the strongest armed forces and are the only member states with nuclear weapons. Moreover, they are the only member states to occupy a permanent seat in the UN Security Council. Without them, any EU foreign policy remains toothless, but these two member states also have the most to lose from giving up more powers to the EU.
- In foreign policy, the EU has to compete against a well-established other international organization, the North Atlantic Treaty Organization (NATO). Since NATO includes the US, many EU member state governments see it as the best guarantor of security in Europe. The building up of a stronger EU foreign policy and military capability is then seen as a threat to the security offered by (the US through) NATO. In addition, some neutral member states (that is, EU member states that are not members of NATO) prefer to work through the United Nations.
- Finally, there are also differences in the way foreign policy is organized within political systems. In some member states, such as France and the UK, the executive plays a central role while in other member states, such as Germany, parliamentary control is stronger.

As a result, the development of EU foreign policy has remained a difficult and slow process. Foreign policy issues were part of discussions in the European Council and the Council of Foreign Ministers from the 1970s, in a process known as 'European Political Cooperation'. This remained strictly a matter between member state governments and limited to discussions and information exchange. This changed with the Maastricht Treaty, in which a Common Foreign and Security Policy (CFSP) was given a specific place within the newly created European Union, as the second of the EU's three 'pillars' (see Chapter 1).

This pillar structure mainly served to insulate foreign and security policies from the 'normal' decision-making procedures and instruments of the first pillar. In the Treaty of Lisbon, the distinction between the pillars was formally abolished, but as we saw in Chapter 4, procedures and instruments in the field of foreign and security policy remain different from those in other policy areas. Generally speaking, *procedures* in the field of foreign and security policies put much more weight on member state governments, to the exclusion of the European Commission and the European Parliament (as well as the Court of Justice). Also, the *instruments* (types of decisions) in this field are distinct and have weaker legal effects for the member states.

Soft power EU

As a result, cooperation in the field of foreign and security policy has gone much less far than in many other policy areas. This is most visible in times of major international security crisis, when EU member states often have difficulties arriving at a common position, let alone agree on some form of intervention. Perhaps most shamefully for the EU member states, this was the case in the series of wars in Yugoslavia during the 1990s, when in the end NATO and the US gave the decisive political and military pushes for settlements.

It also became apparent in the aftermath of the 9/11 attacks, when the UK and some other member states supported the US invasion in Iraq, while France and Germany were vehemently opposed. Most recently, EU member states have found it difficult to come to a joint and clear position towards Russia's involvement in Ukraine and its annexation of the Crimean peninsula. Differing political and economic interests vis-à-vis Russia, coupled with the demanding decision-making procedures at EU level, led to slow responses and sometimes weak compromises.

Many observers have therefore noted a vast discrepancy between the EU's economic power and its military-diplomatic weakness. In a well-known phrase, the EU is often described as 'an economic giant and a political dwarf'. Others have sought to conceptualize the EU's role in the world in more positive terms, stressing not the lack of military power but the use of alternative sources of influence. In this vein, the EU has alternatively been described as a 'civilian power', a '**soft power**' or a 'normative power', which does not rely on military force but on its economic power and the example of peaceful international cooperation it has set.

> **Soft power** is the ability to wield influence, not through the use of force or money, but through the attractiveness and legitimacy of one's values, culture and policies.

The incremental development of EU foreign policy

This general picture of EU foreign and security policy notwithstanding, several notable developments have taken place over the past decades:

- Since 2003, the EU has been involved in a number of civilian and military missions abroad. As of October 2014, the EU had engaged in twenty-one civilian missions, nine military missions and one combined civilian/military mission. Fact file 8.2 gives some examples of missions. Military missions are

Fact file 8.2

Examples of civilian and military missions under the CFSP (as of 1 November 2014)

Examples of civilian missions:

- EUPOL Proxima: Former Yugoslav Republic of Macedonia (2004–5).
  Aim: to build up the country's police, in line with the Ohrid peace agreement.
- EUJUST LEX-Iraq: Iraq (2005–13).
  Aim: to strengthen the rule of law in the Iraqi criminal justice system.
- EUMM Georgia: Georgia (since 2008).
  Aim: to monitor compliance with the agreement reached between Georgia and Russia.

Examples of military missions:

- Artemis: Democratic Republic of Congo (2003).
  Aim: to provide military stabilization in East Congo. This was the first autonomous EU military mission to be conducted.
- Concordia: Former Yugoslav Republic of Macedonia (2003).
  Aim: to allow the implementation of the Ohrid peace agreement between the government of FYROM and the Albanian minority.
- EUTM: Mali (since 2013).
  Aim: to train the Malian armed forces.

Source: EEAS website (www.eeas.europa.eu/csdp/missions-and-operations).

typically used to provide military stabilization of a country or area, often after a peace agreement has been reached. In addition, they are also used to train the armed forces in a country. Civilian missions are mostly used to provide assistance for the build-up of police forces and/or the rule of law in a country, and also to monitor compliance with peace agreements. Sometimes, both a military and a civilian mission take place in the same area, each with its own focus. This is, for instance, the case for the missions in the Former Yugoslav Republic of Macedonia that are mentioned in the fact file.

- The EU has sought to build up some military capabilities of its own, as part of the Common Security and Defence Policy (CSDP), which falls under the CFSP. This takes the form of EU Battlegroups, of 1,500 soldiers each. Forces for these Battlegroups are provided by member states and, at any time, two battlegroups are supposed to be ready for deployment. Decisions on deployment are taken by the Council of Ministers.
- The Treaty of Lisbon included a mutual defence clause (now Article 42(7) of the Treaty on European Union), which obliges member states to come to the aid of another member state that is the victim of armed aggression.

- In 2004 the European Defence Agency (EDA) was created to support the build-up of a European defence capability and cooperation in armaments.
- Based on a provision in the Treaty of Lisbon, in 2011 the European External Action Service (EEAS) was established, headed by the EU's High Representative for Foreign Affairs and Security Policy. The EEAS operates as the diplomatic service of the EU. Before the EEAS, the European Commission already had a number of 'embassies' (officially called 'delegations') in states outside of the EU. These have now been brought under the aegis of the EEAS, which has the task of coordinating the EU's diplomatic activities.
- EU member states have also started to cooperate in the field of border control. This has not been linked to foreign and security policy, but to immigration policy. In response to immigration into the EU and the difficulties some member states had in controlling their borders, the EU has provided support in terms of money, equipment and, most notably, personnel. This is organized through FRONTEX, an EU agency set up in 2004. Although not part of the CFSP per se, this, too, is a significant development, as it touches on member states' border control.

Impressive as these developments may look, one should be careful not to overestimate the transfer of powers to the EU level. In all forms of military cooperation (battlegroups, missions, cooperation within the EDA), member state governments ultimately retain the right to opt in or out of specific initiatives. No member state can be forced to participate in a military mission or other military initiative. As a result, national sensitivities remain central in decision-making, as is exemplified by the fact that, as of late 2014, no EU Battlegroup has ever been actively deployed.

In that sense, the developments outlined above are still very limited and may serve symbolic purposes more than operational ones. Still, the fact that these developments have been set in motion, and have become official policy options, is meaningful in itself. We can now witness a number of developments that go well beyond anything that seemed viable in the early or mid-1990s. In the longer term, they may form the kernel of a further transformation of the EU.

There are now routine attempts to coordinate the response of the EU to international crises and developments. This, in itself, is already quite an achievement for a group of twenty-eight states, most of which have a long history of war with each other. Even though the EU looks slow and impotent in the highly publicized cases of international crisis, it has succeeded in establishing a coordinated position and playing a meaningful role in other, less visible cases.

Arguably, the litmus test for any foreign policy is how it deals with the most serious and threatening crises, and it is here that the EU has often fallen short. For the EU to become a fully fledged player at the international level, member states would have to be willing to give up much more authority to the EU. In the absence of a major, acute and shared security threat to all EU member states (see Chapter 12 on the role of crises in the EU's development), this is unlikely to happen soon.

■ Summary

This chapter has given an overview of policies and policy-making in the European Union. It has argued that:

- The EU is strongly involved in some issue areas but less or hardly involved in other areas.
- EU policy-making focuses primarily on regulatory policies. (Re-)distributive policies are much less important than they are for member state governments.
- The EU budget amounts to some 1% of European GDP.
- The EU receives its revenues primarily from the member states. It does not levy its own taxes, and it is prohibited from running a budget deficit.
- Around 75% of the EU budget is spent on two policy areas: agricultural policy and regional policy.
- Some member states are net contributors to the EU budget while other member states are net recipients. The distribution of contributions and benefits between the member states has led to recurring budgetary battles that pit net contributors against net recipients and member states with large agricultural sectors against member states with small agricultural sectors.
- Regulatory policies in the EU can be divided into three groups: regulation aimed at market regulation, regulation aimed at mitigating the negative impacts of economic activity, and regulation not (directly) related to economic activity.
- Market integration occurs through a combination of 'negative' and 'positive' integration.
- Over time, the EU has developed from an economic union to a political union.
- In a quantitative sense, Regulations form the largest part of EU regulatory output. However, in a qualitative sense, Directives are often more important because they cover broader issues.
- Economic and Monetary Union (EMU) and foreign policy are two areas of EU policy that have been subject to important developments over the past decades.
- In EMU, monetary policies have been centralized at the EU level, while economic policies are primarily decided within the member states. Since the 2008 financial crisis, several measures have been adopted to strengthen the coordination of economic policies within the EU.
- The development of EU foreign policy has been a slow and gradual process, because it goes to the core of member state sovereignty. Nevertheless, since

the late 1990s several steps have been taken to strengthen foreign policy and military cooperation at the EU level. Despite these steps, the EU is still seen as an 'economic power' and a 'soft power', rather than a military power.

Further reading

A good overview of EU policy-making and of EU policies in a range of issue areas is Helen Wallace, Mark Pollack and Alasdair Young (eds), *Policy-making in the European Union* (Oxford University Press, 7th edn, 2014). Jeremy Richardson (ed.), *European Union: Power and Policy-making* (Routledge, 4th edn, 2015) also offers an advanced introduction to EU policy-making processes. A textbook on the EMU's economic underpinnings, written by a leading economist in the field, is Paul de Grauwe, *Economics of Monetary Union* (Oxford University Press, 9th edn, 2014). A good book to learn more about EU foreign policy is Stephan Keukeleire and Tom Delreux, *The Foreign Policy of the European Union* (Palgrave Macmillan, 2nd edn, 2014).

Websites

- Overviews of EU legislation and decisions can be found in EUR-Lex: http://eur-lex.europa.eu/homepage.html
- Overviews of proposals for legislation that are currently being discussed are available through Pre-Lex: http://ec.europa.eu/prelex/apcnet.cfm?CL=en
- Information on the EU budget can be found at: http://europa.eu/pol/financ/index_en.htm
- Statistics on government expenditures in the member states of the EU are compiled by Eurostat, the EU's statistical office: www.ec.europa.eu/eurostat
- A website with a lot of resources on EU foreign policy is Exploring EU Foreign Policy: www.eufp.eu.

Navigating the EU

On the website www.navigatingthe.eu you will find online exercises for this chapter.

9   Agenda-setting

■ Introduction

On 8 December 2005, the European Commission published its Green Paper on obesity, the health condition more commonly known as 'overweight'. The Green Paper outlined the prevalence and underlying causes of obesity within the European Union, identified possible EU actions to reduce obesity, and invited member state governments and stakeholders to submit comments. Earlier that year, the Commission had already launched the European Platform for Action on Diet, Physical Activity and Health, which brought together representatives from industry, consumer organizations and health NGOs in order to arrive at mutual commitments to reduce overweight. On the basis of the responses to the Green Paper, the Commission released a White Paper with more concrete proposals in May 2007, which was embraced by the Council of Ministers and the European Parliament and formed the basis for further initiatives in this field.

The sudden attention to the issue of obesity at the EU level was not self-evident. To begin with, why the EU? Overweight would not seem to be the most logical issue to be taken up by the EU. Cross-border aspects, the self-proclaimed rationale for EU initiatives, are not immediately clear in this case. Moreover, health (care) issues are firmly under the member state governments' remit. The EU Treaty even explicitly prohibits harmonization of legislation on health grounds. In addition, why 2005? The problem of overweight, and the health conditions associated with it, was apparent long before that time. Why, then, did it take so long for the issue to be taken up?

These types of questions are questions about the EU's political agenda. The political agenda is the set of issues that policy-makers give serious attention to. At any given point in time, some issues are 'on' the agenda (that is, they receive attention), while other issues are 'off' the agenda (they receive no or very little attention). Understanding why issues are on or off the agenda is crucial for understanding policy-making, because paying attention to an issue is a necessary condition for doing something about it.

In this chapter, we will take a closer look at agenda-setting in the EU. In so doing, we will discuss the following questions:

- Why is agenda-setting politically important?
- What types of 'agenda' can be discerned and how do they relate to each other?
- Why do political actors try to move an issue on to the EU agenda?
- How do agenda-setting processes evolve in the EU?
- What determines whether issues do or do not come on to the EU's agenda?

We will see that agenda-setting is a highly political process because it has important consequences for the issues on which decisions are taken and the policy options that are considered. As a result, political actors actively try to bring issues on to the EU agenda or keep them off that agenda. The process through which issues come on to the EU agenda is complex and largely informal. Nevertheless, it is not purely random or idiosyncratic. Common elements and drivers can be discerned in many agenda-setting processes. We will see that certain (combinations of) motives explain why actors try to place an issue on the EU agenda. In addition, there is a 'typical' sequence of steps that are taken in EU agenda-setting processes, albeit with variations in specific cases. Finally, the agenda-setting literature has unveiled a number of factors that determine whether or not an issue will actually make it on to the agenda. At the same time, because of their informality agenda-setting processes always include elements of surprise and chance. This is what makes agenda-setting such a fascinating area of study.

■ The political importance of agendas

Above, we defined a **political agenda** as 'the set of issues that policy-makers give serious attention to'. The crucial element in this definition is 'attention'. Attention is basically about what is on policy-makers' minds: what they think about and discuss with each other or, stated differently, what they consider to be important issues to which they accord priority.

> The **political agenda** is the set of issues that policy-makers give serious attention to.

The fact that there is such a thing as an agenda at all stems from a simple fact: people (and organizations) cannot attend to all things at the same time. The number of issues that could be taken up is almost limitless. There is always a vast array of issues that could be addressed or that merit attention. At the same time, policy-makers can only do so many things in a day so they need to make choices about what to attend to and what to ignore (at least for the moment). This is as true for EU policy-makers as it is for politicians in a municipal council or managers in an organization. These choices result in an agenda: a set of issues that receive attention and, by implication, a set of issues that do *not* receive attention.

Agendas can be the result of a deliberate choice, when a policy-maker decides to give priority to some issue over another. They can also be a response to outside events, when policy-makers respond to what is happening around them. For instance, when the financial crisis started in 2008 governments in many Western countries immediately started to focus on issues of banking stability that had previously received much less attention, including wide-scale financial support for and even the nationalization of banks in distress. This choice was hardly the result of a deliberate trade-off between different issues but was almost forced on those governments as a result of the impact of the crisis on the financial markets.

In either case, agenda-setting is a highly political process. Agendas do not simply 'happen': they have enormous political implications. Some groups and politicians gain if an issue comes on to the political agenda while others lose. To return to the example of obesity given in the introduction, this was an issue that the food industry had little interest in raising. For them, it could only entail greater (regulatory) burdens in order to curtail the production and sale of unhealthy foods. For health NGOs, on the other hand, it was an important issue because obesity is related to a range of health conditions that they sought to combat. Hence, health NGOs wanted to get the issue on to the EU agenda, while the food industry wanted to keep it off.

As a result, political actors actively seek to influence the political agenda. They try to push the issues they want to have on the agenda, but also try to keep issues off the agenda if they have little to gain by greater attention. This kind of political struggle even occurs when an issue more or less forces itself on to the agenda. This was the case, for instance, with the terrorist attacks of 9/11, which dominated the political agenda in many Western countries in the period that followed. There were different ways in which the attacks could have been conceived. Were they an act perpetrated in a specific place by a small network of extremists or were they an attack on the values of Western civilization by a global movement of Muslim fundamentalists? In the end, the latter definition 'won', which led, among other things, to the invasions of Afghanistan and Iraq. This outcome was the result of a political struggle between proponents of different courses of action that tried to 'use' the attacks to push forward their own agendas. Even though policy-makers were forced to respond to the attacks themselves, they still had a choice as to which aspect or interpretation of the events they emphasized.

All in all, then, agendas are not self-evident but politically highly consequential and the outcomes of political processes. This is no different at the EU level than within domestic political systems (or, for that matter, local politics). That is why it is important to understand how agendas are formed within the EU.

■ Types of agendas and agenda dynamics

The political agenda, the media agenda and the public agenda

So far, we have only talked about the political agenda. However, we can discern at least three important types of agendas in democratic societies:

- the political agenda, which consists of the issues that policy-makers pay attention to;
- the media agenda, which consists of the issues that receive attention in newspapers, on television and on the Internet;
- the public agenda, which includes the issues that citizens find important at a given point in time.

These agendas may influence each other but they are not identical: policy-makers may discuss issues that hardly appear in the media and are not on many people's minds, while some issues may be important in public opinion or the media but resonate much less in the political arena.

In addition, within the broader category of the 'political agenda', there are several more specific agendas. Thus, the European Commission has an agenda but so do the European Council and the European Parliament. Although they will overlap to a greater or lesser extent, these agendas are usually not identical. Even within these institutions, there are multiple agendas. For instance, the agenda of the Commission's DG Internal Market may feature issues such as the competitiveness of European firms or reducing the regulatory burden on enterprise, while DG Environment may focus on issues such as air pollution or dangerous chemicals. The same is true for different committees in the EP or different configurations of the Council of Ministers. When discussing political agendas, it is therefore important to be clear about which agenda is meant: is it the agenda of the EU as a whole (i.e. the issues that are being discussed in all EU institutions), of one of the institutions or of some part of an institution?

Linkages between the types of agendas

Above, we discussed different types of agendas. The interaction between these agendas is important for understanding agenda-setting dynamics, not just in the European Union but in every political system. In order to elucidate these different dynamics, agenda-setting scholars Roger Cobb, Jennie-Keith Ross and Marc Ross distinguished between three ways in which the various agendas may interact:

- In the 'outside initiative model', issues arise within groups in society, which then seek to reach, first, the public agenda and, next, the political agenda.

- In the 'mobilization model', policy-makers take the initiative to place an issue on the political agenda and then try to gain support for the issue by also placing it on the public agenda.
- In the 'inside access model', issues arise within government and stay there. Thus, they are placed on the political agenda without attempts being made to place them on the public agenda.

Roger Cobb, Jennie-Keith Ross and Marc H. Ross, 'Agenda Building as a Comparative Political Process', American Political Science Review, 70, 1, 1976: 126–38.

The media agenda may play an important role in between the political agenda and the public agenda: societal groups may use media attention to put pressure on policy-makers (in the outside initiative model), while policy-makers may use the media to place an issue from the political on the public agenda (in the mobilization model).

Examples of each model can easily be found in political reality. An example of the outside initiative model was the protests by French farmers on 27 April 2010, who rode into Paris on tractors in order to raise awareness of falling grain prices and demand government action. An example of the mobilization model is US President Bush's decision to invade Iraq. This had been discussed (perhaps even decided) within his government before he sought to obtain public support by raising the 'Iraqi threat' on the public agenda. The example of obesity in the EU, which we gave in the introduction to this chapter, exemplifies the inside access model. This is an issue that has arisen primarily within the EU's health policy communities and has been developed there without a great deal of public attention.

Agenda-setting dynamics in the EU

According to Cobb, Ross and Ross, political systems differ in the prevalence of each of these dynamics. Therefore, a good starting point for understanding agenda-setting in the EU is to identify how often each model of agenda-setting occurs and how this compares with other political systems. In so doing, we can use several insights from other chapters in this book.

Outside initiatives in the EU

The outside initiative model is closely linked with the strategy of outside lobbying that we discussed in Chapter 6. There we explained that outside lobbying consists of attempts by interest groups to put pressure on policy-makers by mobilizing public opinion through protests and media attention. The French farmer protests in Paris that we mentioned above are a typical example of this strategy. In Chapter 6, we saw that outside lobbying is less widespread at the EU level than within the EU's member states, because EU policy-makers are less vulnerable to public opinion than domestic politicians. Insofar as outside lobbying occurs, it takes place mainly within well-specified groups, such as farmers.

Similarly, in Chapter 5 on public opinion it was noted that the EU is not very prominently on most EU citizens' minds and public opinion in (and on) the EU is shaped more by national than by EU circumstances. This makes it more difficult to mobilize 'EU public opinion' in support of a cause than to mobilize national public opinion within a member state.

As a result, the outside initiative model is less common at the EU level than within its member states. This is not to say that it does not occur at all. Examples of issues that came on to the EU agenda through outside initiatives can be found and there is some evidence that outside lobbying has become more important over time. Yet, this is not a 'typical' way for issues to reach the EU agenda.

Mobilization in the EU

For the same reason, the mobilization model is less common than it is in domestic democratic systems. There are several reasons why policy-makers may want to mobilize public opinion. First, policy-makers may do so because they need public interest and public support in order to have an issue implemented. However, as we will see in greater detail in Chapter 11, practical implementation in the EU usually occurs through member state governments. Implementation at the EU level itself then remains limited to refining regulatory standards and monitoring member state performance. This means that EU policy-makers have relatively little use for mobilizing public support in order to facilitate implementation.

It is instructive in this regard to compare agenda-setting around obesity in the EU and the USA. In the EU, the issue of obesity was placed on the agenda within the EU's institutions. Subsequently, it was further developed within the European Platform for Action on Diet, Physical Activity and Health, which included representatives of organizations. Hence, the whole process remained limited to a relatively small circle of policy-makers, health experts and direct stakeholders. In the USA, by contrast, after obesity had reached the political agenda strong attempts were made to involve the general public by raising awareness of the issue (in other words: by placing it on the public agenda). To this end, First Lady Michelle Obama headed a large public campaign named 'Let's Move' that had as its stated objective to eliminate obesity among youths within a generation. This made sense as part of an effort to implement obesity policies, because in the end citizens (consumers) decide what food to buy and eat. However, within the EU's political system such large-scale awareness-raising is much less common and would normally be left to member state governments.

In addition, policy-makers may seek to mobilize public opinion in order to overcome resistance within government itself. By claiming public support for their position, they may be able to override the objections of their opponents. Here, the same restrictions apply as for interest groups engaged in outside lobbying. Because EU policy-making is more 'immune' to public opinion, mobilizing public opinion is as ineffective a strategy for policy-makers as it is for interest groups.

Inside access in the EU

Just as the smaller role of public opinion in the EU limits the prevalence of outside initiatives and mobilization, it increases the importance of *inside access*. This ties in with the observation in Chapter 6 that, in contrast to outside lobbying, inside lobbying is relatively more important in the EU. Inside lobbying means that interest groups try to work through and with the EU's institutions in order to have their voices heard.

The same is true for agenda-setting. Because EU policy-making largely takes place within the EU's institutions, many issues are typically raised there. Exactly who raises an issue may vary. In some cases, the EU institutions themselves (for instance, Commission officials) take the initiative. In other cases, member state politicians and/or the heads of government in the European Council take the lead. In still other cases, member state civil servants try to plug an issue at the EU level. Yet, in all of these cases the issue is raised and developed within the EU's policy-making institutions, without a direct link with the public agenda(s) in the EU.

■ Why do political actors attempt to bring issues to the EU agenda?

Agenda-setting always involves attempts by political actors to bring issues to the EU agenda. When we want to understand agenda-setting in the EU, it is therefore important to know why actors prefer to deal with issues at the EU level rather than within a member state or an international organization. In this section, we will take a closer look at these motives.

Tackling cross-border issues

The first reason is the most straightforward one: actors may want to bring issues on to the EU agenda because the problem they seek to address can only be solved at the EU level. This is the case when the issue has cross-border aspects. The classic example is cross-border pollution: if a factory in one member state pollutes water or air in other member states, the issue cannot be solved at the national level of one country alone but needs to be tackled internationally. EU policies are then a logical answer to the problem. The same is true for a wide range of issues that, to a greater or lesser extent, have cross-border implications, such as international crime or issues related to trade between member states.

Tackling cross-border issues is not only a logical explanation for the appearance of issues on the EU agenda, it is also the official rationale for EU action. The European Commission often goes to great pains to argue that the initiatives it takes are meant to address cross-border problems. This principle has been codified in EU law as the 'subsidiarity principle', which states that issues can only be dealt with at the EU level if they cannot be handled at least equally well by the member states themselves.

Official ideology as this may be, the reality of EU policies does not always conform to this 'rule'. In fact, as we already saw in Chapter 8, the EU also deals with issues that have no or only very limited cross-border aspects. Just think about issues such as animal welfare, non-contagious diseases (such as obesity), smoking in public places, the quality of drinking water, the protection of natural areas, occupational health and safety, and discrimination between men and women (or discrimination more generally). These are all issues that could also be dealt with by the member states individually. What the EU does in these fields is not to address cross-border problems but to establish a European minimum level of protection that each of the member states is required to follow.

Why would politicians, civil servants, interest groups or other actors from the EU member states want to bring these issues to the EU level? Several motives may be at play here, which we can divide into political, economic, universalistic and institutional motives. We will discuss each in turn.

Political motives

A political motive for moving an issue to the EU level arises when political actors want to circumvent political opposition 'at home'. During the 1970s, for instance, British women's groups deliberately went to the EU level to fight for equal rights between men and women because they felt the EU would be more receptive to their claims than British politicians. Likewise, it has been argued that during the 1990s national immigration officials deliberately sought to establish EU immigration policies because at the EU level they would be able to adopt much more restrictive policies than in their respective member states.

The reason for this is that the playing field is often very different at the EU level than within a member state. Opponents that are strong domestically may be much weaker at the EU level – for instance, because they have no access to EU decision-making. To give an example: EU environmental policies are decided upon by the Environment Council, which only includes environmental ministers. This may make it easier for environmental ministers to have ambitious policies adopted at the EU level, where they are 'among themselves', than in their own member states, where they have to face colleagues from other departments (such as agriculture or economic affairs) in their government. By using the EU to adopt policies, they can circumvent this domestic opposition.

In addition to opposition within their ranks, member state governments as a whole may also prefer to bring an issue to the EU level because it allows them to avoid blame for unpopular decisions. If, for example, a government cuts back on unemployment benefits, that measure is politically much more palatable if the government can point to EU requirements that limit the deficits member states are allowed to run (for instance, in relation to the Euro and the associated Stability and Growth Pact). Rather than take full responsibility for a measure, they can then argue that 'Brussels made us do it'.

Economic motives

The economic motive for bringing an issue to the EU level has to do with the effects of differences in regulation on the competitiveness of firms. Firms from member states with stringent standards incur higher compliance costs than firms from member states with less stringent standards. In order to create a 'level playing field', they may therefore argue for EU regulation. Often, this is not (only) done by affected firms themselves, but by member state governments that seek to create beneficial competitive circumstances for 'their' industries. For instance, equal pay between men and women was included in the 1957 EEC Treaty at the behest of the French government, which feared that French industries would be disadvantaged by the fact that in other member states women tended to have lower wages than in France.

Universalistic motives

Universalistic motives involve a belief on the part of a political actor that all citizens within the EU should enjoy the same rights or arrangements. For example, many environmental groups believe that the protection of endangered species is a value in itself, regardless of national borders. Hence, they believe the EU should protect endangered species, even if those species live within national borders and there are therefore no cross-border aspects to the issue. Likewise, some groups and politicians argue that all workers have a right to decent working conditions and that this cannot be left to individual states to decide. This, then, is a reason to take the issue up at the EU level.

Institutional motives

The European institutions themselves often have specific motives to try to bring issues to the EU level. Like national groups or politicians, they can be motivated by universalistic motives: the idea that EU policies will bring benefits that all citizens are entitled to, regardless of nationality. In addition, the Commission and the European Parliament have clear institutional motives to attract certain issues. Dealing with more as well as more prestigious issues enhances their power and status, increases the resources they command and, in general, makes their lives more interesting. For this reason,

Controversy 9.1

A competence catalogue for the European Union?

The allocation of tasks between the EU and its member states has been subject to continuous shifts. Over time, the EU has taken up new tasks and acquired new competences. Partly, this has been the result of treaty changes, in which member states deliberately attributed new competences to the EU (and EU institutions) because they felt the EU needed to deal with certain issues. Partly, however, it has also been the result of strategic attempts by the EU institutions (in particular the European Commission) to increase the scope of existing competences and venture into fields that had hitherto not been part of the EU's remit. This has led some observers and politicians to warn against a process of 'creeping competence', in which the EU gradually acquires ever-expanding competences, even if these competences are not explicitly granted to it.

One proposed solution against creeping competence has been to include a 'competence catalogue' into the EU treaties. After the Treaty of Lisbon, such a catalogue is defined in Title I of the Treaty on the Functioning of the European Union (Articles 2–6). It enumerates which issue areas fall under the exclusive remit of the EU and which are shared between the EU and its member states. This is a method that has been widely used in the constitutions of federal states such as Canada, Germany and the United States.

Do you think a competence catalogue will make a difference to the ability of political actors to put issues on the EU agenda? To what extent do you think there is a problem of 'creeping competence' within the EU? If so, do you think a competence catalogue could help stop it?

most government organizations seek to extend their tasks and take up new, interesting issues. The EU institutions are no exception to this rule, which leads them actively to develop and push for new issues.

Combinations of motives

This overview shows the varied and complicated nature of the motives behind issues on the EU agenda. In reality, many issues are brought up as the result of a combination of motives and different actors may have different motives for bringing the same issue to the EU agenda: there may be some cross-border aspects, it may be politically convenient to discuss an issue at the EU level, firms that incur high costs support a 'level playing field', other groups may feel the EU offers a chance to 'spread the word', and EU institutions want to extend their activities. This complexity is one of the reasons why it has remained difficult strictly to demarcate the competences and responsibilities of the EU from those of the member states. Controversy 9.1 introduces one suggestion that has been put forward in this regard: the construction of a 'competence catalogue' for the EU.

■ From idea to proposal: the process of agenda-setting in the EU

Agenda-setting is, almost by its nature, not a formal process. The process through which policy-makers start giving attention to issues is influenced by many factors. Because it lies at the very 'origin' of policy-making, there are few procedures to follow and political actors have a lot of room for manoeuvre. Nevertheless, certain steps in the process occur in many cases and form a sort of 'common sequence' in EU agenda-setting processes. To set the stage for the subsequent discussion of agenda-setting dynamics it is useful to outline these steps. In so doing, we will focus on issues for which the European Commission has the exclusive right of initiative (see Chapter 4) because they constitute the majority of cases within the EU and because the steps are most clearly discernible in those cases. We will first sketch the steps in a 'typical' agenda-setting process, and then apply this to the example of EU obesity policy.

The steps in a typical EU agenda-setting process

Figure 9.1 gives an overview of the steps that can be discerned in a typical agenda-setting process. The origins of an issue or idea are often difficult to trace. Issues can come from anywhere. The European Commission itself develops ideas about the issues that should be taken up. Interest groups (see Chapter 6) are constantly plugging issues that they feel need to be taken up. Member state governments (both politicians and civil servants) may try to get things on to the EU agenda, and the same goes for Members of the European Parliament. At some point, however, the issue becomes part of (informal) *discussions* among politicians, policy experts and/or the media within the EU.

The first appearance of an issue in an official EU document depends on the issue area. In some areas, the European Commission publishes *multi-annual work plans* that guide work in the field for periods of five years or longer. For instance, in the field of environmental policy the Commission publishes multi-annual Environmental Action Programmes that are officially adopted by the Council and the EP. The programme currently in force is the Seventh Environment Action Programme, which runs until 2020. Likewise, the Commission's priorities in health policy are laid down in the Third Health Programme 2014–2020. Getting an issue into a multi-annual work plan is one way of placing it more firmly on the EU's political agenda. However, such plans are only published for a limited number of policy areas.

A next step is made when an issue is included in the *Commission annual work programme*. Early each year, the European Commission publishes an overview of all proposals it is planning to put forward in that year. Ideas for issues to be

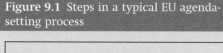

Figure 9.1 Steps in a typical EU agenda-setting process

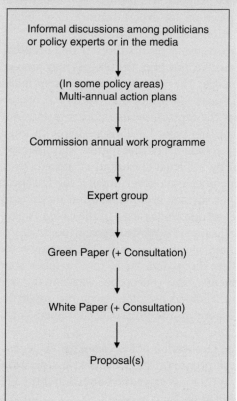

Informal discussions among politicians or policy experts or in the media

↓

(In some policy areas) Multi-annual action plans

↓

Commission annual work programme

↓

Expert group

↓

Green Paper (+ Consultation)

↓

White Paper (+ Consultation)

↓

Proposal(s)

Figure 9.2 Steps in the agenda-setting process around obesity

Prior to 2005: Debates in the medical community and among health experts

April 2005: mention of obesity in EU Health and Consumer Protection Strategy 2007–2013

January 2005: Obesity included in Commission Work Programme 2005

March 2005: Creation of EU Platform on Diet, Physical Activity and Health

December 2005: Commission Green Paper on obesity (+ Consultation)

May 2007: Commission White Paper on obesity

November 2007: Creation of High-Level Group on Nutrition and Physical Activity

included in the work programme come from the Commission's Directorates-General and, within those DGs, specific units. There are always many more suggestions than there is room for within the work programme, so the process of getting an issue into the work programme is an important bureaucratic struggle within the Commission. This is important for Commission officials and outside stakeholders alike, because once an issue is included in the annual work programme, it is officially recognized as one of the priorities for action by the Commission in that year.

When it is decided to develop a proposal, the Commission usually convenes an *expert group* to assist it in drafting a document or proposal. The composition of an expert group is completely at the discretion of the Commission. Normally, it contains policy experts from member state governments and/or interest groups in the field. For the Commission, an expert group is a way to use the best available expertise on an issue when developing proposals. Moreover, it is a way to explore political sensibilities around an issue and to commit important stakeholders to the proposal that is subsequently published. For those stakeholders themselves, an expert group is the best possible way to exert influence on the shape of a policy proposal when much still needs to be decided. This is the reason why a place on an expert committee is highly coveted by governments and groups interested in a certain issue.

In many cases, the work in the expert group results directly in a proposal. When the issue is more complex or sensitive, however, the process may proceed through a number of intermediate steps. The first intermediate step is the publication of a **Green Paper**. Green Papers do not contain specific proposals but chart the terrain, outline policy options and offer a starting point for a discussion with interested stakeholders. For that reason, they are often followed by a formal consultation procedure, in which member state governments, the European Parliament, interest groups and often also individual citizens can respond to the issues and questions raised in the Green Paper.

A **Green Paper** is a discussion document from the European Commission that outlines general issues and options around an issue without presenting specific proposals.

A next intermediate step is the publication of a **White Paper**. In contrast to a Green Paper, a White Paper does contain specific proposals that are presented for further discussion. Here, too, member state governments, the European Parliament and other stakeholders are often given the opportunity to respond to the proposals contained in the White Paper.

A **White Paper** is a discussion document from the European Commission that presents specific proposals for EU action.

Finally, then, this may result in the publication of a *proposal* for EU legislation or other forms of policy. If these proposals are scheduled for decision-making by the appropriate institutions (in most cases the Council and the EP), the issue has moved firmly on to the EU's decision agenda.

This is a 'typical' process but it is not cast in stone. There are many variations, in which some steps do not appear, additional rounds of documents and (formal or informal) consultation are added, or the sequence of certain steps is reversed. We can see how this works in a concrete example by turning to the example of obesity again.

The steps in the agenda-setting process around obesity

Figure 9.2 shows the steps in the agenda-setting process for obesity, linking them to the general steps outlined in Figure 9.1. In the case of obesity, debates on the gravity, determinants and consequences of the problem started well before any mention in an official EU document. A consensus on the significance of obesity developed among medical researchers and practitioners, as well as health policy experts in member state governments, the European Commission and the World Health Organization (WHO), a specialized agency of the United Nations that focuses on health issues. Among these groups, conferences were organized, studies were published and policy options were discussed. This is how interest in the issue gained ground.

Policy work on obesity within the EU took off when the issue was mentioned in the Health and Consumer Protection Strategy for the period 2007–13, which was launched by the Commission in April 2005 and subsequently adopted by the Council and the EP. Even before that, in January 2005, the publication of a Green Paper on obesity had been included in the Commission's work programme for 2005.

In March 2005, the Commission created the EU Platform for Action on Diet, Physical Activity and Health. The term 'platform' was used because this was a more formal institution than a mere expert group. Still, partly the purpose was the same: to bring together expertise and to create support for a certain course of action. In the specific case of obesity, however, the forum was also meant to lead to voluntary agreements on reducing overweight between industry (food, retail and the like), consumer groups and health NGOs, something a regular expert group would not do.

Later that year, in December 2005, the Commission published the Green Paper *Promoting Healthy Diets and Physical Activity: A European Dimension for the Prevention of Overweight, Obesity and Chronic Diseases*. Linked to this Green Paper was a large-scale consultation in which interested stakeholders could give their opinion on the ideas presented in the Green Paper. The results of that consultation were presented in September 2006.

In May 2007, the Commission published the White Paper on *A Strategy for Europe on Nutrition, Overweight and Obesity Related Health Issues*, with more concrete actions to be taken. On the basis of this White Paper, a High-Level Group on Nutrition and Physical Activity was formed that included high-ranking civil servants from each of the member states. The High-Level Group operates alongside the Platform created in 2005, and sometimes the two meet together. So far, no proposals for binding legislation have been adopted because work on obesity is predicated on voluntary commitments by industry and agreements between member states. However, in 2014 an *EU Action Plan on Childhood Obesity 2014–2020* was adopted with further initiatives to reduce obesity among Europe's youths.

Hence, the outlines of the 'typical' agenda-setting sequences of Figure 9.1 are clearly visible in the case of obesity but there are also variations within this scheme. This is the case, to a lesser or greater degree, for many issues that come on to the EU agenda.

■ Why do issues make it on to the EU agenda?

In the previous section, we outlined the steps in agenda-setting processes within the EU. This is a useful starting point for analysing how issues come on to the EU agenda, and it helps to explain the role and status of various types of documents released by the European Commission. At the same time, it does not tell us much about the factors that drive agenda-setting. Why is it that some issues are taken up while others are not? What is the political logic behind agenda-setting processes? In the end, these are the central questions, and they cannot be answered merely by looking at the sequence of events.

Fact file 9.1

A glossary of Commission documents

Commission documents come by different names. Here is a brief guide:

- A *Green Paper* is a discussion document that outlines general issues and options around an issue, without presenting specific proposals. It forms the start of a consultation among stakeholders.

Example: Green Paper *A 2030 Framework for Climate and Energy Policies,* COM (2013) 169.

- A *Communication* informs the other EU institutions, member state governments, advisory bodies and/or stakeholders of the Commission's point of view or intended strategy on a given issue, without inviting a response.

Example: Communication *Enlargement Strategy and Main Challenges 2014–2015,* COM (2014) 700.

- A *White Paper* is a discussion document that presents specific proposals for EU action.

Example: White Paper *An Agenda for Adequate, Safe and Sustainable Pensions,* COM (2012) 55.

- A *Work Programme* sets out the priorities of the European Commission for a given year.

Example: Commission Work Programme 2014, COM (2013) 739.

- An *Action Plan* (or: *Action Programme*) is an overview of activities that the Commission intends to undertake in relation to a given issue or policy area over a period of several years. Normally published in the form of a Communication.

Example: Action Plan for the Future of Organic Production in the European Union, COM (2014) 179.

- A *Report* contains factual information on the state of affairs in a given issue area.

Example: 5th Annual Report on Immigration and Asylum (2013), COM (2014) 288.

In the literature on agenda-setting, several factors have been identified as being particularly crucial in this regard. Below we will review them under three broad headings: issue framing, institutional structures and timing. In discussing these factors, we will use the case of agenda-setting around alcohol abuse to illustrate these factors and to show the possibilities and limitations inherent in EU agenda-setting processes. Briefing 9.1 gives the general background to this case.

Issue framing

A **frame** is an interpretation scheme with which issues and events are defined and given meaning. **Framing** is the activity of (re-)defining an issue in such a way that it fits a particular frame.

Issue **framing** concerns the way in which issues are defined. It determines how an issue is conceived and, consequently, who will be involved in the policy process and whether or not the issue

Briefing 9.1

Getting alcohol abuse on to the EU agenda

Since the mid-1990s, some member state governments and NGOs have tried to get the issue of alcohol abuse on to the EU agenda. For the Swedish and Finnish governments, the EU's internal market rules posed a direct risk to their traditionally strict alcohol policies because their citizens could now import large quantities of alcoholic beverages from other member states. To legitimize restrictions on alcohol sales, they sought to have alcohol abuse recognized as an issue at the EU level. In addition, anti-alcoholism groups from several other member states sought to involve the EU in order to put the issue more firmly on their domestic agendas and bring about more stringent policies.

Proponents of an EU anti-alcoholism policy have had to move carefully because the EU lacks a legal basis to legislate directly on health matters. Moreover, drinking patterns and (cultural) perspectives on alcohol and alcoholic drinks differ widely between member states (contrast the restrictive Nordic policies with the South European 'wine culture'), making it difficult to achieve a consensus on the issue.

Over the years, proponents of an EU anti-alcoholism policy have tried to build up momentum by emphasizing common trends that occur in all member states and that are widely seen as undesirable, such as drink-driving, underage drinking and 'binge drinking'. By highlighting common problems between member states, proponents could argue for an EU-wide approach. Their cause was helped by the rise of 'alcopops', sweet mixes of soft drinks and alcoholic drinks that appealed to (and were explicitly aimed at) teenagers. In that way, the proponents tried to change the prevailing perspective on alcoholic drinks in the EU from one of trade (alcoholic drinks as a tradable commodity like any other) to one of health (alcohol as a source of health risks and crime).

The World Health Organization's (WHO) Regional Office for Europe has also been instrumental in raising attention to the issue, publishing studies, organizing conferences and adopting action programmes. Some of these conferences were jointly organized by the Swedish government, the WHO and the European Commission's DG for Health and Consumer Protection.

After the health effects of alcohol had been included in the EU health action programme for the period 2003–8, DG Health and Consumer Protection worked on an EU strategy to combat alcohol-related harm, which would lay the foundation for an EU role in this area. After the DG had circulated a relatively ambitious draft, lobby groups from the alcoholic drinks industry mounted a fierce campaign in order to water it down (no pun intended . . .). They did so, among other things, by targeting other DGs that were more receptive to the trade and industry side of the issue. In the end, the Commission published a more modest strategy in October 2006 that relied heavily on voluntary measures and industry self-regulation. As a result, alcohol abuse is on the EU agenda now but the role the EU sees for itself is still limited.

will command a lot of attention. Recall the example of the response to 9/11 given above. In the aftermath of the attacks, political actors from different sides offered interpretations of what the attacks constituted and what they implied. These were all attempts at 'framing' the issue: defining it in a certain way that includes some aspects and highlights some factors while ignoring others.

This can also be seen in the alcohol abuse case. Much of the debate around the issue revolved around the question how the issue should be defined. Until the mid-1990s alcoholic drinks, insofar as they entered the EU agenda, were perceived as tradable commodities. Alcohol abuse was seen as an individual problem of a relatively small proportion of all alcohol consumers, which was not related to the general availability of alcoholic drinks. The question was how to ensure free trade in alcoholic drinks as part of the larger drive to create an internal market among the member states. Member state restrictions on the sale and trade of alcohol, such as excise duties to raise prices, were a potential impediment to the creation of such an internal market. The issue then was how to eliminate these impediments.

Proponents of an EU alcohol abuse policy tried to substitute this frame with an alternative frame that focused on the health effects of alcoholic drinks. According to this frame, alcoholic drinks were not 'like any other good' but required special treatment because of their negative side-effects. In this frame, alcohol abuse was not a problem of individual alcohol consumers but inherent in the wide availability of alcoholic drinks. Hence, restrictions on the sale of alcoholic drinks were necessary to reduce these negative effects and the issue was how to formulate an EU-wide policy that would support (or, indeed, require) such restrictions.

From an agenda-setting perspective, these different frames have two important consequences. To begin with, they change the focus of the policy debate and the types of policy that are deemed appropriate and viable. When it is accepted that alcoholic drinks are primarily an internal market issue (that is, the point is how to ensure their free trade among member states), then the logical next step is to consider policy options that liberalize trade in those drinks. It makes no sense to contemplate EU-wide restrictions because that would not fit into the frame. When alcoholic drinks are primarily viewed from a health perspective, the opposite is true. Hence, frames set the agenda in terms of which policy options will be considered.

Second, framing determines who participates. If an issue can be linked to a value that people find important, they will tend also to find that issue important. Thus, as long as alcoholic drinks are seen as an internal market issue, it will only command attention from people who care about internal market issues (or trade and economic issues more generally). However, when the issue is linked to health concerns, it will become relevant to people who take a (professional and/or personal) interest in health matters. This will change the participation around the issue. Because new participants bring with them new ideas, new preconceptions and new interests, this has important consequences for the way agendas are set and policies are made, thus completely altering the balance of proponents and opponents around an issue.

In addition to the substantive aspects of frames (such as the question whether alcoholic drinks are mainly an issue of trade or of health), agenda-setting in the EU also involves aspects of scale or authority: whether or not the issue is *European* in scope. This is particularly important in the EU because most EU policies need to be justified in terms of cross-border effects or common EU-wide problems. If they cannot, the question arises why the EU should be dealing with them, rather than the member states themselves. This becomes even more important when the EU has no clear competence in a certain policy area, such as health policy in the alcohol abuse case.

As a result, proponents of new issues on the EU agenda also need to construct a story about why the issue is European in scope. In the alcohol abuse case, they did so by pointing at problems that occurred in most member states, such as drink-driving, underage drinking and binge drinking. The argument ran such that if these problems occurred in all EU member states they were common problems, and hence all member states could benefit from a joint, EU-wide response. Opponents of an EU-wide alcohol abuse policy, by contrast, could argue that the issue was best addressed at the national (or even local) level given the nature of the problem and the differences between member states.

Institutional structures

Institutional structures greatly affect the receptiveness of political systems to certain (types of) issues. Political scientists Frank Baumgartner and Bryan Jones have used the term **venue** to explain this (Frank R. Baumgartner and Bryan D. Jones, *Agendas and Instability in American Politics*, University of Chicago Press, 1993). Venues are locations where policies are made. As we saw above, there is a great variety of venues (with their own agendas) within the EU: the Commission, the EP, the European Council, the Council of Ministers, and within each of these institutions different DGs, committees, Council configurations and the like. Each of these venues is a place where issues are discussed.

A policy venue is an institution that has the authority to make decisions about an issue.

Which issues are discussed and how they are discussed depends largely on the characteristics of a venue. The reason for this is that venues have specific (institutional) remits that they are responsible for, care about and have an interest in fostering. As a result, venues in the field of, say, foreign policy, will focus on issues that are related to foreign policy concerns. Likewise, venues that deal with economic affairs will focus on issues that are relevant to that domain. In turn, the venue that deals with an issue has important consequences for the type of policy that is being made because each venue will produce policies that 'fit' its remit.

This means that the way venues are organized is not neutral. By creating venues with a certain remit and by granting or withholding resources to existing venues, the receptiveness of a political system to certain (types of) issues is affected. This is why the American political scientist Elmer E. Schattschneider said that 'organization is the mobilization of bias' (Elmer E. Schattschneider, *The Semi-Sovereign People: A Realist's View of Democracy in America*, Holt, Rinehart and Winston, 1960: 71). Every political system will, as a result of its institutional set-up, be more receptive to some issues than to others. Thus, through the way a political system is structured, some issues are 'organized in' while others are 'organized out'. This is as true of the EU as it is of other political systems.

As a result, many of the activities of prospective agenda-setters are aimed at attracting the attention of the 'right' venue for their cause. If they deliberately do so, they engage in what is called 'venue shopping': deliberately 'plugging' issues in such a way as to place them on the agenda of the venue that is most receptive to their claims. In the alcohol abuse case, proponents of EU-wide policies tried to involve DG Health and Consumers because that DG was most receptive to their cause. Conversely, when that DG circulated an ambitious draft, producers of alcoholic drinks tried to involve DGs in the field of the internal market and economic affairs because they were more sympathetic to *their* claims.

This does not only work between venues within the EU. As we saw in Briefing 9.1, the World Health Organization (WHO) also played a role in putting the issue on the EU agenda. For proponents of a restrictive approach to alcoholic drinks, the WHO was an attractive venue because it is unequivocally committed to health issues and (therefore) highly receptive to claims that are based on health concerns.

This is where venues and framing come together: by framing an issue in a way that appeals to a certain venue, it is possible to attract the attention of that venue and involve it in policy debates. By defining an issue in terms of health concerns, DG Health and Consumer Protection became involved in the issue. However, when opponents of EU alcohol abuse policies emphasized the internal market frame, other DGs became involved again and were able to limit the role of the EU in this field.

The concept of venue shopping implies that outside actors shop around more or less passive venues that are waiting for issues to come to them. This is only half of the story, however. In addition, venues are also actively looking for new issues that they can deal with. They do so for the 'institutional motives' that we discussed above. As a result, they are not (only) recipients of issues but also active players in the agenda-setting process themselves, framing and reframing issues, seeking allies and trying to build impetus for their pet issues.

Timing

In addition to framing and venues, timing plays an important role in agenda-setting processes. Sometimes an issue builds up gradually, gaining impetus over time. In most cases, however, there are moments or (short) periods in which an issue rises quickly on the agenda. These are what American agenda-setting scholar John Kingdon has called **policy windows** or 'windows of opportunity' (John W. Kingdon, *Agendas, Alternatives and Public Policy*, 2nd edn, Longman, 2003). After a short while, the policy window closes, and the issue slides down the agenda again. Major

> A **policy window** is a short period in which an issue commands a lot of attention and decisions on that issue can be taken.

initiatives will then have to wait until the opening of a new policy window.

According to John Kingdon, a policy window opens when three 'streams' of events come together:

- There is wide recognition of the importance of some *problem*.
- A viable and acceptable *solution* to that problem is available.
- *Political circumstances* for the adoption of that solution are favourable.

In some cases, there may be recognition of a problem but no solution is available. Or there is a solution, but it goes against the core ideological beliefs of the current government. In those cases, issues will remain low on the agenda. Yet, when all three streams are 'aligned', an issue will move to the top of the agenda.

This alignment of streams may happen suddenly because some event may dramatically highlight the severity of a problem. This is what Kingdon calls a **focusing event**. A good example of a (very strong) focusing event were the terrorist attacks of 9/11, which pushed terrorism issues to the top of agendas all over the Western world. Another example was the sovereign debt

> A **focusing event** is an occurrence that draws strong attention to a problem.

crisis that hit several EU member states from 2009 onwards and which brought the design of the EU's Economic and Monetary Union back on the agenda again (see Chapter 8). For political actors, focusing events are important opportunities to put an issue on the agenda. In the aftermath of 9/11, for instance, many issues and proposals that had been lingering without gaining much attention suddenly rose to the top of the agenda if they could be linked to (combating) terrorism.

In addition to focusing events, changes in political circumstances may also open a window of opportunity. For example, when a new European Commission is installed that expresses a novel set of policy priorities, all issues related to those new priorities rise on the agenda. Sometimes, the same can happen when government coalitions change in (the larger) EU member states. For instance, when Green parties entered governing coalitions in France and Germany in the 1990s, the issue of genetically modified organisms became much more important at the EU level.

Although the alcohol abuse issue of Briefing 9.1 did not experience a strong focusing event or sudden changes in political circumstances, several events helped the issue forward. The appearance on the market of alcopops from 1995 onwards focused attention on the (European-wide) problem of underage drinking. In addition, the issue gained considerable impetus when

Sweden assumed the Presidency of the EU in 2001. By organizing conferences and consistently raising the issue during its presidency, the Swedish government was able to create more favourable political circumstances for the consideration of alcohol abuse on the EU agenda. This resulted in the publication of the EU alcoholism strategy in 2006. For the issue to move forward again, it would probably need another such push in order to overcome opposition by the alcoholic drinks industry and its allies within the Commission.

These examples show that timing is crucial in agenda-setting. Advocates of an issue may take years (sometimes dozens of years) to build up problem awareness and develop policy options, but the crucial moves to the top of the agenda typically take place in short periods of time. These windows of opportunity open quickly but they also close quickly, leading to fast changes in the content of the political agenda.

■ Summary

This chapter has taken a closer look at agenda-setting in the EU. It has argued that:

- The political agenda is the set of issues that policy-makers give serious attention to.
- Agendas are important in politics and policy-making because they determine which issues will be taken up for decision-making and which will not.
- Political actors actively seek to place issues on the agenda or keep them off. As a result, agenda-setting is a highly political process.
- Besides the political agenda, we can also discern the media agenda and the public agenda. Political systems differ in the way these three types of agenda are related. Cobb, Ross and Ross distinguished between three models in this regard: the outside initiative model, the mobilization model and the inside access model. In the EU, the inside access model is relatively more important than in other political systems, although the other two models also occur.
- Political actors may have various reasons for wanting to put an issue on the EU agenda: tackling cross-border problems, circumventing domestic political resistance, creating a 'level playing field' between competing firms, 'spreading the word' for an issue they believe in strongly, or satisfying institutional interests in expanding organizational tasks and resources. In reality, many issues are pushed on to the EU agenda out of a combination of motives.
- Although agenda-setting processes are not formalized, certain steps tend to occur in many EU agenda-setting processes. These steps form the sequence of a 'typical' agenda-setting process. In concrete cases all kinds of variations on this sequence may occur.

- Three (sets of) factors are particularly important in understanding why issues (do not) make it on to the EU agenda: issue framing, institutional structures and timing.
- Issue framing consists of defining an issue in such a way that some aspects are emphasized while other aspects are ignored.
- The existence and remit of institutional venues determine how receptive policy-makers are to certain claims and issues.
- Issues rise to the top of the political agenda during so-called policy windows or windows of opportunity. These windows often occur suddenly, as the result of a highly publicized focusing event or a change in political circumstances.

Further reading

Key texts on agenda-setting (in general) include John Kingdon, *Agendas, Alternatives and Public Policy* (Longman, 2nd edn, 2003), Frank Baumgartner and Bryan Jones, *Agendas and Instability in American Politics* (University of Chicago Press, 2nd edn, 2009), and Bryan Jones and Frank Baumgartner, *The Politics of Attention: How Government Prioritizes Problems* (University of Chicago Press, 2005). On agenda-setting in the EU, see Sebastiaan Princen, *Agenda-setting in the European Union* (Palgrave Macmillan, 2009).

Websites

- Preparatory documents by the European Commission and overviews of the follow-up to those documents are available through Pre-Lex: http://ec.europa.eu/prelex/apcnet.cfm?CL=en
- A wide range of documents on specific policy issues (including Green Papers, White Papers and other agenda-setting documents) can be found on the pages of the various DGs of the European Commission: http://ec.europa.eu/index_en.htm

Navigating the EU

On the website www.navigatingthe.eu you will find online exercises for this chapter.

10 Decision-making

■ Introduction

On 8 February 2013, after twenty-four hours of negotiations, the European Council agreed to the EU's Multiannual Financial Framework (MFF) for the period 2014–20. The Financial Perspectives lay down the size of the EU budget for each year as well as the contribution of each member state and the distribution across major spending categories. This forms the framework within which annual budgets are adopted.

Finding a compromise had been a difficult process because the Financial Perspectives had to reconcile a number of highly diverging interests. To begin with, all member states had had to cut their budgets in the wake of the financial crisis. At the same time, unemployment levels had risen across the EU, leading to a search for ways to stimulate economic growth and, thereby, employment. The ideas about how to do that varied markedly.

In its initial draft, published in June 2011, the European Commission had proposed a rise of the EU budget to 1.08% of the EU's Gross National Income (GNI). The extra money would be spent on research as well as increased investments in infrastructure in the fields of telecom, energy and transport.

The response by the member states followed the lines that were familiar from previous negotiations on the budget. On one side, a group of member states named 'Friends of Better Spending' argued for cuts in the overall EU budget and a reduction of spending on agriculture and cohesion policy to the benefit of policies they deemed important for innovation. This group included most member states that were net contributors to the EU budget (see Table 8.3 in Chapter 8). Even before the first Commission proposal, in December 2010, Finland, France, Germany, the Netherlands and the United Kingdom had already sent an open letter to the Commission demanding a reduced budget.

On the other side was a group called 'Friends of Cohesion', which included some fifteen member states that benefited from the cohesion funds. They argued that cohesion policy was crucial for economic growth and employment and should therefore not be cut in the new MFF. During the course of 2012, this group issued several statements to this effect and made it their priority during the negotiations.

Since all member states had to agree to the final MFF package, prolonged negotiations ensued, during which both the European Commission and the European Council President, Herman Van Rompuy, put forward new proposals. In the end, the overall EU budget was set at around 1% of EU GNI. Expenditures on cohesion policy were largely left alone, while expenditures on the Common Agricultural Policy were further reduced until 2020. This also led to increased expenditures on investments and research, albeit at a lower level than the European Commission had foreseen in its initial proposals. After the decisive European Council meeting, all government leaders declared victory, claiming that they had secured important benefits for their countries.

The MFF offers a good example of the prolonged and high-level negotiations that can accompany EU decision-making. At the same time, the European Council negotiations on the MFF concerned only one type of decision that the EU takes – one at which the stakes for the member states were high. The EU also takes other types of decisions which are much more 'low profile'. Hence, in this chapter we will discuss the following questions:

- What types of decisions are taken in the EU?
- How does decision-making for each of these types work?
- What is the role of expertise and interests in EU decision-making?
- To what types of policy outcomes does EU decision-making lead?

We will see that the EU takes decisions at different 'levels', ranging from history-making decisions that determine the EU's 'constitutional' structure and overall priorities to mundane day-to-day decisions that shape specific policies. Decision-making dynamics vary considerably between these different types. This has important implications for the relative importance of each of the institutions in the decision-making process, as well as the strategies that actors use and the outcomes that characterize the process.

■ Levels of decision-making in the EU

As we noted in the introduction to this chapter, different types of decisions are adopted in the EU. These types of decisions differ in terms of the way in which decisions are taken and the factors that are important in understanding decision-making processes. John Peterson has proposed a threefold distinction that is a useful starting point for exploring these differences (John Peterson, 'Decision-Making in the European Union: Towards a Framework for Analysis', *Journal of European Public Policy*, 2, 1, 1995: 69–93):

- History-making decisions shape the fundamental structure of the EU, by changing the EU treaties or by specifying fundamental, long-term priorities.
- Policy-setting decisions concern the choice between policy alternatives in a specific issue area.
- Policy-shaping decisions deal with the details of policies, including the formulation of policy options and the specification of more general policies.

History-making decisions set the framework within which the EU operates. They are therefore about the EU itself. The other two levels, by contrast, deal with policy-making within that framework. To give an example: the adoption of the Treaty of Lisbon was a history-making decision, while the adoption of the Tobacco Products Directive (see the introduction to Chapter 4) was about policy-making within the EU's existing institutional set-up. The difference between the policy-setting and policy-shaping levels concerns the level of detail at which policies are made. The policy-setting level is about the fundamental choices made within an issue area, while the policy-shaping level is about the detailed instruments and standards applied within the broader policies. Stated differently: policy-setting is about *what* to do, while policy-shaping is about *how* to do it.

The distinction between these three types of decisions runs parallel to the distinction in international relations theory between **high politics** and **low politics**. High politics concerns vital national interests. In a narrow sense, it relates exclusively to issues of peace and security. In a broader sense, it also refers to other issues that a national government finds of prime importance. High politics is played out at the highest political level – that is, the head of government and his or her close advisers. Low politics, by contrast, is about decisions that may be important for the general well-being of society but that do not touch upon these vital interests. Low politics takes place within 'regular' policy-making institutions.

> **High politics** concerns issues that affect vital national interests. **Low politics** concerns issues for which the political stakes are not that high.

History-making decisions are, almost by definition, high politics. They deal with fundamental choices about the distribution of powers and resources between the EU institutions and the member states, and are ultimately decided by the member states' heads of government. Policy-shaping decisions, on the other hand, are typically low politics and involve institutions such as expert groups and Council working parties. Policy-setting decisions are in between. Depending on the issue at stake, they can either be high politics or low politics. This will also determine the main actors in the process. Policy-setting decisions that have a high politics character usually end up in the European Council,

Table 10.1 Types of decisions in the EU

Type of decision	Main actors	Guiding policy-making dynamic	High/low politics
History-making	European Council	Intergovernmental negotiations	High politics
Policy-setting	Commission, Council, EP, interest groups	Interinstitutional bargaining, intergovernmental negotiations, and party politics	
Policy-shaping	Commission DGs, expert groups, Council working groups, interest groups	Technocratic and administrative policy-making	Low politics

Source: Based on John Peterson, 'Decision-making in the European Union: Towards a Framework for Analysis', *Journal of European Public Policy*, 2, 1, 1995: 71.

while policy-setting decisions that remain low politics are decided in the EU's institutional triangle of Commission, Council and EP.

Of course, the distinction between high politics and low politics, like the distinction between the three types of decisions presented above, is not always clear-cut. Some decisions are on the border between two types. For instance, the decision on the 2014–2020 Multiannual Financial Framework was on the border between 'policy-setting' and 'history-making'. It was policy-setting because it laid down choices between broad policy alternatives, but it was also history-making because it concerned long-term EU priorities and fixed the financial relations between the EU and its member states for some years to come. Still, by thinking in terms of these different types, it becomes easier to recognize what is important in decision-making processes and to understand their underlying dynamics. That is why these distinctions offer useful conceptual schemes for organizing our thinking about decision-making.

The main differences between the types of decisions are summarized in Table 10.1. In the next two sections, we will discuss these three types and explain in more detail what they entail.

■ History-making decisions in the EU

Treaty change and high politics

Decisions are **history-making** if they determine the fundamental choices about the course of the EU for years to come. The set of decisions that most closely conforms to this definition involves

> **History-making decisions** are decisions that determine the fundamental choices about the course of the EU for years to come.

decisions regarding treaty change. This is comparable to what, within states, would be called 'constitutional decision-making'. The EU's treaties effectively form its 'constitution', in the sense that they lay down the basic objectives, guiding principles and decision-making procedures that structure the way the EU operates. Changing those treaties requires the consent of all EU member states. Only if all member states ratify a treaty (change), will that treaty (change) come into force.

In addition to treaty change, some decisions within the existing treaties that lay down governance arrangements and political priorities for a longer term can also be called 'history-making'. This is the case, for example, for the Multiannual Financial Framework, which determines the broad outlines of EU policy-making for a period of seven years.

History-making decisions are typically high politics, because they involve the power relations between member state governments in future decision-making as well as the extent to which the EU will be able to wield power over its member states. Therefore, they touch directly upon the core interests and the sovereignty of member state governments. This has three implications for the way decision-making in history-making decisions takes place:

- The basic decisions will be made by the highest political level in each member state, normally the head of government with some senior ministers and advisers.
- The basic considerations will concern the national interest as perceived by those top politicians.
- The basic mode of reaching decisions will be bargaining.

This means that in order to understand the outcome of history-making decision-making we need to understand the dynamics of bargaining between member states. It is to these dynamics that we now turn.

What is at stake in negotiations?

The basic idea behind bargaining is simple: if two (or more) actors have different preferred outcomes, they engage in bargaining in order to achieve an outcome that is closest to their most-preferred outcome. However, in order to achieve any outcome at all, that outcome needs to be acceptable to all parties. We can depict this graphically as in Figure 10.1.

In Figure 10.1, A, B and C are the preferred outcomes of three member states. Let's make this more concrete by taking an example, such as the negotiations on the Multiannual Financial Framework. Let's say, for simplicity's sake, that the positions of A, B and C on the vertical axis represent the preferences regarding the overall budget (higher or lower) and the positions on the horizontal axis the preferences regarding expenditures on agricultural policies (also higher or lower). In that case, A could represent the position of the UK or Sweden, B the position of France and C the position of Hungary or Greece.

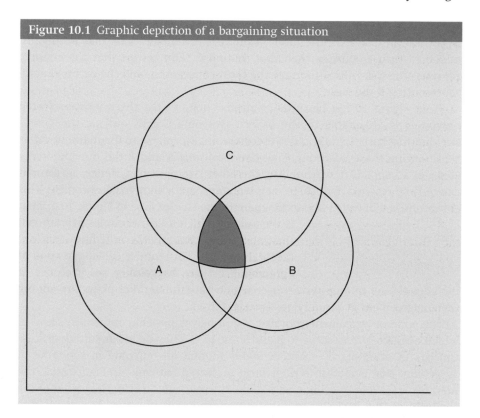

Figure 10.1 Graphic depiction of a bargaining situation

A, B and C represent most-preferred outcomes: the combinations of overall expenditures and expenditures on agricultural policies that various member states would ideally like to achieve. In negotiation analysis, the circle around each of the preferred outcomes is called that member state's **zone of acceptability**: the set of outcomes that each member state is willing to accept (agree to). Any outcome outside of the circle is not acceptable because it is too far removed from the most-preferred outcome. For instance, although France would have preferred an outcome with low overall expenditures but no change in the agricultural policies, in the end it accepted an agreement that entailed reduced spending but also some reductions in CAP spending. At the same time, there were probably limits to the cuts on CAP spending that France was willing to accept. Beyond those limits, it would not have accepted the MFF deal.

> The **zone of acceptability** is the set of bargaining outcomes that a participant in a negotiation is willing to accept.

The zone of acceptability may not be equally large for all member states. Some member state governments may be willing to accept compromises that are further removed from their most-preferred outcomes than others. In

Figure 10.1 this is shown by the different sizes of the circles. In this (purely hypothetical) example, the circle around B is smaller than that around A, which in turn is smaller than that around C. This means that the country representing C is willing to make the most concessions, and the member state representing B the least.

From Figure 10.1 it becomes clear that none of the three most-preferred outcomes is acceptable to the others. Outcome C falls outside the circles surrounding both A and B and is therefore not acceptable to the member states representing those positions. Likewise, positions A and B fall outside of the zones of acceptability surrounding the other two positions. Hence, agreement can only be reached if all three member states are willing to compromise. This compromise will have to lie somewhere in the shaded area in Figure 10.1. That is the area in which all three circles overlap and that, therefore, contains the outcomes that are acceptable to all. This zone is called the **zone of agreement** or the **bargaining set**, because it includes the set of alternatives over which bargaining takes place and among which agreement eventually needs to be found.

> The **zone of agreement** or **bargaining set** is the set of bargaining outcomes that all participants in a negotiation are willing to accept.

The zone of agreement contains a number of possible outcomes, some of which are closer to A, some to B and some to C. The whole bargaining process consists of attempts by member states to find an outcome in the zone of agreement that is closest to their most-preferred outcome. In Figure 10.1, the member state representing A would like the outcome to be in the corner of the shaded area that is closest to its most-preferred outcome and the same is true for B and C. The situation becomes more difficult when the zone of agreement is difficult to identify or when there is no area of overlap. In the latter case, no agreement is possible at all unless some zone of agreement is created during the negotiations. This manoeuvring to find zones of agreement and to determine which of different possible outcomes will be attained is what is at stake in bargaining situations and it is for this reason that negotiations may take so long, as they did in the case of the Multiannual Financial Framework. In the next subsection, we will see how member states play this game or, in other words, what bargaining tactics they use.

Bargaining tactics in negotiations

On the basis of Figure 10.1 and the explanation above, it becomes easier to understand what types of bargaining tactics can be used. Below, we will discuss five tactics that are used in negotiations between EU member states (and are applicable in other bargaining situations as well):

- coalition formation;
- persuasion and the 'management of meaning';
- challenging other member states;
- issue linkage and side-payments;
- splitting the difference.

Coalition formation

A basic strategy in any EU decision-making process is the formation of coalitions with like-minded counterparts. In the case of the Multiannual Financial Framework, we saw clear examples of this with the 'Friends of Better Spending' and 'Friends of Cohesion', which banded together to present unified demands during the negotiations. Within each of these two coalitions, there were small differences of opinion on exactly how much the budget should be reduced (Friends of Better Spending) or the specifics of cohesion policy (Friends of Cohesion), but the joint interests among their members were similar. By coming together and agreeing on one single demand, they were able to make their point much more forcefully and form a block that could not be ignored when negotiating a deal. The success of these coalitions was exemplified by the fact that, in the end, the EU budget was indeed reduced but cohesion policy was largely left untouched.

Persuasion and the management of meaning

Persuasion and the management of meaning involve giving arguments and/or (re-)framing proposals in order to make them more (or less) attractive for opponents. One actor then tries to persuade another actor that the latter should support (or oppose) a proposal because it is in the other actor's own self-interest. This tactic is particularly useful when it is not altogether clear what the implications of a proposal are. In financial negotiations, such as those over the Multiannual Financial Framework, it is possible to quantify the consequences of a proposal (how much it will cost and who will benefit). This makes it more difficult to reframe the proposal.

For many other issues, however, the consequences are much less clear. What does it mean when the Court of Justice receives jurisdiction over a policy area that was previously excluded from judicial scrutiny? Is that a victory for the rule of law, a safeguard against runaway Commission actions, or a threat to member state sovereignty? The answer to this is not always clear, and by skilfully presenting the issue in one light or another adversaries in the negotiations can try to convince each other of their point of view. The important point with this tactic is that it plays on the self-interest of one's opponent. The argument is not that the opponent should change their mind to do you a favour but that they should change their mind because it is in their own interest.

The management of meaning is not just important in the negotiations between member states at the EU level, but also in the subsequent ratification of the outcomes of the negotiations within the member states. Every treaty change needs to be ratified by all member states. Even when no formal ratification is required, as in the case of the Multiannual Financial Framework, member state politicians need to make sure that they do not lose the support of their domestic constituency. Negotiators for a member state are therefore not only concerned with what other member states want but also with what is acceptable to their constituency 'back home'. Framing and reframing the outcome of negotiations is very important in this regard. This is why after the decisive European Council meeting on the MFF, all participants went to great lengths to explain why the deal was such a victory for their own country.

Hence, in terms of Figure 10.1 above, management of meaning can lead member states to redefine which proposals they find acceptable and thereby enlarge the zone of agreement or it can create a zone of agreement where none existed before.

Challenging other member states

Challenging an opponent is another way of achieving a better outcome during negotiations. In that case, one member state tests the firmness of another member state by 'calling its bluff'. A member state may refuse to agree to a proposal, even when it lies within its zone of acceptability, because it hopes to achieve an even better outcome. Rather than trying to convince that member state or offering something in return for agreement, other member states can also mount a challenge by holding firm and forcing the opposing member state either to block the entire agreement or abandon its opposition. If the proposed agreement is indeed within a member state's zone of acceptability, it will most likely not want to block the entire agreement for one or a few minor issues. In that case, it will give in and the challenge by the others will have succeeded.

Challenges are a delicate matter because they rely on the assumption that one's opponent's resolve is weak, which need not be the case. If it turns out that the opponent holds firm, a challenge can therefore lead to a stalemate. Member states may also try to improve the impression that others have of their resolve by openly committing to certain demands. If a government openly declares in its home country that it will not give up some demand, it becomes much more difficult for that government to backtrack at a later stage because it would incur an important loss of face vis-à-vis its own constituency. For governments, this may exactly be the reason why they make such a public announcement: by committing themselves to a demand at home and thus making it more difficult to retreat, they signal to other member state governments that they are not likely to give in. This is probably one of the reasons why the Friends of Better Spending and the Friends of Cohesion sent open letters and published public statements during the negotiations on the MFF. In terms of Figure 10.1, by doing so they reduced their zones of acceptability, which increased the likelihood that the outcome of the negotiations would lie closer to their most-preferred outcome. The drawback (and hence delicacy) of this strategy can also be seen from Figure 10.1. If a member state makes its zone of acceptability smaller, the zone of agreement becomes smaller. However, if it goes too far the zone of agreement may completely disappear, and agreement is no longer possible.

This is why good negotiators offer a 'graceful' way out for their opponents, so they can agree to a compromise without losing face vis-à-vis their constituency. A good example of this can be found in the negotiations around the predecessor of the 2014–2020 Multiannual Financial Framework, the 2007–2013 Financial Perspectives. Negotiations on the Financial Perspectives had evolved along similar lines to the ones we saw for the MFF. In the end, the final deal had to be struck in an around-the-clock meeting of the European Council. During this final round of negotiations, Poland had demanded more money under the EU's cohesion policy. This threatened to unsettle the compromise that had been found until Angela Merkel, the German Chancellor, offered Poland €100 million that had been earmarked for Germany. This convinced the Polish Prime Minister, Marcinkiewicz, to agree to the compromise. Marcinkiewicz and other leaders present at the meeting declared afterwards that Merkel's move had been a sign of true solidarity that had made possible a deal. Substantively, however, the amount of €100 million paled in comparison with the total of €60 billion that Poland would receive under the EU's cohesion policy in the 2007–2013 Financial Perspectives (let alone the €91 billion it would receive in total), so it is unlikely to have been such a major point for the Polish government. It is more likely that Merkel's offer, and the subsequent efforts by all parties to present it as a breakthrough move of great statesmanship, were meant to allow the Polish government to agree to the compromise text without being accused back home of 'selling out' Polish interests.

Issue linkage and side-payments

Another strategy that can be used to make agreement more likely is to link issues into one package. **Issue linkage** works if one issue is important to one side and another issue to another side. Then, by linking the issues in such a way that each side wins on

> **Issue linkage** occurs when the outcome of the decision on one issue is made contingent on the outcome of the decision on another issue.

the issue it feels most strongly about, a deal can be brokered in which both sides win. In this way, even if there is no zone of agreement on each of the separate issues, a zone of agreement can be found for two (or more) issues together.

A variant of issue linkage is the use of **side-payments**. When a member state is not willing to agree to a proposal, the opposition can sometimes be overcome by offering financial compensation. This happened during the negotiations leading up to the 1992 Treaty of Maastricht, which included both the introduction of a common currency (what was to become the Euro) and the creation

> **Side-payments** are monetary compensations given to a participant in a decision-making process in order to secure the support of that participant for a proposal that is unrelated to the payments.

of the EU's cohesion fund, which gives financial support to the EU's poorer member states. For Greece, Ireland, Portugal and Spain, the creation of the cohesion fund was a condition for agreeing to the establishment of a common currency. Stated differently, creating the cohesion fund was a side-payment with which the EU's richest member states secured the support of these four member states for the introduction of a common currency.

Issue linkage is not always used to make agreement easier. By contrast, it can also be used defensively, to fend off a challenge. In the negotiations leading up to the 2007–2013 Financial Perspectives, France at some point raised the issue of the rebate on the UK contribution to the EU budget, arguing it was an anomaly that should be abolished. The UK government countered by linking a reduction in the rebate to a fundamental overhaul of the EU's agricultural policies. This effectively ended the debate on the rebate. By linking an issue that was unacceptable to it (reduction of the rebate) to an issue it knew was unacceptable to the French government (fundamental change in the CAP), the UK government was able to remove the issue of the rebate from the negotiation table.

Splitting through the middle

A final tactic that is often seen in negotiations is simply splitting the difference between two positions through the middle, so each party obtains something but not everything. This is what most people think of as a true 'compromise'. It can be a good way to reach a mutually acceptable outcome, as long as that outcome is within the zone of agreement between the parties involved.

At the same time, splitting the difference through the middle is not always as straightforward as it seems, because it may not be clear what each member state's 'real' preferences are. As a result, it may pay for a member state to exaggerate its demands. Then, if the difference is split through the middle, the final outcome may actually be quite close to what that member state really wanted to begin with.

■ Policy-setting and policy-shaping in the EU

Low politics and high politics in EU policy-making

History-making decisions are the most visible and most widely publicized events in EU decision-making. At the same time, they are quite rare: decisions that lay down the fundamental structures of the EU and set its overall long-term priorities are taken only once every so many years. The vast majority of EU decisions are taken within the existing frameworks of the EU and concern specific policy fields. This is what we may call 'policy-making' decisions.

Policy-making decisions can be divided into two. **Policy-setting decisions** are about the choices between alternatives on a given issue. Does the EU strive for a reduction of greenhouse gas emissions or not and, if so, by what percentage? Will the EU participate in a

Policy-setting decisions are about the choices between alternative courses of action for dealing with a given issue.

new global navigation satellite system to compete with the American GPS system? Are member state governments allowed to give financial support to banks that are on the brink of bankruptcy? These are the major 'what' questions of policy-making: from a range of possible alternatives, what policy option will be pursued?

Policy-shaping is about the development of alternatives for decision-making. For instance, if it is decided to reduce greenhouse gases, how will this be done: by introducing higher taxes on energy, by subsidizing more fuel-efficient cars, or by setting ceilings on the emissions of greenhouse gases by factories? And if emission ceilings are defined, how are they allocated to firms and can firms sell their 'rights to pollute' to other firms if they do not completely use them up? These are the types of specific questions that need to be answered to give content and meaning to the more general choices that are made in policy-setting.

> **Policy-shaping decisions** are about the choices between alternative policy instruments to tackle a given issue.

The institutional framework governing policy-making in the EU was detailed in Chapters 3 and 4. In Chapter 4, we saw there is a variety of decision-making procedures, which differ in terms of the institutions involved (e.g. does the EP have to approve a proposal?) and the decision rule applicable in the Council (unanimity or qualified majority voting). Moreover, in Chapter 3, we saw that even when a decision is formally made by one of the EU institutions, the actual decision may be taken at a lower level: Coreper or a Council working party for the Council, a parliamentary committee in the EP or a DG within the Commission. In these cases, the decision by the Council, the EP or the Commission is merely a formality.

Therefore, although the institutional procedures lay down the playing field for EU decision-making, they do not fully determine the game that is played on that field. As was shown in Table 10.1, policy-setting decisions can be either 'high politics' or 'low politics', depending on the issue at stake. This has profound consequences for the way decision-making evolves, both between the EU institutions and within each of the institutions. If a policy-setting decision becomes high politics, the interinstitutional centre of gravity in the decision-making process will shift towards the Council of Ministers or even the European Council (although formally the European Council has no role to play in most decision-making procedures). When a decision is low politics, the Commission and/or the EP may play a more important role. Likewise, when an issue becomes high politics, the actual decision within each of the institutions will be made at a higher level.

This dynamic relationship between formal procedures and actual processes can also be observed in the process leading up to the Multiannual Financial Framework. In the introduction to this chapter, we focused our story on the negotiations in the European Council. Formally, however, the Multiannual Financial Framework had to be adopted by two other institutions: the Council of Ministers and the European Parliament. The Council of Ministers merely rubber-stamped the compromise reached in the European Council. Throughout the entire process, the EP tried to have its voice heard but mostly in vain. Already before the first Commission proposal in 2011, the EP had adopted a resolution calling for a significant increase of the EU budget (to around 1.11% of EU GNI) and a replacement of member state contributions by taxes levied directly by the EU itself. During 2012, it repeated this position several times, stating that any deal on the MFF would be unacceptable without these elements. When the compromise reached in the European Council failed to honour any of these demands, the EP initially rejected it in a resolution in March 2013. Yet, about half a year later the EP accepted the agreement reached in the European Council after all, having only secured a mid-term review of the MFF in 2016 and the creation of a working group that would study the possibility of reforming the system of contributions to the EU budget after 2020. Thus, although the EP formally had to agree to the Multi-annual Financial Framework, its impact on the final outcome was minimal. This was such a controversial issue among the member state governments that the crucial point was to find agreement among those governments. Once the European Council had reached such an agreement, there was little the EP could change, even after it had initially (and largely symbolically) rejected the compromise.

Whether a decision is high or low politics cannot always be determined purely on the basis of characteristics of the issue itself. Sometimes, seemingly 'technical' issues may become highly politicized and shift from low to high politics or vice versa. One and the same decision may even alternate between high and low politics over time, with the main locus of decision-making shifting in tandem. Briefing 10.1 gives an example of an issue that has alternated between low and high politics: the use of genetically modified crops in EU agriculture.

Interinstitutional dynamics in EU decision-making

In Chapters 3 and 4, we already looked in some detail at the various EU institutions and their roles in decision-making procedures. From this discussion it will have become clear that the EU has an extraordinarily complicated decision-making structure because many institutions and actors need to agree to a proposal before a decision can be taken. In the terminology of the Greek political scientist George Tsebelis, decision-making in the EU involves many **veto players** (George Tsebelis, *Veto Players: How Political Institutions Work*, Princeton University Press, 2002). Tsebelis discerns two types of veto players: institutional veto players (institutions that need to approve a proposal) and partisan veto players (actors within those institutions that are needed to adopt a proposal). On both types, the EU scores high.

A **veto player** is an actor who can prevent a decision from being taken.

To make this clear, compare the EU to the UK. In the UK, decisions are essentially taken by one chamber of Parliament (the House of Commons). Within the House of Commons, most of the time one party has an absolute majority. Moreover, there is a close liaison (if not fusion) between the majority party in the House of Commons and the government, whereby the leader of the government (the prime minister) has a strong hold on the voting behaviour of his or her party's members of parliament. This means that in the UK, there is essentially one veto player: the majority party, headed by the prime minister.

Briefing 10.1

Low politics and high politics around genetically modified organisms

Genetic modification is a technique whereby genes in an organism are altered in order to introduce some desired trait. An example is genetically modified maize that produces its own insecticides and is therefore automatically protected against pests. The technology was developed during the 1980s but only became operational from the early 1990s onwards. Initially, policy-making on the use of genetically modified organisms (GMOs) in the EU was a low politics issue. It was led by the European Commission and experts from the member states, who met in Brussels but also within the Organisation for Economic Co-operation and Development (OECD). As a result, in 1990, the EU adopted two Directives to regulate the use of GMOs.

All this changed when the first GMOs hit the markets. In the late 1990s, environmental NGOs, such as Greenpeace and Friends of the Earth, mounted vast campaigns against the alleged risks of GMOs for the environment and human health. During that same period, Green parties became part of the governing coalitions in two major EU member states, France and Germany. For them, GMOs formed an important political issue. As member state governments became interested, the issue moved from low to high politics. Decision-making on GMOs became subject to heated debates in the Council of Ministers, with a coalition of member states consistently blocking any new approvals of genetically modified crops and forcing a revision of the earlier EU legislative framework.

This example shows how an issue that initially was treated as 'technical' (because it involved a new technology, the risks of which can only be assessed on the basis of scientific expertise) gradually became more 'political' (because it touched upon fundamental concerns raised by environmental groups and Green politicians). Parallel to this shift in perspective, decision-making on the issue moved to higher political forums and involved more high-ranking politicians.

In most cases, if the prime minister or at least the core cabinet agrees to a proposal, that proposal will be adopted.

Now contrast this to EU decision-making. If the ordinary legislative procedure is used, three institutions can effectively block an agreement: the Commission (without which no proposal can be made), the Council and the EP (which both can reject the proposal). They thus present three institutional veto players. Now to the partisan veto players. Within the Commission, a proposal can only be released if all commissioners agree. In addition, the Council decides by qualified majority, which means that a minority of member states can prevent a proposal from being adopted. This is reinforced by the tendency to search for consensus even when a qualified majority is available (see Chapter 4). In the EP, finally, no party group even comes close to an absolute majority (see

Chapter 7) so a coalition of groups is necessary to reach a majority. As a result, the EU has a large number of (institutional and partisan) veto players, which present many hurdles for the adoption of a proposal.

This has four consequences for decision-making in the EU. To begin with, the larger the number of veto players, the more difficult it is to reach an agreement. Since the EU has an extremely large number of veto players, the threshold for adopting a proposal is also very high. Second, because of the supermajorities required in the Council, participants in EU decision-making tend not to think in terms of majorities but in terms of blocking minorities. The question they ask is not 'Is there a majority?' but 'Is there a blocking minority?' Decision-making is geared at overcoming such a blocking minority. Third, the large number of veto players in EU decision-making has implications for the strategies employed between the institutions. The Commission will (have to) consider what proposal has a reasonable chance of going through the Council and the EP. Likewise, when the EP proposes amendments to Commission proposals, it must not only consider the positions and relative strengths of the EP's party groups but also the acceptability of those amendments to the Commission and (a (qualified) majority of) the member states in the Council.

Finally, the large number of veto players has given rise to a culture of consensus and compromise. If all actors and institutions were simply to reject any proposal they did not fully approve of, no decision would be taken at all. This has led to a severe restraint on the use of blocking votes. Actors and institutions use the threat of a rejection as leverage in negotiations to obtain an outcome that is closer to their preferences. Only seldom, however, do they eventually completely reject a proposal. As a result, the vast majority of Commission proposals are eventually adopted, even if they include many amendments. New players in EU decision-making are quickly socialized into this practice. For instance, after Sweden joined the EU, it voted against a proposal in the Council more than thirty times during the first half year of 1995, an amazing number for EU standards. Quickly, however, the Swedish government realized that this strategy led to its isolation and thereby reduced its effectiveness in negotiations with other member states, and the number of no-votes dropped dramatically to reach more 'normal' levels.

Policy networks in policy-making decisions

Although policies are decided by and in the EU institutions, the range of actors that are involved in policy-making processes is not confined to those institutions. In Chapter 6 on interest groups, we already saw that many groups try to influence EU policy-making, often by becoming part of the process of writing and bargaining over proposals. Therefore, decision-making on EU policies cannot be understood exclusively in terms of inter- and intra-institutional politics. Instead, an approach is needed that captures the interactions between actors within and outside the EU's institutions.

Fact file 10.1

Types of networks in (EU) policy-making

- *Policy communities* are networks of policy experts in a given issue area. Policy communities tend to be rather closed – that is, they have a stable membership and fixed ideas about what is the best policy in their area. As a result, they are not easily penetrated by new ideas or outsiders.
- *Iron triangles* are similar to policy communities, although the term 'iron triangle' is often used in a more pejorative sense. The triangle exists between politicians, civil servants and interest group representatives that stand for the status quo in a given issue area. The triangle is made of iron because it is difficult for outsiders (that is, actors with different ideas or interests) to break the hold it has on existing policies.
- *Issue networks* are like policy communities but they are looser, in the sense that participation is less fixed and actors enter and leave the network over time.
- *Advocacy coalitions* are coalitions of actors that share basic ideas about what policy to pursue in an issue area and that coordinate their activities in order to achieve that policy. Advocacy coalitions may include politicians, civil servants, interest group representatives, journalists and academics. Most issue areas have two or more advocacy coalitions with competing ideas that struggle for dominance.
- *Transnational advocacy networks* are networks of activists that join forces across borders to plead for a shared value or policy. These networks are centred on NGOs, such as Amnesty International and Greenpeace.
- *Epistemic communities* are networks of experts that share a professional understanding of a given issue. They are typically centred on academics and other researchers, but may also include government officials with the same professional background. They argue for their preferred policies on the basis of professional expertise.

In the literature on policy-making, the term **policy network** is often used to describe those interactions. When actors interact regularly, they form a network. When that network deals with

> A **policy network** consists of a set of participants in a given policy field who are connected through regular interactions.

policy-making in a given area, it is a policy network. The literature abounds with terms that refer to policy networks, each laying stress on a particular element. Fact file 10.1 gives an overview of the terms and concepts that are often used.

Conceptualizations of policy networks differ in three respects:

- *The type(s) of actors in the network.* For instance, an 'advocacy coalition' may include a wide range of actors: politicians, civil servants and interest group representatives, but also academics and journalists. By contrast, the term 'epistemic community' is used to denote a specific type of network that includes primarily academic researchers and other professional experts.

- *The stability of the network.* The terms 'iron triangle' and 'policy community' denote stable networks with fixed participation, while the term 'issue network' is meant to denote a much looser configuration with floating membership.
- *The degree of conflict implied.* The literature on policy communities and issue networks normally assumes that there is one network in an issue area (for instance, an agricultural policy community or an issue network around rail transport). On the contrary, transnational advocacy networks are engaged in a fight against some practice that they are opposed to, implying a degree of conflict. Likewise, there are usually several advocacy coalitions in a given issue area, which compete for dominance in that area.

Because these different terms lay emphasis on different aspects of policy-making, they are helpful in understanding different decision-making processes. For instance, one policy area may be characterized by a (stable, status quo-oriented) policy community, while decision-making in another area revolves around a struggle between two competing advocacy coalitions. Likewise, the role of expertise, which is at the heart of the study of epistemic communities, varies between issues and over time.

Nevertheless, all these conceptions have two things in common that are important for understanding policy-making in the EU:

- Decision-making is the result of a wide range of actors that interact, not randomly but in a more or less structured fashion.
- These networks are not confined to specific EU institutions but include actors from various EU institutions plus organizations outside of the EU's formal institutional framework. As a result, the crucial dividing line in policy-making is often not between institutions but between networks that include actors from various institutions and support different courses of action.

Take the example of the regulation of genetically modified crops, which was highlighted in Briefing 10.1 above. Different types of networks can be found in this case. To begin with, there are a number of competing advocacy coalitions. One advocacy coalition sees genetic modification as a way to enhance the efficiency and quality of agriculture and therefore seeks to promote its use. It includes, among others, officials from the European Commission (e.g. from its Directorate-General for Enterprise and Industry), liberal MEPs, interest groups that represent the biotechnology industry, and scientists that work on new applications of genetic modification. The other advocacy coalition argues that genetic modification is intrinsically dangerous because it amounts to 'tinkering with nature' and therefore argues for no or a very restricted use of the technology. This advocacy coalition includes other officials from the Commission (most notably from DG Environment), Green MEPs, environmental

NGOs and journalists and scientists who are critical of the technology. Decision-making in this issue area can be understood as a struggle between these advocacy coalitions. Within these broader networks, more specific networks have evolved. For instance, a transnational advocacy network of environmental groups has campaigned against GMOs across the globe. Transnational networks of scientists who are working on genetic modification and believe in a scientific approach to risk management constitute an epistemic community. Much can be learned about the way policies are made by studying the activities of these networks, both because they develop the alternatives over which subsequent decisions are taken (policy-shaping) and because they influence the balance of power in the choice between policies (policy-setting).

■ Technocracy and politics in the EU

Technocracy in EU decision-making

Decision-making in the EU is often described as **technocratic**. This view implies that policy-making is primarily based on (technical) expertise regarding issues and not on (interest-driven) bargaining or the mobilization of public opinion that is central to domestic democratic systems. Technocracy is thus contrasted with 'politics'.

> **Technocracy** is the view that policies should be exclusively based on knowledge and that policy decisions should be made by scientific experts rather than politicians.

The idea of technocratic policy-making has old roots in the thinking about the EU. The idea of some of the founders of the EU (such as Jean Monnet) was that integration should proceed through concrete steps in specific policy domains rather than through grand 'political' designs. This approach has even become known as the 'Monnet method'. It relies heavily on the theories of functionalism and neo-functionalism that were discussed in Chapter 2. Theories of the EU as a technocracy build on this approach, if not as a normative ideal then at least as a description of how EU decision-making works.

In terms of the concepts introduced above, one could say that technocratic decision-making is quintessentially 'low politics'. From the examples we have discussed so far, it should also be clear that this is true only of part of EU decision-making. Another part (most prominently history-making decisions but also certain policy-setting decisions) is typically high politics and is characterized more by traditional diplomatic bargaining than by technocratic decision-making.

Why, then, is it often claimed that the EU is largely technocratic in nature? Two arguments can be made for this claim. First, the claim is often restricted to what we have called 'policy-making decisions' (policy-setting and policy-shaping) and is not extended to history-making decisions. The argument then is that history-making decisions may be the most visible decisions taken in the EU but they are relatively rare and not necessarily the most important ones for understanding what the EU actually does.

Second, it can be argued that policy-making is relatively less politicized in the EU than in domestic political systems. We have seen examples of this in earlier chapters. For instance, Chapter 5 showed that elections for the EP are based more on domestic than on EU-wide political issues. Likewise, Chapter 6 revealed that 'outside lobbying' (which is based on the mobilization of public opinion) is far less prevalent at the EU level than within the member states. The corollary of this is that 'popular politics' in the EU is replaced by more technocratic forms of policy-making.

This is also exemplified by the bodies in which policy decisions are actually taken. Although formally decisions are taken by the EU institutions as a whole, these decisions are prepared in meetings that do not catch the public eye: the expert groups that we already met in Chapter 9, the Council working parties and Coreper that prepare Council meetings (see Chapter 3), and the 'comitology committees' that we will get to know in Chapter 11. In addition, much of the discussion and work that go into a decision takes place within Commission DGs, informal meetings of experts and conferences of academics and/or policy experts. In reality, most decisions are taken there, and are merely formalized by more visible bodies. To obtain a better understanding of the claim that the EU is a technocracy, we should therefore look at the way in which decisions are taken in these 'preparatory bodies'.

The politics of technocracy

The preparatory bodies mentioned above are called technocratic because the mode of interaction in them can be described as 'consensual' and 'expertise-driven'. This stands in contrast to the 'conflictual' and 'interest-driven' style that we saw in the process leading up to the Multiannual Financial Framework. Decision-making in preparatory bodies is consensual because the outcome is not decided by voting but by consensus: if all participants agree (or at least, do not object) to an outcome, that outcome is adopted. They are expertise-driven because the participants are experts in their field and the main mode of interaction between them consists of exchanging information and expert-based arguments. This stands in contrast with the types of bargaining tactics that we discussed above for history-making decisions (but that also play a role in policy-setting decision-making). There, the focus was on overpowering others, whereas in expertise-based settings it is on arguing and convincing.

Although the distinction between 'expertise-driven' and 'interest-driven' processes is useful in understanding the differences between types of decision-making, it is important not to lose sight of the essentially political character of both. In daily parlance, it is common to juxtapose 'expertise' and 'politics': either something is decided on the basis of our best knowledge (expertise) or it is decided on the basis of bargaining (politics). However, this is too simple a depiction of reality, because interests and expertise are not mutually exclusive.

Even when policy-shaping and decision-making in the EU are based on consensus-seeking between experts, these experts may have very different ideas about the best course of action. Even reasonable people may disagree about what is 'right' and 'true' and they may passionately fight for the approach they believe in. Moreover, most participants have vested interests in certain approaches, either because it would be cumbersome and costly for them or their member state to change the approach to a policy or because they have been socialized into seeing their own approach as superior to alternative approaches.

Decision-making in these circumstances is not some kind of dispassionate search for the 'right' or 'best' solution, but a struggle between participants that sponsor different approaches. The main weapons in that struggle are expertise-based arguments (that is why it is 'expertise-driven') and decisions taken by consensus (so that the process is 'consensual'). The participants who are most skilled at convincing or overruling their counterparts will be the most successful in this process. Thus, technocratic decision-making is as much political as bargaining is – only the means are different.

Besides being used as a term to describe EU decision-making, technocracy has also been presented as an ideal that EU decision-making should strive for. Since 2002, the European Commission has worked under the 'better regulation programme', which is aimed at improving the quality of EU legislation through more rational policy- and decision-making. Controversy 10.1 presents some of the underlying ideas of this programme and the criticism levelled against it.

■ Flexibility and inertia in EU decision-making

All through this chapter, and earlier in this book, we have seen that EU decision-making is very complicated because of a number of characteristics:

- the large number of institutions that are involved in most decision-making processes;
- the relatively high thresholds for taking decisions in the Council (as compared to a simple majority rule);
- the combination of intergovernmental and supranational elements;
- the wide diversity of interests and preferences among the EU member states.

This often makes it difficult to reach decisions, which has led some observers of EU politics to be distinctly pessimistic about the prospects for ambitious or innovative policies. Some have argued that bargaining among member state governments in the Council inevitably leads to an outcome that reflects the 'lowest common denominator' – that is, a level of ambition set so low that it is acceptable even to the most reluctant member state needed to adopt the proposal.

Controversy 10.1

Better regulation in the European Union

In the early 2000s, the concept of 'better regulation' (nowadays also known as 'smart regulation') was introduced by the European Commission as a way to improve the quality of law-making in the EU. It was subsequently institutionalized in the Commission's policy-making process through a number of instruments, such as the requirement to carry out regulatory impact assessments before proposing new pieces of legislation, reviews of existing legislation to enable simplification, and systematic evaluations of the effects of policies after they had been put in place. According to the Commission, this is an approach that the Council and the EP should also adopt when deciding on new legislation.

The ambitions of the better regulation programme tie in with the approach of 'evidence-based policy-making', which has gained a hold in a number of Western countries since the 1990s. The idea behind this approach is that policies should be based on rigorous, scientific assessments of the effectiveness of different policy instruments in relation to the objectives to be achieved.

What do you think of these approaches? Do you think a programme like 'better regulation' can help improve decision-making? Is evidence-based policy-making an ideal to strive for or is it too technocratic?

A **joint-decision trap** arises if the participation of non-central governments in the making of central government decisions leads to policies that are ineffective, inefficient and/or outdated but these policies cannot be changed because at least one non-central government benefits from them.

A more complex argument has been put forward under the name **joint-decision trap** by the German political scientist Fritz Scharpf (Fritz W. Scharpf, 'The Joint-Decision Trap: Lessons from German Federalism and European Integration', *Public Administration*, 66, 3, 1988: 239–78). Scharpf's analysis of the EU was based on his earlier studies of decision-making in Germany's federal system. In Germany, like the EU, the governments of the component states (called Länder) play a direct role in federal decision-making because they participate in the German Senate (the Bundesrat). According to Scharpf, this similarity gives rise to the same kind of decision-making dynamics because federal/EU decisions can only be taken with the consent of the Länder/member states.

According to the joint-decision trap thesis, decision-making in the EU tends to be inflexible and inefficient because, once a policy has been created, it is quite easy for a member state to block reform. Since there are always some member states that benefit from existing policies, this makes it very difficult to change policies that have become outdated or inefficient, even if a majority of participants in the decision-making process are in favour of change. He illustrates this with the example of the Common Agricultural Policy, which was considered to be highly inefficient throughout the 1970s and 1980s but proved almost impermeable to change. The reason for this was that the member states that profited from the CAP were able to block any attempt to reform it. This is a 'trap' because it is impossible to get out of it even when most participants want to, and it is a 'joint-decision' trap because decisions can only be taken jointly.

Although the argument was initially illustrated by the CAP, it has been put forward as a more general description of EU policy-making. At the same time, other students of EU decision-making have pointed out cases in which the EU has actually been able to agree upon innovative policies that move beyond the 'lowest common denominator'. A case in point is the CAP itself, which, after the publication of Scharpf's article, has undergone quite substantial reforms.

There are several reasons why the joint-decision trap may not be a general description of EU decision-making:

- There have been considerable *institutional changes* since the time when the term was introduced. Most importantly, the use of qualified majority voting in the Council has been extended enormously. This has made it more difficult for one or a few member states to block proposals.
- The joint-decision trap may not apply equally to all *types of policies*. The thesis was developed with reference to policy areas that involve large amounts of spending, such as the CAP. In those areas, it is easier for actors to calculate their gains and losses. For regulatory issues, the gains and losses are often more diffuse. As a result, member state governments may be less focused on their narrow self-interests in regulatory issues than in budgetary issues.
- The *locus of decision-making* is not the same for all issues. As we saw above, many decisions are *de facto* made not in the Council but in lower-ranking bodies of experts. In these 'low politics' bodies, decision-making processes evolve differently than in the 'high politics' (European) Council. Therefore, the greater the involvement of lower-ranking bodies, the less likely it is that a joint-decision trap type of situation will occur.
- Decision-making is sometimes speeded up under the influence of *outside events*. For instance, after the financial crisis of 2008/9, it became possible to reach agreement on proposals, such as the monitoring of member state budgets and the regulation of financial markets, that had been inconceivable before. Reform of the CAP was also partly brought about by outside pressure, in this case the desire to reach an agreement on global trade with the United States, which demanded CAP reform in return for the creation of the World Trade Organization.
- Political actors can use specific *strategies* to circumvent the effects of a joint-decision trap. One way to achieve this is to change the decision-making arena so as to reduce the role of member state governments. Another option is to delay the actual implementation of a decision in order to reduce the short-term political costs for the governments of member states that are set to lose by that decision. This can be done by taking a decision now, but only letting it take effect several years into the future.

All in all, then, the joint-decision trap thesis is still a valuable argument about EU decision-making but it applies to a specific type of decision in the EU. It is most likely to occur when an issue is high politics, relates to the budget and needs to be decided by unanimity in the Council or European Council. When one or more of these characteristics is absent, there is more room for policy change as well as ambitious and innovative policy outcomes.

■ Summary

This chapter has described decision-making processes in the EU. It has argued that:

- Three types of decisions can be discerned in the EU: history-making decisions, policy-setting decisions and policy-shaping decisions. Decision-making dynamics vary between these types.
- History-making decisions define the framework within which the EU operates, while policy-setting and policy-shaping decisions are about policy-making within that framework.
- History-making decisions are typically 'high politics', policy-shaping decisions 'low politics', and policy-setting decisions 'high' or 'low' politics depending on the issue.
- History-making decisions are characterized by negotiations between member state governments. During those negotiations, governments use different tactics, including coalition formation, persuasion and the 'management of meaning', challenging other member states, issue linkage and side-payments, and splitting the difference.
- Policy-making in the EU is characterized by a large number of veto players. This has four consequences: (1) it makes it difficult to reach decisions, (2) decision-making in the Council revolves around the creation and dissolution of 'blocking minorities', (3) decision-making within institutions needs to take account of the acceptability of the outcomes to other institutions, and (4) actors within the EU operate under a culture of consensus and compromise.
- Decision-making does not take place only between and within the EU institutions but also includes actors outside the formal institutions, such as interest groups, member state civil servants and academics. The interaction between actors within and outside the EU institutions takes the form of policy networks.
- EU policy-making is often described as 'technocratic'. This means that decision-making takes place on the basis of expertise rather than bargaining or popular politics. This depiction is correct for many 'low politics' decisions but typically not for 'high politics' decisions. Moreover, it is important to keep in mind that 'technocracy' is not the opposite of 'politics' but involves a political struggle that is fought with expert-based arguments.

- The joint-decision trap thesis argues that because of the complexity of, and the direct involvement of member state governments in, EU decision-making EU policies tend to become inflexible and inefficient. Although this argument holds true for some policies and decision-making processes, there are also examples of the opposite.

Further reading

An introduction to the three levels of decision-making with applications to various policy areas can be found in John Peterson and Elizabeth Bomberg, *Decision-Making in the European Union* (Palgrave Macmillan, 1999). A sophisticated, quantitative study of EU decision-making is Robert Thomson, *Resolving Controversy in the European Union: Legislative Decision-Making before and after Enlargement* (Cambridge University Press, 2011). A wide-ranging overview of approaches to international negotiations is offered by Victor Kremenyuk (ed.), *International Negotiation: Analysis, Approaches, Issues* (2nd edn, Jossey-Bass, 2002). A good discussion of technocracy in the EU is Claudio Radaelli, 'The Public Policy of the European Union: Whither Politics of Expertise?', *Journal of European Public Policy*, 6, 5, 1999: 757–74. Fritz Scharpf's joint-decision trap, and a number of ways in which EU decision-making is able to escape from it, is further discussed in Gerda Falkner (ed.), *The EU's Decision Traps: Comparing Policies* (Oxford University Press, 2011).

Websites

- The European Parliament's 'legislative observatory' tracks decision-making processes that involve the EP. It reproduces all steps in decision-making processes (including steps taken by other institutions), gives summaries of what happened at each step as well as links to underlying documents: www.europarl.europa.eu/oeil/
- The steps taken in decision-making procedures that involve the Commission can also be traced through Pre-Lex, with links to underlying documents: http://ec.europa.eu/prelex/apcnet.cfm?CL=en
- The results of votes taken in the Council of Ministers can be found on the Council's website: www.consilium.europa.eu/
- The European Commission's approach to smart (or: better) regulation is explained at: http://ec.europa.eu/smart-regulation/

Navigating the EU

On the website www.navigatingthe.eu you will find online exercises for this chapter.

11   Implementing policies

■ Introduction

In the spring of 2007 the Italian city of Naples experienced an acute breakdown of its rubbish collection system. Because waste landfills were full, rubbish collection became impossible and piles of trash quickly built up in the streets of Naples. Although the region of Campania had been struggling with its waste management system for years, the situation proved to be especially urgent this time. Residents started burning the rubbish in order to alleviate the smell of rotting material, transforming the city's streets into a grim scene with dark clouds of smoke and pedestrians covering their faces to avoid the smell. The crisis not only made headlines in the world news but also incited action on the part of the European Commission, which accused Italy of not living up to the terms of the Waste Framework Directive. A month later the Commission sent a formal warning to Italy because it had 'failed to fulfil its obligations under the directive by not putting in place an appropriate network of disposal facilities ensuring a high level of protection for the environment and public health in the Campania region'.

Although the Italian government succeeded in addressing the most urgent problems – for example, by sending its waste by train to waste incineration facilities in the German city of Hamburg – the Commission later that year still considered Italy to be in violation of the terms of the Directive. After a final warning in January 2008 the Commission started a case against Italy before the

Court of Justice, because it had not provided a satisfactory plan for the disposal of its waste nor presented a timetable for putting in place such facilities. In March 2010 the Court of Justice issued a ruling in which it concluded that Italy had indeed failed to fulfil its obligations. Although the Italian authorities responded to this ruling by making progress in their waste management, the Commission felt that it was still not complying fully with the Directive. The Commission therefore started a new court case in June 2013: this time it asked the Court to impose a daily fine of no less than €256,819 for every day the Italian Republic would not comply with the original ruling of the Court.

The story of Italy's waste problem illustrates how difficult it can be to put EU legislation into practice, a process called implementation. Implementation is the third and final stage of policy-making. In this chapter we examine implementation by answering the following questions:

- Which steps need to be taken to translate EU legislation into actual policies?
- What are the respective roles of the Commission and member states in the process of implementation?
- What are the means to monitor correct implementation of legislation?
- What is the role of agencies in the implementation and coordination of policies?

After reading this chapter you will have learnt that implementing policies is not as straightforward as you might initially think. Implementation consists of three different phases and as a result is in fact as lengthy and complex as the two other stages of the political process: agenda-setting and decision-making. The difficulty is in large part due to the multi-level nature of the EU. The member states need to incorporate the legislation in their own legal systems, which may differ considerably from country to country.

■ The three phases of implementation

In order to understand **implementation** we distinguish between three different phases which we discuss in turn in this chapter:

> **Implementation:** The process of applying policies and putting them into practice.

- *Legal implementation*: this is the phase in which European legislation is made ready for putting into actual practice. It consists of two elements:
  - making EU legislation operational via implementation decisions;
  - transposition of EU legislation into national legislation.
- *Practical implementation*: this is the phase where legislation is actually applied and enforced. While most of this is done by the member states, some policies are directly implemented at the EU level by the Commission and the ECB.
- *Monitoring implementation*: this is the phase where the Commission, courts and others verify whether the legislation is correctly applied.

■ Legal implementation

When it comes to applying EU legislation, it is important to distinguish between Regulations and treaty provisions, on the one hand, and Directives, on the other. Regulations and treaty provisions have direct force after they have been adopted and need to be practically implemented precisely in the manner prescribed. For Directives the situation is different. While in terms of results to be achieved they are as binding as all other types of legislation, member states themselves are responsible for choosing the precise legal instruments to do this. This process is known as the **transposition** of EU legislation. In the next subsection we therefore first discuss the transposition process and then turn to the other aspect of legal implementation: the making of implementation decisions.

Transposition: The process of incorporating the legal provisions of EU directives into national legislation.

From EU law to national law: transposing directives

The major difference between Directives and other forms of EU legislation is that Directives need to be transposed into national laws before they become effective. The reasoning behind this form of EU legislation is that it allows member states some flexibility in choosing the specific way of applying EU laws. Depending upon the contents of the Directive and the legal system of the member state the transposition process may involve a formal adoption of legislation by its parliament (either in the form of a completely new law or the adaptation of existing laws) or other legislative measures such as ministerial decrees or executive orders. It may also be that existing legislation fully covers the terms of the Directive: in such a case a member state does not have to draft any new legislation.

A timely transposition of Directives is essential, because the legislation can only come into force when it has been turned into national law. Every Directive therefore states the maximum amount of time member states have to transpose it into national legislation. This period may range from three months to three years and in some cases even longer, but typically member states have two years to do this.

Although at first sight this seems to give member states ample time, several studies of the transposition process indicate that in more than half of all the cases, the transposition deadline is not met, and in about 20% member states exceed the deadline by more than two years. Although ultimately all member states transpose more than 98% of the Directives, there is a large variation in the timeliness of transposing. Take, for example, Directive 2002/44/EC on the exposure of workers to vibration. While Lithuania needed 616 days to transpose it into national legislation, the UK needed more than three times as much time and only fully transposed it after 1,954 days, almost two years past the deadline that was set for transposition.

Several studies have identified a range of factors that influence the time it takes to transpose a Directive:

- Long and complicated Directives that involve many measures take more time to transpose than short and simple Directives.
- Directives that give member states more options take more time to transpose than those that do not provide any options.
- Member states with a weak administrative capacity take longer to transpose than those with an effective bureaucracy.
- Those member states that disagree to a greater extent with the scope and contents of a Directive take longer to transpose than those who fully agree with its contents.
- Member states where existing legislation differs considerably from the one proposed in the Directive take more time to transpose than those that have compatible legislation or no legislation at all in that policy area.

A timely transposition is a necessary but not a sufficient condition for a successful transposition process. Even if member states have transposed legislation in time, they may have done so incorrectly. They may have failed to incorporate all the provisions of the Directive or they may have included provisions that were not allowed. This is a problem that occurs regularly. For example, a study on the implementation of social policy directives in the EU-15 revealed that in only ten of the ninety cases had a Directive been transposed both in time *and* correctly.

So what makes member states ultimately comply? Political scientist Tanja Börzel has made a useful distinction between what she calls 'pull' and 'push' factors. First, in the case of a mismatch between current legislation and the EU legislation, eventual compliance will be more likely if there is domestic pressure from political parties, interest groups, the media and public opinion with regard to the issues at stake. These domestic actors will 'pull' the government into complying with EU legislation. Second, the Commission may also push member states into compliance by making use of several tools to enforce a correct implementation, such as issuing a formal warning and ultimately bringing the member states to court for non-compliance (see 'Monitoring implementation' below). Often pull and push work in tandem, with interested parties pressing the Commission to push member states into properly transposing the legislation.

From formal laws to operative rules: delegated and implementing acts

Although legislative texts are usually very lengthy and detailed, they are almost never able completely to spell out all the operative details that are necessary to implement them properly. In many cases legislators therefore

Implementation decisions: acts that are adopted by the Commission to put legislation into practice.

deliberately leave it up to the executive branch to make **implementation decisions**. This division of labour ensures that governments have the means to actually implement policy measures, without having to go back to parliament for every small decision they need to take to implement the legislation.

In the EU the Commission has been assigned the task of adopting implementation legislation. The significance of these decisions cannot be overestimated as the bulk of the EU's output in fact consists of these kinds of acts.

Two types of acts can be used to adopt such measures: **delegated acts** and **implementing acts**. Delegated acts supplement or amend legislation, implementing acts are used to ensure a uniform implementation. Returning to the example of waste: while the definition of what constitutes municipal waste should be changed through a delegated act, the format that member states use to provide statistical details on waste is decided by an implementing act.

Delegated acts are acts adopted by the Commission to modify specific details of Directives or Regulations (Article 290 TFEU), as long as they do not change the essence of the legislation. The legislation in question must explicitly state the content of the acts and the Council and/or the EP always have the right to veto the proposed act.

Implementing acts are acts that the Commission adopts in order to make sure the member states implement legislation in a uniform fashion (Article 291 TFEU). Member states control and advise the Commission on the adoption of these acts through the system of **comitology**.

There are clear rules in place to check the Commission's power to adopt these decisions. First, the Commission can only adopt these decisions if the legislation at hand has authorized it to do so. Second, the Commission is subject to different types of control when it wants to adopt such acts. The type of scrutiny depends upon the type of act the Commission needs to adopt. In the case of delegated acts control is exerted by the EU legislative institutions themselves: the Council and European Parliament have the right to veto a proposed measure within a certain period of time. In the case of implementing acts the member states exert control through the system of **comitology** (see Fact file 11.1 for an overview).

Comitology: The system of committees through which civil servants from member states discuss the implementation of EU policy and supervise the Commission's implementation decisions.

In a comitology meeting the Commission meets with specialized experts from the different member states. A typical meeting of the committee for the implementation of the Waste Directive includes representatives from the UK's Department for Environment, Food and Rural Affairs, the Hungarian Környezetvédelmi és Vízügyi Minisztérium and the Italian Ministero dell'Ambiente e della Tutela del Territorio e del Mare. There are no fewer than 250 committees that each focus on a certain policy area.

Comitology is a very complex affair in several respects. Due to the topics that are discussed and the congregation of highly specialized experts, the meetings themselves are long and most of the time puzzling to outsiders. Second, a single piece of legislation may provide for different types of committee procedures, depending upon the type of implementation decision. Finally, although the Commission has established a comitology register and an online database

Fact file 11.1

Comitology procedures

Advisory procedure: the committee gives its opinion on a draft measure of the Commission and uses simple majority voting to accept or reject the measure. The Commission decides, 'taking the utmost account of the conclusions drawn from the discussions within the committee and the opinion delivered' (Article 4 (2)).

   Examination procedure: the committee can issue a positive, negative or no opinion on a draft measure using qualified majority voting.

- In the case of a positive opinion the draft is adopted and enters into force.
- In the case of a negative opinion the Commission may not adopt the draft. If it finds the implementing measure necessary it can submit a revised draft to the committee within two months or can refer the matter to an appeal committee, which consists of representatives of the member states and can decide on the issue.
- In the case of the committee delivering no opinion the Commission may adopt the measure unless it is about issues of taxation, financial services, certain trade protection measures or the safety and health of humans, animals and plants.

Source: Regulation (EU) No 182/2011 laying down the rules and general principles concerning mechanisms for control by Member States of the Commission's exercise of implementing powers.

as part of its transparency initiative, it is still very hard to find relevant documents and useful information in this register. The publicly available reports of the meetings tend to be rather procedural and short. The official transcripts of the meetings are lengthy and detailed, but only available to the members of the committee.

Still, despite the highly fragmented and specialized nature of comitology and its complexity to outsiders, the system in practice works quite efficiently. Voting records show that committees almost always support the Commission's proposals. Of the 2,500 to 3,000 implementing measures which are presented to the committees every year, less than 1% require a referral to the appeals committee, usually because the committee is unable to express an opinion on the issue (almost all of these cases concern the highly contested issue of approving new genetically modified organisms to be placed on the market). This then also sheds light on the purported role of member state representatives as watchdogs on the activities of the Commission (see Briefing 11.1). Although the system clearly has been designed to scrutinize implementation decisions, it should as much be seen as a forum in which the Commission and member states deliberate and consult on the details of implementation. Comitology helps the Commission to assess the impact of implementation decisions

Briefing 11.1

The evolution of comitology

The history of comitology provides a nice illustration of the way the EU seeks a balance of power between intergovernmental and supranational interests. The committees find their origins in the earliest days of the EEC and the implementation of the Common Agricultural Policy. The CAP required that target and intervention prices for a variety of agricultural products (grain, pork, wine, etc.) had to be set on a day-to-day basis, something the Commission would be best able to do. The Commission proposed to set up committees for each of the products and give member states an advisory role. Most member states found this unacceptable and demanded some kind of safeguard which would enable them to collectively block proposals or veto them. In the end a compromise was wrought in which a proposal of the Commission could be referred to the Council if a qualified majority of the member states in the committee disagreed with its contents. The Council would then act as an arbitrator between the Commission and the representatives of the member states in the committee and be allowed to make a final decision on the matter. Hence the first type of comitology committees emerged, which were called management committees.

As a result of the growing body of EU legislation during the 1970s and 1980s the number of committees rose accordingly. Because there were no fixed rules, an idiosyncratic system emerged with each committee having its own peculiar set of procedures. In 1987 the number of committee procedures was streamlined into seven different variants and rules were given on the choice of the appropriate procedure for each legal act.

Despite these changes, many people still criticized the system for being very closed to outsiders and not giving the European Parliament any say, even on legislation it had passed itself. In 2006 the EP managed to obtain the right to scrutinize some decisions, after it threatened to block the funding for the comitology system. The Lisbon Treaty revised the system of implementation legislation by introducing a distinction between delegated acts and implementing acts and further simplifying the comitology procedures (see Fact file 11.1).

on member states and provides it with the expert knowledge of member states and their views on the feasibility of the proposals to fine-tune implementation decisions. Expertise and a spirit of deliberation for finding the best solution are part of the operation of comitology as are meetings in which member states zealously guard their national interests.

■ Practical implementation: enacting policies

The second phase of implementation consists of putting the policies into practice. For the bulk of EU legislation the actual carrying out of policies takes place at the national level. Most of the work is done by civil servants in the member state: from the implementation of policies to supervising these policies and reporting results and statistics. This then also explains why the size of the European civil service can be relatively limited. Returning to the example of the Waste Framework Directive, the member state governments are responsible for drafting waste management plans and for making sure that appropriate waste disposal facilities are set up. The Italian government thus had to allocate funds to build plants, start a tender procedure to select a construction company and make sure that the facilities would become operational. Still, this does not mean that Brussels is not interested in what happens at this stage: in the next section we will see how the Commission monitors implementation by the member states.

Before turning to that subject, we briefly outline the three policies that are implemented directly at the EU level: competition policies, expenditure policies and monetary policies.

Competition policies

In order to ensure an efficient operation of the common market and to ensure fair competition the Commission has extensive executive powers in the area of competition policies. The Commission keeps a close eye on the smooth functioning of the market and checks whether free competition is threatened. This may be the case if companies form a cartel and secretly limit the supply of a product or fix its price, or if companies have such a large share of the market that they can dictate price conditions and force competitors out (abuse of a dominant position), or if it turns out that companies unjustly receive financial aid from their government (violation of state aid rules).

As part of the implementation of competition policies the Commission reviews intended mergers between companies if such a merger exceeds certain thresholds in turnover (smaller mergers are dealt with by national competition authorities). It also regularly issues memos in which it provides guidance on issues related to competition, mergers or state aid. For example, during the financial crisis in 2008 the Commission provided guidance to member state governments on which types of financial support would be allowed for ailing banks.

Expenditure policies

In addition to competition policies one other policy area where the Commission can be said to be actively involved in the practical implementation stage concerns the management of the expenditure policies. As was outlined in Chapter 8 the EU's relatively modest budget is spent for the largest part on expenditures relating to the structural funds, the Common Agricultural Policy and the fisheries policies, and – to a lesser extent – on neighbourhood policy, humanitarian and development aid. The largest part of these expenditures consists of payments to, for example, farmers who may be entitled to price support for specific crops and of expenditures on, for example, goods for humanitarian aid such as tents, food and medicine. As the administrator of the EU budget, the Commission is responsible for the actual payments of the funds. In most cases such payments are made to the member states, who in turn distribute the funds amongst the final recipients. Within the structural funds there is a small category of programmes directly managed by the Commission itself. Also, if money is transferred to recipients outside of the EU, as in the case of development aid, the Commission provides the payments directly and as such can be considered the practical implementer of these policies.

Monetary policies

The last policy which is practically implemented at the EU level concerns the **monetary policies** for those countries which are members of the Eurozone. In the EU these decisions are taken by the European Central Bank (ECB). The main task of the ECB is to maintain price stability in the Eurozone, taking into account the Union's objective to attain a high level of employment and sustainable growth (see Chapter 3 for a full overview of its tasks).

> **Monetary policy:** policy aimed at ensuring financial stability through managing the supply of money and controlling the interest rates at which banks can borrow and lend money.

■ Monitoring implementation

Earlier in this chapter we showed that there are many instances where member states do not implement EU legislation correctly or in a timely fashion. Monitoring implementation thus forms the necessary third phase of implementing policies. The EU has by now developed an elaborate system to identify, communicate and redress problems with the implementation of legislation. Below we discuss the two major monitoring efforts that take place. First, the Commission can start infringement procedures against any member state that does not correctly implement legislation. Second, courts in member states can ask the Court of Justice for advice on any cases that involve the application of EU legislation through a reference for a preliminary ruling.

Monitoring via the Commission: infringement proceedings

The Commission has the formal authority to monitor the correct application of EU law. Article 258 TFEU gives the Commission the right to start an *infringement procedure* against a member state that fails to correctly implement EU legislation. Three types of problems may occur:

- *Non-communication*: the member state fails to report to the Commission that it has transposed a Directive.

- *Incomplete or incorrect transposition*: the Directive has been transposed but not in the proper way or not fully.
- *Incorrect or no application of legislation*: the policies that need to be carried out are not in line with what has been prescribed or policies are not enacted at all.

For the Commission it is relatively easy to identify cases of non-communication. Member states have to notify the Commission of the transposition of EU legislation through an electronic database. As soon as a deadline for the transposition of a Directive passes, the Commission can tally the violations (non-communication) with the push of a button.

Spotting the incorrect or incomplete transposition of Directives requires more substantial effort on the part of the Commission. The Commission needs to analyse the texts of the national legislation and check their commensurability with EU legislation. For example, the Directorate-General for the Environment, which also oversees the implementation of the Waste Directive, employs a team of no more than thirty-five lawyers who are continuously scrutinizing the implementation of environmental legislation by the member states. They will have to examine national legislation and compare the texts with the provisions of the Directive and check for any errors in transposition.

Lastly, an even greater challenge for the Commission is to identify problems with the practical implementation of legislation. It has to rely on the willingness of member states to cooperate and to put policies into practice, as well as enforcement agencies that oversee the correct implementation. This has led to repeated calls for more direct monitoring powers by the EU, but until now these have been resisted by the member states. Although in many policy areas the Commission does have authority to monitor the application of legislation in the member states – such as fisheries, veterinary and regional policies – it does not have these powers in all policy areas, such as environmental policy.

All in all, it is clear that the Commission's resources are not sufficient to comprehensively oversee the practical implementation of legislation by the member states. It therefore also invites individuals and organizations to report any possible problems with implementation. These so-called complaints constitute a very important additional source of information next to what the Commission gathers on the basis of its own research.

Figure 11.1 gives an overview of the suspected infringements according to the three different sources of information just discussed: non-communication, the Commission's own investigations and complaints received from external parties. The figure indeed makes clear that complaints constitute an important source of information. It also shows some policy areas are much more prone to such complaints than others. In the area of the internal market many complaints come from companies who believe a member state is posing unjustified barriers to the free market. In the area of environment many complaints come from concerned citizens and environmental groups who notice violations of EU legislation 'on the ground'. (Here we see the combination of push and pull at

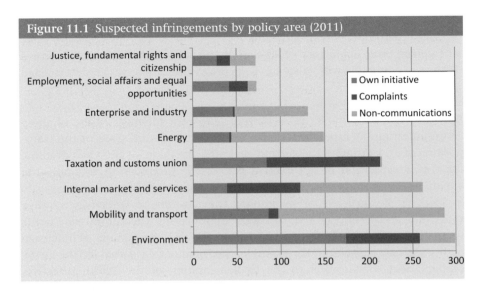

Figure 11.1 Suspected infringements by policy area (2011)

work, which we discussed earlier: organizations alerting the Commission on infringements in the hope that this will lead to steps by the Commission to remedy the problem.)

Figure 11.1 also shows that in environmental policies the Commission seems to have been much more active in actively searching for infringements than in the case of the internal market, where it can rely to a much greater extent on input from interested parties.

It is up to the Commission to decide which complaints merit further investigation and are worthy of an infringement procedure. In its annual report on the application of community law, the Commission provides some insight into the priorities it sets in choosing which infringement cases to pursue. As a general principle it gives preference to those cases 'having the greatest impact on the general good', such as those which violate the four fundamental freedoms of the internal market or those environmental issues which constitute a direct and imminent threat to the health and safety of citizens, as was the case in the waste crisis which we discussed at the beginning of the chapter.

Once the Commission has decided to pursue an infringement case, it starts a multi-staged procedure which consists of the following steps:

- The Commission sends a *letter of formal notice* to the member state in which it sets out the results of its investigation and asks the member state for its viewpoint on the matter. On the basis of the answer of the member state the Commission decides whether it wants to pursue the case further or not.
- If it decides to proceed, the Commission sends a *reasoned opinion*, which specifies in detail what needs to be done to redress the problems and within which timeframe this has to be done. The reasoned opinion once again

provides a framework for an exchange between the Commission and the member state, which may involve negotiations as well. If successful these may lead to an agreement which states what the member state will do in order to satisfy the Commission's demands.

- If the member state fails to provide a satisfactory plan or simply fails to respond to the Commission's demands, the Commission formally indicts the member state and refers the case to the Court of Justice (*referral to the Court*).

Once the Commission has forwarded the case to the Court, the infringement proceedings have entered the litigation stage: the Commission brings the case to court. These court cases can be recognized by a phrasing which pits the Commission against any of the member states. Hence, the waste crisis in the region of Campania ultimately led to the case of *Commission v. Italy* (C-297/08) which was lodged in July 2008. The Commission asked the Court to establish that Italy indeed violated the terms of Articles 4 and 5 of the Waste Directive because it did not put in place a sufficient number of waste disposal installations in the region of Campania. The Court heard the case and issued a ruling in March 2010 in which it concluded that the Italian Republic indeed had failed to properly act upon its obligations.

The initial ruling of the Court thus formally confirmed the existence of an infringement. The Court does not have any other powers at this stage than simply to establish the infringement. Member states are expected to respect the Court's judgment and act in accordance with its conclusions. However, if a member state fails to do so, Article 260 TFEU enables the Commission to start a new court case – a *post litigation infringement proceeding* – in which it can ask the Court to impose fines for every day the member state fails to live up to its obligations. Once again the Commission will first remind the member state of its obligations by sending a warning letter. After two warnings the Commission is allowed to bring a new case to the Court and demand fines be imposed. In the case against Italy the Commission did so in March 2013. This happens only rarely (about ten times a year), because most member states will make sure to take appropriate measures following the rulings.

Figure 11.2 shows the number of cases open at the end of a given year (2011), distinguishing between the problem of late transposition and that of incomplete and incorrect transposition. The figure shows that at that moment Italy, Spain and Greece had the most open cases, whilst countries such as Latvia, Malta and Denmark had the fewest.

Throughout the whole procedure the Commission attempts to get member states to fulfil their obligations, so that it is able to close a case. This is facilitated through an intensive exchange of views between the Commission and the member states, which takes place in between the formal steps of the procedure and is facilitated via a dedicated information system, EU Pilot. Accordingly the Commission can close more and more files, the further it progresses in the proceedings. For example, in 2013 the Commission was able

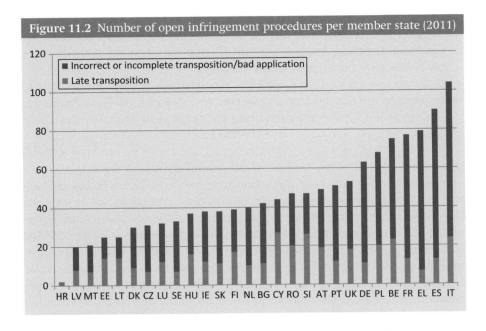

Figure 11.2 Number of open infringement procedures per member state (2011)

to close 484 cases after it had sent the letter of formal notice, 200 after having sent a reasoned opinion and another 47 before it had to decide to refer the case to the Court of Justice. Member states will feel more and more pressed to get their act together in the wake of a possible court case and hence seek to find a solution to avoid further procedures. Given the fact that the Court tends to rule in favour of the Commission in a majority of cases, this seems to be a wise strategy.

Infringement procedures can last for quite some time from the stage of suspecting an infringement to a final judgment of the Court. The phase which involves the Commission – from spotting an infringement to ultimately bringing a case to the Court – lasts on average around two years. A subsequent procedure before the Court lasts another seventeen months on average. Infringement proceedings, however, are not the only way to monitor a correct implementation of EU law. In all of the member states thousands of courts are applying EU law on a daily basis. We discuss their role in monitoring implementation in the next section.

Monitoring via national courts

Next to the Commission as the pivotal player in infringement proceedings, national courts provide the second channel via which the application of EU law is monitored. Given the fact that by now the principles of supremacy and direct effect subordinate national legislation to EU legislation (see Chapter 1), courts in the member states are empowered to apply EU law directly in relevant cases and to declare national legislation invalid if it conflicts with EU law.

This decentralized route of monitoring has been actively promoted by the Commission for several reasons. First, the sheer number of national courts and their proximity to citizens and organizations makes this route much more accessible to these interested parties. The route also provides for a faster resolution of the problem, compared to the lengthy infringement procedures that were discussed above. Finally, such verdicts can be much better enforced than those of the Court, because rulings of a national court will in general be directly enforced by the national authorities.

There are, however, cases where national courts are uncertain about the precise judicial implications of a certain case and need to ask the Court for advice. Article 260 TFEU grants the Court the power to provide a preliminary ruling on cases referred to it by national courts. The preliminary character of the ruling refers to the fact that it is the referring court and not the Court which will issue the ruling, incorporating the advice of the Court. The referral thus yields a binding interpretation of the Court on the case at hand (see Briefing 11.2 for an example).

Figure 11.3 shows that the number of references has been steadily rising since the first reference was made in 1961. The rise can be attributed to both the expanding body of legislation as well as the steadily increasing number of member states over the decades. There are obviously differences between member states in the extent to which their courts refer cases to the CJ. One factor is simply the size of the member state, with courts in larger member

Briefing 11.2

Is spilled oil waste?
In the case of *Commune de Mesquer* v. *Total*, the French municipality of Mesquer had brought proceedings against the oil company Total in a French court. The municipality argued on the basis of the Waste Framework Directive that Total should bear the costs of cleaning the city's coastline, after the oil tanker *Erika* sank in 1999 and spilled oil. The Cour de Cassation, the French supreme court, referred the case to the CJ because it needed to know whether the spilled oil, which in its original form does not constitute waste, would fall under the terms of the Directive. In its 2008 preliminary ruling the Court argued that the 'mixture of the oil, water and sediment' which emerged as a result of the shipwreck indeed constituted waste. It further ruled that the charterer of the ship should be considered the producer of this waste and could be held liable for the costs of cleaning up the coast, if it could be shown that its conduct contributed to the risk of the pollution taking place. The Court's ruling has created additional liability for oil transporters and sellers.

Source: Case C-188/07 *Commune de Mesquer* v. *Total France SA and Total International Ltd.*, 24 June 2008.

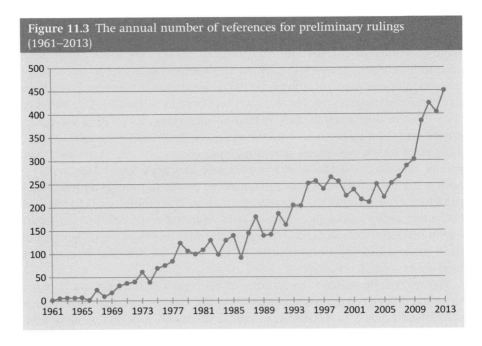

Figure 11.3 The annual number of references for preliminary rulings (1961–2013)

states being confronted with a higher number of cases to deal with than those in smaller states. Another factor is the size and openness of the economy of a member state. Higher levels of trade will generate more cases on the free movement of goods in those countries and hence more referrals to the Court. The rising volume of references also gives an indication of the growing importance of EU law in national legal systems. As such the references can be seen as the tip of an iceberg: while we can observe those cases which are referred to the Court, there is certainly a much larger number of cases which are dealt with by member state courts on their own. National courts, in other words, are the workhorses of the judicial monitoring of EU legislation, with the Court providing authoritative guidance on all issues which are too complex for the former to handle independently.

All in all, it is safe to say that the EU has an elaborate and sophisticated system to monitor the implementation of legislation. One path runs via the Commission and its use of infringement proceedings. The other path runs via national courts which directly apply EU legislation as well as refer some of their cases to the Court to get authoritative guidance. The system's sophistication derives from the fact that both trajectories to a very large extent make use of the efforts of actors in the member states to monitor the application of legislation. Citizens and other interested stakeholders inform the Commission, enabling it to discover a much greater number of infringements than it could on its own. National courts handle the bulk of the monitoring of EU legislation, once again allowing for a much broader monitoring effort than would be possible if everything had to be handled by the Court. The system's sophistication also derives from the multi-staged nature of the procedures which allows for a lot of negotiation and reconciliation before formal procedures are started.

■ Agencies

Given the often high level of specialization and expert knowledge needed to implement legislation, the EU has set up specialized bodies, called **agencies**, which play various roles in the implementation process. Ever since the first two agencies were set up in 1975 more than forty agencies have been established. Most of these are decentralized agencies: they carry out technical, managerial and scientific tasks and are located across the EU. A smaller group consists of executive agencies which are located in Brussels and assist the Commission in the management of programmes.

> **Agencies** are administrative organizations set up by the EU that provide technical expertise in different policy areas and assist in coordinating, implementing and monitoring policies.

Collectively the agencies employ 3,100 staff members and command a budget of around €500 million. Within these aggregate figures there is an enormous diversity in the scope, mission and size of separate agencies. The smallest agency, the Institute for Security Studies (ISS), only employs about twenty people while the European Police Office (Europol) counts more than 500 staff members.

The decentralized agencies can be categorized into four groups. A first group of agencies seeks to foster 'social dialogue'. An example is the European Agency for Safety and Health at Work, which seeks to improve conditions in the workplace by exchanging best practices and making companies aware of risks at work. A second group of agencies consists of so-called observation centres which gather information on specific topics. The European Environmental Agency, for example, collects information on the state of the environment and makes this available to member states, interest groups and citizens. A third group of agencies, called suppliers, focuses on providing specific services, such as the European Training Foundation, which helps countries in transition to strengthen human capital development in education and training. Regulatory agencies form the fourth category of agencies. Of the four types of agency these regulatory agencies are most closely involved in both the legal and the practical implementation of EU policies. The European Medicines Agency, for example, evaluates medicines before they can be marketed in the EU, while the European Food and Safety Agency (EFSA) assesses the risks in the area of food and feed. The Commission will in general follow the scientific advice from regulatory agencies and use it as the basis for decisions.

Regulatory agencies are not unique to the EU, but can be found in any member state. Their names suggest a close resemblance to their national counterparts (the corresponding national agencies for the EFSA are, for example, the UK Food Standards Agency or the German Bundesamt für

Verbraucherschutz und Lebensmittelsicherheit). Still, even though national and European agencies deal with the same topics and cooperate quite extensively, there are two important differences between them:

- National agencies are usually involved in actively monitoring the implementation of legislation in their area. Food safety agencies send inspectors to restaurants, factories and canteens to see whether the cooks follow food safety procedures and protocols. European agencies, on the contrary, are hardly involved in such activities. They may occasionally join national agencies to familiarize themselves with the practice of monitoring, but it is not their core task.
- A second and more important difference concerns the competences of the agencies. While national regulatory agencies enjoy autonomous decision-making powers and are themselves authorized – for example, to approve the marketing of a pharmaceutical product – EU regulatory agencies only have advisory powers. Formal decision-making remains always in the hands of one of the official Community institutions: in the case of Community agencies, the Commission, often assisted by the appropriate comitology committee. There are only three agencies that do have autonomous decision-making powers (OHIM, CPVO and EASA), but only to the extent that these are strictly technical implementation decisions (such as the registration of intellectual property rights to plant species by the CPVO).

This lack of discretionary decision-making authority for agencies can be attributed to the so-called Meroni doctrine, which holds that agencies should never be involved in 'political' decisions involving the weighing of different interests and the exercise of discretionary power (see also Controversy 11.1).

Regulatory agencies at the EU level thus lack the regulatory clout of many of their national counterparts. This is not only a result of the Meroni doctrine, but also because member states have been reluctant in transferring regulatory powers to the European level, as this would reduce both the powers of national regulators as well as the ability of national governments to control those agencies. In 2008, for example, the Commission clashed with the member states over the mandate that should be given to a new Body of the European Telecoms Regulators (BERT). In its original proposal the Commission would have been able to independently enforce the opening up of the telecommunications market if member state regulators failed to do so. However, member states objected to this plan and succeeded in slimming down the size and mandate of the new agency. Half of the members of the new agency would consist of employees from national regulatory agencies, which would need to agree with the Commission before any measures against member states would be taken. Just as is the case with the set-up of comitology, the organization and remit of agencies reflect a deliberate balancing of powers between the supranational actors and the member states.

Controversy 11.1

Meroni versus Majone

Regulatory agencies are severely constrained in their decision-making powers due to the Meroni doctrine, which emerged as a result of a landmark case ruling of the Court. In 1954 the Italian steel company Meroni had been requested to pay import duties on scrap by the Imported Ferrous Scrap Equalization Fund, the name of the agency to which the High Authority (as the Commission was called in those days) had delegated this task. Even after the High Authority itself summoned them to pay, Meroni kept refusing and instead asked the Court to annul the decision. The Court annulled the decision of the High Authority and not only criticized the lack of transparency of the agency but also disputed the legality of the agency's mandate. The Court concluded that many of the agency's decisions involved the use of 'discretionary power' and as such would involve it in actual policy-making. It argued that the delegation of powers 'can only relate to clearly defined executive powers, the use of which must be entirely subject to the supervision of the high authority'. The Court's ruling has served as the foundation of the so-called Meroni doctrine, which severely limits the possibilities to delegate tasks to regulatory agencies.

Political scientist Giandomenico Majone has been highly critical of the Meroni doctrine, because it inhibits the effective implementation of regulatory policies. In Majone's view the Commission is unable to neutrally enforce and monitor rules because of political pressure from member states and political differences of opinion between commissioners. In addition to being politicized, the Commission is also increasingly becoming parliamentarized, as the European Parliament has asserted a greater influence on determining the composition of the Commission over the past decades. Hence in order to increase the credibility of policy implementation, agencies should be empowered to enforce the rules and make regulatory decisions, instead of the Commission. Majone envisages a system of 'transnational regulatory networks' in which national agencies and a European-level agency would work together in ways similar to that of the operation of the European Central Bank, and would be empowered to make regulatory decisions in the same manner as the ECB sets the interest rates for the Eurozone.

The controversy between Majone and the Meroni doctrine revolves around this fundamental question: should we consider implementation decisions as a purely technical exercise or do they involve the allocation of values and hence require the approval of politically accountable bodies?

Source: Giandomenico Majone, 'The Credibility Crisis of Community Regulation', *Journal of Common Market Studies*, 38, 2, 2000: 273–302.

■ Summary

This chapter has examined the implementation of EU policies.

- Implementation is the third phase of policy-making and refers to the putting in practice of policies once appropriate legislation has been passed. The phase of implementation is as lengthy as the phases of agenda-setting and decision-making. Just like in the two other phases, it often involves struggles between the various EU institutions and the member states because their interests may conflict.

- Implementation in the EU can best be understood by distinguishing between three phases: legal implementation (involving the transposition of Directives and making implementation decisions), practical implementation (involving the actual enactment of policies) and monitoring.

- The Commission adopts implementation legislation in the form of delegated and implementing acts. Delegated acts may be vetoed by the Council and/or the EP, whilst member states supervise the adoption of implementing acts via the system of comitology.

- The Commission actively monitors the implementation of policies both with respect to a timely and correct transposition of legislation into national law, and with respect to a correct and complete practical application of policies. If member states fail on any of these aspects, the Commission has the discretion to start an infringement procedure.

- The courts provide the second important channel through which the implementation of policies is monitored. The principles of supremacy and direct effect require the courts in member states to apply EU law where relevant, ensuring a correct implementation of EU policies. National courts may refer cases with an EU dimension to the Court, which will provide a binding interpretation of the case in the form of a *preliminary ruling*.

- In order to assist the EU and the member states in the implementation of policies a diverse range of agencies have been set up. Regulatory agencies are the most important type of agencies and provide expert advice on implementation, while leaving the formal decisions on these to the Commission.

Further reading

The distinction between various phases of implementation and the push and pull model is taken from Tanja Börzel's collection of essays *Environmental Leaders and Laggards in Europe: Why There is (Not) a 'Southern Problem'* (Ashgate, 2005). A detailed study of the transposition of EU legislation in social policy is Gerda Falkner *et al.*, *Complying with Europe: EU Harmonisation and Soft Law in the Member States* (Cambridge University Press, 2005). Falkner's study has been criticized most notably by Robert Thomson in 'Time to Comply: National Responses to Six EU Labour Market Directives Revisited', *West European Politics*, 30, 5, 2007: 987–1008. A classic collection of essays on comparing regulation in member states to European regulation is Giandomenico Majone (ed.), *Regulating Europe* (Routledge, 1996). For a more recent account of the role of agencies see Madalina Busuioc, Martijn Groenleer and Jarle Trondal, *The Agency Phenomenon in the European Union* (Manchester University Press, 2012).

Websites

- Specific information and documents on comitology: http://ec.europa.eu/transparency/regcomitology/
- Information on the application of Community law as well as statistics on transposition and infringements: http://ec.europa.eu/community_law/index_en.htm
- All the EU's agencies can be accessed through the Commission's agency website: http://europa.eu/agencies/index_en.htm
- Information on the litigation state of infringements and on references for preliminary rulings can be found on the website of the Court and in its annual report which highlights the most significant cases: http://curia.europa.eu
- Political scientists have been engaged in a lively debate on which factors affect transposition of Directives. The results of different analyses are collected in a database at: www.eif.oeaw.ac.at/implementation/

Navigating the EU

On the website www.navigatingthe.eu you will find online exercises for this chapter.

Conclusions and reflections

12   Reflecting on the EU as a political system

■ Introduction

When the crisis on the financial markets hit Europe in late 2008, this was generally seen as a grave test for the European Union. Would it be able to respond in the face of crisis? Would member state governments be able to overcome their longstanding differences of opinion on economic and financial policy in finding new solutions? And would the EU's institutional framework of budgetary and free-trade rules be able to withstand the flurry of national support measures and calls for economic protectionism that occurred throughout the member states? The situation became even more serious when the Euro itself came under attack from financial markets after fears had arisen that Greece, and possibly a number of other member states, would be forced to default on their (fast-rising) government debts.

As it turned out, the financial crisis proved a tremendous impetus for European cooperation. Even though member state governments took an unprecedented number of far-reaching measures (nationalizing banks, letting government debt rise in order to stimulate their economies), the lapse into protectionism and unilateralism did not occur. Instead, in most cases member state governments closely consulted on the steps to take and tried to find solutions that would keep up existing EU rules while taking account of the special circumstances.

The lead in all this was taken by the European Council. When fears of a Greek default mounted and interest rates for the Greek government soared, the other member states agreed to give financial support in order to prevent a collapse. The Greek government, in return, committed to rigorous spending cuts even in the face of strong domestic political resistance. At later stages, financial support was also given to Ireland, Portugal, Spain and Cyprus, and a permanent European Stability Mechanism was set up.

In addition, as we saw in Chapter 8, a number of proposals that had been too controversial before suddenly became realistic options. The Council and the EP reached agreement on the creation of a set of EU financial market authorities and the European Central Bank was made responsible for the supervision of banks in the European Union. Also, the regulatory framework around the Euro was strengthened. As part of this, the European Commission obtained the right to review member state budget proposals to check their consistency with EMU's budgetary rules even before they went to national parliaments.

These developments after the financial crisis, and the roles of the various institutions in them, raise a number of questions that we will discuss in this final chapter:

- What are the prospects for the EU and European integration in the future?
- How democratic is the way decisions are taken in and about the EU?
- How do the analyses presented in this book help us to understand the way the EU functions?

In this concluding chapter we will show how the insights and theoretical tools presented in the previous chapters may help you understand developments in EU politics. At the same time, the financial crisis is also a good illustration of the contingencies inherent in the way the EU evolves. Before 2008, no one in their right mind could have predicted the steps taken in the years after the start of the crisis. These contingencies have often been important in determining the future of the EU and will continue to do so. Nevertheless, it is important to look beyond the most visible part of EU politics – that is, the European Council meetings and the 'grand decisions' that make the headlines. Much of what goes on in the EU takes place below that surface but is equally important for understanding what the EU is and does.

■ Deepening the EU: towards 'ever closer Union'?

The Danish physicist Niels Bohr once said: 'Prediction is very difficult, especially about the future.' So it is with the EU. In fact, this unpredictability is one of the EU's characteristics. In terms of the range of policies it pursues, developments in the institutional framework and membership (the three main themes in the EU's history that we discerned in Chapter 1), the EU is still 'under construction'. The pace and direction of that construction process is determined by a combination of inside and outside events. Hence, there is always a degree of contingency in the EU's development that defies all-too-self-confident prediction. Nevertheless, there are a number of recurring themes in the way the EU develops that can be used to understand how the EU is evolving and why it is evolving in that direction. In this section, we will highlight some of these lessons for the domains of policies and institutions. In the next section, we will then turn to the EU's membership and the future of enlargement.

Article 1 of the Treaty on European Union speaks of 'the process of creating an ever closer union' that underlies the objectives of the EU. These words go back to the Treaty of Rome establishing the European Economic Community, whose preamble opened with the stated ambition 'to establish the foundations of an ever closer union among the European peoples'. As we have seen in Chapter 1, the history of the EU has been far from an uninterrupted development towards ever closer union. Rather, the EU has developed in fits and starts, alternating periods of quick expansion with periods in which the project seemed to be caught in gridlock. The sources of these developments have been both internal and external. Below, we will take a closer look at these internal and external sources, and draw a number of more general lessons about the (future) development of the EU.

Internal sources of institutional and policy developments

As internal sources of development, the EU institutions have used the opportunities offered in the EU treaties to build up policies and new institutions where they did not exist before. A few examples may illustrate this dynamic:

- In the early 1960s, the Court of Justice established the doctrines of direct effect and supremacy of EU law, which considerably strengthened the legal status of EU law and have defined the relationship between EU and member state law ever since.
- On the basis of a few provisions on competition policy in the initial EEC Treaty, the European Commission sought to develop a system of merger control, which was later formalized by a Regulation in 1989.
- Formally, the EP can only reject a new European Commission as a whole but not individual commissioners (see Chapter 3). Nevertheless, since the 1990s, the EP has used this power as a leverage to demand the removal of individual commissioners that it did not approve of, threatening to reject the entire Commission otherwise. By now, the right to reject individual commissioners has been accepted as part of the EP's prerogatives. Going even further, after the 2014 EP election, the EP succeeded in having the candidate of its largest party group designated the new Commission president (see Chapter 7).

These types of 'internal' developments depend on the activism of the EU's supranational institutions. Each of them has, at various times, been quite resourceful in exploiting the room that the EU treaties offer. This is the case in specific policy areas (as we have seen in Chapter 9 on agenda-setting) but also in strengthening their own position within the EU's institutional framework.

The implicit, but crucial, necessary condition for this activity has been the acquiescence of member state governments in the face of the *faits accomplis* that the supranational institutions sought to present them with. For example, after the Court of Justice developed the doctrine of direct effect, the member states could have included an explicit provision in the treaties stating that EU law does not automatically have direct effect in national legal orders (as is the case for 'regular' international law). But they did not. Likewise, the member state governments (and the Commission itself) have accepted as a fact of life that the EP uses its powers of approving the European Commission to demand the removal of individual commissioners.

External sources of institutional and policy development

Externally, the EU has often been propelled forward (or held back) by crises facing it. Again, a number of examples come to mind:

- the financial crisis, as shown in the introduction to this chapter;
- the attacks of 9/11, which gave an enormous impetus to the development of joint policies in the field of terrorism and crime fighting;
- the fall of communism in 1989 led member state governments and the EU institutions to redefine the role of the EU, which provided an important push towards the Treaty of Maastricht.

Developments following such major external events show a similar pattern. Initially, member state governments take the helm, in particular the Heads of State and Government assembled in the European Council. In the end, they are the only ones within the EU with the political clout to provide leadership in times of crisis. This could also be observed during the financial crisis, when the major initiatives were taken by member state governments. It was national governments that put unprecedented amounts of money into supporting banks and other sectors of the economy and that deliberately violated the EMU's Stability and Growth Pact by letting government debt rise far beyond the ceilings contained in it. At the time, it seemed as if the EU institutions were simply bypassed and had lost control.

In the longer run, however, crises often lead to a strengthening of the EU's institutional framework. Again, the financial crisis provides an illustration. The European Commission plays an important role in the European Stability Mechanism created in 2012, expanding its financial capabilities with a stroke of the pen. Likewise, the EP played an important role in strengthening the powers of the new European financial market authorities. Only after the EP had amended the proposal during the ordinary legislative procedure (see Chapter 4) did the Council agree to giving the authorities the power to intervene directly in financial institutions.

A similar pattern can be observed in other crises. After the fall of communism, it was politicians such as Germany's Helmut Kohl and France's François Mitterrand who decided on German unification. After 9/11, the European

Council took the initiative to formulate an EU response in a series of meetings in the last four months of 2001. But here, too, the EU institutions in the end came out stronger, with new policy initiatives being incorporated into existing institutions and decision-making procedures.

This pattern is not unlike what can be observed in domestic politics. There, too, the position of key politicians, such as the prime minister or the president, is considerably strengthened during a crisis. During crises, citizens (but also most politicians) tend to look for leadership and demand a single focal point for response. Just as the European Council took the initiatives within the EU after 9/11, so US President George Bush was able to initiate a large number of measures, with the US Congress appearing merely a passive bystander. However, after a while, as things cool down, politics returns to normalcy and the 'usual' institutions of politics and administration resume their work. That this also happens in the EU shows the strength of the EU's institutional framework.

Lessons for the future?

Although we cannot predict the course of the future as such, this reflection on the development of the EU does teach us a number of lessons that can help us to understand future developments. Below we will discuss three such lessons:

- the creative tension between formal rules and informal behaviour;
- the dynamics of crises;
- the importance of 'daily politics'.

Formal rules and informal behaviour

It is important to be aware of the creative tension between formal rules and informal behaviour. Formal rules define the playing field for political actors but at the same time political actors strategically manipulate the rules for their own purposes. In that regard, treaty changes are both a starting point and an end point. They are an end point because they formalize existing practices. And they are a starting point in the sense that they provide new opportunities for political actors to pursue their ideas and interests. Exactly how this will work out depends on the strategic interplay of actors, aided or hampered as they may be by outside events.

Take, for example, the permanent President of the European Council, an office that was created by the Treaty of Lisbon. Even though the Treaty defined the powers and tasks of the office, it was unclear what actual political role the new president would play alongside the Commission president and the rotating member state presidencies of the Council. Much of what the first European Council president (Herman Van Rompuy) and the Commission president (José Manuel Barroso) did in the period after the entry into force of the Treaty was to carve out their respective roles in the EU's new institutional framework, trying to gain the upper hand vis-à-vis the other. Many observers agreed that Van

Rompuy came out as the 'winner' of this struggle, both because of his political acumen and because the financial crisis put the European Council (and hence its president) centre stage. Because these processes are inherently contingent, the outcome cannot be predicted. Yet, when one is aware of the interplay between formal rules and political strategies, one is much better able to understand what is happening and why.

The dynamics of crises

We have seen that crises are important in driving the EU forward. This is what makes it dangerous to give overly confident predictions of the course of the EU. Before the outbreak of the financial crisis, the EU seemed to be in a period of stasis. The rejection of the Constitutional Treaty in France and the Netherlands had revealed a broader trend of Euroscepticism among EU citizens. The first Commission led by Barroso (2004–9) explicitly took it as its leading principle that the EU should refrain from taking on too many new initiatives. Instead, it was time to consolidate what was there and critically review new initiatives in the light of subsidiarity and efficiency. Moreover, the difficulties of negotiating treaty change had convinced many observers that there would not be a new treaty soon after the Treaty of Lisbon. As a result, the EU appeared set for a prolonged period of relative inertia. The financial crisis changed all this, giving new impetus in a policy area that had for a long time been 'too hot to handle'.

Nevertheless, it is important to keep in mind that crises are not merely outside events that 'happen' to political actors (as was already stressed in Chapter 9 on agenda-setting). Rather, crises are opportunities for political actors to get things done that they already wanted to do but were not able to get accepted before. For example, the idea of having an EU authority oversee European financial markets had been proposed a number of times already before 2008. However, it never stood a chance of adoption because member states with strong financial centres (most prominently the UK) were not willing to have an EU body regulate their financial industry. The financial crisis convinced politicians that something needed to be done. As a result of this, the proposal that had previously been deadlocked was revived again and finally even adopted. In that sense, the financial crisis meant an enormous support for those political actors within the EU (member state governments, Commission officials and MEPs) that already supported the creation of an EU authority before the financial crisis. If you are aware of and understand these political uses of crises, the development of the EU can be seen to be less random than it may at first appear.

The importance of daily politics

Finally, it is important to be aware of the relation between 'large events' and 'daily politics'. What people hear and read about the EU is mainly related to the high-profile events that punctuate the development of the EU, such as

European Council summits during which important decisions are taken, and the signing of new treaties. These events are certainly important. But they are not the only things that matter. Much less visible is the day-to-day politics and policy-making that take place within the EU. These activities are often about more mundane issues that do not catch the public eye. Yet, they are equally important for understanding the way the EU works. In the end, the sum of these 'small decisions' adds up considerably and determines what the EU does and how it affects firms and citizens within the EU member states (and often also outside of the EU).

In this book, we have focused primarily on this type of 'daily politics', looking at things like the internal functioning of the European Parliament (Chapter 7) and the implementation of EU policies (Chapter 11). Because daily politics consists of a wider array of actors and activities, its development is often less 'erroneous' than the high politics of large events. For instance, as we saw in Chapter 7, the internal cohesion of political groups in the EP has gradually and consistently been strengthened since the 1980s. The role of the EP vis-à-vis the Commission and Council has also continuously been strengthened over the past decades (see Chapters 1 and 3). As a final example, in Chapter 11 we described the rise of EU agencies in policy implementation, a development that has taken place gradually since the early 1990s and that seems to reflect a longer-term trend in the evolution of the EU. It is the importance of the EU's 'daily politics' and the resilience of the trends in this domain, even in the face of external crises, that underscore the necessity to study the EU not just in terms of 'large events' but also in terms of the underlying political system.

■ Enlarging the EU: towards an ever wider Union?

Another contentious issue in the future development of the EU is the enlargement with new member states. The EU has grown quite rapidly over the past decades, from twelve members before 1995 to twenty-eight in 2013. In addition, a number of countries have applied for membership, while there has been talk at certain points in time of expanding even further to include, for instance, Ukraine.

In the meantime, citizens in the 'old' EU member states (in particular the Western European 'EU-15') have grown weary of further enlargements, giving rise to a mood of 'enlargement fatigue'. A number of observers have linked opposition to further enlargements to more general feelings of Euroscepticism. As was discussed in Chapter 5, citizens have tended to be more critical of the EU and European integration than political elites. With the shift from a 'permissive consensus' to a 'constraining dissensus', public opinion on enlargement has also become more articulate and has had a greater impact on member state politicians. Conversely, the 2004/7 enlargement wave may also have fuelled the constraining dissensus because, at least in some Western European member states, the influx of workers from Eastern Europe was seen as a threat to employment and social cohesion.

The most divisive candidate member state has been Turkey. The prospect of Turkey entering the EU has led to more emotional responses among citizens in the existing member states than the impending membership of any other country. A number of reasons have been cited for this: from the alleged 'cultural difference' between Muslim Turkey and Christian Europe, to the economic challenge posed by a country that would become the EU's largest member state. As a result, negotiations on accession between Turkey and the EU have been protracted and difficult, with no clear perspective on successful conclusion.

The debate on Turkish membership touches upon a fundamental unresolved question in the European Union: What is 'Europe'? Now that the EU includes most countries that belong to the 'core' of the European continent (both in the South, East and North), more and more potential member states belong to the shady area between 'Europe' and 'non-Europe'. The EU has never been able, or willing, to draw a clear line in this regard. Only once, when Morocco applied for membership, was the application refused on the grounds that Morocco was not a 'European' country.

Drawing a firm line in Eastern and South-Eastern Europe is much more difficult because of the different interests and historical experiences of member states. For instance, Poland has strong historical ties with Ukraine (if only because parts of present-day Ukraine used to be part of Poland) and the idea of Ukraine becoming part of the EU is looked upon sympathetically in that country. For citizens in, say, Ireland or France, this is very different.

In the end, the concept of Europe is more cultural and historical than geographical, but since cultures are not monolithic or unambiguous there is a range of countries that partly belong to Europe and partly not. This also goes some way towards nuancing the alleged 'enlargement fatigue'. It is not enlargement per se that seems to be causing controversy. When Iceland applied for membership in 2009 and was granted candidate status in 2010, this did not give rise to any opposition. On the contrary, it was the Icelandic government that put the talks on hold in 2013, out of what could perhaps be called 'EU fatigue'. Likewise, should Norway and Switzerland decide they wanted to join the EU after all, that would probably not meet with a lot of opposition among EU citizens or their governments either. Hence, the current controversy on the enlargement of the EU is more about identity than about the size of the EU per se. The fact that these issues of identity have gained such prominence and that opposition among citizens is playing a greater role in decisions on enlargement than it used to do, goes to show that the constraining dissensus is indeed beginning to have its influence felt in EU politics.

■ Democracy and the European Union

To many people, the EU is an impersonal and impenetrable bureaucracy that affects the lives of citizens without many opportunities for input by those citizens. In the popular media, this image is reinforced by references to

'Brussels' as the outside source of constraints on national policy-makers. Issues of democracy can also be raised in relation to the response to the financial crisis that we discussed in the introduction. Most crucial decisions were taken by the European Council, a body that takes decisions behind closed doors without any real input from the European Parliament or national parliaments. In general, the role of the European Council in EU politics has increased over the past decades, with the European Council acting as both the initiator of important new initiatives and the de facto decision-maker on contentious issues. Some even argue that the European Council should be (or already is) the EU's 'government'.

These types of development have clear implications for democracy, in the EU and in the member states. Is the European Council the right place to make major decisions on the EU's future? If the European Council acts as the EU's government, should it not be **accountable** to the European Parliament, just as domestic governments are accountable to parliaments? And if the EP were to play a greater role, can it rightfully claim the same democratic credentials as national parliaments? Below, we will discuss these questions, taking a few steps:

> An actor is **accountable** to another actor if the actor needs to explain and justify its behaviour to that other actor, and the other actor can impose consequences if it considers the behaviour to be inadequate or inappropriate.

- First, we will discuss the question of whether the EU should be democratic. We will see that the answer to this question is not as self-evident as it may seem.
- Second, we will delve into the debate regarding the EU's 'democratic deficit': the claim that the EU falls short of basic democratic standards.
- Third, and finally, we will confront this criticism with some of the evidence that has been presented in this book.

Should the EU be democratic?

Democracy is a typical 'hurray word': it is a good thing, of which we can never have enough. Saying that something is 'undemocratic' almost immediately implies a negative judgement, while arguing that something is 'democratic' automatically means it is 'good'. In these statements, the precise meaning of 'democratic' may vary, but the general underlying idea is that decision-makers should be accountable to citizens, either directly (e.g. through referendums) or indirectly (through accountability to elected representatives).

Still, even in countries that consider themselves eminently democratic, not all parts of government are placed under democratic control. For instance, in all European countries, but also at the US federal level, judges are not elected but appointed. In fact, they are meant not to be accountable to citizens because they should base their judgements on the merits of the case, not on popular sentiments. The same is true for independent government agencies, such as central banks and competition authorities. They, too, are deliberately placed at a distance from citizens and elected representatives in order to ensure their independence and foster even-handed decision-making. Most citizens do not find this problematic so, apparently, there are situations in which democracy is seen as commendable and situations in which it can be dispensed with (or, actually, is better avoided).

Several arguments have been put forward in support of placing parts of government outside of democratic control. One argument is that some tasks require impartiality and independence. If someone is sentenced by a judge, this should be based on the law. Criminal sentences that depend on the political convictions of a judge will be seen as unjust by most people. Likewise, firms should be able to predict when they will be fined by a competition authority and when not. If the decisions of competition authorities depended on the political mood of the day, this would lead to unpredictability and instability, which would deter firms from making investments and developing business.

Another argument is that some tasks require specific expertise. The idea then is that expertise is possessed only by trained professionals, whose (expert) judgement cannot be properly evaluated by non-professionals. Hence, democratic control (which is almost by definition control by laymen) is not compatible with expert-based decision-making. The application of the law by judges is, yet again, an example of this. This is also an argument for not letting grades for university courses be determined by a democratic vote among students (but some readers of this book may disagree!).

Issues of independence, expertise and democracy are inherent in any decision-making situation. How, then, is the distinction made between situations that require democratic control and situations that do not? To be sure, political thinkers, and citizens more generally, differ in their answer to this question. Some argue for much broader forms of democracy than are currently in place, while others believe that greater independence of politicians from voters would be a blessing. Yet, the basic idea underlying current arrangements is that it is permissible to place a governmental task outside of democratic control if that task (1) requires independence (as explained above) and (2) does not concern fundamental trade-offs but only the attainment of one well-specified objective.

Thus, central banks are tasked with a set of relatively straightforward objectives such as preventing inflation and safeguarding the stability of the financial system. They do not have to weigh these goals against other objectives, such as reducing unemployment or redistributing wealth among citizens. These trade-offs are made elsewhere; central banks just need to make sure their tasks are fulfilled properly. The same is true for competition authorities. They just need to make sure firms do not violate competition law. Although a whole range of other values may be affected by their decisions (employment, protection of vulnerable groups in society, environmental protection, etc.), in principle they do not have to (indeed often are not allowed to) take these other consequences into account. These trade-offs are made by parliaments, who determine broad economic priorities as well as the content of competition

Briefing 12.1

Input legitimacy and output legitimacy

One of the fundamental principles of democratic government is that it should rest on the support of its citizens and is considered to be legitimate. But what makes people support their government? Following Abraham Lincoln's famous definition of democracy as 'government of the people, by the people and for the people', Fritz Scharpf makes a useful distinction between input legitimacy and output legitimacy as two possible sources of support (Fritz W. Scharpf, *Governing in Europe: Effective and Democratic?*, Oxford University Press, 1999).

Input legitimacy (government *by* the people) depends upon the extent to which political systems succeed in translating the preferences of their citizens into policies, and hence give voters the feeling that the government listens to them. In the words of Scharpf: 'Political choices are legitimate if and because they reflect the "will of the people".' Output legitimacy (government *for* the people) refers to the capacity of governments to effectively solve collective problems. In this perspective the actions of governments are justified if they are able to show that they can tackle problems that people cannot solve on their own.

The legitimacy of judges, central banks and independent agencies derives from the fact that they do their job well. They solve problems and deliver useful 'goods' for citizens. Hence, they rely on output legitimacy. Democratic institutions, by contrast, derive their legitimacy from the fact that citizens have been able to give their input into the decision-making process. Even though not everyone may agree with the outcome, at least citizens will accept the decision because it has been arrived at in a democratic way. Therefore, they rely on input legitimacy.

The distinction between input and output legitimacy improves our understanding of the debate on democracy in the EU. When people criticize the EU for making decisions without sufficiently taking account of the wishes of the people, they focus on a lack of input legitimacy. When politicians justify the existence of European legislation by pointing out that it has, for example, led to a reduction in environmental pollution across Europe, this is an argument that focuses on output legitimacy.

law itself. This is why it is believed governments should be democratic but independent agencies should not. Two important concepts in this regard are 'input legitimacy' and 'output legitimacy'. They are introduced in Briefing 12.1.

These arguments are also relevant in the context of the EU. According to some, the EU performs tasks that are similar to those of independent agencies domestically. It does a relatively limited number of things that are, again relatively, technical in nature. Take another look at Table 8.1 in Chapter 8, which lists the policy areas in which the EU is most active and those in which it is least active. Arguably, the most controversial issues in politics (those relating to the welfare state and cultural identity, and those closest to citizens) are exactly the issues that have remained (almost) exclusively at the member state level. The issues that the EU deals with most intensively are further removed from citizens, such as competition policy and harmonization of technical requirements. Hence, the key question to be asked of the EU is whether it does this job well and efficiently. In this line of reasoning, there is no need for further democratization of the EU.

Others disagree with this assessment. They point out that the EU has evolved over time to deal with a much wider range of issues. The EU is increasingly involved in determining the content and application of criminal law in its member states (touching directly upon civil liberties) and, as we saw in the introduction to this chapter, in guiding, if not directly setting, basic economic policy choices. These are things that, in domestic political systems, we would expect democratic bodies to do. Why, then, should this be different at the EU level? The question then becomes whether the EU is actually democratic the way it is. This is the question we will turn to next.

How democratic is the EU?

If one believes the EU should, in principle, be democratic, how democratic is it then? This is the central issue in the debate over the EU's alleged 'democratic deficit'. The argument behind the 'democratic deficit' thesis is that the EU falls short of the basic democratic standards that may be required of a political system. Several arguments have been put forward to substantiate this claim:

- Compared with national parliaments, the EP has a limited role. It is excluded from a number of important policy areas, most notably foreign policy.
- Decision-making in the Council of Ministers and in lower level committees that prepare decisions or check the Commission is often rather secretive and the bodies themselves are not subject to direct accountability to the EP or national parliaments.
- The accountability of individual ministers in the Council (or of individual Heads of State and Government in the European Council) to their national parliaments is often quite weak because they can hide behind the fact that they had to compromise with twenty-seven other colleagues. In those circumstances, it is impossible to hold an individual (prime) minister accountable for the outcomes of a (European) Council meeting. As a result, the Council and the European Council suffer from what accountability scholars have called 'the problem of many hands': when many individuals are jointly responsible for the outcome of a process, no single individual can be held accountable for that outcome, which implies that in the end no one is held accountable.
- In domestic parliamentary systems, parties try to form coalitions after the elections with a view to forming the government. As a result, parliamentary

elections in practice evolve around the question of who will be in government and who will become the next prime minister. This gives voters a clear choice, because their vote helps determine who will be in power after the elections. This is not the case in the EU, because the European Commission, which can be seen as the EU 'government', is not formed directly on the basis of EP elections. After the 2014 elections, the President of the Commission was appointed on the basis of the election results, but the rest of the Commission still was not.

According to proponents of the democratic deficit thesis, the EU should become much more democratic if it is to live up to the standards we may require of it given the wide range of tasks it performs. This would include the further expansion of EP powers, an improvement in the accountability of the Council and European Council and a full politicization of the European Commission by basing it on a parliamentary majority in the EP.

Assessing the democratic deficit in the EU

Having outlined the arguments for the democratic deficit thesis, we can now turn to the 'evidence' presented in this book. Does it support the allegation that the EU is undemocratic or not? To start with, it should be clear that no definitive answer can be given to this question. Much depends on one's assessment of the EU's political system. As we have seen throughout this book, many aspects of how the EU works are subject to ongoing (scholarly) debate. In addition, and more fundamentally, different positions can be taken on what constitutes 'true' democracy. This is not the place to review all possible theories of democracy but one should be aware of the great diversity in conceptions of democracy, ranging from the ideal of direct democracy, in which citizens themselves take important decisions, to conceptions of democracy that lay greater stress on the protection of minorities and the rule of law. Obviously, which conception of democracy one chooses is crucial for determining whether or not one will find fault with the way the EU works.

Nevertheless, it helps to clarify and review some of the empirical assumptions underlying the debate on democracy in the EU. In the other chapters, we have presented several insights that are relevant to this debate. Some of these insights support the claim that the EU suffers from a democratic deficit:

- In Chapter 3, it was noted that about 80% of all decisions in the Council of Ministers are in reality taken at lower levels of preparatory bodies, be it Coreper or Council working parties. Proceedings in these bodies are largely hidden from public view and accountability mechanisms are all but absent.
- In Chapter 5, EP elections were characterized as 'second-order' elections. Because citizens feel little is at stake in these elections, voter turnout is low and voting behaviour tends to be determined by domestic political considerations rather than EU-level issues. This lends credence to the claim that the composition of the EP does not reflect preferences on EU

policy choices. Moreover, it ties in well with the argument that too little is at stake in EP elections because they do not determine the composition of the EU 'government'.

- Also in Chapter 5, it became clear that there is a gap in opinions between citizens and domestic political elites regarding the EU and European integration. Citizens tend to be more sceptical of the EU than political elites, but it is the latter who take the decisions in and on the EU.

- In Chapter 6, we saw that political protest is much less common at the EU level than at the domestic level. Insofar as groups mount political protests against EU policies, they overwhelmingly direct those protests against their national governments, not the EU institutions. An important part of the explanation for this pattern is that the political opportunity structure offered by EU institutions is unfavourable to political protest because EU policy-makers are less vulnerable to public opinion. This is another indication that citizens play a smaller role within the EU than within domestic politics, which makes the EU less democratic.

- Finally, in Chapter 7, it was argued that European political parties do not perform the same set of functions as their domestic counterparts. Most notably, they do not provide the types of links between citizens and the political system that domestic political parties have traditionally provided.

At the same time, there are also a number of arguments against the democratic deficit thesis:

- The EU's institutional set-up has evolved enormously over the past decades. Whereas the EP had no real decision-making powers until the late 1980s, it has now acquired the power to amend and veto legislation in the vast majority of issue areas. Since the Treaty of Lisbon, the number of areas in which the EP has no say at all has diminished even further and these areas are now limited primarily to foreign and defence policy.

- In Chapter 5, we argued that a shift has taken place from a 'permissive consensus' on the EU among citizens towards a 'constraining dissensus'. The picture in this regard is not the same in all member states. In some public opinion has moved from (implicit) support for the EU to Euroscepticism, in others the trend has been the other way around. In general, however, there seems to be a shift in which political elites need to take public opinion more into account when making choices regarding the EU. This hints at a move towards a more 'democratic' public debate.

- The EP itself functions increasingly like domestic parliaments, with its political groups being the key players in parliamentary decision-making. In Chapter 7, it was shown that the voting cohesion of these groups has steadily increased over the past decades. This is an important precondition for a democratic parliament because it allows voters a real and clear choice among a limited set of alternative parties. Similarly, although European political parties do not perform the same functions as domestic political parties, they have developed more in that direction recently, with some parties even opening up membership to individual citizens.

Whatever one's final assessment of the EU's democratic qualities, it is important to keep two points in mind. First, one should be aware that there are two aspects to democracy: institutions and practices. Institutions are important for democracy because they determine the formal roles that citizens play in politics or at least in determining who will govern them. Indeed, for some people democracy is synonymous with a set of institutions, most notably free and fair elections. Yet, democracy is more than institutions. It is also a set of practices that determine how the political 'game' is actually played. In the review of arguments above, we encountered both institutions (e.g. the powers of the EP) and practices (e.g. the behaviour of political groups in the EP). It is important to keep both aspects in mind when assessing the democratic quality of the EU (or of any political system, for that matter).

Second, it is important to compare the EU to other political systems and not just to some abstract ideal of democracy. Useful as ideals are for maintaining a critical stance towards politics, they may easily lead to judgements that are not placed within a proper context. If, for instance, EU decision-making is criticized for being insufficiently transparent, one should also take into account that domestic politics is often far from transparent. How much do citizens see of what goes on in Whitehall, the German Bundeskanzleramt or the French Elysée? For a fair and balanced assessment of the EU, as well as for a well-founded analysis of the background to how the EU works, comparisons with other political systems are therefore essential. In an absolute sense, no political system is fully democratic but another question is how it fares when compared with other, reasonably democratic systems.

■ Between state and international organization: the EU in comparative perspective

The final point of the previous section brings us back to the starting point of this book: studying the EU from a comparative politics approach. In the preface and Chapter 2, we argued that a number of benefits are to be had from comparing the EU with other (domestic) political systems. In particular, comparisons allow us to see (hidden) similarities but also to highlight more clearly the specificities in each system.

Using a comparative approach does not imply, therefore, that the EU is 'like a state' or even 'in the process of becoming a state'. It merely means that by systematically comparing the EU to other political systems, we can gain a better understanding of the characteristics of EU politics. This was apparent, for instance, in Chapter 3, where we analysed the institutional set-up of the EU. By comparing this to other political systems, using well-known classifications such as 'presidential system' and 'parliamentary system', we can obtain a better view of what the EU has in common with those other systems and where

Table 12.1 The EU as a state and as an international organization: five examples

The EU as a (proto-)state	The EU as an international organization
Wide range of policy areas	No EU taxes, army or police
Important role of supranational institutions	Central role of the Council of Ministers and European Council
Directly elected European Parliament	Second-order character of EP elections
Qualified majority voting in many areas	(De facto) unanimity in many areas
Supremacy of EU law and direct effect	Member states implement most policies

it differs. Thus, we can see what the European Parliament has in common with other parliaments (its legislative role, its approval of the Commission) but also what its specificities are (its lack of legislative initiative, the absence of a 'governing coalition').

The end result is a political system that is indeed unique, just as the political systems of, say, France and the United States are unique. The uniqueness of the EU stems from the fact that it seeks to marry the characteristics of a 'traditional' international organization with many of the tasks and institutions that have always been characteristic of 'states'. Formally speaking, the EU is an international organization. It has been created on the basis of an international treaty, under international law, by sovereign states. However, in its institutions and the tasks it undertakes, the EU has also developed a number of characteristics that are typical of a state.

If we use 'state' and 'international organization' as two ideal-typical concepts to describe political entities, we can find characteristics of each in the EU. Table 12.1 highlights five of these characteristics. In the column on the left-hand side are a number of points on which the EU is similar to a state. In the column on the right-hand side are the corresponding points at which the EU is more like an international organization. Below, we will discuss each of these five points to obtain a better idea of how the EU relates to other political systems.

The scope of policies

The EU is more like a state (and very much unlike other international organizations) in the sense that it covers a broad range of policy areas (see Chapter 8). International organizations typically only deal with one policy or issue area: NATO does defence, the WHO does health, the International Atomic Energy Agency (IAEA) atomic energy, the WTO trade, and so on. The EU, by contrast, does all these things plus a lot more. In that regard, the scope of its activities is more like that of a state than like that of an international organization.

At the same time, the EU lacks three capabilities that are seen as the cornerstones of state sovereignty: it does not levy its own taxes, it does not have an army and it does not have its own police force. For these things, the EU still relies on its member states. The same goes for policy areas that are closely related to the power to levy taxes, most prominently policies related to the welfare state. That is why Italian political scientist Giandomenico Majone called the EU a 'regulatory state': even if it is 'state-like', it is a state that focuses almost exclusively on regulation as a means to exert influence.

The role of the EU's supranational institutions

The same ambiguity can be found in the EU's institutional set-up and decision-making processes. The EU's supranational institutions (Commission, EP, Court of Justice) play important roles, much more so than the secretariats and adjudication bodies of other international organizations. A longstanding controversy among students of EU politics is to what extent these supranational bodies have real power vis-à-vis the member state governments (see Controversy 2.1 in Chapter 2). Much of this debate has focused on the 'high politics' of European integration, such as treaty revisions. It is undeniable, however, that in the daily policy-making processes of the EU the supranational institutions play key roles, which leads to very different policy-making dynamics than in other international organizations.

Nevertheless, member state governments remain crucial actors in EU decision-making, involved as they are in almost every decision through the European Council and the Council of Ministers or one of its subordinate bodies. This degree of involvement of constituent governments in 'central' policy-making is different to what can be found even in the most decentralized federal states. In developing his 'joint-decision trap' thesis (see Chapter 10), Fritz Scharpf pointed out that EU decision-making in the Council shows clear affinities with the role of the Bundesrat (the 'Senate') in Germany, which is composed of representatives of the German Länder. Still, important as the role of Länder may be in German politics, member state governments are much more central to EU politics. In that regard, the EU remains a typical international organization.

The central role of the member states is also reflected in the source of the EU's competences. The competences of a state (or of the federal government in a federal state) are defined in a constitution that the state itself can change (albeit often with a special, more demanding procedure). The competences of the EU, by contrast, have been specifically delegated to it by the member states and have been laid down in the EU treaties. The EU cannot change these treaties itself. This can only be done by the member states, acting unanimously. Even if the EU 'constitution' had been adopted, this would not have changed because in legal terms it would still have been a treaty. Therefore, the EU lacks what German lawyers call 'Kompetenz-Kompetenz': the competence to define its own competences. This is typical of international organizations.

Citizens and the salience of EU politics

The central role of member states is also reflected in the saliency of EU politics in the minds of European citizens. As we saw in Chapter 5, political interest

Controversy 12.1

Constitutional patriotism and the European Union

According to several political thinkers, some form of political allegiance and common identity is necessary for a political system to function. How else can citizens be mobilized for a common cause and can their support for the political system be assured? In nation-states, allegiance often takes the form of nationalism: a feeling among citizens of belonging to one nation, with a shared history, language and cultural identity. In the EU, such a type of 'European nationalism' is unlikely to arise.

Political thinkers have therefore looked for alternative types of allegiance that could underpin the European political project. One proposal in this regard has been the concept of 'constitutional patriotism'. It denotes an allegiance that is based on the norms, values and procedures inherent in a liberal-democratic political system, rather than some shared 'ethnic' background.

The notion of constitutional patriotism was developed in Germany after the Second World War. Initially, it was put forward as a proposal for a new German identity, as an alternative to the violent 'ethnic' nationalism that had led to two world wars and mass destruction. Later, the German philosopher Jürgen Habermas translated this idea to the European level and argued that it could provide a good basis for a European allegiance.

What do you think of this idea? Do you believe there should be some form of 'European identity'? If so, do you find 'constitutional patriotism' an attractive idea for building a European identity? And what do you think of the sequence between European identity and democratic politics: is some form of European identity necessary to foster citizen participation in EU politics or is participation by citizens in EU politics necessary for creating a European identity?

and loyalty remain overwhelmingly concentrated on the national (or in some parts of Europe, regional) level. Hence, even though the EP is the only directly elected international legislature in the world, EP elections remain 'second-order', reflecting domestic political concerns and developments rather than European ones.

Unlike most national states, the EU does not yet inspire much political loyalty, let alone patriotism. Quite apart from the EU's institutional set-up, this lack of European patriotism is an important political fact that has placed severe limits on the extent to which politicians have been able to mobilize pan-European support for political initiatives. As a result, member state politics and member state governments continue to be important focal points in EU politics. The issue of EU patriotism has also come up in debates on a 'European Constitution'. Controversy 12.1 presents one proposal put forward in that debate: the idea of 'constitutional patriotism'.

Voting in the Council of Ministers

A key characteristic of international law and politics is the idea that states cannot be bound against their will. That is why binding decisions can often only be reached by unanimity. Moreover, states may include reservations, in which they state that they do not consider themselves bound by certain provisions in a treaty. In terms of the underlying treaties, the EU works in the same way. Yet, in terms of daily decision-making many decisions are now taken by qualified majority, which effectively means that individual member states can be outvoted and cannot unilaterally declare reservations to EU legislation. With the new voting rules included in the Treaty of Lisbon, the threshold for reaching a qualified majority has been lowered even further (see Chapter 4). In that sense, the EU has developed towards the kind of majority voting that is characteristic of domestic politics.

Still, here too there is a qualification. Apart from the fact that a qualified majority is still more than a simple majority, qualified majority voting itself is not as common as one might assume. As was noted in Chapter 4, member state governments tend to look for consensus, even when a qualified majority has been reached. Voting is only used as a measure of last resort, when consensus cannot be reached. This is typically 'diplomatic' practice, in which the sovereignty of member state governments takes precedence over the simple majority calculus that is often seen in domestic politics, and it shows the diplomatic roots of the EU.

EU law and member state law

As a final defining characteristic, we have seen that EU law takes precedence over member state law (the doctrine of the 'supremacy of EU law') and that EU firms and citizens can directly invoke their rights under EU law before a national court ('direct effect'). In this regard, the EU resembles a federal state, with its hierarchy between federal law and the law of the constituent units. The fact that EU law can be directly invoked before national courts sets the EU apart from other international organizations. Under 'normal' international law, states can determine themselves whether and to what extent they allow international law to become part of their national legal system. In the EU, however, they do not have that choice. This was the truly revolutionary quality of the Court's *Van Gend en Loos* and *Costa/ENEL* rulings (see Chapter 1).

Having said this, the implementation of EU law largely remains a matter for member state governments. Not only do they have to transpose EU Directives, but they also undertake the application and enforcement of most EU Directives and Regulations (see Chapter 11). This means that the effects of EU law and policies 'on the ground', which materialize in and through implementation processes, are still very much determined by member state governments and administrations.

Putting the threads together?

What type of political system, then, is the EU? This is a question that keeps occupying scholars of EU politics and will continue to do so in the foreseeable future. In the end, it is a question to which there is no easy answer. There are at least two reasons why this is so. First, the EU is continually evolving. Throughout this book, we have seen examples of developments that changed, or had the potential to change, the shape of EU politics. The example of the financial crisis with which we opened this chapter is a case in point. Some of the responses to the crisis have constituted fundamental shifts away from established practices and political equilibriums. However, the lasting effects of those shifts can only be assessed properly with the benefit of several years of hindsight. The same goes for more gradual developments, such as the rise and increasing powers of EU agencies. This may affect the balance between the EU and its member states, but this is a process that will continue to unfold over the coming years and whose outcome is not predetermined.

Second, and more fundamentally, reasonable people can differ in their assessment of the EU's political system or elements of it. Is the EP a 'real' parliament or a toothless institution vis-à-vis the Council? Can we call the Commission the EU's 'government' or is this a misrepresentation of its role and activities? Is the process of European integration moved forward by 'daily politics' or by 'grand bargains'? These are just some of the questions to which political scientists have given vastly different answers. The reason is that politics (and social life in general) is multifaceted and statements on it are as much a matter of interpretation and perspective as of 'pure facts'.

In this book, we have sought to show some of these debates and their underlying perspectives. In doing so, we hope to have provided more insight into the way the EU works as well as a number of conceptual and theoretical tools that can be used to analyse EU politics. In addition, we have sought to extend an invitation: an invitation to continue to think critically, empirically and comparatively about EU politics in order to gain better-informed, better-founded answers to the important questions of EU politics. We hope you will take up that invitation in your future studies.

■ Summary

This chapter has provided a reflection on the future development of the EU, democracy in the EU, and the benefits of using a comparative approach in studying EU politics. It has argued that:

- Developments in the EU's institutional framework and policy scope have resulted from both internal and external sources.
- The internal sources of developments have come from attempts by the EU institutions to increase their remit and authority. It has rested crucially on the acquiescence of member state governments.
- The external sources of developments have come from crises facing the EU and its member states. The initiative in responding to these crises has normally been taken by member state governments and the European Council, but in the longer run these responses have often led to a strengthening of the EU's institutional framework.

- It is important to keep in mind that, besides 'large events', the EU is also about 'daily politics'. Developments in this domain are less visible but highly consequential for the course of European integration. In comparison with large events, they are often more gradual.
- Enlargement of the EU has recently been characterized by 'enlargement fatigue' on the part of many citizens and member state governments. This has not just been the result of further enlargements per se but also of the fact that a number of new candidates (in particular Turkey) have given rise to questions about the European 'identity'.
- Critics have accused the EU of suffering from a 'democratic deficit'. This assessment depends on two separate arguments: that the EU *should* be democratic and that the EU in fact *is not* democratic.
- The answer to the question whether the EU should be democratic depends on one's perspective on the tasks of the EU: does it execute a number of relatively technical and clearly predefined tasks or does it make policies that imply trade-offs between important values?
- The answer to the question whether the EU is in fact democratic depends on one's assessment of the democratic credentials of both institutions and practices in the EU.
- In comparison with other political systems, the EU shows characteristics of both a state and an international organization. It is this ambiguity that makes the EU unique.

Further reading

A further introduction to the comparative study of EU politics is provided by Simon Hix and Bjørn Høyland, *The Political System of the European Union* (Palgrave Macmillan, 3rd edn, 2011). For the debate on democracy in the EU, a key text is Andrew Moravcsik, 'In Defence of the "Democratic Deficit": Reassessing Legitimacy in the European Union', *Journal of Common Market Studies*, 40, 4, 2002: 603–24. In this article, Moravcsik argues that the EU does not suffer from a democratic deficit. For a response and critique, see Andreas Føllesdal and Simon Hix, 'Why There is a Democratic Deficit in the EU: A Response to Majone and Moravcsik', *Journal of Common Market Studies*, 44, 3, 2006: 533–62. For a penetrating yet complex argument about the type of political system the EU is in comparative perspective, see Sergio Fabbrini, *Compound Democracies: Why the United States and Europe are Becoming Similar* (Oxford University Press, 2007) or his article 'A Single Western State Model? Differential Development and Constrained Convergence of Public Authority Organizations in Europe and America', *Comparative Political Studies*, 36, 6, 2003: 653–78.

Navigating the EU

On the website www.navigatingthe.eu you will find online exercises for this chapter.

Key terms and concepts

Accountability Situation where an actor needs to explain and justify its behaviour to another actor, and the other actor can impose consequences if it considers the behaviour to be inadequate or inappropriate.

Action for annulment Case brought before the Court of Justice in which an interested party asks the Court to declare a decision by any of the EU's institutions to be void.

Agencies Administrative organizations set up by the EU that provide technical expertise in different policy areas and assist in coordinating, implementing and monitoring policies.

Bicameral legislature Legislature consisting of two houses. In federal systems one house represents the national population, whilst the other house represents regional populations.

Coalition Set of parties that work together to achieve some political objective – for instance, to create a government (in parliamentary political systems) or to coordinate voting behaviour (in the EP).

Cohesion The extent to which MEPs of the same political group vote together. If all MEPs from a political group vote exactly the same, cohesion is high. If some MEPs in a political group vote for a proposal or amendment while other MEPs from that same group vote against, cohesion is low.

Cohesion policy Set of EU policies designed to reduce economic disparities between regions by giving financial support to economically underdeveloped regions in the EU member states.

Comitology The system of committees through which civil servants from member states discuss the implementation of EU policy and supervise the Commission's implementation decisions.

Common Agricultural Policy (CAP) Set of EU policies designed to regulate agricultural markets and provide financial support to farmers.

Common Assembly Predecessor of the European Parliament that was created as part of the ECSC in 1951.

Common position In the first reading the Council adopts a common position when its viewpoint on a proposal differs from the EP's opinion and/or the Commission's modified proposal.

Community method Way of making decisions in which the EU's supranational institutions (Commission, EP) play an important role.

Conciliation committee Committee consisting of representatives of the Council and the EP, assisted by representatives of the Commission. Its task is to produce a compromise text if the Council and the EP have not reached an agreement after the second reading of the ordinary legislative procedure.

Copenhagen criteria Fundamental conditions regarding institutions, human rights and economic readiness aspiring member states have to meet before being able to join the EU.

Coreper Committee of permanent representatives. Highest preparatory body for meetings of the Council and European Council.

Corporatism System of interest representation in which a limited number of interest groups have privileged access to governmental decision-making.

Cues Cognitive short-cuts offered by political parties, the media or opinion leaders that allow voters to make up their mind about an issue.

Customs duties Charges levied on imports or exports, resulting in higher prices for consumers buying those products.

Delegated acts Acts adopted by the Commission to modify specific details of Directives or Regulations (Article 290 TFEU), as long as they do not change the essence of the legislation. The legislation in question must explicitly state the content of the acts and the Council and/or the EP always have the right to veto the proposed act.

Direct effect Major legal principle in EU law holding that individuals can directly invoke EU legislation in cases before national courts.

Directive Type of EU legislation that needs to be transposed into national law by the member state governments.

Economic and Monetary Union (EMU) includes the coordination of economic and fiscal policies, a common monetary policy and a common currency.

Enhanced cooperation Procedure through which a group of EU member states can adopt legislation (or a decision under the CFSP) that only applies to them and not to the other member states.

Eurosceptic Term used for people, member states or political parties that have been highly critical of European integration.

Focusing event Occurrence that draws strong attention to a problem.

Frame An interpretation scheme with which issues and events are defined and given meaning.

Framing The activity of (re-)defining an issue in such a way that it fits a particular frame.

Governance Term used to refer to a mode of governing characterized by collaborative and networked forms of policy-making.

Green Paper Discussion document from the European Commission that outlines general issues and options around an issue without presenting specific proposals.

Gross Domestic Product (GDP) Measure of the size of an economy, which equals the total value of goods and services produced in a country in a given year.

High politics Politics concerning issues that affect vital national interests.

History-making decisions Decisions that determine the fundamental choices about the course of the EU for years to come.

Ideology More or less systematic and comprehensive set of ideas and beliefs about politics that guides the positions of politicians, political parties and/or citizens on specific political issues.

Implementation The process of applying policies and putting them into practice.

Implementation decisions Acts that are adopted by the Commission to put legislation into practice.

Implementing acts Acts that the Commission adopts in order to make sure the member states implement legislation in a uniform fashion (Article 291 TFEU). Member states control and advise the Commission on the adoption of these acts through the system of comitology.

Infringement procedure Legal procedure set in motion against a member state if it does not comply with EU legislation.

Inside lobbying Strategy in which interest groups seek to influence policies through direct contact with policy-makers.

Interest group Group of people that share certain preferences regarding the outcomes of governmental decision-making and organize in order to influence those outcomes, without seeking elected office.

Intergovernmental Conference Meeting of the member states to discuss and decide a revision of treaties. As its name indicates an IGC is a purely intergovernmental affair that only involves representatives of the member state governments.

Intergovernmental institutions EU institutions that represent the member states: European Council and Council.

Intergovernmental method Way of making decisions in which member state governments play a central role.

Intergovernmental organizations Organizations in which member states work together on policies of common concern but retain their full sovereignty.

Intergovernmentalism Integration theory which holds that member states are fully in charge of cooperative steps they take and only collaborate with a view to their direct self-interest.

Interinstitutional agreement Binding agreement between the Commission, the Council and/or the EP, in which the institutions define arrangements for their cooperation.

Issue linkage Constellation when the outcome of the decision on one issue is made contingent on the outcome of the decision on another issue.

Joint-decision trap Constellation that arises if the participation of non-central governments in the making of central government decisions leads to policies that are ineffective, inefficient and/or outdated but these policies cannot be changed because at least one non-central government benefits from them.

Judicial activism Type of judicial behaviour where judges take a broad and active view of their role as interpreters of the law.

Legitimacy The condition of being in accordance with the norms and values of the people.

Lisbon Strategy Agreement made at the 2000 European Council meeting in Lisbon with the aim to make the EU the world's most competitive economy by 2010.

Lobbyist Individual engaged in attempts to influence governmental decision-making on behalf of an interest group.

Low politics Politics concerning issues for which the political stakes are not that high.

Luxembourg Compromise Agreement allowing a member state to block a decision in the Council if it declares the matter to be of 'vital national interest'.

Monetary policy Policy aimed at ensuring financial stability through managing the supply of money and controlling the interest rates at which banks can borrow and lend money.

Negative integration Abolition of trade barriers that are imposed by member states.

Neo-functionalism Integration theory which states that member states will work together to reap economic benefits, setting in motion a process in which ever more tasks are delegated to the supranational level.

Non-attitude Expression of opinion which is not rooted in strongly held beliefs and hence can be very volatile.

Non-tariff barrier All kinds of conditions, restrictions or regulations that do not consist of tariffs, but still make the import or export of products difficult or impossible.

Open Method of Coordination Mechanism which aims at convergence of member state policies through a process of benchmarking and policy learning.

Opt-outs Specific exceptions that are granted to a member state when it is unwilling or unable to fully accept all provisions of a treaty or a law.

Ordinary legislative procedure Decision-making procedure that is most commonly used in the EU for adopting legislation, giving equal powers to the European Parliament and the Council.

Outside lobbying Strategy in which interest groups seek to put pressure on policy-makers by mobilizing public opinion.

Parliamentary committee Subdivision of parliament dealing with specific policy areas. Prepares and debates proposals before sending them to the full, plenary parliament for final decision-making.

Permanent representatives Member states' ambassadors to the EU who reside in Brussels and prepare much of the work of the European Council and Council.

Pluralism System of interest representation in which a large number of interest groups compete with each other for access to governmental decision-making.

Policy entrepreneur Actor which successfully influences decisions made by others, by skilfully mobilizing support, building coalitions and proposing solutions in the direction of an outcome close to its own preferences.

Policy network Set of participants in a given policy field who are connected through regular interactions.

Policy venue Institution that has the authority to make decisions about an issue.

Policy window Short period in which an issue commands a lot of attention and decisions on that issue can be taken.

Policy-setting decisions Decision on choices between alternative courses of action for dealing with a given issue.

Policy-shaping decisions Decisions about the choices between alternative policy instruments to tackle a given issue.

Political agenda Set of issues that policy-makers give serious attention to.

Political agreement A constellation in the first reading stage of the ordinary legislative procedure where the Council already communicates its views on a proposal before the EP has formally adopted its opinion.

Political cleavage Stable conflict dimension between political groups that is rooted in social differences between groups in society.

Political elites The relatively small number of people at the top of a political system who exercise disproportionate influence or power over political decisions.

Political opportunity structure Institutional and political context within which an interest group operates and that determines the receptiveness of decision-makers to the claims of that group.

Political participation All activities that are aimed at influencing policies and/or the selection of politicians.

Political party Group of like-minded people who organize in order to influence politics through winning political office.

Positive integration Adoption of EU laws to reduce the differences between member state laws in a given area (also known as **harmonization** or the **approximation of laws**).

Preferential trade agreement Agreement between countries on lowering the tariffs they charge for importing goods.

Preliminary ruling Binding interpretation on a matter of EU law delivered by the Court of Justice at the request of a member state court.

Principle of proportionality Principle stating that the burden to implement legislation should be minimized and commensurate with the objective to be achieved.

Qualified Majority Voting Decision-making rule in the Council which requires a majority that is substantially larger than a simple majority of (50%+1), but does not require unanimity.

Race to the bottom Process in which states lower their regulatory standards in fields like environmental, social and consumer protection in order to attract firms or prevent them from moving abroad (also known as social dumping).

Rapporteur Member of Parliament responsible for summarizing a committee's opinion and its modification proposals on a specific piece of legislation.

Ratification Procedure through which a member state formally commits itself to a treaty, in most countries via a majority vote by its parliament.

Regulation Type of EU legislation that is directly applicable in the EU and in all member states.

Side-payments Monetary compensations given to a participant in a decision-making process in order to secure the support of that participant for a proposal that is unrelated to the payments.

Soft power The ability to wield influence, not through the use of force or money, but through the attractiveness and legitimacy of one's values, culture and policies.

Spillover The way in which the creation and deepening of integration in one economic sector creates pressures for further economic integration within and beyond that sector and greater authoritative capacity at the European level.

Strategic culture The set of assumptions and values through which a country typically interprets and reacts to international events.

Subsidiarity principle Principle stating that the EU is only allowed to act if the objectives of that action can be better reached at EU level than at member state level.

Supranational institutions All those EU institutions that represent the general interest of the EU (Commission, Court of Justice, European Central Bank and Court of Auditors) as well as the European Parliament.

Supranational organizations Organizations in which countries pool their sovereignty on certain matters to allow joint decision-making.

Supremacy Major legal principle in EU law holding that if national legislation is in conflict with EU law, EU law overrides national legislation.

Technocracy The view that policies should be exclusively based on knowledge and that decisions on them should be made by scientific experts rather than politicians.

Transnational organization Organization that connects subnational levels of governments or brings together any other type of organization (businesses, civil society groups) from different countries.

Transposition The process of incorporating the legal provisions of EU directives into national legislation.

Trilogues Regular meetings of representatives of the three institutions (Commission, EP, and Council) that are convened in order to identify points of agreement and differences, and find a compromise on a legislative text.

Veto player Actor who can prevent a decision from being taken.

White paper Discussion document from the European Commission that presents specific proposals for EU action.

Zone of acceptability Set of bargaining outcomes that a participant in a negotiation is willing to accept.

Zone of agreement Set of bargaining outcomes that all participants in a negotiation are willing to accept (also known as bargaining set).

Index